Sophia Studies in Cross-cultural Philosophy of Traditions and Cultures

Volume 44

The Sophia Studies in Cross-cultural Philosophy of Traditions and Cultures focuses on the broader aspects of philosophy and traditional intellectual patterns of religion and cultures. The series encompasses global traditions, and critical treatments that draw from cognate disciplines, inclusive of feminist, postmodern, and postcolonial approaches. By global traditions we mean religions and cultures that go from Asia to the Middle East to Africa and the Americas, including indigenous traditions in places such as Oceania. Of course this does not leave out good and suitable work in Western traditions where the analytical or conceptual treatment engages Continental (European) or Cross-cultural traditions in addition to the Judeo-Christian tradition. The book series invites innovative scholarship that takes up newer challenges and makes original contributions to the field of knowledge in areas that have hitherto not received such dedicated treatment. For example, rather than rehearsing the same old Ontological Argument in the conventional way, the series would be interested in innovative ways of conceiving the erstwhile concerns while also bringing new sets of questions and responses, methodologically also from more imaginative and critical sources of thinking. Work going on in the forefront of the frontiers of science and religion beaconing a well-nuanced philosophical response that may even extend its boundaries beyond the confines of this debate in the West—e.g. from the perspective of the 'Third World' and the impact of this interface (or clash) on other cultures, their economy, sociality, and ecological challenges facing them—will be highly valued by readers of this series. All books to be published in this Series will be fully peer-reviewed before final acceptance.

Govert J. Buijs • Jordan J. Ballor
Editors

In Search of the Spirits of Capitalism

World Religions on Markets & Morality

Springer

Editors
Govert J. Buijs
Faculty of Social Sciences and Humanities
Vrije Universiteit
Amsterdam, The Netherlands

Jordan J. Ballor
Center for Religion, Culture & Democracy
First Liberty Institute
Plano, TX, USA

ISSN 2211-1107 ISSN 2211-1115 (electronic)
Sophia Studies in Cross-cultural Philosophy of Traditions and Cultures
ISBN 978-3-032-01136-7 ISBN 978-3-032-01137-4 (eBook)
https://doi.org/10.1007/978-3-032-01137-4

This Springer imprint is published by the registered company Springer Nature Switzerland AG
The registered company address is: Gewerbestrasse 11, 6330 Cham, Switzerland

Acknowledgements

This volume originates with the subproject 'World Religions on Markets, Morality & Human Flourishing', coordinated by Dr. Jordan J. Ballor, which was part of a larger research project 'What Good Markets Are Good For', conducted by representatives of four Dutch universities, Vrije Universiteit Amsterdam, Radboud Universiteit Nijmegen, Erasmus Universiteit Rotterdam and the University of Tilburg, Tilburg.

The project was led by a team consisting of Prof. Dr. Govert J. Buijs (VU-Amsterdam) and Prof. Dr. Johan J. Graafland (University of Tilburg), as academic coordinators, and Eefje de Gelder, MA, and Dr. Ilse Oosterlaken as project coordinators.

See Moralmarkets.org

The project was funded by a grant from the Templeton World Charity Foundation, Inc.

Contents

Contributors

Jordan J. Ballor Center for Religion, Culture & Democracy, First Liberty Institute, Plano, TX, USA

Victor van Bijlert Vrije Universiteit, Amsterdam, Netherlands

Govert J. Buijs Faculty of Social Sciences and Humanities, Vrije Universiteit, Amsterdam, The Netherlands

Amitava Krishna Dutt Notre Dame University, Notre Dame, IN, USA

Waleed El-Ansary Xavier University, Cincinnati, OH, USA

Hershey H. Friedman Brooklyn College, New York, NY, USA

Jennifer A. Herdt Yale University, New Haven, CT, USA

Carsten Herrmann-Pillath Erfurt University, Erfurt, Germany

Cornelis van der Kooi Vrije Universiteit, Amsterdam, Netherlands

Joseph Isaac Lifshitz Shalem College, Jerusalem, Israel

Joel Magnuson Independent scholar, Portland, OR, USA

Ayman Reda University of Michigan-Dearborn, Dearborn, MI, USA

Candauda Arachchige Saliya Sri Lanka Institute of Information Technology, Malabe, Sri Lanka

Mary Szto Syracuse University College of Law, Syracuse, NY, USA

Chapter 1
Introduction: With Weber, Beyond Weber—The Search for the Future Spirit(s) of Capitalism

Govert J. Buijs and Jordan J. Ballor

Abstract Although we live in a globalized world, there has still been little interreligious dialogue about markets and morality in relation to human flourishing and even less so in connection with economic theory. The field of comparative study on the economic ethic of the world religions which Max Weber around 1905 initiated with his studies published as *Die Wirtschaftsethik der Weltreligionen,* has not progressed much since the early twentieth century and is still fragmentary. This essay introduces the theme of this edited volume and explains in what way Weber's questions are revisited in a new way. The sociological approach of Weber is complemented here by asking what moral insights each religion and worldview has to offer, both positively and critically, in dialogue with the market economy today.

Keywords Max Weber · Capitalism · Flourishing · World religions · Market economy

1.1 In Memory of Max Weber

In 2020 it was exactly one hundred years ago that the great sociologist Max Weber (1864–1920) passed away and in 2025 it is 120 years ago that his famous essay on 'The Protestant Ethic and the Spirit of Capitalism' was published. The achievements of his rather short lifetime are immense. He is, for example, rightly identified as one of the founders of modern sociology. Within his entire oeuvre, arguably his project on the economic ethics of the world religions (*Die Wirtschaftsethik der*

G. J. Buijs (✉)
Faculty of Social Sciences and Humanities, Vrije Universiteit, Amsterdam, The Netherlands
e-mail: g.j.buijs@vu.nl

J. J. Ballor
Center for Religion, Culture & Democracy, First Liberty Institute, Plano, TX, USA
e-mail: j.ballor@crcd.net

G. J. Buijs, J. J. Ballor (eds.), *In Search of the Spirits of Capitalism*, Sophia Studies in Cross-cultural Philosophy of Traditions and Cultures 44,
https://doi.org/10.1007/978-3-032-01137-4_1

Weltreligionen) stands out as his most ambitious and thorough endeavor. Starting with the already mentioned 1904/05 essay on Protestantism and Capitalism (in German: *Die protestantische Ethik und der Geist des Kapitalismus*), his work branched out to in-depth treatments of Confucianism and Daoism, Hinduism and Buddhism, as well as ancient Judaism. Weber did not live to produce planned volumes on Islam and medieval Christianity. But although they are unfinished, the three volumes of *The Economic Ethic of the World Religions* that were completed are impressive achievements.

The purpose of this present volume is not a mere retrospective or an attempt to validate Weber's own conclusions and methods in detail. While that would be a very valuable undertaking, particularly in light of the recent new emphasis in the social sciences on replicability of results, a very informing volume with that very goal has been published recently (Ertman 2017).

To be clear from the start: our goal is different. We have asked ourselves the question: given the still extant variety of world religions, as Weber analyzed, and given that they all have given rise to moral reflections on the economy, that is an economic ethic (*Wirtschaftsethik*), what is there for us in the twenty-first century to learn from them, as we now possibly, even likely, face the task of redirecting capitalism? Assessments and analyses of the current and future directions of the world economy abound. Notable in this regard are the calls to somehow adjust capitalism to new realities (Barton et al. 2016; Roche and Jakub 2018; Barnes 2018; Collier 2018; Stiglitz 2019, 2024; Wolf 2023; Balkenende and Buijs 2024). But at the same time we face *anno* 2025 a very heavy backlash against all attempts to put even the slightest correction on (the outcomes of) capitalist markets: a group of 'anarcho-capitalists' have taken over the American government, with as one of their primary goals the prohibition of any critical debates on and corrections of capitalism. Jeff Bezos, owner of the Washington Post, has even with a Soviet-type 'ukase' ordered the editors that from now on no critical discussion of the free market will be allowed!. So much for freedom of speech, the gloves are off, apparently. This is no coincidence: under the cover of 'free speech defense' in recent years a form of capitalism has emerged that deeply intrudes the private life of billions of people, more and deeper, more capillary, than any, even totalitarian, governments in world history, "surveillance capitalism" (Wu 2016; Zuboff 2019) and there is even talk about a new feudalism, hence the reemergence of what once was thought to be the opposite of capitalism (Kotkin 2023).

As Weber focused mainly on the supposed obstacles or propellers of capitalism within the various world religions, we ask the question of possible moral guidance and moral orientation that world religions may offer for capitalism, that is, free markets. Hence the contributions in this volume are meant as an answer to the question:

> From the perspective of one of the world religions, do free markets contribute to human flourishing, and what from these perspectives is the role of morality and especially virtues, in realizing this contribution?[1]

That we ask this question in this way is in part a reflection of the substantially different context in which we find ourselves today, in the first half of the twenty-first century than Weber's context was in the early twentieth century. In this introduction we first give a brief reconstruction of how Weber saw capitalism and then we sketch what we see as the main differences between Weber's context—and the way he interpreted it—and the present context as we see it. This shift of context can be described (with Ulrich Beck) as the move from "high modernity" to "reflexive modernity". We will identify four major issues/developments we are facing today that Weber did not, and perhaps could not, envisage. After that we give some reflections on the role of religions and worldviews in the public sphere: whether they should be allowed to participate anyway (something which some recent branches of liberalism deny). In the penultimate section we elucidate our key terms and general approach. We conclude this introduction with a brief overview of the volume.

1.2 Weber's 'end of history': A Grim and Monolithic Picture of Capitalism

Weber's fascination with capitalism was at least partly triggered by his analysis of the process of modernization. Next to the rise of bureaucratic government, it was the rise of capitalism that for him embodied virtually the end stage of history, the outcome of a world-historic process of rationalization, or, as Weber in his later stages came to call it "disenchantment" (*Entzauberung*).

Weber's view of history clearly derived from Enlightenment sources. Several Enlightenment thinkers had designed an overall narrative about the human race, in which mankind developed from a primitive, mythological, or religious phase (concrete, imaginary thinking, considered characteristic of the age of childhood), via the great religious-metaphysical and philosophical systems that emerge in the metaphysical age (typified by abstract thinking and characterized as the age of youth) toward a final stage of pure rational thinking, the positive age (marked by the priority of evidence-based, empirical thinking, and the age of maturity). The view was most clearly elaborated by August Comte (1798–1857), often called the father of sociology, but was anticipated already by De Saint-Simon (1760–1825) and Turgot (1727–1781) (Löwith 1949). A mild form of this we can trace as well in Immanuel Kant's famous 1784 dictum according to which mankind is now not yet

[1] The triangle Markets—Virtues—Human Flourishing was the heart of our research project 'What Good Markets Are Good For', funded by the Templeton World Charity Foundation, Inc., the project that provided as well the opportunity to work on the present volume. In a subsequent book we will expand on this triangle.

"enlightened" but certainly lives in an "age of enlightenment," characterized by the "courage to use one's own reason" (*sapere aude*). This is "man's emergence from his self-incurred immaturity" (Kant 2009, 1). There is a distinctly optimistic tone in Kant's statement. Using reason, mankind can grow up and liberate itself, at first in the world of thought, scholarship as the true public sphere, but this will eventually trickle down in society at large. This is as well the time of Adam Smith and his expectation of the growing wealth of nations—if we organize our economies well. Rationalization is expected to greatly enhance human flourishing.

In Weber, one can clearly hear the echoes of these sentiments. However, in his work the optimistic overtones have vanished entirely. The emergence of a fully rationalized world has now become as much our fate as it is our choice, and it is as much a prison as it is liberating—perhaps even more so. This is clear already from the very term *disenchantment* in itself: growing up is not all that easy, as in the process we moderns lose a sense of meaning and of cosmic embeddedness.

Weber's analysis of capitalism and its rise captures this perspective very well. Why did it arise in the West and nowhere else? This was Weber's famous research question. His answer is well known. Although many preconditions for the rise of capitalism (technology, rational book-keeping, trade, and so on) can be found elsewhere (especially in China), what really triggered capitalism was a certain *Geist*, a "spirit," a mentality. This was provided by the Protestant ethic: working hard as a duty, but not spending the surplus, work for work's sake, not for consumption or luxury. In this way a constant surplus is created that cannot be spent but should only be re-invested in a rational way, a way that will turn out to foster the creation of further useful things. Moreover, for the English Puritans in particular, creating prosperity was as well a way of ascertaining their election and eternal salvation by God, for otherwise there weren't too many signals humans receive about Gods eternal decrees.

Although Weber strongly emphasized the role of Protestantism—hence religion—as the birth ground of capitalism, he was as explicit and adamant that capitalism, once in place, did not need any of this background any longer (Weber 2005, 123–125). The monster of disenchantment was devouring its own father, and it could continue very well without it. So capitalism does not need the Protestant ethic for its sustenance. Protestantism has served as the launchpad where the satellite of capitalism has lifted off, but now it circles in its own orbit, for ever and ever, totally detached from its origin. The spirit of capitalism maintains itself, without recourse to the originating Protestantism. Capitalism is self-sustaining—and increasingly universal. As Weber states immediately at the beginning of *The Protestant Ethic and the Spirit of Capitalism*, he wants to study phenomena that may have started in European civilization but that "lie in a line of development having *universal* significance and value" (Weber 2005, xxviii). That is capitalism.

That implies as well that as a self-sustaining system, capitalism does not give humans any choice as to participate in it or not. Capitalism encapsulates us (therefore Weber would not be surprised at all by the emergence of the aforementioned "surveillance capitalism"). Weber writes, "The Puritan wanted to work in a calling; we are forced to do so" (2005, 123). When this ethic, at first formed and strengthened in medieval monasteries (*ausserweltlich*, still somewhat outside of the world), via Protestantism entered the everyday life of work and economy (*innerweltlich*), it became part of a process in which "the tremendous cosmos of the modern economic order" was built. Once the process is complete, there is no escape anymore, and Weber even seems to anticipate the depletion of ecological resources in the process:

> This order is now bound to the technical and economic conditions of machine production which today determine the lives of all the individuals who are born into this mechanism (not only those directly concerned with economic acquisition) with irresistible force. Perhaps it will so determine them until the last ton of fossilized coal is burnt. (Weber 2005, 123)

Ceaseless economic activity, which for the Puritans still was considered to be a "light cloak" now for us late-moderns has become an "iron cage". Material goods now have an inexorable power over the lives of men, in a degree which has never happened before. The spirit is gone; the show goes on.

> To-day, the spirit of religious asceticism – whether finally, who knows? – has escaped from the cage. But victorious capitalism, since it rests on mechanical foundations, needs its support no longer. (Weber 2005, 124)

The end result may well be a world full of, as Weber says (perhaps quoting some kind of standard expression in his days) "specialists without spirit, sensualists without heart," boasting of their own world historic superiority, while they have left behind all these outdated and old-fashioned religious fairy tales, and are only pursuing wealth for wealth's sake.

In this respect Weber's work shows a remarkable paradox: he assumed that all the religions he had studied so meticulously had already been rendered superfluous, outdated, and irrelevant for the further development of the modern world. History has moved on, beyond mythological and religious phases, into pure empirical rationality. So religion was doomed to disappear as a public phenomenon. Of course, for those weak souls who in private crave for spiritual guidance, the doors of the churches (and today we could easily add the mosques, the synagogues, the sanghas, the temples, or the books of Confucius) are still open, ready to be consulted. But their public relevance is nil, as he stated very emphatically in his dramatic lecture on "Science as a Vocation." The public world is the world of rationality, of facts, of procedures and rules, not of values, not of meaning, not of these *Weltreligionen* he had studied (Weber 1946). The rationalized systems have reached their own orbit in outer space and will be there, determining our lives, but being untouched by whatever moral consideration we might have or might be willing to have. Capitalism will no longer ask anyone to have a 'spirit'; it will not ask anyone to have moral considerations; it will not require anyone to formulate ideas about human flourishing and then somehow hold capitalism accountable for realizing this yes or no. The system is morally and religiously immune. Indeed, the system is *ein stahlhartes Gehäuse*, "a house as hard as steel," or an "iron cage," Weber's grim and gloomy image to denote this situation.

So, in summary, Weber paints a rather grim and monolithic picture of modern capitalism. It is one clearly identifiable phenomenon which has occurred in the

West, is now spreading worldwide, and which has developed into a steel-hard system, impervious to religious or moral considerations, no longer amenable for human action and direction, occurring in a world in which religion is withering away anyway.

There is a slight reservation in Weber. It is contained in this little interjected question in one of the quotes above: "whether finally: who knows?" Weber elaborates on this briefly when he ponders the possibility that "entirely new prophets will arise," or a "great rebirth of old ideas and ideals" that may occur (Weber 2005, 124). But it seems only a kind of academic-empirical courtesy to express these reservations. At no moment he gives the impression that this may be a real possibility.

1.3 Beyond Weber: Four Major Changes Calling for a New Reflexivity

However, we can see Weber's slight reservation as a pointer to new developments that he did not foresee, but that we see ready at hand before us. We believe that there are four key differences between Weber's situation (and the incisive interpretation he gave of it) and ours.

1.3.1 The Interpretation of Capitalism

A hundred years after Weber, we have become aware that capitalism is not just one thing, but that there are varieties of capitalism and that hence, capitalism interacts with culture (van Geest 2021; Zsolnai and Kovacs 2021).

For quite some time Weber's interpretation of world history in terms of the rise of rationality, disenchantment, and capitalism as a universal, monolithic phenomenon, a kind of end-state of history, was more or less the standard view within Western philosophical and social science circles. The early work (although not the later work) of Francis Fukuyama (1992) can be seen as representative of this view. However, what has shown itself during the last hundred years is a *variety* of capitalisms, partly as a result of specific interaction between some general tenets of capitalism and the older background cultures that were studied by Weber (Hall and Soskice 2001; Hancké et al. 2007; see also Albert 1991, 1993; Sheikh 2017). So we need another theoretical model than the one we exemplified with the idea of a launchpad and the satellite in its orbit, the ground (the Protestant ethic) which is then left behind forever. Apparently, capitalism is open to cultural, even religious, influences! It is for this reason that a more recent Weber-inspired sociologist, Shmuel Eisenstadt, coined the phrase "multiple modernities" (Eisenstadt 2000). Capitalism in China is rather different from capitalism in Russia, and capitalism in Italy is different from capitalism in the Netherlands. We could even say that capitalism in one formerly Protestant area, say northwestern Europe, where the Arminian theology of the free will never gained primacy, is different from capitalism in the USA, the country of Arminianism and hence individual free will, free choice, spiritual self-determination. Capitalism is always socially and culturally embedded (Granovetter 2011).

In particular the so-called Axial Age religions and worldviews—a term that goes back to Karl Jaspers (2021, or. 1949/1953) but that has regained impressive prominence in recent years in the field of sociology of religion and adjacent fields—appear to have immensely impacted the respective cultures in which they emerged (Voegelin 1956–1987; Eisenstadt 1986; Arnason et al. 2005; Taylor 2007; Bellah 2011; Bellah and Joas 2012). And the rise of some form of modernity (including some form of capitalism) does not simply wipe away and equalize all those deep backgrounds. We can still see China as the culture where—apart from Marx and modern science—Confucianism is indispensable for understanding it; and even in the immensely technologically progressive Arabian Emirates, Islam deeply influences the shape of its modernization, to say nothing of other Islamic countries. Hinduism is still a key for understanding India, as Protestantism is for Northern Europe and the USA, and so on. Samuel Huntington (1996) was largely right in pointing at "civilizations" as identifiable spheres of shared mentalities (though we do not necessarily have to buy into his rhetoric of an imminent or even unavoidable "clash" between them). The World Values Survey is still able to show rather divergent value orientations in the world, along civilizational lines, as is shown in their "Cultural Map of the World" (Inglehart and Welzel 2005; Inglehart and Welzel 2009) (Fig. 1.1).

What does this imply? First of all, it shows that the transition to modernity (and the rise of capitalism) apparently is not a monolithic, one-way process, but allows for intricate interaction with specific cultural contexts. What Weber could probably not imagine was the extent to which capitalism is—and remains—amenable to "non-systemic" influences, which may even come for example from cultural and religious traditions (de Jong 2009). Capitalism is not a satellite in orbit, but a bird that constantly has to feed itself from the local ground in order to be able to fly. So there is much more interaction between capitalism and culture, much more back and forth, than Weber expected.

Secondly, this implies as well that apparently there is much more room for variation in the way capitalism is fashioned, the way markets are designed and economic activity is embedded, than Weber thought. Reflection on what we, as a society, or as societies, expect free markets to be and what to deliver, what we ask of them in terms of virtues and human flourishing, is a highly relevant matter! Human convictions, hopes, aspirations, ideals, perhaps even moral systems and religions, are not simply something of a distant past, but may bear on the actual present as well as on the future. Capitalism is more diverse and multifaceted than Weber assumed. Of the rise of capitalism—or, more generally spoken "free markets" (more on our terminology later in this introduction)—the same may be said what Alexis de Tocqueville said about the rise of democracy, that it is "so strong that it cannot be stopped, but it is not yet so rapid that it cannot be guided" (de Tocqueville 1954, 7). This guidance may turn out to be critical for our common future on planet Earth. And for this

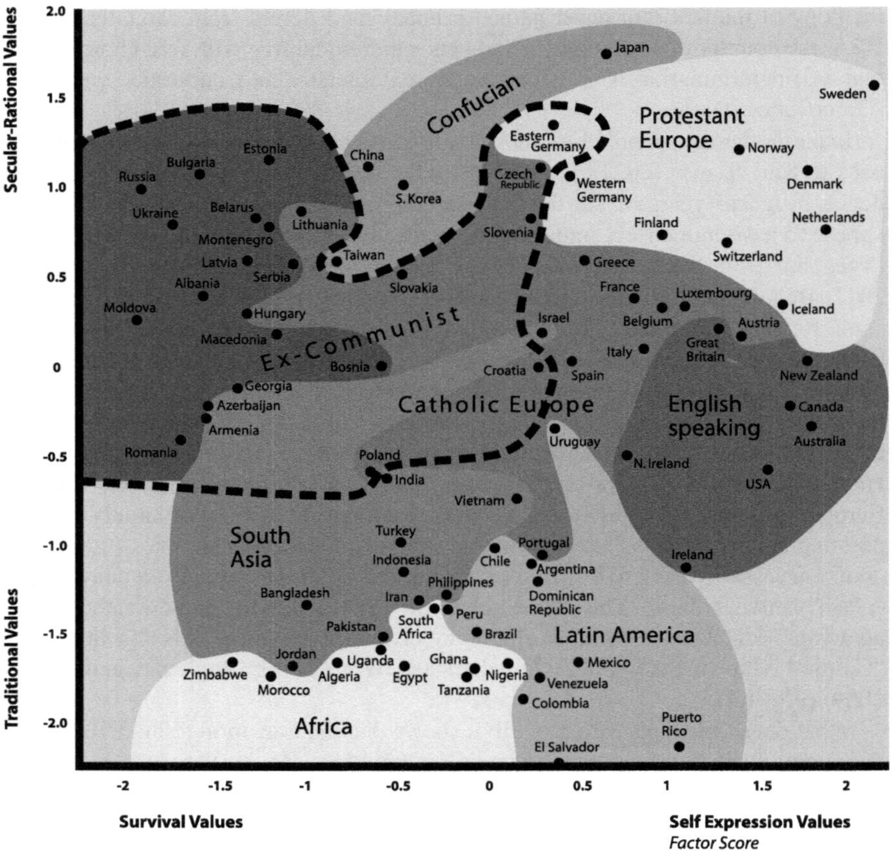

Fig. 1.1 Koyos, CC BY-SA 3.0 https://creativecommons.org/licenses/by-sa/3.0, via Wikimedia Commons

guidance of capitalism, it can be very helpful to look to the very same world religions that Weber studied.

1.3.2 Secularization?

A hundred years after Weber, we have witnessed and are still witnessing a global resurgence of religion as a publicly present phenomenon, with considerable political, and economic, consequences.

Weber could not imagine that religion would play a public role in the future of modern society. The Weberian frame only allowed for the gradual disappearance of religion parallel to the rise of modernity and modern rationalism. This "high modernity" frame prevented Western intellectuals, social scientists, economists, and policy makers from seeing the continuing and even resurging manifestation of religion in the public sphere, particularly once the cloud of the Cold War was starting to be lifted (Casanova 1994; Berger 1999; Thomas 2005, Polinder 2024). Of course, Weber himself had expressed a slight reservation: "whether finally: who knows?" Today, we know, for the moment at least. At least since the 1970s we have witnessed a resurgence of public manifestations of religion. The Catholic Church during the pontificate of John Paul II manifested a new political leverage and a reshaping of church-state relations that perhaps can only be compared with the eleventh-century Investiture Struggle (when in 1077 the Emperor had to acknowledge the political independence of the church). Now, in the 1980-ties numerous dictatorial regimes, both Marxist-totalitarian and right-wing, fascist autocratic regimes, had to give way to democratic change, after the public denunciation (and behind-the-scene activism) of the "Polish Pope," who had a long track record of dealing with communist dictators (Huntington 1991). Around the same time the in the West virtually unknown Ayatollah Khomeini who lived in Paris, suddenly appeared as head of a strong Shi'ite Islamic uprising against the Shah of Persia/Iran. Again, around the same time we saw the rise of Pentecostalism, that had its origins in the early twentieth century but had its breakthrough in South America and Africa in the final third of that century and which has developed a kind of Protestant work ethic on its own, combined with beliefs about the combination of Christian beliefs and worldly success. As Peter Berger memorably put it, "Max Weber is alive and well, and living in Guatemala" (Berger 2010). Later, in the first decades of the twenty-first century, we have seen a new prominence of older religions like in Russia where the Orthodox Church gained a new public presence under Putin. And in India, the "Hinduthva"-program of Modi and the BJP almost seems to enlist the capitalist economy for religious purposes, reversing what Weber expected.

The resurgence of religion is partly a mirage, in as far as religion probably was there before, but the geo-political situation of the Cold War blinded our view. Once the curtain was removed—both the Iron Curtain, but as well the Cold War-curtain in its entirety—we received a new perspective on the world of civilizations in which religions often had a formative role, as Huntington's analysis mentioned earlier has pointed out.

This development has only gained prominence in recent years. What Castells has dubbed the "global network society" seems to have fostered at the same time a longing for what he has called, and what very often still is called, "identity" (Castells 1996–2004; Fukuyama 2018). For a number of reasons, however, we would prefer to speak about various, though often conflicting, conceptions of the good life instead of identities, sometimes reactionary, sometimes progressive. Of course terms are very important here. By using the term *identity* we tend to tap into a discourse that puts religions and worldviews into defensive strategies and social constructions. Mahatma Gandhi, Martin Luther King, and Desmond Tutu are certainly religiously inspired public voices, yet it is not easy to simply categorize them under the term *identity politics* as the phrase is used today, in the first decades of the twenty-first century.

This all has implications as well for debates on (the future of) capitalism. There are new (and in fact many rather old) voices to be heard, which have had and may still have their own impact on the way capitalism is constructed in various contexts. Why not study them in the terms that they want to be studied? Why not invite people who speak from within those traditions? At the same time a critical dialogue between these various voices themselves, as well as between them and economists should be staged, for in a globalized, plural context no one can lay down an absolute truth claim in the global public sphere. As Peter Berger once observed, "Modernity does not necessarily secularize. What modernity necessarily does is *pluralize*." That is, "All the basic forces of modernization bring about a situation where most people constantly encounter beliefs, values and lifestyles different from the ones in which they were originally raised" (Berger 2011, 12). This encounter, dialogue, and sometimes clash of perspectives ought to be acknowledged and may even be welcomed for the possibilities it brings in terms of new insights to be expressed rather than denied and suppressed.

1.3.3 Weber's Method of Interpretation

A hundred years after Weber, we have become aware that the world has become a globalized world in which the West no longer has the exclusive right to interpret the course of the world and to interpret the role of other cultures in one preset template—so the Western interpretation of modernization is not simply the only option on offer.

A third development that we have to take into account compared to Weber's context is the process of globalization itself and its implications for the way we now look at the world. Whereas Weber's picture of the world and world history was still markedly Eurocentric, today we have become aware that the world is a global village in which we have come face to face, from a huge variety of cultural backgrounds and traditions. Therefore we no longer should allow ourselves to analyze all cultures and world religions from a location in a German academic office, but we have to have voices all around the table, so to speak.

This is not just a matter of physical opportunity and logistics, but first of all a mental attitude. For if we look closer at Weber's massive project, it becomes apparent that he did not escape the danger of casting all the religions he studied on his own Western-style Procrustean-bed and cutting them accordingly. Yes, he certainly wanted to immerse himself in the religions and worldviews he was studying—*Verstehen* is the German term, which means something like "sensitively understanding." However, as already indicated before, for Weber the heart of world history was the rise of Western style rationalization in a gigantic struggle with magic. So in spite of this emphasis on *Verstehen*, his research question really boiled down to asking, "How far have they come" along this path? How far is Confucianism, how far is Judaism, how far is Hinduism, and the rest, along the road to modernization? How much magical or superstitious thinking is still there, preventing the rise of capitalist rationalization (or rational capitalism), and how much *ratio* is there to be found? For Weber, everywhere where magic is somehow curbed, it can only be by rationalism. So the devotion to God, as the Eternal One in the Hebrew Scriptures, out of which follows its rejection of magic, soothsaying, fortune telling, consulting of spirits, and so on, is seen by Weber only as rationalization. Judaism, by virtue of its monotheism, automatically becomes a key instance of rationalization. Even when he refers to the Psalms, in which we hear believers express their sorrows, their sadness, as well as their joy in the goodness of God and their surprise at his steadfastness every morning—Weber calls them "perfectly unemotional." They are, apparently, purely *rational* songs:

> The influence of the God-fearing but perfectly unemotional wisdom of the Hebrews, which is expressed in the books most read by the Puritans, the Proverbs and the Psalms, can be felt in their whole attitude toward life. In particular, its rational suppression of the mystical, in fact the whole emotional side of religion, has rightly been attributed... to the influence of the Old Testament. (Weber 2005, 76)

After that Weber concedes that Medieval Christianity could still leave room for emotions, but the Calvinists selected this "unemotional" side and made it central to their religious praxis. And how does Buddhism fare on this flat continuum? For Weber it clearly is rational, if only for the reason that it is not magical.

Moreover, whether there might be something to learn in all these traditions and religions is not Weber's concern. Learning from normative traditions, as distinct from mere studying them, would for him imply a dangerous crossing of the modern boundaries between facts and values, between the world of rationality and the world of meaning, between the objective and the subjective. As Dingxin Zhao has observed, "The mechanisms that facilitated the rise of industrial capitalism are very different from the learning of capitalism under the isomorphic pressure of the Western and Japanese imperialism" (Zhao 2017, 144). Understanding the extent to which different religions and worldviews might "learn" capitalism, and in the process alter it, whether for good or ill, is a central goal of this project.

Indeed, if capitalism is not a natural phenomenon but a human construction, and even to a certain extent can be guided, then why not collect as many candidates for providing guiding ideas as possible, one or perhaps more "spirits"? Even if one wants to maintain the Weberian boundaries between facts and values, then it is still possible to collect, inventory, and study ideas without necessarily choosing between them. One only has to give up the progressivist prejudice that everything from the past is now superseded and irrelevant. But it indeed does require a different hermeneutic than Weber's scheme of magical versus rational thinking. One has to take seriously the moral and even ontological claims that are presented in various worldviews and religions and understand their coherence within the entire framework of that religion or worldview, something that truly can be called *Verstehen*. This brings us to our final point.

1.3.4 The Future of Capitalism

A hundred years after Weber we not only have discovered that capitalism has varieties but that we perhaps even need new varieties that we have to develop in order to meet the requirements of the future. For that we may need a new "spirit of capitalism" that is able to align free markets with ecological, social, and psychological requirements.

A fourth development that we see emerging in recent decades is a growing awareness that we cannot simply continue the economic development of the last two centuries, with free market capitalism-as-we-know-it-now as the leading mode of organizing our economy for another two or more centuries. This awareness in itself is not new. During the last two hundred years there have been extensive debates about the up- and downsides of free markets and capitalism (Fourcade and Healy 2007). Adam Smith himself already assumed the embeddedness of markets in a moral horizon in which the classical virtues are present, as described in his *Theory of Moral Sentiments* (1759). A century later Karl Marx of course vehemently started to criticize capitalism. The debate has continued with oscillating ups and downs, more or less continuously until the fall of the Berlin Wall in 1989, which ushered in a period that seemed to celebrate the final and almost global victory of the free-market idea.

And indeed, capitalism and free markets (we will discuss more precise definitions later) have an impressive track record as it comes to combating poverty and boosting the "wealth of nations." Scholars like Hayek and Friedman certainly have seen correctly that free markets galvanize the creativity and industriousness of people and are able—via supply and demand, mediated by prices—to handle information in a way that no controlling or organizing agency would ever be able to do. So in this fundamental respect free markets are much better positioned to fight poverty and create wealth than state-led or centrally planned economies. What can be called the "Adam Smith-revolution" (a primarily intellectual one, that rather quietly has developed into policies) has lifted millions of people out of poverty in a way that the "Karl Marx-revolutions" (with much more noise and violence) have not been able to do. The connection between global trade and growth are undeniable, although a lot of problems remain regarding the connection between globalization and the reduction of poverty (Collier 2007) (Fig. 1.2).

However, in recent years serious new questions have been asked as to whether we really can continue like this and live within this system forever after? A first trigger for this new debate was the 2008 credit crisis. The growing awareness of the contemporary ecological threats for our planet, in light of the immense population growth worldwide, is another trigger: can we really have 9 or even 10 billion people who consume like Westerners consume today? An added development that is drawn into the discussion is the emergence of new very large concentrations of uncontrolled power especially with the information-processing companies (sometimes called the G-MAFIA: Google, Microsoft, Apple, Facebook, IBM, Amazon) (Webb 2019). Do markets, by constantly stimulating (material) production and by

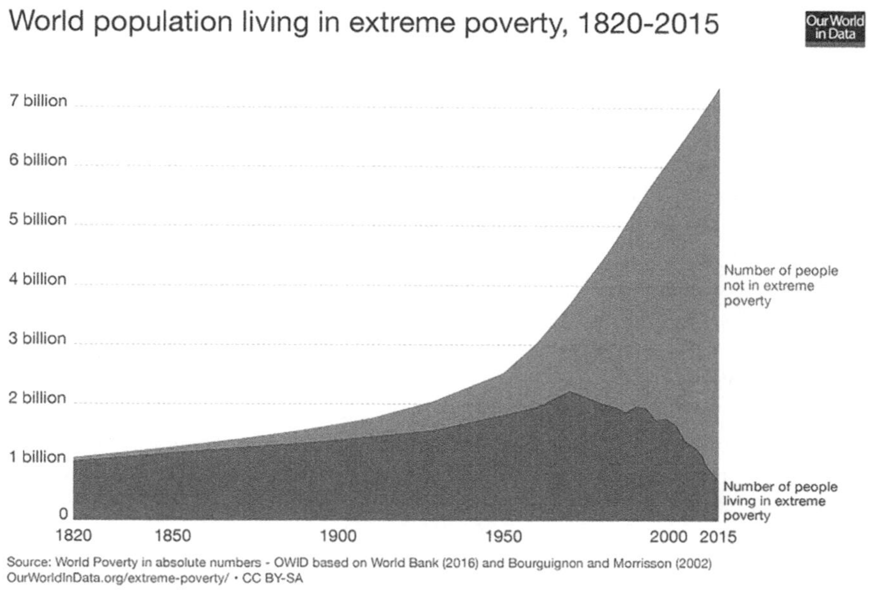

Fig. 1.2 CC BY-SA https://creativecommons.org/licenses/by-sa/, via Our World in Data

constantly stimulating the buildup of concentrated power, perhaps have a built-in tendency toward self-undermining and self-destruction? In Donald Trump's second term, it even seems that Big Tech is almost taking over the government.

The discussion about the consequences and the results of capitalism and free markets is closely tied to the discussion about the moral preconditions and consequences of free markets. Are free markets not based on vice, notably greed and envy (as was asserted in Bernard de Mandeville's famous 'Fable of the Bees')? And are not the moral results of these vices found in materialism, constant dissatisfaction, resentment, anger, and therefore a moral breakdown? Does not this moral breakdown invite people to cheat, to manipulate, to build up double standards, to operate constantly on the verge of hypocrisy? Is it not the case that in capitalism at the end of the day it is only money that counts, pushing people to think that money can buy everything, and act on it, in their business relations, in politics, and also in their private lives? Or if not money (which is preferable because it is measurable) then is it not preferable that we at least have markets in all dimensions of human activity (Brennan and Jaworski 2016)?

Or is all this a distortion and corruption of the free-market idea and not inherently connected to the idea? Can markets be both virtuous and vicious, depending on the moral power and moral resilience of market actors? Is virtuousness perhaps a necessary condition for markets to function well? Can capitalism indeed do without a 'spirit'? And if not, what should that spirit be?

In recent years we have seen an avalanche of attempts to rethink the morality of markets. Ideas and phrases like "moral markets," economics for the common good, economics of mutuality, doughnut economics, sustainable economics, moral capitalism, completing capitalism, rethinking economics, are being developed. By and large we can indeed summarize this search as a search for moral embedding of free markets. How should we develop ourselves morally in order to live well within a free-market society? How will we be able to check ourselves and to check the market? What kind of morality do we need? What kind of view of the world, of the self and of society, do we need to be able to survive our own creation—the free market?

The discussion is raised to an entirely new level by all sorts of attempts to formulate yardsticks for judging, and subsequently redirecting, capitalism, or the overall performance of free markets. Well known are the various happiness indexes, developed in the World Happiness Reports, the capabilities approaches of Amartya Sen and Martha Nussbaum, the OECD Better Life Index, the Legatum Prosperity Index, and so on. The yardsticks somehow presuppose that markets economies can be—at least to a certain extent—influenced, constructed with an eye to intended outcomes. For these outcomes understood as more inclusive than GDP, we use the term *human flourishing* (more on the term below).

So when we take a birds-eye view on current discussions on free markets and capitalism we see the emergence of a triangle: we have *free markets*, which are supposed to contribute to something like *human flourishing*, and in order to make sure that indeed markets do contribute to human flourishing we have to pay attention to the nature of the *market institutions* themselves and above all to a certain morality, *a set of virtues* that need to be present in—at least a substantial number of—actors on the market. Referring to Weber, we can call a certain complex of more or less dominant virtues in a society a *spirit*, a more or less shared mentality.

For a redirection of capitalism in order to make it sustainable, we cannot remain within the confines of Weber's analysis of the spiritless "iron cage," but we need to discuss the possibility that *spirits* are still able to influence the economic system—not in this case Keynes' "animal spirits" but moral- and worldview-spirits—very much in line with what Weber investigated. That is a very good reason to ask representatives of various spirits to articulate what that spirit could be and how it would bear on the economic order. In this sense can what we are doing in this book be characterized as moving with Weber beyond Weber.

In summary: different from what Weber expected, modernity is not as monolithic a process of unilinear rationalization after all. There are different paths of modernization, there are degrees of freedom, there are problems that we can consciously identify. This calls for reflection and orientation. The characterization of our present condition as "reflexive modernity," a term coined by Beck and collaborators (Beck et al. 2003), therefore seems apt. This phrase is used to point to a phase in the modernization process in which the unintended consequences and shadow sides of modernization have become clearer—what Charles Taylor has dubbed the "malaises of modernity"—and in which a cheap postmodernism has run its course and left us dissatisfied (Taylor 1992, 2007; cf. Beck et al. 2003). What characterizes the program of reflexive modernity is the acknowledgment that modernization is a strong force and that in many ways it has given us real progress but that in light of considerable tradeoffs, we as societies need to take back control of modernization, globalization, capitalism, that is, control over the way we as humans, as citizens, organize our world.

Now the word *control* certainly is too provocative and misleading. We use it here to emphasize strongly that there are degrees of freedom in the way we as societies organize free markets, and that therefore it is highly relevant to have reflection and debate on this. Capitalism, the phenomenon that Weber studied so intensely, is neither an iron system (Weber's position) nor a natural phenomenon like the weather (as many neoliberals have suggested). In both interpretations it is unchangeable and unaffectable by human action. However, the debate over varieties of capitalism shows that capitalism is not written in stone, but is a human cultural creation or construction, one that requires human input. For this input the study of and dialogue between various religions and worldviews can be of great aid.

On the other hand, identifying degrees of freedom should not lead us into the temptation of thinking as if century long processes can change their direction overnight, at our simple command. The present situation is much more complicated than that. The metaphor that we find in Beck, when he is reflecting on this, is that of *surfing* versus *drifting* (Beck et al. 2003, 26). Although he primarily applies this to individual behavior in late-modern societies, we may as well expand the metaphor to the public, societal level. *Surfing* is accepting constant changes but always trying to reach your own goals in spite of that, perhaps even using the changes. It accepts uncertainty—expecting the unexpected—but constantly looks for opportunities to move ahead, from whatever side winds and waves are coming (Beck et al. 2003). The surfer has her plan but is aware that this may not be realized as expected. *Drifting* is the attitude that simply regrets the way things go, and that goes with the flow, without seeing or willing to see any possibility for critical action.

Reflexive modernity therefore is about trying to navigate in difficult circumstances, to choose a point of orientation and then try to get to a destination or at least to go in that direction. For this task of choosing of points of orientation, it may be very worthwhile to consult the various traditions that Weber has studied—but clearly with different intentions than he had. In general, for Beck et al., reflexive modernity is characterized by an *and-and* approach instead of a modern *either-or* approach. Instead of either facts or values (Weber's sharp distinction) it is facts *and* values; instead of either nature or technology, it is nature *and* technology; instead of individualization versus community, it is individual *and* community; instead of religion or secularization, it is religion *and* secularization. For us, this idea of reflexive modernity implies a willingness to listen to different voices, to different types of knowledge, to different ideas that may be of relevance to give some reflexive guidance to the future development of capitalism, in order to make it conducive to human flourishing.

1.4 In Search of the Future Spirit(s) of Capitalism: Listening to Different Voices

But then: why give in this new debate specific attention to religious or worldview-inspired perspectives on capitalism, morality, and human flourishing? First of all, it is not up to anyone, either politicians, scholars, or intellectuals, to place themselves in a position to judge who are allowed to give their viewpoints in the public sphere and who are not. It is not up to politicians or up to academics to deny space for adherents of worldviews and religions to give their views. No elite professor can give or deny religions the right to speak out, although liberal thinkers like John Rawls have tried to build a case for excluding these viewpoints from the public sphere (Rawls 1997). In our view, the public sphere is better conceived of as a free space. Everybody can send messages—although there is no concomitant right to be heard or listened to either.

However, while defending the right to speak may be very important from a political-legal point of view, it does not bring us very far in terms of our societal challenges. Just accepting that there are different viewpoints may well result in recognizing a plurality of well fenced-off reserves for endangered species, which are called religions and/or worldviews.

However, the argument developed thus far brings us to the insight that it may be very important to give attention to the actual message of religions and worldviews as the stage of reflexive modernity calls for new orientation, a new search for the future "spirit of capitalism." We can deepen this argument in the following ways.

First of all, there is an independent argument for preserving a variety of viewpoints and to prevent an early closure or force an early consensus. We can call this the Mill argument. In this view, it would be extremely unwise to only foster one world- and lifeview, one conception of the good life, that is, the modern-rational view. Doing so would stifle all difference of opinion, all diversity, all developments of possible alternatives. For purely pragmatic reasons only, that would be very unwise. Thus we find the basic argument of John Stuart Mill, which says that.

> The peculiar evil of silencing the expression of an opinion is, that it is robbing the human race; posterity as well as the existing generation; those who dissent from the opinion, still more than those who hold it. If the opinion is right, they are deprived of the opportunity of exchanging error for truth: if wrong, they lose, what is almost as great a benefit, the clearer perception and livelier impression of truth, produced by its collision with error. (Mill 2015, 19)

This is a pragmatic argument that we could apply as well to the various conceptions of the good life that world history has passed down to us. As long as people find these conceptions worth continuing, worth living, and worth further developing, it may be important to treasure them, and encourage them to express themselves, especially in light of the strong uniformizing power of the modern world.

Of course, we—either as moderns ourselves, or as adherents of another conception of the good life—may find some convictions and practices appalling, others awkward or cumbersome, and we may not be able to see their point. However, it may well be that exactly these mutually strange and inaccessible elements may hide important insights that may not be present in other traditions or run the risk of getting lost.

There is a second reason why attention for what representatives of various religions and worldviews have to say may be highly relevant. As we have come face to face in a globalized world as people from various cultural backgrounds, it turns out that it is not always easy to live together. This is true for individuals as well as societies and institutions. As Berger puts it,

> On the institutional level, this means that different communities of meaning (religious or other) have to find ways of living together unless they want to embroil their society in ongoing, possibly violent conflict. On the level of individuals, it means that they can no longer take for granted the worldview of earlier generations; instead they must make choices between alternative worldviews on offer in their milieu. (Berger 2011, 12, 14)

A simple response might be what Charles Taylor has called the "ethics of inarticulacy" which is characterized by a "method of avoidance": just do not talk about deep differences, remain silent, and assume a superficial consensus; this is actually the Rawlsian procedure. It is truly dubious whether this is enough. This seems to be a reiteration of Weber's analysis, that religions and worldviews are ultimately irrelevant in light of the modern rationalized world.

Charles Taylor himself advocates a different path, dubbed the "politics of recognition" (Taylor 1994). The key idea here is that living together in a common world—which certainly relates to nation-states, but also seemingly to the global community as well—requires some sort of mutual recognition, a basic respect for each other's viewpoints. Simply declaring them irrelevant, relegating them to the private sphere, will not do. On the other hand, a facile recognition in the form of feigned admiration or respect, is demeaning and humiliating as well. True recognition calls for hard work. For Taylor the distinction between *a priori* and *a posteriori* is crucial here. Everyone in the public sphere, especially those who represent the majority-position, is obliged to *a priori* respect for other viewpoints, the "presumption of equal worth." However, this may become different after one has thoroughly acquainted oneself to the position to the other—by a "fusion of horizons," trying to place oneself in the position of that other viewpoint and considering the arguments and reasons that are provided by the adherents of that other viewpoint. Once that is done, one still has the right to criticize or reject the position of the other. The *a posteriori* judgment does not have to repeat the equal worth of the *a priori*: it may well be that one finds the viewpoints of the other unacceptable. But there is as well the option that one at least understands the other's viewpoint, or that one even learns from it.

The German social philosopher Jürgen Habermas, deeply influenced by Weber, has brought this line of argumentation even a step further. He has argued for new space that should be given to religious contributions within the public sphere. He sees the late-modern society as a post-secular society, in which we have to acknowledge that Weber's expectation of a full disenchantment, a completed secularization, has not materialized. However, Habermas adds to this another important element: the awareness that religious groups may have insights that are not yet or not anymore present in the shared public consciousness of a largely secular society and yet may be highly relevant:

> Secular citizens or those of other religious persuasions can under certain circumstances learn something from religious contributions; this is, for example, the case if they recognize in the normative truth content of a religious utterance hidden intuitions of their own. Religious traditions have a special power to articulate moral intuitions, especially with regard to vulnerable forms of communal life. (Habermas 2006, 10)

Habermas envisages the possibility of "complementary learning processes" of religious and secular citizens together (Habermas 2006, 16). The burden of these learning processes should not be on one side exclusively (say, that religious people should learn to tolerate other viewpoints) but should be on both sides, symmetrically, so as to develop a common language of communication. This may imply that religious insights should be translated into non-religious language, but that also secular people should try to understand the deeper, perhaps not always fully explicable concerns of religious people. For Habermas therefore the religious inspiration behind the argument should not have to be hidden at all costs. Here we hit on a key assumption of the revisionist position: religions can learn, secular citizens can learn as well, political orders can learn; all can learn from each other.

Generous as he may be, at the same time Habermas maintains some of the usual liberal reservations. Not all citizens are able to "match up to the yardstick of the public use of reason" and they thereby are "endangering political integration." There is the dim prospect of a world that is characterized by a "collision of fundamentalist and secular camps" (Habermas 2006, 18). Therefore, representatives of religious traditions should be aware that they live in a plural world, where they cannot claim an *a priori* monopoly on truth, and where they can be legitimately criticised by others. For us, this is an important insight for this volume as well.

1.5 The Central Purposes and Concepts of This Project

Let us summarize our argument thus far. Capitalism is not a one size fits all-phenomenon or a natural phenomenon. There is a variety of capitalisms, each feeding on cultural and historically even religious traditions. As we are now entering into a phase that we can call reflexive modernity, where we need to revisit and look for a reorientation of capitalism-as-we-know-it, it may even become an urgent matter to listen to what has been said or can be said from various religious and worldview backgrounds on markets, morality, and human flourishing. Let us repeat here the specific orientation for this volume, the central question, is, as simply put as possible:

> From the perspective of one of the world religions, do free markets contribute to human flourishing, and what from these perspectives is the role of morality and especially virtues, in realizing this contribution?

1.5.1 Terminology: Capitalism and Free Markets

In this introduction we have mostly used the term *capitalism*, a choice inspired by Weber's project. Most free-market economies that we know of today are characterized as capitalist. Definitions of capitalism abound and no single one will be able to generate consensus (Hodgson 2015). However, most definitions refer to an economic system in which individual persons and enterprises can exchange goods and services by mutual consensus, guaranteed by a legal system of individual property rights, and in which those who provide the capital for investments by enterprises are psychologically, morally and legally seen as the owner of the business/enterprise and hence are the ones who are entitled to its profits. In capitalist economies there is a tendency that the capital transactions are the only relation that the investor has with the entrepreneur/businessman, and the expectation of profit the only concern that the investor has. Moreover, as Van Bavel has emphasized, there is a tendency in (later phases of) capitalism that land, labor, and capital itself become subject to market exchanges and that both property-less wage laborers and property-owning entrepreneurs/investors both become increasingly dependent on output and factor markets (Van Bavel 2016). Eventually this leads to a phase in which accumulation and concentration of capital takes place, together with growing inequality, huge profits, and privileges for capital owners and monopolies.

Given these and similar analyses of capitalism, starting with Marx, in which the term capitalism becomes inherently connected with decay and inequality, it seems adequate to make a distinction between *capitalism* and *free markets*, that is, *free markets economies*. Free markets are actual or virtual platforms where individuals and individual organizations can freely buy and sell goods and services and in this way fulfill their needs and wants. The *free* refers to the absence of government regulations that directly interfere with the transactions between the market actors (e.g., ordering what to produce of buy, or at what price).

Pope John Paul II distinguished between conceptions of *capitalism* that mirror these respective usages. In addressing the question whether capitalism is "the model which ought to be proposed to the countries of the Third World which are searching for the path to true economic and civil progress?," John Paul said that the answer depends on what one means by the term *capitalism*. Thus,

> If by "capitalism" is meant an economic system which recognizes the fundamental and positive role of business, the market, private property and the resulting responsibility for the means of production, as well as free human creativity in the economic sector, then the answer is certainly in the affirmative, even though it would perhaps be more appropriate to speak of a "business economy," "market economy" or simply "free economy."

But, he continues,

> if by "capitalism" is meant a system in which freedom in the economic sector is not circumscribed within a strong juridical framework which places it at the service of human freedom in its totality, and which sees it as a particular aspect of that freedom, the core of which is ethical and religious, then the reply is certainly negative. (John Paul II 1991, §42)

A *free-market economy* then is an economy in which the vast majority of goods and services are produced freely by privately initiated or owned enterprises and are offered to potential buyers and exchanged for a mutually agreed price. In almost all free-market economies there is a legal framework in place that ensures the enforceability of mutually agreed transactions and property rights.

By using the terms in the way just indicated, we imply that free-market economies are not necessarily capitalist, though in the course of the last 200 years, capitalism and free-market economies are almost co-extensive. Yet, there are varieties of capitalism, or, as we would prefer to say varieties of free-market economies. The variety usually has to do with two axes, one institutional and one moral:

(a) *The institutional axis*: the extent in which governments regulate, influence, or coordinate the economy, often in order to make sure that societally held ideas of human flourishing or other standards are indeed realized by the market system (e.g., employment figures; social security arrangements; viability of certain economic sectors that are seen as vital for the nation). Hall and Soskice, key authors in the varieties of capitalism debate, make a distinction between Liberal Market Economies (LME) and Coordinated Market Economies (CME) (Hall and Soskice 2001). It seems wise to add to this typology at least another type that can be called Hierarchical Market Economies (HME) (de Jong 2021). The underlying issue seems to be here the question whether in a given society the generally shared idea is that the outcomes of the market process are in themselves the best possible outcomes or whether there are clear market failures that need correction, by other societal actors or by the state.

(b) *The moral axis*: the extent in which the partners in the market, notably the enterprises, are legally obliged or morally nudged to develop a broader perspective on added value than mere financial profits. In a society the dominant opinion can be that market actors are morally obliged to embed the market activity in a network of various stakeholders, or the dominant opinion can be, as Milton Friedman famously phrased it, "that there is one and only one social responsibility of business—to use its resources and engage in activities designed to increase its profits so long as it stays within the rules of the game" (Friedman 2009, 133; see also Friedman 1970). Both perspectives have moral underpinnings and a set of concomitant virtues.

In the first approach the basic idea is that the entrepreneur and his business can only do what they do because of a preestablished context in which there are already good laws in place, where potential employees already have a certain level of education, where there is a physical (or recently a digital) infrastructure that makes it possible to do whatever the business sets out to do. No one is self-made, and therefore one always has a social responsibility to help sustain the common good. Moreover, as an entrepreneur or as a business always participates in a society, there is always the responsibility to involve various stakeholders in the affairs of the company, employees, NGOs, and neighborhoods that are affected by what the company is doing. Paying taxes is as well a natural element in this approach. Important virtues here are temperance, trust (or love, or solidarity), and justice.

In the other approach, the full emphasis is on the individual creativity and initiative of the entrepreneur or of the business. If they would not have taken this or that particular initiative, nothing would have been there. So the initiator is fully entitled to the results of this initiative. And the financiers of the initiative, the risk-takers, are fully entitled to have their share. Within the constraints of the law, there should be an almost absolute freedom to develop one's own goals—and in this way others can profit as well. Key virtues here are courage, hope, and creativity.

1.5.2 Human Flourishing

Although perspectives on human flourishing may vary among the various world religions that we are dealing with in this volume, we propose here to give a rough framework that sets some boundaries as to what we are looking for in our discussions. Therefore we state some provisional claims.

First, human flourishing brings together *both 'subjective' and 'objective' elements.* We cannot speak of human flourishing when people do not feel happy at all. So happiness—or subjective well-being—certainly is an element of human flourishing. But people may well be happy doing terrible things to others, to the environment, or doing great harm to oneself. So human flourishing is at least a reasonable level of happiness experienced in a socially and ecologically sustainable bedding or life practice.

Second, human flourishing is *multidimensional.* Although sometimes life may be lived in a very narrowminded or focused way—for example, the life of a top athlete—in general people tend to agree on the insight that "there is more to life than *x*." Even top athletes often indicate how important their family life is as support for their activities. Or the team may be very important. So even in that case their flourishing consists of at least two dimensions: the athletic achievements and the social dimension. But in general the multidimensionality of human flourishing asserts itself in the cry for balance: work-life balance, for instance, or a *people-planet-profit* balance, and so on. For some, a sense of transcendent meaning may be a dimension of human flourishing. We pointed already to a variety of recent attempts to develop multidimensional sets of indicators as an alternative for the one-dimensional GDP such as the capabilities approaches of Amartya Sen and Martha Nussbaum, the OECD Better Life Index, the Legatum Prosperity Index, and so on (Balkenende and Buijs 2024, 90ff).

Third, human flourishing is dependent upon certain *'supra-individual' conditions, which our flourishing life should not diminish.* It is almost impossible to describe any notion of human flourishing in, say, a context of civil war or in a context of failing states or in a context of huge shortages in basic life supplies. We have to give account of the conditions for human flourishing that have to be fulfilled: a healthy environment, bodily health, supportive institutions, social relationships, and the possibility to develop a sense of meaning (which implies the cultural presence and recognition of meaningful narratives, life-orientation, rituals, and so on) (Verbrugge et al. 2018).

So based on these three claims we could describe human flourishing as a justified sense of living a fulfilling life within a supporting institutional, ecological, and social context. Our question then becomes: do free markets enhance human flourishing thus described?

1.5.3 Virtues

Virtues we will describe as *acquired or acquirable, socially valued, dispositions or character traits that are being exhibited in the person's habitual behavior.* It is significant for this definition that it concerns both the inward and the outward, both the intentions and motivations of people and their actual behavior. When Weber spoke about the "ethic of Protestantism" and the "spirit of capitalism," he actually was after something very similar: inward convictions and motivations on the one hand and on the other hand outward behavior that can be related to these convictions, or, as we would say, can be related to these worldview traditions. So when we ask the question after the future "spirit of capitalism" we could rephrase it as well as by asking, "What virtues will be needed for people acting within free market economies, in order for human flourishing to be promoted?"

1.5.4 Religion and Worldview

In the search for the future spirit of capitalism, or, more specifically, the spirit of human flourishing enhancing free markets economies, in this volume we examine various *world religions*, in Weber's terminology. How do we define *religion*? Weber was quite generous in this respect. In his project he dealt with Confucianism, Buddhism next to Protestantism and Judaism, all as part of this project on world religions. This opens an immense debate on how to define religion. Is Confucianism properly identified as a religion? Is Daoism? Is Buddhism? The same question applies to the various substreams within these traditions.

In this volume we propose—very pragmatically—to use a wider term that comprises both *secular* and *non-secular religions*, the term *worldview* or *worldview tradition*. We may use this term as the wider term and, if an author wishes to do so, speak as well of religions, usually as a subtype within this broader category.

The term *worldview* has its drawbacks as well, as it may give the impression that it always concerns a primarily intellectual set of ideas. That is not intended here. We may describe a worldview tradition here as *shared basic intuitions about what really counts in life and the concomitant practices as they have developed over an extensive period of time*. In explicating "what really counts in life," we can include what the theologian Paul Tillich used to call *ultimate concern* or what often is referred to as *the sacred*—which then could be interpreted both in a more immanent way and in a more transcendent way (Tillich 1957, 23).

A final word about the very term 'world religions'. In recent years this term has become a contested one, partly due to a new awareness of its roots in colonialism and Eurocentrism, and even 'Protestant-centrism' (Cotter and Robertson 2016). The, as it is now sometimes called, 'World Religions Paradigm' employs a concept of religion that is very much 'text-based' and has specific 'doctrines' and overlooks all kind of forms of 'lived religion', especially what is often called 'indigenous religions' (although in itself another contested term). However, as Max Weber is very much the source of inspiration for this project, we decided to follow his lead and focus on religions that directly or indirectly (e.g. Judaism via Christianity and Islam) have influenced larger civilizational areas. But in subsequent projects, we certainly would prefer to look beyond these, especially when we draw the relationship between humanity and nature into the picture, a key element in the current ecological challenges that capitalism faces, and on which exactly representatives of indigenous religions might have important things to say.

1.5.5 'Emic' and 'Etic'

Worldview traditions have been, for thousands of years, important ways for people to find moral orientation in life. They help identify and define what for humans is a good life, in distinction from mere living. It is for this reason that we should engage in an effort of letting the various religions articulate and develop their own particular views on—in this case—how to evaluate free markets, in terms of what they consider as human flourishing.

In this volume we have chosen to give the floor to both people who consider themselves active adherents of or participant in a certain worldview tradition and to those who are studying, in an academic-critical way, the content and/or some societal effects of certain worldview traditions.

Anthropologists have developed a distinction that may be clarifying in this respect, between *emic* and *etic* interpretations. *Emic* stands for the perspective *from within* a certain tribe, group, or tradition, for whom this tradition is somehow authoritative; *etic* stands for the perspective from without, as sociologist or historians of thought tend to do, not dealing with what a certain tradition might still have to say.

Our background assumption behind this idea is somewhat Habermasian: in our often post-secular world, religions and worldviews should be able to speak out of their own traditions and convictions, but at the same time no religion or worldview can afford to stay away from critical discussion.

Although it was not an explicit requirement, some authors in this volume have taken the opportunity to explicitly contrast their *emic* findings with Weber's *etic* interpretations.

1.6 Conclusion: Max Weber as a Point of Departure

Now what then remains of the role of Max Weber in this project? First of all, we do not assume that the contributors to this volume are Weber specialists, who necessarily directly engage with Weber's work (as mentioned: the Ertman 2017 volume has done exactly that). We are not going to pursue a direct review or recapitulation of Weber's work. What then is Weber's role? We could describe this role as a "point of departure". Most literally, we can say that Weber was the first to ask the type of questions we are asking, but now, a century later, we have to depart from him to ask our own questions and develop our own views.

Weber is thus a direct source of inspiration. He is the one who has asked, virtually for the first time, highly intriguing questions regarding the relation between the way the shape of economies and societies is influenced by religions and worldviews. Moreover, he did not leave it at that, but tried to give rather detailed substance to his claims, by delving into the very content of worldviews and religions, trying to identify not primarily their dogmatic content but the way everyday life, the life lived, looks when the interpretation of the world for a particular group of people is actually shaped by a certain religion or worldview. What does life look like for a Puritan Calvinist? How about for a Hindu? For a Confucian? What are the overriding concerns people had and have when they consider themselves adherents of these conceptions of the good life? What are their fears and hopes? What is their idea of good and bad? Weber's work is an invaluable achievement which we will do our utmost to honor.

Weber's central question was: Why did capitalism arise in the West at a certain time, and nowhere else, although many of the material and technological preconditions for something like capitalism were present elsewhere as well? We make in conclusion three observations regarding Weber's project, that on the one hand clarify somewhat further what Weber was doing (for those who do not know his work in some depth) and on the other hand give some further contrasts with what we are trying to achieve in this volume.

First, Weber's focus is primarily—or better, almost exclusively—on *explanation, not on evaluation*. Weber nowhere explicitly endorses or rejects capitalism, or takes any other normative position regarding capitalism. However, as shown above, between the lines, it is clear that he had great doubts about the normative validity of capitalism. Will it really contribute to human flourishing? One can really wonder whether Weber succeeded in his goal of being value-free. Already by defining capitalism purely and exclusively in terms of rationalization and not in terms of either oppression and class struggle on the one hand, or freedom and creativity on the other hand, he takes a stance that is not purely value-free.

In our project, we are not as afraid as Weber was to be explicit about normative positions and normative evaluations. Put even more strongly, part of our investigation is an attempt to critically develop a notion of human flourishing that we can apply as a normative yardstick for evaluating capitalism. Does capitalism, or, our terms, do free markets, do what we as human beings can and may expect them to do? Does this phenomenon enhance human flourishing? And do religions and worldviews have particular views on human flourishing, views that perhaps are worth listening to by adherents of other views, for they may enhance their understanding of the human condition?

Second, in accordance with his attempt to be value-free, Weber does not give any real attention to the content of what religions and worldviews might have to say regarding economics and (potentially) regarding capitalism. For Weber, religions and worldviews are just systematically observed, contingent constructions, that do not shed light on the human condition, that do not have something to say in their own right about the good life or about human flourishing. The basic question is at the end of the day for Weber is only, "Does religion *x* give way to capitalism or not?" And this for him is very much related to the degree of magic that is still to be found there. Why it might promote or resist capitalism, or what qualifications and moral requirements it puts on the table, Weber does not analyze. There is no content that is to be found that may direct capitalism. Religions and worldviews are explanatory factors, not conceptions of the good life that may be of intrinsic interest for humans qua humans. In this volume we take a different route: there may be something to learn in religions regarding the nature of human flourishing and virtues, that may turn out to be worthwhile in our context of reflexive modernity and the search for the future spirits of capitalism.

Third, what Weber explicitly intended to do is what he calls *Verstehen*. This is a conscious attempt to understand a certain way of life or a certain action from within, from the perspective of the people studied. He explicitly does not want to press his own template on the materials he is dealing with. And indeed, if one reads Weber, one can be impressed on the one hand by the richness of the materials that he is presenting. However, on the other hand, one gets at various instances the impression that he indeed has somewhat imposed his own template on the materials, what we referred to above as his Procrustean bed. For our project, a true effort at *Verstehen*, which we could translate as "sensitively interpreting", or "staying as closely as possible to the adherents' own interpretation of a certain worldview or religion", is crucial, provided that this does not preclude further critical examination.

However, in conclusion, in spite of the criticisms, Weber was the first to deal in such an extensive and considerate way with religions and worldviews in relation to markets, trade and labor. Thus, even if we depart from him in some ways, doing so is at the same a tribute to his work. With apologies to MacIntyre, we might say that today we await another, albeit undoubtedly different, Max Weber (MacIntyre 1984, 263). Well over a century later, it is our humble hope that we can pay tribute to him with a volume that is truly worthy of his pioneering work.

1.7 An Overview of This Volume

The order of the contributions in this volume roughly follows the order in which Weber has executed his project and was planning to continue it, as related by his then widow Marianne Weber in the brief 'Preface' (*Vorwort*) to the third volume of the studies on the Economic Ethic of the World Religions. He started with Protestantism, a branch of Christianity. The initial plan to have a larger study of Christianity lost its urgency after publication of *Die Soziallehren der christlichen Kirchen und Gruppen* by his friend Ernst Troeltsch in 1912, although Weber still wanted to do this from his own point of view at a later stage (Troeltsch 1931/2009). So Weber continued with his studies on China (Confucianism and Taoism), followed by India (Hinduism and Buddhism) and the studies in ancient Judaism, which he saw as preparing the way for more extensive studies in early Christianity and Islam. Neither the studies on early Christianity nor these on Islam were actually carried out although Marianne Weber speaks of preparatory work that was done.

Given that Weber did start with Protestantism and intended his studies of Christianity to provide the background for the work on Protestantism, we decide to start as well with pre-Reformation Christianity, and then continue in the order that was laid down by Weber.

Jennifer Herdt gives a broad overview of some key tenets of reflection on business, wealth, and poverty within the Christian tradition, starting with the early church, moving on to the Mendicant Orders, and moving toward Calvin and eventually Adam Smith. Cornelis van der Kooi picks up on this by focusing on the Protestant tradition, starting with Calvin, then interrogating the social ethics of the Dutch theologian, political leader and prime minister Abraham Kuyper, ending with a discussion of views that have emerged in the World Council of Churches.

From the (modern) West Weber moved to the ancient East and we follow suit. Carsten Hermann-Pillath shows that Confucianism has had a determining influence on the formation of the Chinese economy, though in an entirely different, and less market-hostile way than Weber thought. Moreover, he asks, why treat capitalism as the pinnacle of human rationality, as Weber did? In this section we included also an entirely different piece by Mary Szto, who provides a collection of key passages from the Confucian *Analects*, dealing with virtues in markets.

Weber's next stop was India, where he encountered Hinduism and (at least in its origins) Buddhism. Contrary to the often-invoked claim that Hinduism is primarily an 'otherworldly' spirituality, Amitava Dutt uncovers a substantive amount of ethical reflection in key Hindu sources, that come close to what can be called a virtue ethics, leading toward 'liberation' *(mokṣa),* and there are many implications drawn and to be drawn for the pursuit of wealth and market behavior. Victor van Bijlert sketches the contours of a distinct Hundy modernity, in which there was a key role for Raja Rommohan Roy, whose work can be seen as a kind of parallel to Western Protestantism, although leading less to pro-capitalist behavior as to a combination of world-renunciation with a new emphasis on community values, freedom and justice.

Joel Magnuson gives a comprehensive sketch of 'socially engaged Buddhism', drawing from Buddhist insights cornerstones for a thorough critique of 'greed is good' economics and pathways for renewing our thinking about economics and market behavior. Candauda Arachchige Saliya provides us with an exploration of commonalities as well as differences of emphasis between Theravada and Mahayana Buddhism regarding their basic attitude toward business and markets, the one more individual-oriented, the other more focused on the community.

The last great studies more or less finished by Weber concerned 'ancient Judaism'. In this volume a Judaic perspective is outlined by Hershey Friedman who draws from Torah, Midrash, and Talmud to sketch the attitude toward not only businesses and markets, but as well elaborates the concept of social and environmental responsibility. Joseph Isaac Lifshitz highlights the concept of 'creativity' as key element of humans being created in the image of God, which has important implications for the view on business and entrepreneurship.

As indicated, Weber never completed his journey that would have brought him to the heartlands of Islam, but we do continue in the same direction in this volume. Ayman Reda shows that in Qu'ran and Hadith the appreciation for markets and business is strongly dependent on whether they allow for and pursue virtues. If they do, they are highly praised, if not, they have to face strong condemnation. Waleed El-Ansary provides a deep analysis of the Islamic wisdom tradition and the spiritual cosmology that is articulated in it. With this background human work, and the larger scope of economic activity, becomes a special vocation to manifest the Divine artistic creativity.

In an Epilogue we as editors briefly look back on some insights that the volume has brought. Is there contradiction, complementarity and/or convergence in what the various religions have to say? Where will the search for the future spirit(s) of capitalism lead?

References

Albert, Michel. 1991. *Capitalisme contre capitalisme*. Paris: Seuil.

Albert, Michel. 1993. *Capitalism Against Capitalism*. London: Whurr.

Arnason, Johann, Shmuel N. Eisenstadt, and Björn Wittrock. 2005. *Axial Civilizations and World History*. Leiden: Brill.

Balkenende, Jan Peter, and Govert Buijs. 2024. *Capitalism Reconnected. Toward a Sustainable, Inclusive and Innovative Market Economy in Europe*. Amsterdam: Amsterdam University Press.

Barnes, Kenneth J. 2018. *Redeeming Capitalism*. Grand Rapids: Eerdmans.

Barton, Dominic, Dezso Horvath, and Matthias Kipping, eds. 2016. *Re-Imagining Capitalism: Building a Responsible Long-Term Model*. New York: Oxford University Press.

Beck, Ulrich, Wolfgang Bons, and Christoph Lau. 2003. The Theory of Reflexive Modernization. *Theory, Culture and Society* 20 (2): 1–33.

Bellah, Robert. 2011. *Religion in Human Evolution*. Belknap: Cambridge.

Bellah, Robert, and Hans Joas. 2012. *The Axial Age and Its Consequences*. Belknap: Cambridge.

Berger, Peter. 1999. *The Desecularization of the World: Resurgent Religion and World Politics*. Grand Rapids: Eerdmans.

Berger, Peter. 2010. Max Weber Is Alive and Well, and Living in Guatemala: The Protestant Ethic Today. *The Review of Faith and International Affairs* 8 (4): 3–9.

Berger, Peter L. 2011. *Dialog zwischen religiösen Traditionen in einem Zeitalter der Relativität*. Tübingen: Mohr Siebeck.

Brennan, Jason, and Peter M. Jaworski. 2016. *Markets Without Limits: Moral Virtues and Commercial Interests*. New York: Routledge.

Casanova, José. 1994. *Public Religions in the Modern World*. Chicago: Chicago University Press.

Castells, Manuel. 1996–2004. *The Information Age: Economy, Society and Culture*. 2 vols. Oxford: Blackwell.

Collier, Paul. 2007. *The Bottom Billion: Why the Poorest Countries are Failing and What Can Be Done About It*. New York: Oxford University Press.

Collier, Paul. 2018. *The Future of Capitalism: Facing New Anxieties*. New York: HarperCollins.

Cotter, Christopher R., and David G. Robertson. 2016. *After World Religions. Reconstructing Religious Studies*. London/New York: Routledge.

Eelke De Jong. 2009. Culture and Economics: On Values, Economics and International Business. London: Routledge.

Eelke De Jong, ed. 2021. Economic Ideas, Policy and National Culture: A Comparison of Three Market Economies. New York: Routledge.

de Tocqueville, Alexis. 1954. Author's Introduction. In *Democracy in America*. New York: Vintage Books.

Eisenstadt, S. N., ed. 1986. *The Origins and Diversity of Axial Age Civilizations*. Albany: State University of New York Press.

Eisenstadt, Shmuel N. 2000. Multiple Modernities. *Daedalus* 129 (1): 1–29.

Ertman, Thomas C., ed. 2017. *Max Weber's Economic Ethic of the World Religions: An Analysis*. New York: Cambridge University Press.

Fourcade, Marion, and Kieran Healy. 2007. Moral Views of Market Society. *Annual Review of Sociology* 33:285–311.

Friedman, Milton. 1970. The Social Responsibility of Business Is to Increase Its Profits. *The New York Times Magazine*.

Friedman, Milton. 2009. *Capitalism and Freedom: Fortieth*. Anniversary ed. Chicago: University of Chicago Press.

Fukuyama, Francis. 1992. *The End of History and the Last Man*. New York: Free Press.

Fukuyama, Francis. 2018. *Identity: Contemporary Identity Politics and the Struggle for Recognition*. London: Profile.

Granovetter, Mark. 2011. Economic Action and Social Structure: The Problem of Embeddedness. In *The Sociology of Economic Life*, ed. R. Swedberg and M. Granovetter, 3rd ed., 46–61. Boulder: Westview Press.

Habermas, Jürgen. 2006. Religion in the Public Sphere. *European Journal of Philosophy* 14 (1): 1–25.

Hall, Peter A., and David Soskice, eds. 2001. *Varieties of Capitalism: The Institutional Foundations of Comparative Advantage*. Oxford: Oxford University Press.

Hancké, Bob, Martin Rhodes, and Mark Thatcher, eds. 2007. *Beyond Varieties of Capitalism: Conflict, Contradictions, and Complementarities in the European Economy*. Oxford: Oxford University Press.

Hodgson, Geoffrey M. 2015. *Conceptualizing Capitalism: Institutions, Evolution, Future*. Chicago: University of Chicago Press.

Huntington, Samuel P. 1991. The Third Wave: Democratization in the Late Twentieth Century. In *New York: Simon & Schuster*. Norman: University of Oklahoma Press.

Huntington, Samuel P. 1996. *The Clash of Civilizations and the Remaking of World Order*. New York: Simon & Schuster.

Inglehart, Robert, and Christian Welzel. 2005. *Modernization, Cultural Change, and Democracy: The Human Development Sequence*. Cambridge: Cambridge University Press.

Inglehart, Robert, and Christian Welzel. 2009. How Development Leads to Democracy: What We Know about Modernization Today. *Foreign Affairs* 88:33–48.
Jaspers, Karl. 2021. [1949 Or./1953 Eng. Tr.]. *The Origin and Goal of History*. New York: Routledge.
John Paul II. 1991. Encyclical letter *Centesimus Annus*.
Kant, Immanuel. 2009. *Answer to the Question: 'What Is Enlightenment?'*. New York: Penguin.
Kotkin, Joel. 2023. *The Coming of Neo-Feudalism. A Warning to the Global Middle Class*. New York: Encounter.
Löwith, Karl. 1949. *Meaning in History: The Theological Implications of the Philosophy of History*. Chicago: University of Chicago Press.
MacIntyre, Alasdair. 1984. *After Virtue*. 2nd ed. Notre Dame: University of Notre Dame Press.
Mill, John Stuart. 2015. *On Liberty, Utilitarianism and Other Essays*. New York: Oxford University Press.
Polinder, Simon. 2024. *Towards a New Christian Realism. The Amsterdam School of Philosophy and the Role of Religion in International Relations*. London: Routledge.
Rawls, John. 1997. The Idea of Public Reason Revisited. *The University of Chicago Law Review* 64:765–807.
Roche, Bruno, and Jay Jakub. 2018. *Completing Capitalism: Heal Business to Heal the World*. Oakland: Berrett-Koehler.
Sheikh, Haroon. 2017. *Embedding Technopolis: Turning Modernity into a Home*. Amsterdam: Boom.
Stiglitz, Joseph. 2019. *People, Power, and Profits. Progressive Capitalism for an Age of Discontent*. New York: Allen Lane.
Stiglitz, Joseph. 2024. *The Road to Freedom. Economics and the Good Society*. New York: W.W. Norton & Co.
Taylor, Charles. 1992. *The Ethics of Authenticity*. Cambridge: Harvard University Press.
Taylor, Charles. 1994. The Politics of Recognition. In *Multiculturalism*, ed. A. Gutman, 25–73. Princeton: Princeton University Press.
Taylor, Charles. 2007. *A Secular Age*. Belknap: Cambridge.
Thomas, Scott. 2005. *The Global Resurgence of Religion and the Transformation of International Relations: The Struggle for the Soul of the Twenty-First Century*. Basingstoke: Palgrave Macmillan.
Tillich, Paul. 1957. *Systematic Theology*. Vol. 2. Chicago: University of Chicago Press.
Troeltsch, Ernst. 1931/2009. *The Social Teaching of the Christian Churches*. Louisville: Westminster John Knox Press.
van Bavel, Bas. 2016. *The Invisible Hand? How Market Economies Have Emerged and Declined Since AD 500*. Oxford: Oxford University Press.
van Geest, Paul. 2021. *Morality in the Marketplace: Reconciling Theology and Economics*. Leiden: Brill.
Verbrugge, Ad, Govert Buijs, and Jelle van Baardewijk. 2018. *Het goede leven en de vrije markt*. Rotterdam: Lemniscaat.
Voegelin, Eric. 1956–1987. *Order & History*. 4 vols. Baton Rouge: Louisiana State University Press.
Webb, Amy. 2019. *The Big Nine: How the Tech Titans and Their Thinking Machines Could Warp Humanity*. New York: PublicAffairs.
Weber, Max. 1946. Science as a Vocation. In *From Max Weber: Essays in Sociology*, ed. H. H. Gerth and C. Wright Mills, 129–156. New York: Oxford University Press.
Weber, Max. 2005 [1930]. *The Protestant Ethic and the Spirit of Capitalism*. Translated by Talcott Parsons. New York: Routledge.
Wolf, Martin. 2023. *The Crisis of Democratic Capitalism. New York: Penguin.*
Wu, Tim. 2016. *The Attention Merchants. The Epic Scramble to Get Inside Our Heads*. New York: Vintage.

Zhao, Dingxin. 2017. Max Weber and Patterns of Chinese History. In *Max Weber's Economic Ethic of the World Religions: An Analysis*, ed. Thomas C. Ertman, 137–171. New York: Cambridge University Press.

Zsolnai, Laszlo, and Gabor Kovacs. 2021. Buddhist Values for Creating Mindful Markets. *Journal of Management, Spirituality & Religion* 18 (1): 57–70.

Zuboff, Shoshana. 2019. *The Age of Surveillance Capitalism. The Fight for a Human Future at The New Frontier of Power*. London: Profile.

Govert J. Buijs studied political science, philosophy and theology at various institutions in the Netherlands and Canada and holds a PhD in political philosophy of the VU University ('Vrije Universiteit') in Amsterdam, the Netherlands. He currently holds the Goldschmeding Chair Societal and Economic Renewal which is combined with the Abraham Kuyper Chair for Political Philosophy & Religion at the philosophy department of the Faculty of Social Sciences and Humanities of VU University Amsterdam. His book Het goede leven en de vrije markt ('The Good Life and the Free Market', co-authored with Ad Verbrugge and Jelle van Baardewijk) won the Dutch Socrates Prize for the best book in philosophy in 2019. Recently, he published with the former Dutch Prime Minister Jan Peter Balkenende the book *Capitalism Reconnected. Toward a Sustainable, Inclusive and Innovative Market Economy in Europe.* (Amsterdam University Press, 2024).

Jordan J. Ballor is executive director at the Center for Religion, Culture & Democracy at First Liberty Institute (USA). He has previously held research positions at the Acton Institute for the Study of Religion & Liberty and the Vrije Universiteit Amsterdam as part of the Moral Markets project, and has doctorates in reformation history from the Universität Zürich and in moral theology from Calvin Theological Seminary.

Part I
Christianity

Chapter 2
Commerce and Communion: Business, Profit and the Circulation of Wealth in Christian Thought

Jennifer A. Herdt

Abstract The understanding of trade and business within Christian thought has evolved significantly over two millennia, reflecting broader social changes. Despite this evolution, Christian reflection on business has consistently aimed to assess and transform contemporary practices to better love God and neighbor. This essay focuses on key historical figures and moments, including the Franciscan poverty debates, the Protestant Reformation, particularly Calvin's economic thought and the emergence of political economy alongside capitalism, notably through Adam Smith. Throughout these phases, some notion of the common good remained paramount. The emancipation of self-interest and profit-maximalization as central to the economy is a nineteenth century, post-theological and post-Smith development.

Keywords Christianity · Poverty debates · Ownership · Usury · Virtues · Self-interest

2.1 Introduction

It is hardly surprising that cultural understandings of trade and business have shifted dramatically over the past two millennia, since the social world itself has changed so much in that time. Yet Christian reflection on business has been a constant—an ongoing effort to assess contemporary practices and to guide and transform them so as better to love God and neighbor. Any essay-length treatment of this topic can offer no more than a few broad strokes; I will attempt to give the present discussion

This article has been published earlier in Daniel K. Finn (ed.). 2021. *Business Ethics and Catholic Social Thought*.

J. A. Herdt (✉)
Yale University, New Haven, CT, USA
e-mail: jennifer.herdt@yale.edu

G. J. Buijs, J. J. Ballor (eds.), *In Search of the Spirits of Capitalism*, Sophia Studies in Cross-cultural Philosophy of Traditions and Cultures 44,
https://doi.org/10.1007/978-3-032-01137-4_2

greater definition by focusing on a few key figures and moments in this history: the Franciscan poverty debates, the Protestant Reformation (and Calvin's economic thought in particular), and the founding of political economy in the context of the rise of capitalism with Adam Smith.

Some surprising things emerge when we do. First, the Franciscans' radical reaction to the dislocations introduced by a new money economy was to reject any sort of ownership of property. But the Franciscans were at the same time at the forefront in developing theories of relative price and defending the social value of merchant activity. Second, the Protestant Reformation has been unforgettably linked by Max Weber with the "Spirit of Capitalism" and the notion that the pursuit of profit is a divine mandate and wealth a sign of divine favor. And it is true that the Reformation (in all its forms, Catholic as well as Protestant) reflected a new appreciation that devotion to God could be lived in the world as well as in the monastery. But Calvin regarded wealth not as a sign of divine favor but as a trust to be stewarded in service to one's neighbor and the common good, in continuity with the main channels of Christian reflection. It is true, further, that Calvin pioneered in his willingness to say that usury was not always bad. However, he was simply pointing out that so much room had been carved out for legitimate kinds of lending for profit that the old ban had become a merely semantic matter; what was evil was not obtaining profit through lending, but exploitation and injustice. Third, Adam Smith is seen as the founding figure of laissez-faire capitalism, with his notion of the invisible hand that regulates the market quite apart from the intentions of market actors. But while Smith argued that commercial society maximized wealth, he did not advocate the unfettered pursuit of self-interest. Rather, he insisted that reason and humanity required that the market be regulated with a view to its impact on the poor and disadvantaged. While his moral philosophy reflected a flattening of traditional Christian understandings of God's ends in creating the world, he is not responsible for unleashing free-market capitalism. Understanding the market mechanism was fully compatible with refusing to enthrone the pursuit of unfettered profit maximization.

Sustained themes animate Christian reflection on business, profit, and wealth: just as each has different spiritual gifts for the good of the body of Christ, so the differential distribution of wealth accords Christians opportunities for mutual service and for the mutually beneficial circulation of goods. In part, this takes place by way of charitable giving, in part, by way of buying and selling. Wealth that circulates is wealth that can serve human needs. Private property, commerce, profit, are legitimate only because and insofar as they serve the common good. It can be challenging to discern just how to live out these insights in our own constantly changing social and economic environment. But it was similarly challenging for the mendicant orders to address the new realities of urban life and a money economy, for scholastics to assess new forms of lending that might or might not be usurious, and for Christian thinkers to discern how best to serve genuine human flourishing in the midst of the decline of feudalism and the rise of capitalism. There is wisdom for today in the Franciscan insistence on making need the measure of value, in Calvin's insistence on the stewardship of wealth, and in Smith's recognition that the unfettered pursuit of self-interest does not and cannot redound to the common good, and much to gain from understanding the ways in which Christian economic reflection has unfolded amidst changing contexts in the past.

2.2 Christianity in the Ancient World

Trade and manufacture prospered in the ancient Mediterranean world, and was key to the strength of the Roman Empire. This did not mean, however, that the life of business was respected. Leisure was prized as freedom; work was seen as enslavement. The life of a philosopher was seen as one of leisure; that of a merchant, as work. Plato saw the need for "producers" in his ideal republic, but ranked them below the auxiliaries and the guardians. These values were taken over into early Christianity's elevation of contemplation. But traditional Hellenistic disdain for the merchant life as work rather than leisure was joined with quite different concerns inherited from the Hebrew tradition: notably, an insistence on God's care and concern for the poor.

Jesus proclaimed the poor blessed; he said that it was more difficult for the rich to enter the kingdom of heaven than for a camel to pass through the eye of a needle (Luke 6:20; Matthew 19:24). His advice to the rich young man was to give away all that he had in order to follow Jesus (Matthew 19:21). Even as this was understood as a counsel of perfection rather than as an obligation binding all Christians, it decisively shaped Christian attitudes toward wealth.[1] As Clement of Alexandria remarked in the second century,

> If no one had anything, what room would be left among men for giving? …
>
> He who holds possessions, and gold, and silver, and houses, as the gifts of God … and knows that he possesses them more for the sake of the brethren that (sic) his own … is he who is blessed by the Lord."[2]

While radical voices urged all Christians into a life of voluntary poverty, insisting that wealth taints and corrupts, then, more moderate voices regarded wealth itself as neutral or good, in that it enables sustained giving and provides sustenance to the poor.

Poverty was a central feature of monastic life as it began to take shape in the fourth and fifth centuries. The sixth-century Rule of St. Benedict rejected private ownership by monks, seeking explicitly to recreate the form of Christian community described in the book of Acts (4:32): "the whole group of those who believed were of one heart and soul, and no one claimed private ownership of any possessions, but everything they owned was held in common." (*Rule of St. Benedict*, 123).

---

[1] See Peter Brown's rich discussion in *Through the Eye of a Needle* (2012)

[2] Clement of Alexandria, "Who Is the Rich Man?" 1951: XIII; XVI, 594–595. On Augustine's variation on this theme, see Brown 2012. I have discussed Augustine's views of wealth and almsgiving in Herdt 2015, 97–112.

2.3 The Commercial Revolution

From the sack of Rome in 410 CE up to the eleventh century, Western Europe remained largely a subsistence agrarian economy. This began to change with the cessation of invasions from the north, as trade routes became safer and cities grew (Bloch 1989, 3–56; Little 1978, 7). Over the course of the "Commercial Revolution" of the eleventh and twelfth centuries, the economy became money-based; coins were minted, an interconnected economy developed, and investment grew.[3] Money was seen as having "a mysterious power to represent the value of ordinary useful things" (Todeschini 2009, 13). It made it possible to tally up not simply stocks of various commodities, but wealth as such. The monasteries became major sites for the increase of wealth, and monks took pride in tracking that increase. But tensions existed between different understandings of wealth. All agreed that wealth should be devoted to the service of God and neighbor, not private indulgence. But was monastic wealth best invested in jeweled chalices and elaborate architecture, as at Cluny? Or was it better to reinvest profits in land, accumulating wealth? Bernard of Clairvaux championed the latter, Cistercian, model, as the proper stewardship of talents, leading to their multiplication. Cluny was increasingly seen no longer as suitably glorifying God but rather as hoarding wealth and tying it up unproductively. (Todeschini 2009, 19, 47).

With the emergence of a money economy, and a preoccupation with increasing wealth, usury became a major preoccupation. The prohibition on money lending had deep roots, reaching back into the Deuteronomic prohibition on lending at interest to fellow Hebrews (Deut. 13:19–20). Gratian's *Decretum* defined usury as "expecting to receive back more than you have given" in a loan, focusing on the sinful intention embedded in this expectation.[4] As the discussion evolved, money lending was condemned; the sale of land rents was not, nor was the activity of merchants. The latter forms of activity were regarded not as hoarding wealth, but as using or investing it for the sake of the common good. The private gain was viewed as incidental. In fact, merchants were in the twelfth century directly compared to ascetic monks who impoverished themselves for the sake of something of higher value: "the merchant left his house to go to the market, the cleric left his domains to learn Wisdom: the former sold everything he possessed, the latter gave up everything, even himself."[5] Hence, merchants and monastics could be viewed as cooperating in the pursuit of the common good, over against the greed of money lenders.

The rise of the merchant class went hand in hand with the growth of the cities. Within feudalism, peasants exchanged agricultural products and military service for the use of land and for protection from manorial lords. In growing cities, serfs could

[3] Little 1978, 15–18; Benson and Constable 1991, xvii–xxx; Bloch 1989, 421–437. For an overview of developments in Italy, see Schlag 2013, 180–181.

[4] Gratian 1959, C.14.q.3, c.I: col. 735; see Wood 2002, 159.

[5] Zachary of Besançon, Unum ex quattuor, sive de concordia evangelistarum, *Patrologia Latina* 186: 77, quoted in Todeschini 2009, 21.

escape bondage, but were also subjected to new forms of insecurity, while merchants and craftspeople could become prosperous without owning land. Initially, merchants were merely servant of manorial lords. However, "they would trade, exchange and lend, as much for their own profit as because they were authorized to do so by their lords" (Todeschini 2009, 14). They enriched their lords, to be sure, but also themselves, and they gradually acquired independent power, moving freely about in conducting business: "wealth and its secrets were being mastered more by people who were not masters in the highest meaning of the term" (Todeschini 2009, 15).

2.4 The Mendicant Orders

These far-reaching social and economic changes associated with the rise of cities and merchants, and the dislocations associated with them, stimulated intensive reflection not just on wealth and profit, but also on the meaning of ownership, need, and poverty. Indeed, the first school of moral theology grew up in the late twelfth century around Peter the Chanter as a site for wrestling with conflicts issuing out of the need for credit, alongside the prohibition on usury (Little 1978, 175). None were more fully involved in this reflection than the members of the mendicant orders, the Dominicans and Franciscans (Little 1978, 156–158). The mendicant orders were an urban phenomenon. The older monastic orders had been rooted in place and tied to the land; monks farmed, made wine and beer, and engaged in prayer and contemplation. The mendicants were on the move. Their emergence and identity were thus bound intimately up with major economic shifts associated with the emergence of the cities.

The Dominican order was founded in 1216 to oppose heresy and preach the gospel. Dominic perceived a need for men of God who were free to travel to areas where informed preaching was needed—especially the cities (Todeschini 2009, 31). Dominic and his associates regarded it as quite proper that they, like the apostle Paul, be sustained by gifts from the communities they served. The Dominicans quickly became rooted in the university (a new urban phenomenon), and devoted themselves not just to doctrinal theology, but to reflecting on property, money, price, and profit. Albert the Great and his student, Thomas Aquinas, drew on Aristotle to develop new defenses of private property, over against a patristic consensus that property was nothing more than a concession to sin, needed in order to maintain public order. Private property, they argued, encouraged good stewardship of material resources and effective coordination of human activity; it was beneficial to individuals, families and communities (Little 1978, 176–177; Hirschfeld 2018, 161–190). Economic activity could be a site for the cultivation of virtuous human agency that contributed to genuine human flourishing. Financial partnerships were legitimate so long as shared risk was involved; profit in such cases was acceptable compensation for risk, not usury (Little 1978, 178–179).

Francis represented a more radical challenge to the rising money economy. For Francis, mendicancy did not simply enable a new kind of mission to the people; it *embodied* that mission, expressing a new valorization of poverty as the life lived by Christ and an approximation to the pre-lapsarian state. Whereas the Dominicans regarded voluntary poverty as compatible with accepting endowments in support of the order, the Franciscans did not. Francis regarded physical separation from money and ownership as essential: to be poor was to wear rags, to wander, to beg, to touch animals and outcasts, those outside civil human existence (Todeschini 2009, 61–64). Having stepped outside of the ordinary structures of human life, Francis questioned the capacity of money to measure value. Only poverty, he argued, allowed one to grasp the true value of things, and to see that needs can be satisfied only through relational connections (Todeschini 2009, 69).

2.5 The Franciscan Poverty Debates

Money itself, then, was viewed as a form of hoarding, impeding the direct circulation of goods. Poverty freed one for loving relationships with others. The Franciscan Rule of 1223 therefore specified: "Let the Friars appropriate nothing for themselves, not a house, nor a place, nor anything else."[6] This was understood as a rejection of both individual and common property; Franciscans rejected any *proprietas* and accepted only *usus*, only the use of those things needed to support life (Mäkinen 2001, 193). This radical stance elicited intense discussion over more than a century. Pope Gregory IX, in a 1230 bull, *Quo Elongati*, insisted against early critics that the Franciscans were indeed living without any rights but only had the use (*usus*) of things. Pope Innocent IV added that this was possible because what the Franciscans used were things properly owned by the Roman Church.[7] Critics such as William of Saint-Amour argued that Christian perfection does not require giving up all property; the early Christians owned property in common, and hence Franciscan poverty did not represent an improvement on the usual practice of monastic life.[8] Without property, he pressed, how could the Franciscans perform acts of charity to the poor? Gerard of Abbeville went farther, arguing that the Franciscans could not possibly avoid owning property: insofar as a share of the common possessions of the Church rightfully belong to the poor, a share rightfully belongs to the Franciscans.[9] Further, it was not legally possible to "use" food and other consumables without owning them, since *dominium* without use applied only to objects the substance of which was not diminished through use (Mäkinen 2001, 196). Whenever the Franciscans were given gifts, ownership was thereby transferred to them (Mäkinen 2001, 197).

[6] Francis of Assisi, *Regula Bullata*, c. 6, in *Die Opuscula des Hl. Franziskus von Assisi*, ed. K. Esser (Spicilegium Bonaventurianum XIII), Frottaferrata (Rome) 1989, cited in Mäkinen 2001, 11.

[7] Innocent IV, *Ordinem Vestrem*, in *Bullarium Franciscanum*; Mäkinen, 2001, 193–4

[8] William of Saint-Amour 1995, 328–329; Langholm 1992, 146.

[9] Langholm 1992, 278.

Bonaventure argued that this represented a misconception of "use." "Simplex usus," he argued, was legally indifferent, not a mode of *dominium*; it was simply "permission to use for the substance of life," not a transfer of ownership (Mäkinen 2001, 198).[10] The created state of humankind was not one of common property but of simple communion of goods, *communio*. The Franciscans, like Christ and the apostles, were approximating this prelapsarian state. Pope Nicholas III, sanctioning Bonaventure's views, added the notion of factual use, "*usus facti*": the use of those things necessary for sustenance, quite apart from having or acquiring any rights to these things. But the attacks continued through the 1270s and 1280s, led by the secular theologians at Paris, Henry of Ghent and Godfrey of Fontaines, culminating in a 1322 papal declaration that the order was heretical. Pope John XXII insisted that it was not possible to distinguish between *dominium* and *usus facti* when it came to consumables. To deny that the Franciscans had the right to use those things which they consumed was to say that they were committing an injustice in using them. The Franciscans could not claim to be exemplary without admitting that they did in fact have property rights (Mäkinen 2001, 203; Langholm 1992, 147–148). While the Franciscans continued to defend themselves, it was this position that finally prevailed.

Alongside their theoretical refusals of property ownership, the Franciscans were also forced to create new forms of practical relationship. They needed to rely on others who did not aspire to Christlike poverty, and who were willing to handle money on their behalf, receiving donations intended for their support and buying the goods they required (Little 1978, 165). The Franciscans harbored no illusions that all Christians would embrace voluntary poverty. Indeed, some defended their way of life in part because it meant that more resources would be left for the rest of the populace (Todeschini 2009, 83). They also depicted themselves as experts on use and value who could thereby be of service to others in analyzing market society from a disinterested point of view. Bonaventure, for instance, argued that even ostentatious clothing might not be useless for some, but rather an appropriate sign of authority (Todeschini 2009, 85). By the end of the thirteenth century, the Franciscans had developed quite a sophisticated understanding that need, and therefore value, were not absolute but rather context-dependent. They also grasped how markets determine prices: "the value of things and professions, of goods, and people, is formed by considering, case by case, the generally recognized usefulness, the variable abundance, and also the subjective degree of appreciation these realities receive from people" (Todeschini 2009, 115).

2.6 The Franciscan Role in the Rise of a Credit Economy

This understanding of relative price paved the way for a surprising development: the Franciscans could view merchants as, like themselves, experts in evaluating value. Hence, merchants were to be regarded as socially useful and as rightfully earning compensation for their expertise, in the form of profit. Peter Olivi wrote:

[10] The relevant text of Bonaventura is his *Apologia pauperum* 1882–1902, 1269.

> As the artisan's ability and activity legitimately procure him profit, so the merchant's activity, evident in his careful examination of the value and price of things, and his ability to determine a fair price by paying attention to the smallest details rightfully enable him to earn a profit, since, staying in a variable range of fair prices, he is useful to others just because, in this way, they will learn to calculate more accurately the prices and values of things.[11]

Hence, somewhat paradoxically, the Franciscans contributed to a new valorization of the merchant way of life. And while the Franciscans proper could of course not become merchants, laypeople who joined the lay confraternities linked to the Franciscan order were often merchants, and in fourteenth-century French and Italian cities, members of the Third Order of the Franciscans were often given particularly sensitive public responsibilities, since they were seen both as public-minded and disinterested and as having a refined grasp of the art of understanding price and value.[12]

The Franciscan Alexander Lombard, writing at the end of the thirteenth century, wrote a tractate on usury that identified twelve sorts of cases in which it was legitimate to receive more in return from an original amount paid.[13] Over the course of the 13th and 14th centuries, further exceptions were carved out. If a loan caused real damage to a lender, for instance, he could claim compensation in the form of *damnum emergens* (Noonan 1957, 115–116). If a lender lost out on an opportunity to buy something and sell it at profit by virtue of having made a loan, he could require of his debtor an equivalent, *lucrum cessans* (Noonan, 116). And if a loan involved risk of loss, the lender could demand a compensatory *periculum sortis* (Noonan 1957, 129).

Even as theological argument created theoretical space for a credit-based economy, merchants, who circulate wealth in service to the common good, were sharply distinguished from usurers, those who immobilize capital by lending money simply in order to gain more. This distinction was bound up with a self-serving and hypocritical Christian anti-Judaism. Jews were invited to settle in European cities because they were not bound by Christian prohibitions against usury. They therefore served a critically important urban role as bankers for societies increasingly dependent on the availability of capital. However, their activities, unlike those of merchants, were not viewed as forms of service to the common good. How could they serve the common good when they were not properly members of the community at all, and rarely full citizens? Traditional Christian anxieties about the presence of Jews in their communities were in the fourteenth and fifteenth centuries increasingly focused on regarding Jewish usury as the foil over against which Christian merchant activity could be exonerated from critique and valorized as socially beneficial (Todeschini 2009, 151–156).

---

[11] Peter John Olivi, *De contractibus, de emptionibus et venditionibus* (1980), quoted in Todeschini 2009, 118.

[12] Todeschini 2009, 130; Little, 1978, 207. On Olivi's contributions, see Schlag, 2013, 184–190.

[13] Alexander Lombard, *Tractatus de usuris*, 1307, discussed in Little, 1978, 182.

One final development is worth mentioning in connection with the Franciscans. In late fifteenth century Italy, they created the *Monte di Pietà*, a new kind of financial institution that formed the basis of modern banking. As originally conceived, merchants donated money to the *Monte* to be lent at very low interest to the poor. In this context, money-lending was a form of charitable activity and service to the poor; the interest charged served only to cover the costs of the enterprise. This sort of money-lending, unlike that of the Jews, was framed as public service, which helped to eliminate poverty by enabling the poor to establish small businesses (Todeschini 2009, 174–178). Controversy raged nonetheless, with Dominicans (against the Franciscans) insisting that the expenses of the institutions should be borne by the lenders, not the borrowers. The legitimacy of charging interest to borrowers was affirmed by the Fifth Lateran Council in 1516. Once the payment of interest was allowed, the *Montes* had a way to sustain themselves apart from ongoing charitable gifts, and gradually became institutions that lent to businesspeople as well as to the poor. Thus the road was paved for the acceptance of noncharitable lending institutions, and for the charging of interest that is used to sustain a business (Noonan 1957, 294–310).

Despite their own embrace of radical poverty, then, the Franciscans played a key role in legitimating the activities of merchants and the rise of a credit-based economy. Always, the criterion was service to the common good: "poverty and wealth could appear contiguous and complementary in building the common good, if they gave substance to the choice of acting, every day, in sight of a definition of common welfare." (Todeschini 2009, 194).

2.7 The Protestant Ethic and the Spirit of Capitalism?

Important as it is to recognize the Commercial Revolution of the 11th and 12th centuries, and to see the economic changes from this time up to the Industrial Revolution as gradual in kind, this does not mean that no significant shifts took place in the early modern period. The fourteenth century witnessed the decline of manorialism in Western Europe; serfs were freed in efforts to increase the yield of land, resulting in migration to the cities and a large urban proletariat, often unemployed (Biéler 2005, 4). The Hundred Years' War (1337–1453) spurred on the centralization of the French and English states, accompanied by increased rates of taxation that burdened populations decimated by the Black Death (1347–1351). Social unrest mounted. In commercial cities, tensions developed between powerful merchants and craft-guilds, and between these and the urban poor. The guilds tended to enact restrictions on trade; monarchs, who relied on credit from wealthy merchants, supported their efforts to evade these restrictions. Hence commerce grew and the gap between rich and poor expanded. The influx of precious metals from the New World fed the development of banking and caused price increases that further burdened the poor during the course of the sixteenth century; wages did not keep up with the price of living. It was hardly surprising that movements for religious renewal were often bound up together with social and political movements, even as the former can in no way be reduced to the latter.

The powerful influence of Max Weber's *Protestant Ethic and the Spirit of Capitalism* has made it difficult to bring into proper focus the changes introduced into economic thinking and practice in the Reformation era.[14] According to Weber, Protestantism (particularly the Reformed traditions), drove the development of capitalism by way of its notion of vocation or calling (Weber 1905/1958, 155–64, 170–72, 180). No longer were "vocations" limited to those who accepted the counsels of perfection and turned their backs on the world, embracing lives of poverty, chastity, and obedience. Each individual received a divine calling, and that vocation might well be to a life of business. Further, Weber argued, Calvinists regarded economic prosperity as a sign of divine election, and their affirmation of double predestination drove a restless pursuit of assurance of election. Protestants were "inner-worldly ascetics," who labored in a highly organized and disciplined fashion, while condemning luxury and self-indulgence (Weber 1921/1968, 542). Since profits could not be consumed, they were re-invested, driving economic growth.

Perhaps the first thing to be noted in taking stock of Weber's thesis is simply how much continuity there was between Protestant and Catholic and between early modern and late medieval economic thought. Critiques of luxury continued unabated. Catholics and Protestants alike affirmed the right for a merchant to receive a profit adequate to compensate for cost, time, labor, and risk, while insisting that merchants were not justified in exploiting the plight of others and selling their goods at prices as high as possible.[15] Luther, echoing earlier Franciscan reflection on the just determination of prices, argued that this sort of exploitation could be avoided if goods were "valued at the price for which they are bought and sold in the common market, or in the land generally."[16] Much has been made of Calvin's departure from tradition in refusing to condemn usury as such.[17] However, Calvin's innovation was less dramatic than it is often depicted as being. The process of defining usury in ever-narrower terms had been underway for centuries, carving out space for the growth of credit-based economies. Calvin simply pointed out that the argument had become merely semantic. Usury was rightly condemned wholesale if understood as lending practices that exploited the poor or extracted interest in cases in which the borrower acquired nothing more from the loan than the actual price of the money (Biéler 2005, 403–416; Valeri 1997, 123–42). If usury so defined is condemned, however, this leaves room for approving forms of lending at interest that put money to productive use. Alternatively, one might say that usury itself is not always bad, but only when exploitative. Calvin endorsed the latter approach, arguing that scrip-

[14] Ernst Troeltsch advanced a similar argument in 1911, emphasizing the significance of the blessing Calvin gave to lending at interest and hence to capitalism, 1912. Max Stackhouse offers a brief overview of some of the most influential responses to Weber's thesis in 2014, 310–314.

[15] Luther 1524, 248.

[16] Luther 1524, 250.

[17] See, e.g., Tawney 1926; Visser 't Hooft 1928. For a balanced discussion, see Noonan 1957, 365–367.

ture did not intend to rule out all lending at interest. In doing so he contextualized and historicized biblical texts condemning usury, and rejected scholastic arguments concerning the unproductive character of money. This built on groundwork developed gradually within the context of the medieval Commercial Revolution.

The rejection of monastic life, and the concomitant affirmation of ordinary lay occupations, constituted the most significant cultural shift in Protestant territories. Calvin rejected both luxury and asceticism: "if we ponder to what end God created food, we shall find that he meant not only to provide for necessity but also for delight and good cheer."[18] Similarly for grasses, trees, fruits, wine, and flower—they are intended to delight as well as sustain life, and to lead human beings to God: "all things were created for us that we might recognize the Author and give thanks for his kindness toward us."[19] This does not mean that wealth is to be equated with spiritual blessing. Calvin unequivocally rejects the notion that wealth is a sign of God's favor or poverty a sign of divine rejection:

> As, on the one hand, the most of men, judging of the favor of God from an uncertain and transitory state of prosperity, applaud the rich, and those upon whom, as they say, fortune smiles; so, on the other hand, they act contemptuously towards the wretched and miserable, and foolishly imagine that God hates them, because he does not exercise so much forbearance towards them as he does towards the reprobate. The error of which we speak, namely, that of judging wrongfully and wickedly, is one which has prevailed in all ages of the world.[20]

Wealth tempts us to rely on ourselves and our own power rather than on God; poverty can teach us to trust in God.[21]

Possession is rightly understood as stewardship. All the things that we have are "as it were, entrusted to us, and we must one day render account of them."[22] Wealth is to be consecrated to God, and this consecration is shown in generosity to those in need. The rich are God's deputies; by virtue of the fact that they have been given more than they need, they are charged with the responsibility of acting in God's own person, to distribute good as God does. It is theft to defraud poor neighbors of good things one has been given in trust in order to benefit them. God distributes wealth unequally in order to provide opportunities for the circulation of wealth, for reciprocal exchanges of God's good gifts, such that human society will be built up by its imaging of God's own generous giving and taught how to accept God's good gifts: "while they communicate to each other mutually according to the measure of gifts and of necessity, this mutual contribution produces a befitting symmetry, though some have more, and some less, and gifts are distributed unequally."[23] The institution of private property fosters virtuous agency, in particular, responsibility and diligence, and it is appropriate that property be used first to take care of the needs of

---

[18] Calvin 1559, III.X, 720.

[19] Calvin 1559, III.X, 721.

[20] Calvin 1979a, Matthew 6:24.

[21] Calvin 1979a, Matthew 6:27.

[22] Calvin 1559, III.X, 723.

[23] Calvin 1948a, 2 Corinthians 8:14.

one's own household, but beyond this, it is legitimized only by its circulation, not its accumulation.[24] Here there was substantial continuity with medieval economic thought, with its refusal to regard property rights as absolute; private property is legitimate because and insofar as it serves the common good. The magisterial Reformation in this respect maintained a traditional position over against humanists who appealed to Roman law to justify largely unfettered rights to private property and movements of the Radical Reformation that regarded private property as itself sinful and sought to establish new forms of common ownership, in effect extending to laypeople some of the ideals embodied in medieval monasticism.[25]

It was in this context that Calvin emphasized vocation: "each individual has his own kind of living assigned to him by the Lord as a sort of sentry post so that he may not heedlessly wander about through life."[26] By embracing this vocation and its associated duties, the Christian can be confident that she is acting as a good steward. Further, even the most lowly occupations are elevated when lived as callings: "no task will be so sordid and base, provided you obey your calling in it, that it will not shine and be reckoned very precious in God's sight."[27] There is no special value in voluntary poverty or asceticism; God's good gifts are to be used productively, neither hoarded, nor squandered, nor exploited unsustainably.[28] Contemplation is not essentially better than work, for in working in ways that serve the common good, human beings serve and glorify God and share in God's own productive activity.[29]

This is not the place to attempt a thorough assessment of Weber's causal claims concerning the Protestant Ethic and the development of capitalism. Suffice it to say that Weber's thesis has been roundly criticized from a number of directions. R. H. Tawney, one of Weber's early critics, noted that Weber's analysis was focused primarily on later Calvinism, which had been transformed by intervening economic developments which could not be attributed to Calvinism (Tawney 1926, xi, xiii). Calvin's emphasis on work as participating in God's providential care for the common good is quite alien to the mindset that captivated Weber, one in which the pursuit of profit is taken as an end in itself. Historians have argued convincingly that the divergence between the economic fortunes of East and West did not occur until the Industrial Revolution, and indeed that parts of China and India were more prosperous and productive than western Europe prior to that time (Pomeranz 2000). And Renaissance Italy has been defended as the real birthplace of European capitalism (Cohen 1980). Indeed, some have argued that capitalism developed in a more unregulated fashion in Catholic territories which continued to pay lipservice to the prohibition of usury.[30]

---

[24] Calvin, 1979b, Acts 2:45.

[25] However, the view that Roman law defended absolute property rights is largely a construction of the nineteenth century, Jakab 2015, 106–31.

[26] Calvin 1559, III.X, 724.

[27] Calvin 1559, III.X, 725.

[28] Calvin 1948b, *Commentary on Genesis* 2:15.

[29] Calvin 1852, Exodus 20:8.

[30] André-E. Sayous, "Calvinisme et capitalism à Genève de la Réforme à la fin du 18e siècle," *Annales d'histoure économique et sociale*, Paris, 1935, 227; cited by Bieler 2005, 447.

Some scholars still find aspects of Weber's thesis compelling. For it was cities in which Reformed Protestantism was strong that became economically dominant in the sixteenth century—successively, Antwerp, Amsterdam, and London (Gorski 2005, 167). This may not have been due directly to greater industriousness on the part of Protestants, but it does seem to have resulted in part from a decreased number of religious holidays, a lengthening of the workday, and the economic impact of the dissolution of monasteries and sale of monastic lands (Gorski 2005, 168; De Vries 1994, 249–70). These social changes were indeed related to the Protestant sanctification of worldly existence, extending even to business activity. Weber wrongly attributed the economic vitality of Reformed cities, and Reformed industriousness, to anxiety over election, but there was a kernel of truth to his analysis, and his provocative thesis continues to spur scholarly inquiry to the present day.[31]

2.8 Political Economy and the Rise of Capitalism: Adam Smith

Adam Smith is recognized today as the founding father of "political economy," predecessor to modern-day economics. While not the first to use the term "division of labor," he articulated with persuasive clarity how the division of labor enhanced national wealth and prosperity.[32] He was writing in the context of the Scottish Enlightenment, which represents the high water mark of enthusiasm regarding the positive social effects of commerce. Commerce was valued as a civilizing force, which by bringing distant peoples into contact with one another and fostering sympathetic understanding would ensure not just prosperity, but also virtue.[33] Today we appreciate the dark side of this discourse of "civilizing" commerce, which served to legitimate colonial empires (see e.g. Chakrabarty 2008). In the eighteenth century, many Scots, regarding Scotland essentially as a British colony, saw in commerce both a path to economic independence and flourishing and to the healing of religious and political factions (Herdt 1997, 12–13).

Smith is best known, however, not for his account of the economic impact of the division of labor, but rather for his notion of the "invisible hand"—despite the fact that he used the term only three times, and only once in the *Wealth of Nations*. The passage has made him the darling of free market economists, for it seems to support the notion that public good is promoted most effectively when individuals pursue their private self-interest unencumbered by regulation:[34]

---

[31] Among recent works, in addition to those already noted, see Lehmann and Roth 1993, Ghosh 2014, Barbalet 2008.

[32] Campbell and Skinner suggest that the first exposition of the term "division of labor" was Sir William Petty, writing in 1690; 1976, I, 13.

[33] See Hont and Ignatieff 1983 and Phillipson 1974, 407–448.

[34] See, e.g., Friedman 2002, Stigler 1982; Stigler remarked of Smith's *Wealth of Nations* that it "is a stupendous palace erected upon the granite of self-interest," 136. For a powerful critique of this narrative, see Kleinbard 2015 31.

> As every individual, therefore, endeavours as much as he can both to employ his capital in the support of domestic industry, and so to direct that industry that its produce may be of the greatest value; every individual necessarily labours to render the annual revenue of the society as great as he can. He generally, indeed, neither intends to promote the public interest, nor knows how much he is promoting it. By preferring the support of domestic to that of foreign industry, he intends only his own security; and by directing that industry in such a manner as its produce may be of the greatest value, he intends only his own gain, and he is in this, as in many other cases, led by an invisible hand to promote an end which was no part of his intention. Nor is it always the worse for the society that it was no part of it. By pursuing his own interest he frequently promotes that of the society more effectually than when he really intends to promote it. I have never known much good done by those who affected to trade for the public good. It is an affectation, indeed, not very common among merchants, and very few words need be employed in dissuading them from it. (Smith 1776, IV.ii, 456)

Despite scattered texts implying that the pursuit of self-interest may be providentially turned to common benefit, Smith makes clear that ordinarily it is up to human beings to scrutinize policies to avoid distortion by special interests. Commercial society, on Smith's account, has two primary benefits: it maximizes wealth, raising the welfare of both rich and poor, and it fosters freedom, by transforming patterns of dependency. Where the vast majority were once directly dependent on the powerful few, in a commercial society, all are indirectly dependent on many, as markets develop and interlock in complex ways.[35] Smith did not, however, believe that commercial society or any "invisible hand" operating within it would guarantee equality or social justice. Further, he argued that such a society generates a host of vices: vanity, pride, duplicity, indifference (Hanley 2009, 102–103). We must combat these vices by cultivating countervailing virtues, notably the virtue of beneficence (Hanley 2009, 175–208). And we must intervene in markets in order to redress the inequality and suffering that arise even within the most flourishing commercial society. Smith insisted, for instance, that "no society can surely be flourishing and happy, of which the far greater part of the members are poor and miserable. It is but equity, besides, that they who feed, cloath and lodge the whole body of the people, should have such a share of the produce of their own labour as to be themselves tolerably well fed, cloathed and lodged." (Smith 1776, 96). A living wage, he argues, is the lowest wage "consistent with common humanity." (Smith 1776, 86). He worries that workers paid by the piece will overwork themselves, and argues that employers should "listen to the dictates of reason and humanity" in allowing adequate time for rest (Smith 1776, 100). He was struck by the unintended effects of human actions, and by the way in which the pursuit of profit works through market determinations of price in publicly beneficial ways. But he certainly did not conclude that no one need be directly concerned with promoting the public good. The self-interest of merchants leads them to seek to form monopolies, for instance, and Smith regarded these as clearly detrimental to the public and in need of regulation (Smith 1776, 267).

[35] On these two benefits identified by Smith, see Hanley 2009, 15–22.

2.9 Beyond Smith: Emancipating Self-Interest

If Smith is not to blame for giving his blessing to unrestrained capitalism, who was? We need to place Smith in a broader context. Smith was hardly alone in linking the analysis of the workings of political economy with reflection on divine providence. Indeed, this is a striking characteristic of European economic thought during the seventeenth and eighteenth centuries. The modern natural law tradition from Grotius onward had reasoned from observed features of human social behavior to conclusions concerning God's intentions and design for humankind. For instance, that human beings were needy and vulnerable, lacking in thick fur or sharp claws, was taken as an indication that God intended them to band together for mutual security, building societies. The discourse of political economy grew out of a context shaped by this sort of providentialist natural law reflection.[36]

Another piece of this puzzle has been explored by Albert Hirschman in his classic text *The Passions and the Interests: Political Arguments for Capitalism Before Its Triumph* (1977). Seventeenth-century thinkers became intrigued with the possibility of using one set of passions to control another, and in particular, for using the "calm" passion of profit to control or displace warlike passions. These useful passions came to be described as "interests" and regarded not as fallen and sinful but as part of humankind's created endowment and as essentially beneficial, if properly balanced. Weber might lead us to expect that it was Protestant thinkers who led the way in this elevation and transformation of the passions. In fact, this was an ecumenical movement. Thomas Wright (1561–1624), English Catholic author of *The Passions of the Minde in Generall* (1601; 1604), is a striking case in point. Wright argued that the concupiscible and irascible passions had been given to humankind by God in order to allow them "to provide for themselves all those things that are profitable, and to avoid all those things which are damnifiable."[37] Wright regarded self-interest and virtue as going naturally hand-in-hand: "What can more deterre men from wickedness then their own private losse, or move them more to virtue than their owne present gaine?"[38] We tend to think of Mandeville, and his catchphrase "private vices, public benefits" as the origin of the even more striking notion that vicious behavior itself serves the common good.[39] However, other thinkers several decades earlier were exploring similar notions; John Houghton, for instance, wrote in 1681 that "those who are guilty of Prodigality, Pride, Vanity, and Luxury, do cause more wealth to the Kingdom, than loss to their own estates."[40]

Insofar as thinkers regarded the workings of political economy as a product of providential design, recognition of the ways in which this system gave rise to

[36] On the *Wealth of Nations* precisely as natural theology, see Waterman 2004, 88–106; also Haakonssen 1996.

[37] *The Passions of the Minde in Generalle*, 1604: 21, quoted in Barbalet 2008, 95.

[38] Wright, *Passions of the Minde*, 326; quoted in Barbalet 2008, 96.

[39] Bernard Mandeville 1714.

[40] Quoted in Appleby 1978, 171.

suffering and inequity created theodicy problems (Oslington 2018, 112–113). Malthus's pessimistic focus on scarcity and diminishing returns played an influential role here (Waterman 1991, 114–118; 2004, 58–112). One tack was to try to show that benefits outweighed harms. Another was to relieve economic thinking of the burdens of theodicy. Over the course of the nineteenth century, it was the latter tack that won out. One might have expected that this would release reformist energies, that a system no longer viewed as divinely designed to benefit automatically the common good would have been regarded as demanding human intervention. And this was in fact the case to some extent. In England, the 1850s witnessed the Christian socialism of F.D. Maurice, Charles Kingsley and others.[41] Leo XIII initiated the tradition of Catholic social teaching with his 1891 encyclical, *Rerum Novarum*. During the same time period, Abraham Kuyper sought to develop a thoroughly Christian form of economic thought from within a Dutch Calvinist perspective (Kuyper 1898). Yet mainstream economic thinking came during this period to be wholly detached from theological reflection. Indeed, nineteenth-century British theologians themselves fed the development of political economy as an autonomous science, by arguing that it is simply a realm of value-neutral fact, to be used as a means to the pursuit of ends identified by theology (Waterman 1991, 107–126; 2004, 113–170). They failed to anticipate how aggressively market logic would take over, defining human flourishing in purely material terms and abandoning any further reflection on the ends of economic life. The door was opened for the glorification of the pursuit of profit and of free-market capitalism.[42]

2.10 Concluding Reflections

Where, then, does this narrative leave us? On the one hand, the economy has changed dramatically. Where households could once upon a time aspire to relative self-sufficiency, and "economy" refer to the management of the household, systems for the production and consumption of goods and services have now become something that can be fathomed only in light of interdependencies that extend around the globe. Yet human beings remain much the same—creatures that can be harmed by want and violated by injustice, whom Christians understand as cherished and summoned by God to participate as agents in the self-gifting communion of the divine life. The creative activities of making, buying, and selling goods and services are rightly understood as part and parcel of human response to this divine summons. Work is not slavery. Neither wealth nor ownership nor profit are intrinsically evil. These things can be humanly fulfilling and good when they are not exploitative, when they take their place in a mutually beneficial circulation of goods and services

[41] For an overview, see Preston 1993.

[42] On the rise of neoliberal economics proper, see Jones 2012, esp. 113–115. For a nuanced theological assessment, see Hirschfeld 2018.

that builds up community and serve the common good—a common good we must now grasp as extending to the earth and its creatures (Cloutier 2021; Hirschfeld 2021). Work should leave room for contemplation and fellowship. Wealth should be held in trust. Ownership is not an unlimited right. There is no invisible hand to prevent human selfishness from doing harm, or guarantee that efficient markets will be just markets. The challenges of holding corporations responsible are immense, and extraordinarily complex. The first, critical step is taken in acknowledging that we may not evade this shared responsibility, that we have been placed in the garden to till and keep it, to live in harmony with one another and with our fellow creatures, circulating for common nourishment what earth has given and human hands have made.

References

Appleby, Joyce. 1978. *Economic Thought and Ideology in Seventeenth-Century England.* Princeton: Princeton University Press.

Barbalet, Jack. 2008. *Weber, Passion, and Profits*. Cambridge: Cambridge University Press.

Benson, Robert L. and Giles Constable, eds., with Carol D. Lanham. 1991. *Renaissance and Renewal in the Twelfth Century*. Cambridge, MA: Harvard University Press, 1982; Repr. Toronto: University of Toronto Press.

Biéler, André. 2005. *Calvin's Social and Economic Thought*. Geneva: World Council of Churches.

Bloch, Marc. 1989. *Feudal Society*, 2 vols. London: Routledge.

Bonaventura, *Apologia pauperum contra calumniatorem*. Vol. VIII. *Opera Omnia*. 11 vols. Quaracchi 1882–1902.

Brown, Peter. 2012. *Through the Eye of a Needle: Wealth, the Fall of Rome, and the Making of Christianity in the West, 350–550 AD*. Princeton: Princeton University Press.

Calvin, John. 1559. *Institutes of the Christian Religion*. Translated by Henry Beveridge. 1990. Grand Rapids: Eerdmans.

Calvin, John. 1979a. Calvin, *Commentary on a Harmony of the Evangelists*. Translated by William Pringle. Vol. 1. Orig. Pub. Calvin Translation Society. Grand Rapids: Baker Book House.

Calvin. 1979b. *Commentary on the Acts of the Apostles*. Translated by Henry Beveridge. Vol. 1. Orig. pub. Calvin Translation Society. Grand Rapids: Baker Book House.

Calvin, Jean. 1948a. *Commentary on the Epistles of Paul the Apostle to the Corinthians*. Grand Rapids, Eerdmans.

Calvin, Jean. 1948b. *Commentaries on Genesis*. Grand Rapids: Eerdmans.

Calvin, Jean. 1852. *Commentaries on the Four Last Books of Moses*. Charles Bingham. Edinburgh: Calvin Translation Society.

Campbell, Roy H., and Andrew S. Skinner. 1976. Introduction to Adam Smith. In *An Inquiry into the Nature and Causes of the Wealth of Nations*. Oxford: Clarendon Press.

Chakrabarty, Dipesh. 2008. *Provincializing Europe: Postcolonial Thought and Historical Difference*. Princeton: Princeton University Press.

Clement of Alexandria. 1951. Who Is the Rich Man That Shall Be Saved? In *The Ante-Nicene Fathers*, vol. 2. Grand Rapids: Eerdmans.

Cloutier, David. 2021. How Consumers and Firms Can Seek Good Goods. In *Business Ethics and Catholic Social Thought*, ed. Daniel K. Finn, 141–162. Georgetown: Georgetown University Press.

Cohen, Jere. 1980. Rational Capitalism in Renaissance Italy. *American Journal of Sociology* 85:1342–1350.

Francis of Assisi. 1989. Regula Bullata. In *Die Opuscula des Hl. Franziskus von Assisi*, ed. K. Esser. Rome: Grottaferrata.

Friedman, Milton. 2002. *Capitalism and Freedom*. 40th Anniv. ed. Chicago: University of Chicago Press.

Ghosh, Peter, ed. 2014. *Max Weber and the Protestant Ethic: Twin Histories*. Oxford: Oxford University Press.

Gorski, Philip S. 2005. The Little Divergence: The Protestant Reformation and Economic Hegemony in Early Modern Europe. In *The Protestant Ethic Turns 100: Essays on the Centenary of the Weber Thesis*, ed. William H. Swatos Jr. and Lutz Kaelber, 165–190. Boulder/London: Paradigm Publishers.

Gratian. 1959. *Decretum. Corpus Iuris Canonici*. Graz: Akademische Druck- u. Verlaganstalt.

Haakonssen, Knud. 1996. *Natural Law and Moral Philosophy: From Grotius to the Scottish Enlightenment*. Cambridge: Cambridge University Press.

Hanley, Ryan. 2009. *Adam Smith and the Character of Virtue*. Cambridge: Cambridge University Press.

Herdt, Jennifer A. 1997. *Religion and Faction in Hume's Moral Philosophy*. Cambridge: Cambridge University Press.

Herdt, Jennifer A. 2015. Eudaimonism and Dispossession: Augustine on Almsgiving. In *Augustine and Social Justice*, ed. Teresa Delgado, John Doody, and Kim Paffenroth, 97–112. Lanham: Lexington Books.

Hirschfeld, Mary. 2018. *Aquinas and the Market: Toward a Humane Economy*. Cambridge: Harvard University Press.

Hirschfeld, Mary. 2021. What is the Technocratic Paradigm and Must Business Be Structured By It? In *Business Ethics and Catholic Social Thought*, ed. Daniel K. Finn, 93–113. Georgetown University Press.

Hirschman, Albert. 1977. *The Passions and the Interests: Political Arguments for Capitalism Before Its Triumph*. Princeton: Princeton University Press.

Hont, Istvan, and Michael Ignatieff, eds. 1983. *Wealth and Virtue: The Shaping of Political Economy in the Scottish Enlightenment*. Cambridge: Cambridge University Press.

Jakab, Eva. 2015. Property Rights in Ancient Rome. In *Ownership and Exploitation of Land and Natural Resources in Ancient Rome*, ed. Paul Erdkamp, Koenraad Verboven, and Arjan Zuiderhoek, 106–131. Oxford: Oxford University Press.

Jones, Daniel Stedman. 2012. *Masters of the Universe: Hayek, Friedman, and the Birth of Neoliberal Politics*. Princeton, NJ: Princeton University Press.

Kleinbard, Edward. 2015. *We Are Better Than This: How Government Should Spend Our Money*. Oxford: Oxford University Press.

Kleinbard, Edward. 2018. "The Reification of the Social Mortgage." Invited paper, Agency, Self-Interest and the Moral Legitimacy of Business conference, Institute for Advanced Catholic Studies, University of Southern California. (publication in process).

Kuyper, Abraham. 1898/1931. *Lectures on Calvinism*. Grand Rapids: Eerdmans.

Langholm, Odd. 1992. *Economics in the Medieval Schools: Wealth, Exchange, Value, Money and Usury According to the Paris Theological Tradition 1200–1350*. Leiden/New York: E.J. Brill.

Lehmann, Hartmut, and Guenther Roth, eds. 1993. *Weber's Protestant Ethic: Origins, Evidence, Contexts*. Cambridge: Cambridge University Press.

Little, Lester K. 1978. *Religious Poverty and the Profit Economy in Medieval Europe*. Ithaca: Cornell University Press.

Luther, Martin. 1524. Trade and Usury. In *Luther's Works*, ed. W. I. Brandt and H. T. Lehmann. 1962, vol. 45. Philadelphia: Muhlenberg Press.

Mäkinen, Virpi. 2001. *Property Rights in the Late Medieval Discussion on Franciscan Poverty*. Leuven: Peeters.

Mandeville, Bernard. 1714. *Fable of the Bees; or, Private Vices, Publick Benefits*, ed. F. B. Kaye.. 1924. Oxford: Oxford University Press.

Noonan, John T. 1957. *The Scholastic Analysis of Usury*. Cambridge: Harvard University Press.

Olivi, Peter. 1980. Tractatus de emptionibus et venditionibus, de usuris, de restitutionibus. In *Un trattato di economia politica francescana*, ed. Giacomo Todeschini, 51–108. Rome: Istituto storico italiano per il Medio Evo.

Oslington, Paul. 2018. *Political Economy as Natural Theology: Smith, Malthus and their Followers*. London/New York: Routledge.

Phillipson, Nicholas. 1974. Culture and society in the 18th-century province: the case of Edinburgh and the Scottish Enlightenment. In *Europe, Scotland, and the United States from the 16th to the 20th Century*, ed. Lawrence Stone and The University in Society, vol. 2, 407–448. Princeton: Princeton University Press.

Pomeranz, Kenneth. 2000. *The Great Divergence: China, Europe, and the Making of the Modern World Economy*. Princeton: Princeton University Press.

Preston, Ronald H. 1993. Christian Socialism. In *The Blackwell Encyclopedia of Modern Christian Thought*, ed. Alister McGrath. Oxford: Blackwell.

Rule of St. Benedict. 2011. Edited and translated by Bruce L. Venarde. Cambridge: Harvard University Press.

Sbaralea, J., and C. Eubel, eds. 1759–1908. *Bullarium Franciscanum*. Vol. I–VIII. Rome.

Schlag, Martin. 2013. Economic and Business Ethics in Select Italian Scholastics (ca. 1200–1450). In *Handbook of the Philosophical Foundations of Business Ethics*, ed. Christoph Luetge, 179–204. Dordrecht: Springer.

Smith, Adam. [1776]1976. *An Inquiry into the Nature and Causes of the Wealth of Nations*, eds. Campbell Roy H. and Andrew S. Skinner, 1976. Oxford: Clarendon Press.

Stackhouse, Max. 2014. Weber, Theology, and Economics. In *The Oxford Handbook of Christianity and Economics*, ed. Paul Oslington, 307–336. Oxford: Oxford University Press.

Stigler, George J. 1982. *The Economist as Preacher and Other Essays*. Chicago: University of Chicago Press.

Tawney, R. H. 1926. *Religion and the Rise of Capitalism*. New York: New American Library.

Todeschini, Giacomo. 2009. *Franciscan Wealth: From Voluntary Poverty to Market Society*. Translated by Donatella Melucci. Saint Bonaventure: The Franciscan Institute.

Troeltsch, Ernst. 1912/1976. The Social Teachings of the Christian Churches. Translated by Olive Wyon. Chicago/London: University of Chicago Press.

Valeri, Mark. 1997. Religion, Discipline, and the Economy in Calvin's Geneva. *Sixteenth Century Journal* 28:123–142.

Visser 't Hooft, W.-A. 1928. *The Background to the Social Gospel in America*. Haarlem: Bethany Press.

Vries, De. 1994. The Industrial Revolution and the Industrious Revolution. *Journal of Economic History* 54:249–270.

Waterman, Anthony Michael C. 1991. *Revolution, Economics, and Religion: Christian Political Economy, 1798–1833*. Cambridge: Cambridge University Press.

Waterman, Anthony Michael C. 2004. *Political Economy and Christian Theology since the Enlightenment: Essays in Intellectual History*. New York: Palgrave Macmillan.

Weber, Max. 1905/1958. *The Protestant Ethic and the Spirit of Capitalism*. Translated by Talcott Parsons. New York: Charles Scribner's Sons.

Weber, Max. 1921/1968. Asceticism, Mysticism and Salvation. In *Economy and Society; An Outline of Interpretive Sociology*. New York: Bedminster Press.

Werhane, Patricia. 1989. The Role of Self-Interest in Adam Smith's *Wealth of Nations*. *The Journal of Philosophy* 86:669–680.

William of St. Amour. De quantitate eleemosynae. A. Traver, ed. 1995. William of Saint-Amour's Two Disputed Questions De Quantitate Eleemosynae and De Valido Mendicante. *Archives d'histoire Doctrinale et Littéraire du Moyen Age* 62:295–342.

Wood, Diana. 2002. *Medieval Economic Thought*. Cambridge: Cambridge University Press.

Jennifer A. Herdt is Gilbert L. Stark Professor of Christian Ethics at Yale University's Divinity School and has published widely on virtue ethics, early modern and modern moral thought and political theology. She serves on the editorial boards of the Journal of Christian Ethics, Studies in Christian Ethics and the Journal of Religion, and served as the 2020 President of the Society of Christian Ethics. From 2013 to 2021, she served as the academic dean of Yale Divinity School, and is now Senior Associate Dean for Faculty Affairs. Among her recent books are *Assuming Responsibility: Ecstatic Eudaimonism and the Call to Live Well* and earlier *Putting On Virtue: The Legacy of the Splendid Vices* (selected as a Choice Outstanding Academic Title). Her forthcoming book on more-than-human creaturely agency stems from research funded by a Templeton Foundation collaborative grant for science-engaged theological anthropology.

Chapter 3
Protestant Thinking on Markets, Morality, and Human Flourishing: Calvin, Kuyper, and the Ecumenical Movement

Cornelis van der Kooi

Abstract The Reformed tradition, identified closely with the reformer John Calvin, puts distinctive emphases on the relationship between economics and theology. Tracing the thought of Calvin through to the nineteenth-century Dutch theologian and politician Abraham Kuyper and most recently to the economic teachings of the World Council of Churches, distinct themes emerge, including the importance of acknowledging God's sovereignty and authority, the relative rights of property, the relationship of humanity as a communion, the dignity of every person, the role of institutions in intellectual, moral and spiritual formation, a balanced view of hierarchy, and the priority of the role of love. In this way a variegated and yet generally consistent picture emerges of the Protestant understanding of the relationship between economic realities and human flourishing.

Keywords Ecumenical movement · Protestant ethic · John Calvin · Economic ethics · Abraham Kuyper

3.1 Introduction

In 2018 the World Council of Churches (WCC) marked the 70th anniversary of its founding in Amsterdam. Since its beginning the ecumenical movement has grown and flourished for many decades, particularly from the 1950s through the 1980s. As an ecumenical body that included many of the Protestant churches around the world it has been very prolific on questions of work and life, on race and gender, on poverty, social justice, and ecology. Poverty, discrimination, gender issues, and political suppression, or together, a lack of human flourishing, have been prominent on its agenda, and the ideology of the free market and economic neoliberalism has often stood at the front of its criticism. One of the latest examples is *Economy of Life*, the

C. van der Kooi (✉)
Vrije Universiteit, Amsterdam, Netherlands

G. J. Buijs, J. J. Ballor (eds.), *In Search of the Spirits of Capitalism*, Sophia Studies in Cross-cultural Philosophy of Traditions and Cultures 44,
https://doi.org/10.1007/978-3-032-01137-4_3

report of the WCC theological consultation held from 27–30 October 2014 in India. It is an example of a protest against situations of injustice, the structures and imbalances of power that suppress people, that render them dependent, and that rob them of access to the basic resources for a decent human life. The title itself hints at the statement's religious and theological background. The economy should be good for human life. The very word life is redolent of John 10:10 where Jesus says: "I have come that they may have life, and have it to the full."

In its emphasis on fair and humane social and economic conditions, this report does not stand on its own. The Protestant tradition from the start has addressed the topic of human flourishing concerning the economy, markets and social relations. In this contribution I have chosen to discuss three voices in this tradition from different eras: John Calvin, Abraham Kuyper, and the above-mentioned report of the WCC. I will feature them as a triangle, in which Calvin stands at the top and the other two are the legs, which in some way are related to the top. Each of them explores the relationship between theology and thinking about social and economic relations. Each posits a relationship between socio-economic relations and a broader set of virtues or vices, and each suggests how good relationships should promote virtues and contribute to human flourishing. And, as I will argue, there are good reasons to use these three for answering the central question of this essay: is there something that can be called a characteristically Protestant line of thought on markets, morality, and money?

First, we will discuss John Calvin, the second-generation Reformer and organizer of the city of Geneva. He functions as the top of the triangle, from which lines can be drawn to the other two, Kuyper and the WCC. Why Calvin? Max Weber's choice for Luther in his seminal work *The Protestant Ethic and the Spirit of Capitalism* is understandable in so far this reformer was responsible for an understanding of daily work as a vocation, thereby bringing ordinary life and work into the force field of religion and obedience to God. Calvin, however, can be regarded as the reformer whose work and thoughts have had the most transformative power in moral and social issues. It is not without reason that André Biéler's dissertation *La pensée économique et social de Calvin* from 1959 was translated and published by the WCC in 2005. Calvin's emphasis on sanctification and renewal of society links up with the search within the ecumenical movement for a 'responsible society' and was regarded to have more revolutionary power than Luther with his penchant to societal conservatism (Thévenaz 2005, xxi–xxix). In Calvin's exegesis of the law of Moses, the keel may be laid for what we are looking for, the basic features of a Protestant line of thought on markets, virtues, and human flourishing.

Next we will examine the contribution of Abraham Kuyper, the long-time leader of the Neo-Calvinist movement, who sought to relate Reformed faith and life to the new circumstances of the modern industrial economy in the last four decades of the nineteenth century. Kuyper stands out as the main public theologian and political ideologist who launched a Reformed tradition of Christian social thought in what in the introduction to this volume is characterized as high modernity; this movement not only had its effects in the Netherlands, but also abroad. The recent translation project of the collected works in public theology of Kuyper is a sign of its vitality and fruitfulness. His indebtedness to Calvin is also clear. In his political manifesto *Our Program*, for example, he explicitly refers to Calvin's influence numerous times (Kuyper 2015).

Finally we will give attention to the already mentioned report *Economy of Life* because it represents the critical voice on work, life, and human well-being that the international ecumenical movement has issued from its start until now. This report reflects the confusing situation in what the introduction calls hypermodernity. As said, the publication of Biéler's work is a clear proof of the inspiration that this ecumenical body draws from Calvin. We will close with a few conclusions about the main question of this volume, the relation of markets, virtues and human flourishing.

3.2 John Calvin

The name of John Calvin has often been related to only one book, his *Institutes*, and to the doctrine of double predestination in which God is everything and humanity means nothing. Both images are wrong and long outdated among scholars. A better approach is to see Calvin as the organizer of Geneva, a principal Swiss city which, in the early decades of the sixteenth century, had won its independence from the bishop and wanted to avoid coming under the dominion of Bern. Today we might label Calvin an interim manager who was called to act in a situation where the split from the structures of the medieval church had left a vacuum (Biéler 2005, 75). It was in this situation of total transformation—social, economic, and religious—that Calvin worked. It was, as will be laid out later, a time of new market conditions, initiated by free cities, a stronger citizenry and better logistical means. He re-organized local institutions, carried on a heavy daily correspondence with the leaders of his times, wrote various treatises, and—most important but too often forgotten—wrote his commentaries on the books of the Bible and delivered thousands of sermons. It was there, and not first of all in the *Institutes*, that one finds how Calvin's theology addressed all kinds of societal issues. In his commentary on the eighth commandment we find some basic features of how he treated the issues of market, lending at interest, virtues and human flourishing. Calvin was really what we nowadays call a public theologian. Only in this broader context the *Institutes* remain as well an important source that we can, and will, use.

What is decisive in Calvin's thought on economic and social relations? Four basic convictions deserve to be mentioned right at the outset.

First is the conviction of God as authority. God transcends all human and this-worldly powers who claim sovereignty, and as such he is a well and source for righteousness. The critical potential of this statement should not be underestimated. Human rule and power is never absolute, it is subjected to higher authority, to God. The prime foundation of human righteousness and justice is therefore the right worship of God. To illustrate this with a quote from the *Institutes*: "We call it source and spirit because from it men learn to live with one another in moderation and without doing injury, if they honor God as Judge of right and wrong" (Calvin 2011, 1:377).

In the second place: to correctly grasp Calvin's explanation of the law in general and of the eighth commandment in particular we need to remember that the law can only be rightly understood when the relationship between law and lawgiver is taken into account. The law in itself is not God; it is given and ordained by God. For Calvin the whole law—the commandments and all regulations flowing from them—must be interpreted within the covenant that God made with Abraham, that was confirmed on Mount Sinai, and that was confirmed in Jesus Christ. The Lawgiver is not a bare, distant God; he is the Father of Jesus Christ (Hesselink 1992). This has a bearing on the way the eighth commandment—"You shall not steal"—is to be understood. For Calvin these few words must be regarded as a synecdoche: it is a short statement that only partially indicates a larger and positive content. The positive content is formulated by Calvin in the first words of his comment: *Quande caritas est finis legis,* that is: Because love is the goal of the law. It must be emphasized that caritas should not be interpreted as our modern word charity. Caritas is much more, it is care or even obligation to give care and involvement.

The third point flows from the acknowledgement of God's sovereignty and relates to property. The God of Israel is the only one God and as such He is the owner of the earth and all that is in it (Ps. 24:1). In his famous response to Cardinal Jacopo Sadoleto Calvin wrote a sentence that became an adage in the Reformed tradition: *Deo enim, non nobis, nati imprimis sumus, sed Dei,* "For we are born first of all for God, and not for ourselves" (Olin 2000, 52). This adage is not only a general theological statement about the human situation, but also applies to all that humans have available to them and possess. God is the giver of life and has entrusted human beings with all kinds of goods. Nevertheless, God remains the owner; humans have been given a loan. Absolute property does not exist for human beings. This qualification of life, capacities, and goods as a gift has an immediate bearing on the way people are to deal with their possessions and behave on the market. It furthers virtues like gratitude, generosity, and solidarity. From a contemporary point of view it may launch indignation that Calvin takes it as a given that there are rich and poor people, but then the different cultural and theological context must be taken in consideration. God has distributed goods and property unequally, but he binds all human people, rich and poor, together in one spiritual and moral order in which they are bound together. The rich are supposed to freely give or lend to those who are poor and needy. The rule to learn is that the poor "should know how to bear poverty peaceably and patiently" and the rich "how to bear abundance moderately." (Inst. II.10.4). In his comment on 2 Cor. 8:14 he writes: "For the system of proportional right in the Church is this — that while they communicate to each other mutually according to the measure of gifts and of necessity, this mutual contribution produces a befitting symmetry, though some have more, and some less, and gifts are distributed unequally." That is the kind of justice formed by living within the covenant. It should be practiced with a free heart and serve as the point of departure among people in social and economic affairs.

The fourth point relates immediately to the message of redemption. Because God has delivered human beings from servitude to sin and the powers of death, any kind of servitude to other human beings should be avoided and stands forbidden as theologically and morally impossible. All human beings stand on the same level with each other in their relation to God, with no exceptions. From this flows a deep sense of equality of all human beings.

3.2.1 The Eighth Commandment

What this means for social and economic relations in daily life Calvin specifically explained in his discussion of the eighth commandment in his *Commentaries on the Four Last Books of Moses*: "You shall not steal." In Calvin's view this commandment is not just negative. Underlying it is radical positive outlook; it is "ultimately a command to love." (Hesselink 1992, 124). He starts his exposition with the already cited words: "Since charity is the end of the Law, we must seek the definition of theft from thence" (Calvin 1852–1855, 3:110). He continues, "This then is the rule of charity, that everyone's rights should safely be preserved, and that none should do to another, what he would not have done to himself" (Calvin 1852–1855, 3:110). These last words evoke the Golden Rule as stated in Matthew 7:12, where they were put in a positive voice: "In everything, do to others what you would have them done to you, for this sums up the Law and the Prophets." For Calvin the Golden Rule is a description of equity. Taken in general the Law of Moses exposits what justice will mean in different situations, but all these regulations, too, should be regarded as falling under the broader norm of the goal and essence of the law, that is, love for neighbor. It is not only a civic duty not to harm others; it is a command to grant other human beings life and to support them through the possessions and possibilities available to them. So the law is not a number of norms and regulations important in itself but is part of the covenant that God made with the people of Israel. Thus Calvin, interpreting the law by love, undermines thinking of justice by the logic of *do ut des* [*quid pro quo*]. Taking love as our starting point, it is no longer possible to think of justice as something essentially negative, restrictive; rather, it is a dynamic virtue that favors charity. The matrix of justice may be constituted by reciprocity and equality, but at the same time Calvin emphasizes that *justice goes beyond contractual relations*. This means that the rich have specific obligations toward the poor, because they are poor. Here the meaning of equity in Calvin's thought becomes important: Equity refers to the distinction between the letter of the law and an appropriation of the law imbued "by a transformed life flowing from the union with Christ" (Haas 1997, 2). Equity is however not to be confused with equality.

This entails a different way of thinking, one that brings the heart of the human being into play. The commandments of the second table are part of a life that is called to serve and worship God, showing gratitude to God for our own life and good. Therefore the meaning and range of the eighth commandment goes far beyond the prohibition of theft. The negative carries with it a more positive meaning. In his exposition of this commandment in the *Institutes* Calvin states the positive goal of this commandment very briefly:

> let each man consider what, in his rank and station, he owes to his neighbors, and pay what he owes. Moreover, our mind must always have regard for the Lawgiver, that we may know that this rule was established for our hearts as well as for our hands, in order that men may strive to protect and promote the well-being and interests of others. (Calvin 2011, 1:411)

The believer should take care for the needs of those who are poor and in want.

So far so good. But suddenly the exposition of Calvin takes a turn that the modern reader, who may be familiar with what today is often called "philanthropy", may hardly expect. For Calvin states as well that those who refuse to show care where they had a possibility of doing so are the real thieves condemned by the commandment. They take away from the poor what is essential for living. Commenting on Deuteronomy 24:6 Calvin writes,

> He then, is as cruel, whosoever takes in pledge what supports a poor man's life, as if he should take away bread from a starving man, and thus life itself, which, as it is sustained by labor, so, when its means of subsistence are cut off, is, as it were, itself destroyed. (Calvin 1852–1855, 3:123)

In other words, one should not take away another's means of making a living, even if it is permitted by the law of the land. So not only is giving recommended, not giving is strongly condemned.

This statement of Calvin comes from a passage where he discusses at length the question of lending at interest, or as it is often put, the question of usury. As is widely known, Calvin took a decisive step in theological thinking on charging interest. He broke with the church's long-time conviction that lending at interest was forbidden. On the ground of texts like Ex. 22:25, Lev. 25:35–38, and Deut. 23: 19–20, it was clear for the church that charging interest was not allowed. Against this venerable church teaching Calvin came openly to another attitude. And he had still to defend it.

What were the reasons for this move? To name a few causes briefly, the social and economic situation had changed rapidly in recent centuries (Biéler 2005, 122–129). The European voyages of discovery, the invention of new tools, the rise of independent cities, the opening and growth of new modes of transportation, and the increasing importance of citizens with political rights had transformed the character of society. One of the biggest effects was the breakdown of the old framework of a closed economy. Production was no longer only used for local consumption; trade and transportation of goods over long distances became the new reality and created an open market. With that came the need for a new financial system. International trade required large funds and an increasing concentration of capital, and the need for credit spurred the growth of banks and credit systems (Biéler 2005, 145). The city of Geneva was particularly affected by these transformations. It was built at the crossroads of several trade routes. It had to deal with the challenges of sharp increases in population, refugees, and accordingly want of food. Commerce and trade therefore became vital arteries for the life of the city. It was in this changed context that Calvin came to a more differentiated view on the question of interest (Biéler 2005, 139–179). He accepted the new reality of a market, of which lending at interest was a necessary element—however, at moderate rates, and not in all cases.

In the context of his reinterpretation of certain Old Testament passages Calvin frequently refers to the word that we already came across: equity (*aequitas*). In our times the word might be associated with equity funds and big profit-making, but in Calvin we encounter an older meaning. The Latin word *aequitas* brings us into an ethical realm, where the outcome of a judgment cannot be equated with a straightforward application of a rule but requires a cautious and mindful deliberation. As such, it comes close to what today is often called, with reference to Aristotle's notion of *phronesis,* "practical wisdom". Equity being situated in the realm of ethics and religion, however, does not resolve the matter of its application. Calvin writes, "But if we would form an equitable judgment, reason does not suffer us to admit that all usury is to be condemned without exception" (Calvin 1852–1855, 3:131). What follows in Calvin's exposition are not direct statements in favor of charging interest, but questions to his critical contemporaries. He brings the question of lending at interest into debate by giving examples where it would be unfair not to give any compensation:

> If the debtor has protracted the time by false pretenses to the loss and inconvenience of his creditor, will it be consistent, that he should reap advantage from his bad faith and broken promises? Certainly no one, I think, will deny that usury ought to be paid to the creditor in addition to the principal, to compensate his loss. (Calvin 1852–1855, 3:131)

This is an interesting deliberation. In opposition to older views (von Hagen 2014), Calvin is of the opinion that money in the contemporary market situation is indeed productive; it is used as an investment and therefore the rule of equity requires a further step beyond repaying the principal. He then draws an interesting distinction between two sorts of loans. The one is for basic needs like food, clothing and shelter; the other is for investment and production. In the latter case a moderate rate of interest may be charged. In the former, charging interest violates the virtues of love and equity. Later he adds that the same logic should be extended to widows, orphans, and strangers in remembrance of the fact that they (Moses's original Israelite audience) had been bondmen in the land of Egypt (see Deut. 24:17).

Does Calvin's shift in thinking on interest mark the birth of a 'capitalist spirit' (Biéler 2005, 423–454)? The foregoing has made clear that Calvin's thought on markets, virtues, and human flourishing are far from that; social and economic life should be formed and regulated by a life in agreement with the covenant, by the virtues of love and equity. That will promote a humane and flourishing society.

Calvin warns repeatedly in these passages of the risks of wealth, and he does so not only as theologian. As a humanist scholar he reminds the reader that heathen authors saw that "since all men are born for the sake of each other, human society is not properly maintained, except by an interchange of good office" (Calvin 1852–1855, 3:126). This means that one "who does not relieve the necessities of his brethren when he can" should be deemed unrighteous. In another place Calvin draws from Proverbs 5:16 the lesson that "those who have abundance do not enjoy their possessions as they ought, unless they communicate them to the poor for the relief of their poverty" (Calvin 1852–1855, 3:126).

By way of conclusion we can say the following: In thinking about society and economic relations Calvin starts with the notion of community and covenant. For people to be good servants of others there should be "an interchange of good office," which means that humans have to apply all their gifts, including reason and imagination, to find ways to creatively and productively serve one another. This is an obligation placed on society by God and one that is absolutely necessary for the maintenance and flourishing of society. The poor, too, belong to that society; they are created by God and should therefore be regarded and treated as brothers. Calvin accepts lending at interest in cases of investment. In his times this was a brave move; he was breaking with a centuries-old Christian teaching. His primary concern, however, remained the protection of the weak and the damage that lenders can do to the borrowers. Underlying economic relations are human relations, and they should be determined first of all by love and equity. It was clearly beyond Calvin's scope to see that lenders also can be injured and that two-sided protection is needed in a well-balanced society (Biéler 2005, 421).

3.3 Kuyper: A Modern Calvinist View

Now I will turn to the second example of Protestant thinking which also stresses human dignity and the importance of ordinary, even marginalized people. In the last decades of the nineteenth century Abraham Kuyper, a theologian, journalist, politician, and opinion leader, emerged as the foremost leader of a renewal movement in the Netherlands which, like Neo-Thomism on the Roman Catholic side, strove to retrieve and renew its tradition for a new context (Bratt 2013). It is the time of high modernity. Rationalization and industrialization have caused major changes in society and the free-market system has plunged large numbers of workers in a continued and blind-alley situation of poverty. In *Our Program*, a collection of articles that he published in 1879, Kuyper issued a political and cultural manifesto for the first modern political party in the Netherlands, the Anti-Revolutionary Party (Kuyper 2015).

This manifesto set forth a holistic view of the state, society, and politics, particularly defining the responsibility of the state and the role of the people in a dramatically changing society. *Our Program* was foundational for the thought and ideas of what became the Christian-democratic wing of Dutch society from the last third of the nineteenth and into the first decades of the twentieth century. The piece is still impressive for the political-cultural principles that it laid out and for its stimulation of Christian thinking about modern society, including industrialization and the mobilization of ordinary people—and including as well the shadow sides of modern development. In this context Kuyper addressed the issues at the heart of social and economic relations: not least, the question of how to strengthen the virtues so as to promote the genuine flourishing of society. In his thought virtues are not only person-related, but also related to societal structures and last but not least, to theological doctrine.

Crucial to Kuyper's discussion of a just society and right relations is the issue of authority (Kuyper 2015, 16–28), and here lies a strong connection to some of the characteristics of Calvin's thought, as laid out above. Who will have power and authority? What is decisive for Kuyper in the formation of virtues and human flourishing is recognition of the *source* of authority. Recognition of the right authority will help to build righteous structures and develop virtues. He opposes two positions that he identifies as negative effects of the French Enlightenment: the idea of popular sovereignty on the one hand and of state-sovereignty on the other. The first was inscribed on the banner of the French Revolution. Power and sovereignty should no longer be the privilege of the high classes, of the nobility, or the king, or the church and its clerics. No, the people's will should be decisive, the people themselves sovereign. The second position was embodied in Hegelian idealism, in which the state is regarded as embodying and guarding the fruits of Reason, humanity, and a flourishing nation. Both positions, according to Kuyper, are offspring of the Revolution which wanted to abolish every form of divine authority. Modernity in the French style wants to get rid of the deepest conviction of Christianity, that the human being is not the first and final authority but occupies a secondary position. In fact, held Kuyper, human beings are created by God and it behooves their humanity that they acknowledge God as sovereign over them. Paul's words in Romans 13:1 are central for him and his modern version of Calvinism: the governing authorities have been instituted by God. As Kuyper himself put it, "the source of sovereign authority does not reside in the law or the will of the people but in God" (Kuyper 2015, 19). Therefore, no human authority has authority in itself; it has been given or bestowed on humans, and only for a function, for a task.

This principle has deep and important bearings upon the way one should think about economy, society, and the division of power. Authority is never the absolute possession of the human being; it is a grant, a loan without end. Kuyper worried about the problems that ensue if this position is not accepted. If the secondary and endowed status of human authority is denied, then the source of power must be sought elsewhere, and that source will naturally assume a godlike power next to God. Kuyper saw Hegel and his progeny putting the state in that position; alternatively, those who located sovereignty in the people's will left the state subject to whatever the voters and their representative bodies might say. In our own time we see public opinion having come to occupy the emptied throne.

Instead, right at the outset of *Our Program*, Kuyper appeals to the Word of God and suggests the existence of eternal principles and ordinances that could be drawn from the Bible. That is typical for Kuyper; the search for such principles and ordinances for every sphere of life was part of his ideological agenda throughout the years (Kuyper 2015, 336). By setting that goal he sought a ground of authority that stood above the state on the one hand and beyond the reach of political manipulation on the other. Kuyper went even further than political authority here. He saw these principles to be foundational for creation in all its diversity, and he posited their ground to be in the mind of God.

Let me pause for a moment and make an historical and a critical comment at this point. The search for eternal principles in this renewal movement has not proven to be successful. Forty years out from *Our Program* Herman Bavinck declared that the search for such distinctively Reformed foundational principles had failed (Harinck et al. 1994). Besides, we have to say that in the twentieth century the search for eternal ordinances came under suspicion in that it only endorsed a conservative attitude. Historically speaking, we must say that the search for eternal principles was itself steeped in idealistic thought of a Hegelian cut. However, our critical evaluation can be more appreciative: Kuyper offered something that, in my opinion, we should not lose, namely, an appeal to the sphere of ethics and moral judgment also in regard to politics, economics, and social relations. The advancement of virtues cannot be separated from this moral sphere nor from religion. It is from this spiritual sphere that the human heart is addressed and the relation with God is at stake. Here the narrative of the Bible becomes important for all that can be said about the dignity of the human being, beneficial social structures, virtues, and human flourishing.

Kuyper's statements on authority and power set the stage for what he had to say about society, labor, property, and power structures. We will restrict our consideration here to *Our Program*, keeping in mind that it laid out the foundations of what he elaborated years later in *The Social Question and the Christian Religion*, his famous opening address to the first Christian Social Congress held in Amsterdam in November 1891 (Kuyper 1891; Ballor 2016). That was a moment of dire crisis in Dutch society and marked the birth of the Christian Social Tradition in the Netherlands (Hazenbosch 2016). For Kuyper the 'social question' of the late nineteenth century had many facets and implications. One of the biggest problems was the mal-distribution of power in contemporary society. Those who have wealth are always in a better position, for example, to obtain quality education for their children, to get justice in the courtroom, and to defend their interests. They have more power. Kuyper argues explicitly for increasing the influence of ordinary people, which in his time meant greater power for the lower, non-tax-paying class. In this way, by building better, virtuous structures, the life of ordinary people will improve.

Our Program also decried the modern state's penchant for centralization and argued for decentralization instead. Kuyper likewise resisted top-down governance where not absolutely necessary. Centralization and top-down dominion of the state destroy the vitality, energy, and responsibility of the different domains of life, and are the characteristic bane of modern society (Kuyper 2015, 146). Instead Kuyper advocated putting responsibility as low on the social scale as possible, beginning with the family. He related this model to his theological anthropology which held that every human being had been created in the image of God and therefore endowed with dignity, conscience, and responsibility. It is this theological doctrine that fuels the courage to stand up, frank and without fear, and to ask for a fair share in society, access to political, economic, and societal resources. It has a bearing on the way the members of society relate and behave toward each other, and the way the relations are structured. Society in general, and relations between employers and employees in particular, should not be regarded as a bare contractual relationship. They should be seen instead as embedded in a moral sphere in which the humanity of the other is acknowledged, where "moral ties of trust, solidarity, and attachment bind the wage earner to his employer" (Kuyper 2015, 333). Industrialization requires new and properly oriented structures of the labor market. Kuyper appreciates improvements in industrial development that stemmed from the invention of steam power and machine production. At the same time, he is critical on the new market situation and writes, "this has freed capital almost completely from its earlier dependence on manual labor. It has led the capitalist to regard his employees as nothing but machines of flesh that can be retired or scrapped when they break down or have worn out" (Kuyper 2015, 332–333). In other words, employees should not be regarded merely as *human resources*.

To solve the problem of impersonalized relations and imbalances of power Kuyper did not want "the laws [to] be hastily revised and made to lean more to the side of the lower class." Rather, "the element that is currently shut out has to be given a voice in nation's representative bodies" (Kuyper 2015, 343). That is, Kuyper advocated a democratization of social and economic power. He also argued for the formulation of a Code of Labor to supplement the already existing Code of Commerce. If in older times such a written code was hardly necessary because employer and employee lived and worked closely with each other, in the new circumstances of urban industrial society such a Code had become necessary. The job market had changed tremendously, so relations between people in terms of labor, wages, and working conditions had become more complicated. In short, the way to a better future and the flourishing of the whole of society is a transformation in power relations—thus *protection*, not *regulation*. What does that mean? Kuyper stipulates regulation to be a process in which the government decides everything in a top-down manner, or what he called "the regulatory mania of the meddlesome state" (Kuyper 2015, 339). He rejects this carryover from traditional hierarchical society. *Protection*, by contrast, obtains when society has open spaces, markets, and negotiating tables where workers and employers can together work out fair wages and decent labor conditions. It is clear: Kuyper does not focus in the first place on personal virtues; he advocates better and just structures. These structures will help people to be involved, to contribute to society, and to develop personal virtues as well.

This proposal of balancing influence among different interest groups fits with Kuyper's broader political and social theory. In his view society consists of different "spheres" which are in principle sovereign and equal. This equality applies also to the State. The sphere of the State does not stand hierarchically higher than other spheres. Only in case of emergency and only temporarily is the State allowed and called to interfere in other spheres—for example, in the sphere of the family if the interests of the children are under serious risk or threat. Ordinarily, however, the State should facilitate the flourishing of the spheres of education, industry, family, and religion but not interfere in them. Kuyper was obviously afraid of too much State power, when it comes to economic and social relations as well. He writes:

> The fanatic for state omnipotence, or to put it more mildly, the statesman who leans toward expanding the power of government, is not pursuing the moral goal of protecting the weak, but has the doctrinaire objective of recasting society according to an ideal model. (Kuyper 2015, 339)

Kuyper obviously did not believe in such a model. Instead, the government has a restricted task and the classes and groups of citizens should be able to organize life and work on their own terms.

Kuyper's contribution to the question of labor markets and human flourishing focuses directly on the division of power. Power should not be held by an elite group, a single class, or investors alone. Those who have to offer their labor should have a fair share of power and influence as well. Kuyper promoted a model of representative governance from the bottom up. Every human being, every sphere, should have a say—and, accordingly, responsibility—for its own business.

A strong penchant for democratization thus surfaces across Kuyper's thought. This assumes, again, a Protestant emphasis on the human person, but definitely not in the sense of an ideological individualism. In fact, he identified individualism as one of the evils that the French Revolution brought into the world. The human individual, apart from God, is set on the throne as first authority. Kuyper viewed the human person as part of the wider organism of humanity. Every human being, as a creature of God, has dignity and thereby responsibility, but she should never and nowhere be separated from the community of human beings. She is part of an organism, the body of Christ, the church, and the wider society. The human being is called to act as steward in God's world as part of the wider community.

Linking up with what we already found in Calvin, Kuyper in his political manifesto also cites passages in the Old Testament on social and economic issues. He writes,

> The antirevolutionary, after all, who reckons with God's ordinances, can never overlook in Israel's social laws, which had God himself as their author, the presence of a broad series of provisions that made the relationship between haves and have-nots different from what it would otherwise have been if left to itself. Israel's laws touching usury, lending against collateral, creditors, day laborers, after-harvest gleaning, the return of alienated fields, the tithe, leaving the fruit of the land for the poor every so many years, and so much more, made for a system of social institutions that unquestionably served to restrict the powerful and to raise a protective shield over the weak. This encouraged the higher principle of mercy and charity to come to expression also in civil life. (Kuyper 2015, 338)

Society cannot be left to itself. It needs structural protections against imbalances of power in accordance with the higher law of charity and equity.

3.4 *Economy of Life*: A Document of the World Council of Churches

As a third step I want to discuss the WCC document on *Economy of Life* (Mshana and Peralta 2013). As already mentioned, this report mirrors in many respects the diffusing situation of high modernity: economic and technological progress, globalization, but also market liberalization resulting in a monopoly of some internationally operating companies and exploitation of huge masses, particularly in southern countries. What is its message? Is there a continuity in what we found in Calvin and Kuyper?

Significant in this report is again the theological basis. A basic and repeatedly used term in this report is the New Testament Greek word *koinonia*. *Koinonia* means not only community but also communion. According to the report *koinonia* means that people "have a dignified, clean and safe place to live and die among family and friends who love and share life with them; where work has dignity and wages are fair and just, where justice is done, mercy is loved, and all walk humbly with God (Micah 6:8); and where the Earth's beings ... live in the integrity God has made." What is described here could also be phrased in terms of *shalom*: a situation of peace, or better, a situation where life-giving relations are built up and maintained so as to make human life flourish. Directly after laying out this hopeful and positive vision, the report describes today's reality to be the opposite. Indeed, the situation wrought by the modern free market system is gloomy:

> In today's world, we do not see God's vision of koinonia. The liberalization and deregulation of markets over the last three decades as part of the sweeping process of neoliberal globalization have allowed the build-up of a system which promotes insatiable consumption of human and natural resources and thus ever-growing economic, social and ecological imbalances. Today, just 67 people own half the world's wealth. Religious traditions of the world have long warned us against the greed that leads to this utter disruption of the divine vision. In the midst of the poverty, suffering, oppression, economic exploitation, and abuse of power that shape life for the majority of the world's people, as well as the torture and increasing death of the Earth and all her beings, God weeps with us in our pain and vulnerability.

The report continues in dark tones when speaking about markets, globalization, and the world economy and identifies it all with plundering the earth. By contrast an *economy of life* is characterized by cooperation and collaboration. It lifts up the values of solidarity, mutual inter-dependence, and relationship. It is safeguarded by taking seriously the dignity of all creatures, not only humans but also for our whole life system.

It may be concluded that this report depicts quite eloquently the general feeling within the ecumenical community about markets and economy (Ballor 2010). The modern economics of free-market capitalism are cast as dangerous powers. They are not evaluated for decreasing poverty, child mortality, and social injustice. Rather, modernity and global developments of the last decades have only caused more problems and have not solved anything. One wonders what the authors of this report would answer to the quite different approach of, for example, Deirdre McCloskey, whose work emphasizes the humanizing effects of the idea of bourgeois virtues (McCloskey 2006). This element is completely absent. The Christian answer found in this report lies in the ritual of baptism, where the Christian community is taught a different way of life. Just as in baptism "we learn renunciation and detachment from the dominating powers, so we are called to a renunciation of economic power and detachment from consumerism. We are called to a life where Jesus Christ is Lord, not the gilded sham of the market." Later, the report emphasizes the principle of relationship:

> A holistic Economy of Life rejects homogenization which denies differences in identity, ethnicity, culture, tradition, values, history and systems of governance and economics. Rather it conserves and celebrates ways of life and economies practiced by marginalized communities. These ways of life depend on need rather than greed and respect the integrity of all living beings who are considered of equal importance. They are rooted in the understanding that we belong to the land and that land does not belong to us, that we are all part of one wondrous organic web of life.

Positively speaking, this report puts first and foremost the values of solidarity, communion (*koinonia*), and a willingness to fight the destructive hegemony of economies of death. It thus stands in line with the basic theme for a Protestant view of social and economic relations in the thought of Calvin and Kuyper. However, it must be noted that the WCC report, in contrast to those earlier voices, remains very abstract and shows only the dark side of the coin; all kinds of evil are lumped together and almost rendered identical. It offers little differentiation, no awareness or mention of the positive effects of modernization and free enterprise, no acknowledgement of the diminishment of the numbers of people who live in poverty or the decrease in infant mortality. The evils of social injustice, situations of poverty and oppression fill the canvas. At the same time, it must be emphasized that this report ushers in a new and highly needed concern for our time in expanding the notion of *koinonia* to all living beings, to creation and thus to ecology. This elaboration urgently needs to be integrated into a Christian view on markets, virtues and human flourishing. A reformed and catholic approach will encompass this widened idea of *koinonia.*

3.5 What Is Typical for Protestant Thinking?

What can we conclude? Is there such as a Protestant line of thought on markets, virtues, and human flourishing? The Protestant world has no magisterium, no council that delivers authoritative statements on social and economic issues. Compared to the Roman Catholic world it stands at a disadvantage in this respect. The World Council of Churches neither fills that gap nor has a similar status. All that said, we can still draw seven conclusions from the voices we have discussed.

First, the acknowledgment of *God as the supreme Authority* and Lord of life. Not the state, the market, or capital or any other blind or anonymous power should be given this place. God is the source of all authority and human executive authority has its standard and rule in God.

Second, there is *no absolute property*. All that humans possess, invent, make, or gather is not strictly their own. It is loan, a gift for this life, part of this creation; and this creation with all that is in it is God's. This not only affects claims on property in goods or the issue of intellectual property, but also brings the way we deal with anything we possess to a spiritual and ethical level. The concept of stewardship corresponds to this sense of ownership; thus it underscores an important moral mandate that is placed on human beings to manage our resources appropriately and productively for the common good.

Third, Protestant thinking according to these three voices is characterized by a deep awareness of *humanity as communion*. Foundational in Calvin's thought is God's covenant; Kuyper speaks of humanity as an organism; and *Economy of Life* centers on the concept of *koinonia*. This report expands the concept of *koinonia* to include our ecological life system as well. Individualism does not hold center stage here; rather, active participation in the body of Christ in baptism and eucharist radiates into the wider society and creation.

Fourth, *koinonia* and covenant include the *dignity of every person,* and correlatively the dignity of all morally legitimate work and every calling. This tenet has clear and direct economic effects. Calvin emphasizes that nobody should be subjected to servitude or stripped of means. God has delivered humans from servitude to sin and dehumanizing powers. Kuyper in his time elaborated these notions in a democratic direction. Society consists of different spheres and networks where all the different participants—such as employers, employees, and providers of capital—should have access to power and influence. He argues for a society with open places, markets, and meeting tables, in other words, a civil society, where no one party—state, capital, public opinion—dominates and imposes its will. Modern society does not only need personal virtues in order to promote human flourishing; good, virtuous structures are also fundamental, structures that give the people a voice to speak and to have a share in power.

Fifth, the foregoing thoughts on the participation of all members of society correlate significantly with the strong emphasis on *catechesis*, *education*, and *learning* in general in the Protestant tradition. Everyone has a calling to contribute to society and to take their due share of responsibility for its well-being. These notions of stewardship and calling require the formation of moral virtues such as trustworthiness, responsibility, charity, justice, equity, courage, and perseverance. They prepare and shape people to be active and critical members of society, in its political and societal institutions, and at work. Virtues enhance good work; so also, good work will help character formation and contribute to individual and societal flourishing (Ballor and Cooper 2015). Apart from its deep criticism of the free market and neoliberalism, the WCC report *Economy of Life* offers a new and, for our time, necessary element. The abuse of creation and depletion of resources are deeply problematic and are part of a distorted market. The concept of stewardship should explicitly encompass all living beings and our creation as a whole. New life-giving initiatives will not come from great institutions with power, this report expects; they will come from the margins, from people with no power.

Sixth, all these Protestant sources show a critical sensitivity to hierarchy. If all forms of authority and executive power are endowed by God, entrusted to divinely appointed ends, and have their criterion of valuation in God's love and benevolence, then the persons and bodies in charge may be duly questioned about their use of power. Checks and balances are vital in this respect; where these are absent, power will degenerate.

Seventh, central and recurrent in Protestant thinking on social and economic issues is the word *love*. Love not understood as an unrealistic, sentimental or romantic ideal that has nothing to do with real-life issues, but love as mutual honor in broader forms of interdependency. Love should not be restricted to simple I-Thou relations (Welker 2014, 106). Love provides a critical perspective on power relations, behavior, transactions, and undertakings; it leads to an application of the Golden Rule. The ideal here is not the Silver Rule, which says that we not should do to others what we do not want for ourselves, but the Golden Rule which calls for active investment in mutual benevolence. Economics are not an independent reality; at its center are real human beings, created in the image of God and thus for love. This kind of love is a highly critical criterion for our current economic system, and any other.

References

Ballor, Jordan J. 2010. *Ecumenical Babel: Confusing Economic Ideology and the Church's Social Witness*. Grand Rapids: Christian's Library Press.

Ballor, Jordan J., ed. 2016. *Makers of Modern Christian Social Thought: Leo XIII and Abraham Kuyper on the Social Question*. Grand Rapids: Acton Institute.

Ballor, Jordan J., and Cary L. Cooper. 2015. Work and Human Development. In *Handbook of Virtue Ethics in Business and Management*, ed. A. J. G. Sison. Dordrecht: Springer.

Biéler, André. 2005. *Calvin's Economic and Social Thought*. Geneva: World Council of Churches.

Bratt, James. 2013. *Abraham Kuyper: Modern Calvinist, Christian Democrat*. Grand Rapids: Eerdmans.

Calvin, John. 1852–1855. *Commentaries on the Last Four Books of Moses, Arranged in the Form of a Harmony*. 4 vols. Edinburgh: Calvin Translation Society.

Calvin, John. 2011. *Institutes of the Christian Religion*. 2 vols. Louisville: Westminster John Knox Press.

Haas, Guenther H. 1997. *The Concept of Equity in Calvin's Ethics*. Waterloo: Wilfrid Laurier University Press.

Harinck, G., C. van der Kooi, and J. Vree. 1994. Als Bavinck nu maar eens kleur bekende. In *Aantekeningen van H. Bavinck over de zaak-Netelenbos, het schriftgezag en de situatie van de Gereformeerde Kerken*. Amsterdam: Vrije Universiteit.

Hazenbosch, Piet. 2016. *De kracht van verbondenheid*. Almere: Parthenon.

Hesselink, I. John. 1992. *Calvin's Concept of the Law*. Allison Park: Pickwick Publications.

Kuyper, Abraham. 1891. *Het sociale vraagstuk en de christelijke religie: rede bij de opening van het Sociaal Congres op 9 november 1891 gehouden*. Amsterdam: J.A. Wormser.

Kuyper, Abraham. 2015. *Our Program. A Christian Political Manifesto*. Bellingham: Lexham Press.

McCloskey, Deirdre N. 2006. *The Bourgeois Virtues*. Chicago: University of Chicago Press.

Mshana, Rogate R., and Athena Peralta, eds. 2013. *Economy of Life: Linking Poverty, Wealth and Ecology*. Geneva: World Council of Churches.

Olin, John C., ed. 2000. *A Reformation Debate: John Calvin & Jacopo Sadoleto*. New York: Fordham University Press.

Thévenaz, Jean Pierre. 2005. André Biéler: A Portrait. In *Calvin's Economic and Social Thought*, ed. André Biéler. Geneva: World Council of Churches.

von Hagen, Jürgen. 2014. Microfoundations of the Uses of Money. In *Money as God? The Monetization of the Market and Its Impact on Religion, Politics, Law, and Ethics*, ed. Jürgen von Hagen and Michael Welker, 19–41. Cambridge: Cambridge University Press.

Welker, Michael. 2014. Kohelet, a Monetary Economy, and Religion. In *Money as God? The Monetization of the Market and its Impact on Religion, Politics, Law, and Ethics*, ed. Jürgen von Hagen and Michael Welker, 98–108. Cambridge: Cambridge University Press.

Cornelis van der Kooi is a theologian who has published widely in the field of systematic theology and on the theology and impact of (neo)Calvinism. He served as the Head of the Department of Dogmatics and Ecumenics and as Director of the Center of Evangelical and Reformation Thought at the VU University of Amsterdam. After his retirement he joined the Erasmus University Rotterdam as a senior lecturer in the field of Theology and Economics. He is one of the founders of the Erasmus Economics & Theology Institute (EETI).

Part II
Confucianism

Chapter 4
Beyond Confucianism: An Essay on Max Weber, the Religion of China, and the Ritual Economy of Chinese Market Society

Carsten Herrmann-Pillath

Abstract Chinese religion is deeply wedded with the economy and reflects the historical completion of the Chinese market economy in the Qing dynasty. This is where the distinction between market economy and capitalism comes into full significance. Weber already recognized that China had developed a strong commercial culture and markets. Hence, implicitly he distinguished between markets and capitalism. Yet his focus on European history undermined this analytical distinction. But it is essential to explain the apparent contradiction between the two narratives about Confucianism and markets: the Confucian failure story and the Confucian capitalism story. Weber failed both to adequately recognize the nature of Chinese religion and the nature of the Chinese market economy as ritual economy because he projected his grand narrative on capitalist rationalization on China. Chinese religion, in conjunction with the philosophy of Confucianism, may be reinvented today as a way of expressing beliefs about the sacredness of certain pivotal human relations to the world, which enable humans to conduct good life in a way of acting reasonably and responsibly.

Keywords Max Weber · Confucianism · Markets · Rationalization · Capitalism

4.1 Max Weber and China: An Intellectual Giant with Feet of Clay?

Max Weber's work on world religions certainly has been most influential in the field of thinking about China and Confucianism as the 'religion of China'. In this chapter, I want to reflect on some fundamental aspects of his thought that have been recently thematized by the economic and social historian Philip Huang (2015, 2019)

C. Herrmann-Pillath (✉)
Erfurt University, Erfurt, Germany

G. J. Buijs, J. J. Ballor (eds.), *In Search of the Spirits of Capitalism*, Sophia Studies in Cross-cultural Philosophy of Traditions and Cultures 44,
https://doi.org/10.1007/978-3-032-01137-4_4

and relate this with the question what we can learn from Weber about the relationship between religion and economy in China today. This will lead us to reinstate Weber's theses in a substantially modified form and must start out from recognizing Weber's failure to adequately understanding Chinese religion, as distinguished from 'Confucianism and Daoism,' the topic of his famous book. The crucial issue is Weber's notion of capitalism, beyond the narrower scope of his Protestantism thesis, and his general account of rationalization and secularization, often covered by his notion of *Entzauberung* ('disenchantment,' see Joas 2017). For his analysis of Confucianism in relation to capitalism, the idea is fundamentally that Confucianism has been only partially *entzaubert*, 'disenchanted'. Accordingly, my argument also involves his famous *Zwischenbetrachtung*, following his treatment of Confucianism, often interpreted as making the case for functional differentiation of spheres of value, such as the economy, religion, or erotic life. This is the grand narrative of twentieth-century sociology about rationalization and differentiation in the rise of modernity. Weber's approach to religion is entirely governed by this perspective, and accordingly, if we cast doubt on this narrative, our interpretation of Chinese religion will also change.

I will argue that to get the argument right, it is essential to distinguish properly between market economy and capitalism, and to interpret the Chinese case as an alternative trajectory of integrating across value spheres, such as in the case of the topic of this chapter—economy and religion—while at the same time achieving rationalization in substantive ('material') terms. This matches with Weber's view, critically evaluated by Lai (2015), that China represents the most distant antipode to Western development, epitomized in various dualities, such as confronting 'rational adaptation to the world' in Confucianism with 'rational domination of the world' in Protestant Puritanism (Schluchter 1983). Weber, therefore, even claimed that China never attained substantive rationalization, not to speak of formal rationalization, salient in his interpretation of traditional Chinese legal practice as mere *Khadi Justiz* (person-based, not based on formal rules). All these observations focus on Weber's central concern: Explaining China's grandiose historical failure to achieve the transition to capitalism. This failure puts China at the opposite pole to the West in all social domains, including religion.

The topic is of considerable significance for understanding the general relationship between economy and religion beyond the question of the historical origins of capitalism. For example, in their recent synthesis of economic research on religion McCleary and Barro (2019) simply treat 'Confucianism' as state religion in 1900 and assign no religion to China after 1949. They ponder whether Confucianism may be a functional substitute for religion in terms of a secular ethics, which would directly stay in tension with Weber's view, influential until today, to approach Confucianism as religion—even though Weber also saw Confucianism as a kind of 'minimalist' religion, almost completely reduced to a this-worldly practical ethics. Hence, in McCleary and Barro's analysis the most significant development in the world economy, the recent rise of China to a world economic power, might automatically drop out from systematically investigating into religion and economy in general. On first sight, that might be justified in considering the many results from public opinion surveys in China that the majority of Chinese assert as having 'no religion' at all, fitting the image of a secular state combining communist politics with capitalist economy.[1]

My chapter aims at demonstrating that both views are wrong, and that we can develop a more adequate approach in reflecting on Weber's analysis of Chinese religion, without taking it at face value today anymore. My argument dovetails with Yü Yingshi's (2021) masterly reflection of the intellectual history of late Imperial China, showing that the synthesis of Buddhism and Neoconfucianism increasingly shaped the worldview and *Lebensführung* (conduct of life) of its vibrant merchant class. Religion and economy became closely intertwined, yet we must distinguish neatly between 'market economy' and 'capitalism', both in terms of the 'Great tradition' (Herrmann-Pillath and Zhao 2023) and the 'Little tradition' of everyday religious life (Gates 1996; Stafford 2020). The important implication is that markets and morality remain within the same value sphere of envisaging and enacting a good 'life under heaven'. Ultimately, this represents a form of substantive rationality that counters the irrationality of radically disenchanted capitalism (Yang 2020).

Weber's failure in dealing with China results from troubles on two levels. The first is simply that Weber's knowledge about China was limited, not because he was not fully aware of the state of the art in Chinese studies of his time, but because since his time Chinese studies have moved on and have changed, if not revolutionized, many of our views on the economic and social conditions in the Late Empire, which is most relevant for discussing the issue of religion and economy.[2] This has been already documented extensively in the earlier literature on Weber and China and does not need to be repeated in detail here. The other level is more interesting: As Huang points out, there is a highly suggestive gap in Weber's thinking about rationality in excluding the possibility of substantive rationality apart from formal rationality, and hence a fully-fledged systemic alternative to capitalism in the Western sense, not only with reference to the economy, but also state-society relations in general. It is often overlooked that Weber himself, despite his grand narrative of rationalization, recognized that capitalism can and perhaps even necessarily must result in failures of material rationality, such as severe inequality and exploitation (Weber and Tribe 2019, 172, 245). This is the argument that I want to pursue

[1]The most recent data of the Pew Research Center for 2023 confirm that more than 90 percent of the Chinese do not assign themselves to a specific 'religion', in the sense of the confessional self-ascription (Wenzel-Teuber (2024). However, the alternative survey approach is 'god-based' and asks about specific practices. For example, 32.4 percent of Chinese believe in Buddha and Bodhisattvas. The available statistical data would suggest a low presence of religious life in China today, whereas most observers agree that there is a strong and vibrant religious revival. On the problems of Chinese religious statistics, see Chau (2019, 7ff).

[2]The definitive assessment of Weber's China scholarship is the edited volume introduced by Schluchter (1983) which includes contributions from leading China scholars at the time. Since then, however, the debate has even moved further on, especially with regard to social history, because more archives became accessible in the PR China, thus enabling more detailed historical research on social life.

here, but in the context of specific and mainly empirical issue about Confucianism and its status as a religion in China (or possibly, *the* religion of China).

4.2 The Confucian Revival in China Today

Confucianism is the most frequently used concept when trying to sketch essentials of Chinese culture in relation to economic modernization, salient in many systematic value surveys that pursue comparative research (e.g., House et al. 2004 or the ongoing waves of the World Values Survey https://www.worldvaluessurvey.org/wvs.jsp). In this respect, the Weber thesis is still relevant, namely that Confucianism was one of the most important obstacles towards the transition to capitalism in China, interpreted both as a specific institutional form of the economy and as a pattern of technological development, i.e., industrialization (e.g. Landes 2006; Brandt et al. 2014). Of course, with the rise of the so-called 'tiger economies' that thesis was often seen as being refuted, and even the concept of 'Confucian capitalism' became popular (Dirlik 1996; Yao 2002). Yet, basic Weberian ideas are still invoked when explaining China's apparent standstill relative to the West in Qing dynasty times, referring to the specific complex of institutions and ideas about social order that is reflected in the Confucian doctrine of the time. After all, Chinese reformers and revolutionaries in the twentieth century often agreed with this view and hence vigorously battled against Confucianism. These debates still await conclusion: The most recent survey of the literature on religion and growth (Becker et al. 2024) notices the same conceptual difficulties in dealing with Confucianism as McCleary and Barrow and emphasizes that the economics literature is still very limited regarding the macroeconomic aspects beyond the scope of the Abrahamitic religions. There is a pronounced difference between economics and sociology in dealing with these issues since economists look at the transition to modern economic growth as a change in quantitative patterns (extensive to intensive, total factor productivity, demography etc.) and treat all the phenomena that the other disciplines focus on as explanatory variables, such as religion. Sociology and historical sciences look at this transition as the transformation of a totality of institutional and ideational assemblages into 'capitalism', and then asks which factors explain such a fundamental transformation. The distinction between capitalism and market economy falls between those two chairs. In this chapter, we start out from a simple point. Weber treats Confucianism as a 'world religion,' combining it with Daoism. This had the consequence that he projected a developmental yardstick on his comparisons of religions, derived from his views on rationalization and capitalism: Confucianism is conceived as the least developed form of religion in the concert of world religions, as far as these represent a limited set of differentiated value spheres, beyond more atavistic forms of magic beliefs and practices. This reflected the scientific development of his times that resulted in the emergence of modern religious studies, which included the emergence of the concept of 'world religions' (Sun 2013). There were protagonists in the debate that launched the case for treating

Confucianism as the religion of China. This was extremely influential not only for scholarly research but also for the further historical developments in religion and policies towards religion in China. Now, it is intriguing to observe that in China today, Confucianism is not included in the constitutionally recognized list of religions in China: Buddhism, Daoism, Protestantism, Catholicism, and Islam. Yet even today, the Communist Party increasingly acknowledges the centrality of Confucianism to the cultural identity of the Chinese (Billioud and Thoraval 2015; Kubat 2018). So, what is going on here?

Assessing and possibly misrepresenting Confucianism as a religion is influenced by two factors: First, our theoretical lens that identifies 'religion,' and second, the way how we relate empirical and historical facts to that notion. To begin with the first, the official view in China today indeed reflects what emerged as a definition of 'religion' in the late nineteenth century, and which at that time suggested that Confucianism could be regarded as the religion of China. This includes a body of sacred texts and a set of standardized ritual practices which invoke the presence of transcendental entities and forces. From that point of view, the Imperial State cult, including the specific rites devoted to Confucius, would count as religion. If we look at the situation in China today, of course, this state cult does not exist anymore. Does that mean it is a mere political decision to exclude Confucianism from the official list of religions, reflecting the political suppression of that genuinely Chinese belief system which could emerge as the most direct competitor to Communist ideology?

The ongoing Confucian revival in China includes the renaissance of Confucian cults. We need to distinguish between cults devoted to Confucius, the Sage, himself, and cults devoted to values and personalities, both historical and mythical ones, that play an important role in the Confucian canon, without necessarily referring to the Sage directly. At this point, I want to introduce a perspective that will become increasingly significant in the course of my argument: the Confucian revival is partly driven by economic motives. The revival of cults is often part and parcel of local tourism projects, which aim at highlighting certain local monuments and historical sites and creating events that attract visitors to the place (Oakes 2019). Hence, for Confucius' birthplace, the town of Qufu, it is a highly attractive business proposition to advertise the cult, and for the descendants of the Confucius family, it is certainly an advantage to mobilize the shared identity of their most illustrious ancestor.

This observation may cause a deflationary, if not cynical, view about the Confucian revival. But that would throw the baby out with the bathwater. Take an example from my own fieldwork in the megacity of Shenzhen. There was the initiative of a former businessman to establish sacred Confucius halls 'Kongshengtang' in Shenzhen and other cities (Billioud and Thoraval 2015). This initiative is supported by the Confucian Academy of Hong Kong. The Academy is of special interest here because, over many decades, it has pursued the goal of establishing Confucianism as a religion in China and has become especially active in the Chinese mainland since the turn of the millennium (Sun 2013, 88ff). What does that mean? This follows the precedent of Chinese Buddhism in the 1920s, when the charismatic leader Taixu launched, for instance, a reorganization of the Buddhist organizations and practices in textual editions according to the model of Christian churches, especially Protestantism (Goossaert and Palmer 2011, 80ff). This is a direct reflection of the deep impact that the Western notion of 'religion' had in China, which was also maintained by Weber. As reflected in the modern Chinese constitution, a religion should have a certain institutional structure, which includes a phenomenon that is central to Weber's thinking, namely a bureaucratic organization that follows rules that are enshrined in sacred texts. In other words, 'religion' is seen as a system of beliefs that has undergone a process of rationalization, and that is embodied in certain rational organizational forms. This is what Taixu pursued for Buddhism, responding to the threat of organized Christianity and its missionary pursuits. The Confucians followed, yet their initiative remained less successful.

What do we see in Shenzhen today? The municipal government sponsors festive activities in which traditional values are celebrated that are enshrined in the system of 'guo xue,' 'national learning', sometimes translated as 'sinology', such as the festival in 2018 held in front of the 'Kongshengtang.' Indeed, 'guoxue' is deeply rooted in Confucianism, but it cannot reasonably be interpreted as a body of religious texts. In fact, historically 'guoxue' was a project of rationalizing and secularizing traditional Confucian learning (Chen 2015). Yet, what happens in Shenzhen today is that on that festive occasion, a proper ritual ceremony was conducted to worshipping the Sage. Propaganda of traditional culture, entertainment, and religious rites are deeply enmeshed, and most interestingly, one topic of performances was to advertise the role of 'Confucian merchants,' 'rushang' in modern business. That means, and most interestingly for our discussion of Weber, the aspect of business ethics or economic ethics plays an important role in the Confucian revival: Confucian merchants distinguish themselves from other businessmen in terms of what Weber called *Lebensführung*, conduct of life (Feng 2024).[3]

There are many other examples in Shenzhen and all over China that manifest the same ambivalence, such as festivals in Shenzhen that celebrate a Confucian hero of 'filial piety,' Huang Shu (Cheng et al. 2024), or the Grand Rites devoted to the mythical Emperors Huangdi and Shun (McNeal 2011, Guo and Herrmann-Pillath 2019). In all these events, genuine religious ceremonies are combined with celebrating core values of Chinese civilization and hosting events that attract tourists and business. Different groups participating see different things, but one observation certainly holds: Those who really adopt a religious stance towards the event are probably a minority.[4] What can we learn from this? Apparently, the religious revival of Confucianism has a strong instrumental dimension. For many, the ritual and the ceremony are means to pursue certain non-religious goals, such as raising moral awareness in society or doing business, but they have no intrinsic religious

[3] As an example, see the 'Academy of Bright Virtue' which is a Confucian executive education outfit, http://www.mingdeshuyuan.com/gxg.html, accessed November 29, 2019.

[4] The coexistence and interplay of many perspectives on the same ritual event maintained by different participating groups of actors has been often highlighted in the ethnographic literature, see e.g. Kang (2009) and Bruckermann (2016).

significance. Yet, we cannot say that this is a new development reflecting the secular and modernist spirit of Shenzhen, since the pragmatic stance towards religious activities has always been a marker of Chinese religious practices, such as taking part in the construction and maintenance of local temples independent from genuine belief, but even explicitly expressing their function for fostering community spirit and solidarity (DuBois 2005; Chau 2006). For interpreting the observations, we need to move to deeper levels of analysis.

4.3 Is Confucianism a Religion?

Two observations are crucial in assessing Weber's thoughts on China. The first is that Weber indeed emphasized the instrumentalism of Confucianism and Daoism, as he understood them, but mainly referred to magical instrumentalism. In his view, Confucianism was stuck in the magical *Zaubergarten*, and, therefore, remained pre-rational, still partially 'enchanted.' The other is that Weber maintained the idea that religious beliefs are inner states of individuals. Both opinions converge on the idea that rituals are inherently magical and that, therefore, the pinnacle of rationalization of religion was Protestantism, especially Puritanism, which downplayed the role of rituals in battles with Catholicism and focused on the inner states of the individual in her or his direct relationship with God. According to Weber, Puritanism, therefore, was crucial in the historical emergence of capitalism, driven by its 'inner-worldly asceticism.' This concentration of religious beliefs on the inner world of religious subjects paved the way for the comprehensive rationalization of the world, in the shape of the great Western civilizational achievements, science, bureaucracy, and capitalist rationalism in organizing economic life. According to Weber, China failed in all these domains, because Confucianism, despite its pragmatic orientation to the material world, maintained the belief in magical instrumentalism, especially regarding sacred rites, as properly conducted by the Emperor.

We are well advised in comparing this view with the alternative approach to ritual by the other towering figure of the early years of the emerging discipline of sociology, Durkheim. For Durkheim, the emotional effervescence of rituals is essential for realizing their core social function, which is expressing, creating, and affirming the shared identity of social groups and their solidarity. Weber's view, in contrast, reflects the 'disenchantment' of western societies ('excarnation' in Taylor's 2007 wording), fitting his view of the 'iron cage of capitalism' as embodying rationalization of society. In other words, there is a tradition in sociology that represents an alternative view on rituals, even though we need to recognize that this has been circumscribed in the later development of the discipline to special fields, such as, after all, the study of religion, but especially the study of pre-modern societies (Stephenson 2015). Most of the other 'grand theories' of sociology in the twentieth century more or less follow Weber's precedent in envisaging a linear Western trajectory of modernization, functional differentiation, individualization, and all those terms denoting an alleged inherent logic of comprehensive developmental trajectories of societies (Joas 2017).

In our context, Weber's Protestantism hypothesis does not count in terms of historical veracity, which is doubtful, but as a principled point about the relationship between rationalism, religion, and capitalism. It is the alleged pre-rational nature of Confucianism that impeded China's transition to capitalism, even though the level of economic development and marketization had opened the door widely and early. Weber was aware of the pro-business attitudes of Confucianism, as he noticed that China was probably the society where material welfare was most expressively put at the center of social and political values, and he even conceded, in a sort of lucid anticipation of things to come in his final paragraphs of the Confucianism book, that the Chinese might be the people most capable to jump on the train of capitalism, while being completely unable to build it and put it on track. This reveals a certain vacillation in dealing with China, yet Weber, often even in almost offensive terms, again and again, asserts the backwardness of China and her utmost incapacity to achieve progress, mired in tradition as defined by Confucianism. To resolve this conundrum, we need to ask the simple question, what is the religion of China?

Weber had access to the Chinese studies of his time, which mainly was based on historical sources drafted by Confucian scholars and field studies mainly by missionaries. Both created a bias in approaching Chinese realities. In synthesizing both sources, he combined two entirely different perspectives. One is elite and learned Confucianism and the other is practices of ordinary people, as observed by Westerners. The problem is that there were no neutral accounts of practices by Chinese intellectual elites at that time who either viewed them through the lens of moralizing Confucians or increasingly radical modernizers. Both agreed on viewing most of the practices as 'superstition.' 'Superstition', however, was not a term that existed in Chinese and was invented by the Japanese, employing Chinese characters, and then imported back into China, like many other modern concepts, including 'religion' (Goossaert and Palmer 2011, 50ff). One consequence was what already transpired previously: Many intellectuals and scholars at the turn of the century started to believe that China does not have a religion, but only 'superstition': that smacks like a vulgar notion of Weber's *Zaubergarten* thesis. But Weber did not sufficiently acknowledge that even starting with the Master himself, Confucians always distanced themselves from folk religion, even including beliefs in ancestors, which is otherwise an essential element of rituals enshrining filial piety. That introduced a tension in his entire analysis since he was well aware of the fact that one could also interpret Confucianism as the ideology and philosophy of the ruling stratum of scholar-officials, but not as a religion, in the two senses of Confucianism not being a religion at all, and not being the religion of China, in terms of a set of religious beliefs maintained by the majority of Chinese.

China studies have tried to catch the complex relationship between learned Confucianism and folk practices in distinguishing between 'orthopraxy' and 'orthodoxy' (Schmidt-Glintzer 1983; Watson 1985; Sutton 2007). In a nutshell, that means that in Confucian thinking the proper conduct of rituals, orthopraxy, is essential, and not the question of true belief, 'orthodoxy.' In addition, many

Confucians believed that the question of proper ritual is important because this is essential to fulfilling a function, that is, maintaining social order. Beyond orthopraxy, they adopted a functionalist-instrumental attitude towards ritual. This is a view that one frequently meets in China today, too. Religion is seen as having no intrinsic value, but a function in society. That sounds like a *zweckrationale* attitude towards religion that would not evoke the *Zaubergarten* but would also clearly confirm that Confucianism as a doctrine is no religion at all. This is the view that many Chinese have maintained until today: Confucianism is a practical philosophy. But why do religious rituals play such an important role in it? Is it just quasi-Marxian opium for the people?

Orthopraxy does not mean that ritual is a mere mechanism imposing incentives and constraints on individuals: In Chinese intellectual history, this was the position of the major antagonist to Confucianism, the doctrine of Legalism. In the Confucian view, what counts is the sincerity of ritual action, which would then also have a deep civilizing effect on the individual (Sutton 2007). In other words, whereas the Western view, also maintained by Weber, sees inner states as prime drivers of action, and rituals as mere surface phenomena, which could be rationalized away, the Chinese view sees ritual as transformative forces that channel the spiritual and moral development of individuals in their social context, and as such indispensable also for individual moral and spiritual development (Hall and Ames 1998; Seligman et al. 2008). That is why a major Confucian concern was the monitoring, designing, and implementing of proper ritual practices in society. This view on ritual had metaphysical and cosmological dimensions.

The Confucian *Zaubergarten* was apparently embodied in the Imperial pantheon of Gods and Saints that were officially recognized in the state cult, and hence officially endorsed many practices that Weber counts as 'magical.' This pantheon was pivotal in managing religious behaviours and movements in Imperial China, because it formally distinguished between legitimate cults and illegitimate ones, and was even projected into the vision of the realm of gods in folk beliefs (Feuchtwang 1992). But this does not mean that Confucianism as a doctrine adopted the corresponding beliefs. At the same time, however, since Han times Confucianism had adopted a metaphysical and cosmological view in which morality and balances in the physical world were conceived as being deeply enmeshed in the notion of 'tian,' 'heaven'. Moral disorder, societal disorder, and cosmic disorder in 'tianxia,' the (Chinese) 'world under heaven', were interpreted as being manifestations of similar forces, with morality assuming a pivotal role in anchoring order in the totality of being. These views were encapsulated in core notions shared also with the Daoists, such as 'virtue' 'de' and 'dao,' 'way'. These were also the standards according to which one can differentiate between legitimate and illegitimate beliefs, as supported by the long historical evidence about the ups and downs in 'tianxia'. The historical records contain numerous episodes about the synchronicity of the spread of new cults, growing social discontent and uprisings, and the occurrence of natural disasters. In the highly engineered Chinese agricultural system, it is straightforward to diagnose a deep connection between social and natural balances, since the latter were essentially co-determined by human landscape design (Schoppa 1989).

If we weigh in on that cosmological dimension, the religious nature of Confucianism seems more salient. But at the same time, the very unity of the doctrine becomes elusive. This was apparent in the syncretistic and unifying efforts of the Late Empire when many Confucian scholars proposed the unity of the 'three teachings' (Confucianism, Daoism, and Buddhism), and comes to the fore when we consider that today probably the most powerful manifestation of a Confucian religion is not the narrow project of establishing a Confucian church, but the syncretistic new religion of 'Yiguandao' that rapidly spread in China in the 1920s, was then rigorously suppressed and has been expanding rapidly in Taiwan after democratization, now also infiltrating the mainland (Billioud 2020). Yiguandao expressively puts together many elements from various religions, and centers them on a few fundamental Confucian notions, which, however, renders Confucianism in the strict sense almost meaningless.

Yiguandao is an example for the wide range of redemptionist cults and movements that emerged in the early twentieth century, showing a high degree of religious creativity in Chinese society (DuBois 2005). That means, there is a strong dynamism in Chinese religious life, which combines the traditional forms of religious practices in the population with new, sometimes outrightly modernist forms of spiritual movements, of which in the People's Republic certainly the most visible is the Falungong sect, today strictly prohibited and its followers persecuted, but still very active abroad. Falungong emerged as a Qigong cult, which itself was a modernist movement transforming certain practices and elements of traditional folk religion into a new syncretistic belief system with a strong rational component, similar to 'fengshui' practices (hence even Mao Zedong thought of Qigong as being 'scientific') (Chen 2003). But certainly, these cannot reasonably be interpreted as *the* 'Chinese religion.'

In sum, although Confucianism reveals many connections to phenomena that may be labelled as 'religious,' we cannot conclude that Confucianism is a religion, and with emphasis, that it is the religion of China. So, what else fits the bill?

4.4 Chinese Popular Religion and Ritual Economy

Indeed, systematizing redemptionist movements do not cover what is the genuine 'mainstream' in Chinese religion, and which is mostly referred to as 'superstition' by Confucians, Marxian atheists, and modernist agnostics alike. This is the vast and complex domain of what is called 'popular religion' (Clart 2012). There have been terminological suggestions to cover this domain as a 'religion,' most significantly, it seems to me, as 'Shenism', since that in Japanese is very close to Shinto. This is that domain of Chinese religion that one of its leading modern scholars, C.K. Yang (1961) has called 'diffuse.' And that is the domain of magic that seems to survive in the Confucian *Zaubergarten*.

In dealing with popular religion in the context of Weber, I want to jump immediately to foundational and methodological concerns, since this directly ties up with

Weber's notion of rationality. And I want to establish a connection that might appear to be surprising, namely the recent research on religion in Greek and Roman antiquity (Rüpke 2018). In this field, scholars have introduced notions such as 'religion in the making,' 'doing religion,' or 'lived religion' to deal with the difficulty that there was no organized and systematized 'religion' in antiquity, but a loosely structured, highly dynamic sphere of activities of numerous different types of actors which left marks in texts and archaeological records. There were religious specialists, but mostly their knowledge was secretive, and they got into touch with the wider public by providing certain services, such as oracles and fortune-telling. Many activities were highly individualized on the household level, and various groups with different geographical and ethnic background maintained specific cults, which, however, may also attract others in the course of time. There was a plethora of entities, gods, and other transcendental beings that might be invoked in worshipping. To grasp this bewildering richness of religious life, it is analytically powerful to approach religion as a type of activity that involves many different aspects and dimensions of what in Europe later emerged as organized religion and as a separate social and spiritual domain.

This brief characterization evokes many family resemblances with Chinese popular religion, and opens the view on the possibility that this is what we should conceive as 'Chinese religion' in the first place, and all other more organized and formalized forms of religion just as elements in that larger overarching system (Feuchtwang 2010). To that suggestion, a caveat must immediately follow: this cannot include those religions that raise exclusive claims on their believers, such as Christianity and Islam. They inherently define themselves as staying outside the domain of Chinese religion, although, as we observe in many less developed countries in the past until today, they might morph into local idiosyncratic versions that would slowly reintegrate with the indigenous forms of religious life.

The approach of 'doing religion' has been developed systematically by one of the leading scholars on Chinese religion, Adam Chau, as the paradigm of 'religious polytropy' (Chau 2011, 2012), and fits into a general trend in religious studies to focus on individual agency in 'doing religion' (Rüpke 2015). That concept approaches religious behaviour in terms of various 'modalities of doing religion,' which also reflect different functions of religious activities relative to individual and social needs. For example, one modality is conducting ritual services at important life-cycle events, another is spiritual support in case of emergencies, or another one is textual forms of sense-making of the world. Typically, such activities may involve very different types of actors. For example, in case of serious illness, one might approach a local Daoist priest or even spirit medium or Shaman, or in case of conducting a proper funeral one might approach a Buddhist expert. To this analysis of modalities, we might add core notions of religion, such as the recognition of the sacred nature of certain places and objects, or the belief in transcendental entities and forces that are seen as having causal powers, hence agency, beyond the reach of the visible world. Yet, all these elements are only loosely coupled and eventually are anchored in the religious creativity of individuals and communities. As Chau (2014) emphasizes, this has a very important consequence in comparing Chinese religion with Christianity: contrary to Weberian views which would emphasize the individualization of religion in terms of a direct relation with God, Chau argues that Christianity is mainly community based, which springs to the eye when comparing the Chinese situation, where households and even individuals stay at the center. In China, households host the Gods, whereas in Christianity the church is the place where God hosts the community, as manifest in the Eucharist ritual. In this sense, in Chinese religion, a high degree of individualization is achieved, compared to the strict confessionalism of Christianity (Herrmann-Pillath 2020).

Let me develop this argument by introducing some observations on my field site, the city of Shenzhen. This is an important case since many observers argue that the capitalist dynamics of this immigrant city create conditions of anomie and, hence, a strong demand for religious remedies to overcome the loss of orientation and meaning of life (Fan and Whitehead 2011). Indeed, this modernist urban environment also features a strong revival of traditional popular religion. Without being able to go into details here, one conspicuous observation is the reconstruction or new construction of ancestral halls and associated temples, often on highly visible 'cultural squares' that have many purposes, such as allowing for many spare-time activities (such as parents with kids learning to skate) or for conducting large-scale events, such as the previously mentioned 'guoxue'-festival. This example is important against the backdrop of the question whether and how Confucianism plays a role in Chinese religion.

The ancestral halls in Shenzhen number about 500, with about 120 of them officially recognized as historical sites (in detail, see Herrmann-Pillath et al. 2021). Most of them date back to pre-1949 times. They are sacred places in the traditional villages that shaped the landscape before the high-speed urbanization of the special economic zone was launched (compare Lagerwey 2010). Many of these villages turned into so-called 'urban villages,' that is, unregulated urban settlements constructed by the villagers to offer cheap housing to the millions of migrant workers (Wang 2016). These urban villages were built on the collective land of the villages, which in pre-reform times were socialist production brigades. Many villages are so-called 'single-lineage' villages with one dominant surname.

What is the role of the ancestral hall in modern Shenzhen? The native villages in the urban space trace their history back to migration events in the distant past, many even to Song dynasty times. There are many instances of chain-migration within the region, so that certain surnames have spread across various villages, and often set up ancestral halls devoted to the original settler in these series of migration events. Hence, ancestral halls reflect the concept of descent, as embodied in the central sacred spot, the altar and the genealogy in form of a tree of tablets bearing the names of the male descendants from the original settler (Trémon 2015; Herrmann-Pillath and Man 2019).

However, the ancestral hall is only one, though pivotal, element in what we identify as the 'ritual space' of the traditional village. This is where we approach what we could identify as a possible notion of 'system' in Chinese popular religion. This system is the ritual space of the village, implying that the village itself is sacred in nature (Lagerwey 2010; DuBois 2005). A traditional village, created via a migration event in the past, would be located according to a fengshui practice identifying the flow of positive and negative forces in the natural environment of the place. Once the village grows and accumulates the necessary resources, villagers would mark this space with numerous sacred buildings and monuments. Ideal-typically, the most basic structure is the duality of ancestral hall and a temple devoted to an important deity, such as Tianhou (Mazu) in the Pearl River delta, or to the Buddhist deity Guanyin. But there are many other sacred sites, in old China including those ones that connect the village with the Imperial body politic, such as the Earth God shrine. This is an important aspect of Chinese popular religion: The world of gods and saints is seen as a celestial hierarchy, thus directly mirroring the Imperial order (Feuchtwang 1992). Yet, at the same time there would be many shrines, steles, or sacred items such as holy trees that enrich the ritual space of the village and that render it highly idiosyncratic. Often other big temples might be devoted to local deities which go back to historical figures without generic religious roles.

It is very important to add another aspect which is also highlighted by Adam Chau. In everyday life, the sacred space of the village is almost like a fractal replicated on the household level. To give an example from Shenzhen today: Native villagers live in newly built apartment blocks, and the apartment may be systematically dotted with religious items, beginning with a small altar at the entrance protecting the home, and continuing with an altar devoted to a closer ancestor (e.g., deceased grandfather), a private altar devoted to Guanyin, and the Kitchen God altar, which in old China directly connected the household to the Imperial order as the kitchen god reports misdeeds to the Yellow Emperor. That means, not only is the village a sacred space, but also the dwelling of the family, which would also be reflected in doing fengshui analysis of its location.

There are two ways how this ritual space of religious activities was influenced or even shaped by Confucianism, in a way that we can even diagnose in modern Shenzhen. The first is that in Qing dynasty the Imperial government actively supported lineage institutions in terms of disseminating standards for ritual practices or even organizational 'consulting,' for example, via handbooks of managing lineage organizations (Faure 2007). This was part and parcel of the universal Confucian support for family and kinship values that were conceived as roots of social order, and which were also shaped via many interventions, such as editing texts for local operas that celebrate these values (Ebrey 1993). This type of 'family Confucianism' is revived today in the active support of the so-called 'family customs' by the CCP, endorsed by President Xi Jinping, which are texts that enshrine the values that a certain lineage and surname group upholds.

The other channel works via the notion of descent. As we said, many villages trace themselves back to migration events in the distant past. The first wave occurred when the Song dynasty collapsed under the invasion of the Mongols. Many Northern elite families fled to the south, settling down there, and became farmers. However, in their family history, the villagers keep the memory of their elite origin, and that means, a connection to the ideology of the Empire, such as highlighting the Confucian officials in their descent line. A foremost example from my field research in Shenzhen is the Wen clan consisting of seven lineages in Shenzhen and Hong

Kong at different locations and with various origins, however, all ancestors being close relatives to the famous Song general and chancellor Wen Tianxiang, until today celebrated as a 'national hero' in China. Wen is an exemplary Confucian official who sacrificed his life in loyalty to the Emperor and who also was an accomplished poet who expressed his Confucian beliefs in the famous poem 'On duty' that is today carved on a plaque standing in front of the Wen Tianxiang memorial at Fenghuang village, one of the Wen branches in Shenzhen.

The Fenghuan Wen invested in a holiday park centering on a temple complex newly erected on the site where the original village temple was located. This temple complex shows the ritual infrastructure of a traditional village, except the ancestral hall, which is located at the center of the village, whereas the park is located in the hills close to the village. This is an example of what I described previously: Religious activities are deeply enmeshed with economic projects. In this respect, it is highly significant that the villagers decided to devote the holiday park to a temple, and not to anything else. The centerpiece of the complex is a Buddhist temple, which is not just a tourist attraction but 'activated' by proper Buddhist rituals, hence an officially registered religious place of worship. However, as the villagers explain, for them the most important spot in the temple is not the big Guanyin statue at the middle altar hall, but the smaller adjacent hall which hosts the local gods, the most important of which is Wen Tianxiang. Guanyin is for the general public, the smaller altar for the villagers.

The transmission of Confucian values via the notion of descent is a very important factor in sustaining a 'lived Confucianism' in the local population. Beyond the native villagers, it is interesting to look at the two groups of the Hakka and the Chaoshan, because they adopt distinct attitudes towards Confucianism. The Hakka, the 'guest people,' are a group of late immigrants who initially did not define themselves as Hakka but only in the course of the violent battles over land in the nineteenth century (the so-called 'Hakka wars') (Constable 1996). Hakka mostly live also at other regions in Guangdong province, and very substantial numbers migrated to Shenzhen after 1979. The same is true for the Chaoshan people, who, however, were not present in Shenzhen before 1978. Both groups count at least two million each in Shenzhen today.

In terms of religious behavior, the two groups are clearly distinct. Traditional Hakka walled villages were literally centered on the ancestral halls and marginalized other temples. In contrast, Chaoshan beliefs are very inclusive, show a strong impact of folk Buddhism, and refer to many local deities of various Chaoshan groups. If a visitor to Shenzhen wants to see the ritual space of a Chaoshan village in Shenzhen today, she is well advised to visit Hubei village at Luohu district, before it will be completely demolished and renewed (O'Donnell 2019). Hubei village retains the original buildings of the walled village of the local Zhang lineage, a very powerful clan before 1949, who, however, moved out and rented their buildings out to Chaoshan people who moved in as construction workers. The village is replete with religious items and markers of sacred places. The entries are protected by altars where women regularly burn 'ghost money' (see below). There are small installments with incense at every corner of the narrow alleys crisscrossing the incredibly cramped place. There is lack of space, so temples look like makeshift provisional arrangements, but there are many.

When asked directly, Chaoshan people tend to assert that for them Confucianism is not an essential element in their beliefs, but rather Buddhism is. Yet their family values are very conservative and reflect Confucian traditions. In comparison, the Hakka are probably the subethnic group in China which most represents Confucian beliefs. The reason lies in the aforementioned role of descent: Although marginalized in recent times, the Hakka were not 'Hakka' at all in the more distant past, but mostly belonged to Northern elites. Therefore, they emphasize education and scholarship, and tend towards aspiring public office, whereas the Chaoshan people distance themselves from government and are naturally born independent entrepreneurs. This is by no means a stereotype, but is reflected in actual practices: For example, the infamous Shenzhen 'Shanzhai' business (i.e., the pirating and creative imitation of brands) is dominated by Chaoshan people.

These observations reveal the complexity of the roles that Confucianism takes in Chinese religion as popular religion. In the case of the Hakka, it is most significant that the ancestral cult is almost devoid of religious meanings but approaches a community ritual. Accordingly, many Christian missionaries saw no principled tension between ancestor worship and Christianity, and many Hakka indeed converted to Christianity. But would that really imply that ancestor worship is not a religious practice? Certainly not. Indeed, ancestor worship is one of the oldest and defining elements in the open and fluid system of Chinese religion.

I need to add a final building block to our re-assessment of Weber in the face of empirical data, and which is most visible in the Chaoshan case. This is what transpired already, namely the close relationship between religious and economic behavior. Chinese popular religion is deeply enmeshed with the economy. In China studies, sometimes the notion of 'ritual economy' is employed to catch this phenomenon (Faure 2006; Yang 2007). As I have argued elsewhere in much detail, this reflects the congruence between ritual infrastructures and the market system in traditional China: local market centers (such as the historical Shenzhen, Sham Chun), were at the same time ritual centers, with major temples and residing ritual specialists offering their services (Skinner 1964/1965; Herrmann-Pillath 2017). Many ritual institutions were simultaneously business entities, such as lineage trusts (Zelin 2009). But there is an even deeper level.

I mentioned the 'ghost money' which is still visibly used in Shenzhen today: For example, the Fenghuang temple complex also has several burners where you can observe people burning paper money in bag loads. I cannot detail this most interesting religious practice here, but just notice that it reflects the economy of the netherworld, populated with hell's banks and with the spirits of ancestors who would morph into 'hungry ghosts' if they are not adequately supported by relatives. Money establishes a direct economic and ritual connection between the world and the netherworld (for a comprehensive study, see Blake 2011). This is not genuine money, but in the original practice, it is neither printed fake, as is often the case today, to save time. The original paper money is artisanal in the sense that it is cut and folded mostly by women, bill by bill, a time-consuming task. But this is the point: The ghost money represents labor, and in donating highly valuable labor effort, the gods and ancestors receive proper recognition. This world and the netherworld are connected via a continuous flow of exchange and gift relations, in which the agents in the two spheres mutually support each other, and basically stay in structurally homologous networked relations of exchange (Chang 2010).

The centrality of money in Chinese religion is an important phenomenon because most religions show deep mistrust towards money. This was also true for Chinese religion before Qing dynasty. A significant transition in Chinese religious history is the transformation of the god Wutong into the God of Wealth (von Glahn 1991). Wutong was an almost diabolic figure, a cheater and trickster, who gained fame in hunting the chastity of women, and his favorite means was money. But later he became the benevolent God of Wealth, the god of merchants, ubiquitous in all Chinese business outfits. This is remarkable because it represents the accommodation of Confucianism with the economy, even to the extent that money became an important sacred object.

There is an inherent family resemblance between the world of business and the cosmology of Chinese religion, which celebrates the complexity and fluidity of forces of Yin and Yang and the fundamental uncertainty of life, and which is manifest in the widespread practice of gambling, testing 'luck' (Chu 2010). The world is full of opportunities, and individuals need to act in a way that adapts to the unpredictable and unknowable flows, yet not results in passive fatalism but bursts of quick entrepreneurial decisions at a propitious moment. In Shenzhen today, one of the hidden spheres of the economy is fengshui, on which Chaoshan people are especially keen. Real estate business is a major engine of the economy (annually about a quarter of the investment share in GDP), and the project is rare which does not involve advice by fengshui masters.

The gist of my argument is now as following: Chinese religion is deeply wedded with the economy and reflects the historical completion of the Chinese market economy in the Qing dynasty. This is where the distinction between market economy and capitalism comes into full significance. Weber already recognized that China had developed a strong commercial culture and markets. Hence, implicitly he distinguished between markets and capitalism. Yet, his focus on European history undermined this analytical distinction. However, it is essential to explain the apparent contradiction between the two narratives about Confucianism and markets: the Confucian failure story and the Confucian capitalism story.

At this point Weber's reference to the state of Chinese studies at his times necessarily led his theorizing on the wrong track. There have been at least three fundamental insights about Chinese history that were not yet available to him. First, with the landmark volume Elvin (1973), the medieval economic revolution was recognized as a watershed in Chinese economic and social history, which raised principled doubts about the cultural explanation of China's alleged failure to move towards capitalist modernization. Second, the monumental work by Needham showed that the dystopian view on Chinese science was simply wrong. And third, the picture of the mature Chinese market economy in Qing times has changed fundamentally (von Glahn 1991). If we take all that together, this has resulted in the revisionist view of Chinese social economic history championed by the California school (e.g., Pomeranz 2000) that China did not really 'fail' to achieve capitalism, but did adapt efficient and workable institutions and mechanisms of a fully-fledged market economy that enabled the rapid growth of the population and descent well-being for a large part of her population before the onslaught of Western Imperialism.

This view is not undisputed, however. Interestingly, there is a position that somehow reconciles the conflicting views: This is Philip Huang's (1990) concept of economic involution. In this view, China had developed the most efficient and adaptable markets, but this was exactly what fostered the emergence of economic organizations that remained non-capitalist. An important case in point is the decline of the manor which had emerged in the medieval economic revolution, but later was substituted by the family farm, a transformation which Weber already noticed. However, Weber thought that the absence of capitalist agricultural organizations in China resulted from her institutional and cultural, and especially religious context. Huang argues that this reflected economic conditions, and hence highly efficient adaptations to economic forces, and even the almost perfect organization of the Chinese market system, which gave the Chinese family farm the competitive edge over any 'capitalist' alternatives.

In this sense, we can argue that the diffuse nature of Chinese popular religion is a mirror of the highly decentralized, flexible, and fluid market system of old China. That can be even covered in theoretical terms: McCleary and Barro (2019) ground their approach to religion in the 'religious markets' approach as seminally developed by Iannaccone (1991). Indeed, Chinese popular religion comes very close to a religious market, monitored and regulated by the Chinese government, both in Imperial times and today, with Confucianism as a regulatory philosophy. This parallelism includes the acknowledgement that the closest analogy to Western liberalism is Confucianism, partly also recognized by Weber, but again downplaying its role because of a perceived lack of metaphysical grounding of notions such as individual liberty. This view has been challenged by more recent scholarship on Confucian ethics (Metzger 1977; Roetz 1992).

Summing up, I defend the view that market economy and Chinese popular religion manifest certain structural family resemblances, and that Confucianism is a philosophical reflection of this. Since the famous Han dynasty discourse on 'Salt and Iron,' Confucians endorsed the market economy as the soil on which the commonweal can flourish (Chin 2014; Herrmann-Pillath and Zhao 2023)). But different from the Western tradition, they approached this from the perspective of statecraft, and therefore China never developed the distinct merger of liberalism and economics that emerged in the West. Popular religion and market society were deeply interrelated: perhaps the most salient expression of this deep-structural family resemblance is that China did neither develop a unified religion nor a unified monetary system.

4.5 Conclusion

Returning to the general problem of Weber's approach to China, we reach a very significant conclusion. Weber failed both to adequately recognize the nature of Chinese religion and the nature of the Chinese market economy as ritual economy because he projected his grand narrative on capitalist rationalization on China. Like many others, he concluded that since China failed to follow this narrative, something must be deficient with her institutions, culture, and, in our context, even her religion: China is seen as radically 'irrational,' and in this sense the ultimate antipode of the West.

But if we distinguish between market economy and capitalism, we can receive Philip Huang's argument on the 'substantive rationality' of Chinese institutions. China's alleged failure to develop capitalism, in the revisionist California school view, reflects the well-functioning market economy of Qing China, undergirded by reasonably liberal Confucian views on the contributions of markets to the commonweal. If we compare this with the West, we may shift to Polanyi's (2001 [1944]) reconstruction of capitalism: Capitalism is the projection of a capitalist utopia on society, overextending markets into domains where they may eventually even harm the commonweal. Weber, in his commitment to value-free social science, avoids judging capitalism, yet his notion of rationality is loaded with hidden value-judgements. We can turn Weber 'from head to feet,' as Marx claimed to have done with Hegel. Then, capitalism appears to be the ultimate pinnacle of irrationality: This is the belief that the world could be subject to a totalizing sphere of rationality, defined in purely formal terms. Polanyi's view boils down to this radical turn.

In fact, economists have often pointed towards this fundamentally irrational core of capitalism, especially in the case of Schumpeter in his theory of entrepreneurship. There is a logically misplaced conclusion from the apparent developmental achievements of capitalism to its 'rationality.' In fact, believing in growth and progress comes close to a religious belief in the transcending forces of the economy, and if not religion, then a 'culture of growth' (Mokyr 2016). As Beckert (2016) argues, capitalism builds on fictions, which might be rationalized according to the rules of discourse in our modern societies, but remain fictions, after all, dreams of transforming the world according to human desires, defined mainly in terms of material progress. Our current climate crisis raises the specter that this has always been a dangerous delusion about what we can really achieve.

If we think in terms of the market economy, Weber may be right in pointing at the 'adaptive' stance of Confucianism. But we can judge this as a rational stance in substantive terms. The idea that capitalism builds on delusions was firstly and clearly articulated by Adam Smith in the famous paragraphs of his *Theory of Moral Sentiments* where he argues that the delusionary struggle of humans over relative status and social reputation drives economic achievements, and eventually, human mastery about the world. But again, this delusion is irrational. Adam Smith's view on the moral foundations of market society as civic society bears many family resemblances with Confucianism, which also claims that there is a fatal conceit in just striving for material benefit and social status without being bounded by a moral order (Herrmann-Pillath 2014).

Chinese religion, in conjunction with the philosophy of Confucianism, may be reinvented today as a way of expressing beliefs about the sacredness of certain pivotal human relations to the world, which enable humans to conduct the good life in a way of acting reasonably and responsibly. Certainly this tones down the transformative and utopian drives in religion, but perhaps this is what we must appreciate in our troubled times.

References

Becker, Sascha O., J. Rubin, and L. Woessmann. 2024. Religion and Growth. *Journal of Economic Literature* 62 (3): 1094–1142.

Beckert, Jens. 2016. *Imagined Futures: Fictional Expectations and Capitalist Dynamics*. Cambridge, MA: Harvard University Press.

Billioud, Sébastien. 2020. *Reclaiming the Wilderness: Contemporary Dynamics of the Yiguandao*. New York: Oxford University Press.

Billioud, Sébastien, and Joël Thoraval. 2015. *The Sage and the People: The Confucian Revival in China*. Oxford: Oxford University Press.

Blake, C. Fred. 2011. *Burning Money: The Material Spirit of the Chinese Afterworld*. Honolulu: University of Hawai'i Press.

Brandt, Loren, D. Ma, and T. G. Rawski. 2014. From Divergence to Convergence: Reevaluating the History Behind China's Economic Boom. *Journal of Economic Literature* 52 (1): 45–123.

Bruckermann, Charlotte. 2016. Trading on Tradition: Tourism, Ritual, and Capitalism in a Chinese Village. *Modern China* 42 (2): 188–224.

Chang, X. Q. 2010. *Guanxi or Li Shang Wanglai? Reciprocity, Social Support Networks, & Social Creativity in a Chinese Village*. Taipei: Ariti Press.

Chau, Adam Y. 2006. *Miraculous Response: Doing Popular Religion in Contemporary China*. Stanford: Stanford University Press.

Chau, Adam Y. 2011. Modalities of Doing Religion and Ritual Polytropy: Evaluating the Religious Market Model from the Perspective of Chinese Religious History. *Religion* 14 (4): 547–568.

Chau, Adam Y. 2012. Efficacy, Not Confessionality: On Ritual Polytropy in China. In *Sharing the "Sacra": The Politics and Pragmatics of Intercommunal Relations Around Holy Places*, ed. G. Bowman, 79–96. Oxford: Berghahn.

Chau, Adam Y. 2014. Household Sovereignty and Religious Subjectification: China and the Christian West Compared. *Studies in Church History* 50:494–506.

Chau, Adam Y. 2019. *Religion in China: Ties that Bind*. Cambridge/Medford: Polity.

Chen, N. N. 2003. Healing Sects and Anti-Cult Campaigns. *The China Quarterly* 174:505–520. https://doi.org/10.1017/S0009443903000305

Cheng, J., L. Li, C. Herrmann-Pillath, and M. Guo. 2024. Shareholding Cooperative Companies in Shenzhen and the Revival of "Filial Piety" as a Core Value of Chinese Ethical Life. In *East Asian Ethical Life and Socio-Economic Transformation in the Twenty-First Century*, ed. C. Herrmann-Pillath and Q. Zhao, 114–131. Abingdon/New York: Routledge.

Chin, Tamara T. 2014. *Savage Exchange: Han Imperialism, Chinese Literary Style, and the Economic Imagination*, Harvard-Yenching Institute Monograph Series 94. Cambridge, MA: Harvard University Asia Center.

Chu, Julie Y. 2010. *Cosmologies of Credit: Transnational Mobility and the Politics of Destination in China*. Durham: Duke University Press.

Clart, Philip. 2012. Chinese Popular Religion. In *The Wiley-Blackwell Companion to Chinese Religions*, ed. Randall Nadeau, 219–235. Oxford: Wiley-Blackwell.

Constable, Nicole. 1996. Introduction: What Does It Mean to Be Hakka? In *Guest people: Hakka Identity in China and Abroad*, ed. Nicole Constable, 1996. Seattle: University of Washington Press.

Dirlik, Arif. 1996. Critical Reflections on 'Chinese Capitalism' as a Paradigm. In *Chinese Business Enterprise*, ed. Rajeswary A. Brown, vol. 1, 17–38. London/New York: Routledge.

DuBois, Thomas D. 2005. *The Sacred Village: Social Change and Religious Life in Rural North China*. Honolulu: University of Hawai'i Press.

Ebrey, Patricia. 1993. The Chinese Family and the Spread of Confucian Values. In *The East Asian Region*, ed. Gilbert Rozman, 45–83. Princeton University Press.

Elvin, Mark. 1973. *The Pattern of the Chinese Past*. Stanford: Stanford University Press.

Fan, Lizhu, and James D. Whitehead. 2011. Spirituality in a Modern Chinese Metropolis. In *Chinese Religious Life*, ed. David A. Palmer, G. Shive, and P. L. Wickeri, 13–29. Oxford/New York: Oxford University Press.

Faure, David. 2006. *China and Capitalism: A History of Business Enterprise in Modern China*. Hong Kong: Hong Kong University Press.

Faure, David. 2007. *Emperor and Ancestor: State and Lineage in South China*. Stanford: Stanford University Press.

Feng, Xingyuan. 2024. Between Corporate Social Responsibility and Ethical Life: The Ethical Resources of Family Entrepreneurship in China. In *East Asian Ethical Life and Socio-Economic Transformation in the Twenty-First Century*, ed. Carsten Herrmann-Pillath and Q. Zhao, 191–208. Abingdon/New York: Routledge.

Feuchtwang, Stephan. 1992. *The Imperial Metaphor: Popular Religion in China*. London/New York: Routledge.

Feuchtwang, Stephan. 2010. *The Anthropology of Religion, Charisma and Ghosts: Chinese Lessons for Adequate Theory*, Religion and Society 46. Berlin: De Gruyter.

Gates, Hill. 1996. *China's Motor: a Thousand Years of Petty Capitalism*, 1996. Ithaca: Cornell University Press.

Goossaert, Vincent, and David A. Palmer. 2011. *The Religious Question in Modern China*. Chicago: Chicago University Press.

Guo Man, and Herrmann-Pillath, Carsten. 2019. Exploring Extended Kinship in Twenty-First-Century China: A Conceptual Case Study. *Journal of Current Chinese Affairs* 48(1): 50–75. https://doi.org/10.1177/1868102619845244

Hall, David L., and Roger T. Ames. 1998. *Thinking from the Han: Self, Truth, and Transcendence in Chinese and Western Culture*. New York: SUNY Press.

Herrmann-Pillath, Carsten. 2014. A 'Third Culture' in Economics? An Essay on Smith, Confucius and the Rise of China. *The Adam Smith Review* 8:83–110.

Herrmann-Pillath, Carsten. 2017. *China's Economic Culture: The Ritual Order of State and Markets*. New York: Routledge.

Herrmann-Pillath, Carsten. 2020. Religious Individualisation in China: A Two-Modal Approach. In *Religious Individualisation: Historical Dimensions and Comparative Perspectives*, ed. Martin Fuchs, Antje Linkenbach, Martin Mulsow, Bernd-Christian Otto, Rahul Bjørn Parson, and Jörg Rüpke, 643–668. Berlin/Boston: De Gruyter.

Herrmann-Pillath, Carsten, and Guo Man. 2019. Exploring Extended Kinship in 21st Century China: A Conceptual Case Study. *Journal of Current Chinese Affairs* 48 (1): 50–75.

Herrmann-Pillath, Carsten, and Q. Zhao. 2023. The Cultural Meaning of "Market" in China and the Western Tradition. In *"Weltbeziehung". The Study of Our Relationship with the World*, ed. Rosa Hollstein and Jörg Rüpke, 157–188. Frankfurt: Campus Verlag.

Herrmann-Pillath, Carsten, Guo Man, and Feng Xingyuan. 2021. *Ritual and Economy in Metropolitan China: A Global Social Science Approach*. New York: Routledge.

House, Robert J., Paul J. Hanges, Mansour Javidan, Peter W. Dorfman, and Vipin Gupta, eds. 2004. *Culture, Leadership, and Organizations. The Globe Study of 62 Societies*. London: Sage.

Huang, Philip C. C. 1990. *The Peasant Family and Rural Development in the Yangzi Delta, 1350–1988*. Stanford: Stanford University Press.

Huang, Philip C. C. 2015. Morality and Law in China, Pat and Present. *Modern China* 41 (1): 3–39.

Huang, Philip C. C. 2019. Rethinking 'the Third Sphere': The Dualistic Unity of State and Society in China, Past and Present. *Modern China* 45 (4): 355–391.

Iannaccone, Laurence R. 1991. The Consequences of Religious Market Structure: Adam Smith and the Economics of Religion. *Rationality and Society* 3 (2): 156–177.

Joas, Hans. 2017. *Die Macht des Heiligen. Eine Alternative zur Geschichte der Entzauberung*. Berlin: Suhrkamp.

Kang, Xiaofei. 2009. Two Temples, Three Religions, and a Tourist Attraction: Contesting Sacred Space on China's Ethnic Frontier. *Modern China* 35 (3): 227–255.

Kubat, Aleksandra. 2018. Morality as Legitimacy Under Xi Jinping: The Political Functionality of Traditional Culture for the Chinese Communist Party. *Journal of Current Chinese Affairs* 47 (3): 47–86.

Lagerwey, John. 2010. *China: A Religious State*. Hong Kong: Chinese University Press.

Lai, Junnan. 2015. 'Patrimonial Bureaucracy' and Chinese Law: Max Weber's Legacy and Its Limits. *Modern China* 41 (1): 40–59.

Landes, David S. 2006. Why Europe and the West? Why Not China? *Journal of Economic Perspectives* 20 (2): 3–22.

McCleary, Rachel M., and Robert J. Barro. 2019. *The wealth of religions: the political economy of believing and belonging*. Princeton University Press.

McNeal, Robin. 2011. Moral Transformation and Local Identity: Reviving the Culture of Shun at Temples and Monuments Across China. *Modern China* 41 (4): 436–464.

Metzger, Thomas A. 1977. *Escape from Predicament: Neo-Confucianism and China's Evolving Political Culture*. New York: Columbia University Press.

Mokyr, Joel. 2016. A culture of growth: the origins of the modern economy. Princeton University Press.

O'Donnell, Mary-Ann. 2019. Heart of Shenzhen: The Movement to Preserve 'Ancient' Hubei Village. In *The New Companion to Urban Design*, ed. T. Banajeree and A. Loukaitou-Sideris, 480–493. London: Routledge.

Oakes, Tim. 2019. Making Cultural Cities in China: Governance, State-Building, and Precarious Creativity. *Environment and Planning A: Economy and Space* 51 (1): 178–186.

Polanyi, Karl. 2001 [1944]. *The Great Transformation: The Political and Economic Origins of Our Time*. Boston: Beacon Press.

Pomeranz, Kenneth. 2000. *The Great Divergence. China, Europe, and the Making of the Modern World Economy*. Princeton: Princeton University Press.

Roetz, Heiner. 1992. *Die chinesische Ethik der Achsenzeit. Eine Rekonstruktion unter dem Aspekt des Durchbruchs zu postkonventionellem Denken*. Frankfurt a.M: Suhrkamp.

Rüpke, Jörg. 2015. Religious Agency, Identity, and Communication: Reflections on History and Theory of Religion. *Religion* 45 (3): 344–366.

Rüpke, Jörg. 2018. Religious Agency, Sacralization and Tradition in the Ancient City. *ИСТРАЖИВАЊА* 29:22–38.

Schluchter, Wolfgang. 1983. Einleitung: Max Webers Konfuzianismusstudie – Versuch einer Einordnung. In *Max Webers Studie über Konfuzianismus und Daoismus. Interpretation und Kritik*, ed. W. Schluchter, 11–54. Frankfurt a.M.: Suhrkamp.

Schmidt-Glintzer, Helwig. 1983. Viele Pfade oder ein Weg? Betrachtungen zur Durchsetzung der konfuzianischen Orthopraxie. In *Max Webers Studie über Konfuzianismus und Daoismus. Interpretation und Kritik*, ed. W. Schluchter, 298–341. Frankfurt a.M.: Suhrkamp.

Schoppa, Keith R. 1989. *Xiang Lake – Nine Centuries of Chinese Life*. New Haven/London: Yale University Press.

Seligman, Adam B., Robert P. Weller, Michael J. Puett, and Bennett Simon. 2008. *Ritual and Its Consequences: An Essay on the Limits of Sincerity*. Oxford/New York: Oxford University Press.

Skinner, G. William. 1964/1965. Marketing and Social Structure in Rural China, Parts I-III. *Journal of Asian Studies* 24 (1): 3–43, 24(2): 195–228, 24(3): 363–399.
Stafford, Charles. 2020. *Economic Life in the Real World: Logic, Emotion and Ethics*. New York: Cambridge University Press.
Stephenson, Barry. 2015. *Ritual: A Very Short Introduction*. Oxford: Oxford University Press.
Sun, Anna. 2013. *Confucianism as a World Religion: Contested Histories and Contemporary Realities*. Princeton: Princeton University Press.
Sutton, Donald S. 2007. Ritual, Cultural Standardization, and Orthopraxy in China: Reconsidering James L. Watson's Ideas. *Modern China* 33 (1): 3–21.
Taylor, Charles. 2007. *A Secular Age*. Belknap: Cambridge, MA.
Trémon, Anne-Christine (2015) Local capitalism and neoliberalization in a Shenzhen former lineage village *Focaal* 2015 (71): 71–85. https://doi.org/10.3167/fcl.2015.710107
von Glahn, Richard. 1991. The Enchantment of Wealth: The God Wutong in the Social History of Jiangnan. *Harvard Journal of Asiatic Studies* 51 (2): 651–714.
Von Glahn, Richard. 2016. The economic history of China: from antiquity to the nineteenth century. Cambridge University Press.
Wang, Da Wei David. 2016. *Urban Villages in the New China: The Case of Shenzhen*. New York: Palgrave Macmillan.
Watson, James L., and Evelyn S. Rawski, eds. 1988. *Death ritual in late imperial and modern China*. Vol. 8. Univ of California Press.
Weber, Max, and Keith Tribe. 2019. *Economy and Society: A New Translation*. Cambridge, MA: Harvard University Press.
Wenzel-Teuber, Katharina. 2024. Statistik zu Religionen und Kirchen in der Volksrepublik China. Ein Update für das Jahr 2023. *China heute. Informationen über Religion und Christentum im Chinesischen Raum* Jg. XLIII (222): 97–109.
Yang, C. K. 1961. *Religion in Chinese Society: A Study of Contemporary Social Functions of Religion and Some of Their Historical Factors*. Berkeley: University of California Press.
Yang, Mayfair M.-h. 2007. Ritual Economy and Rural Capitalism with Chinese Characteristics. In *Cultural Politics in a Global Age: Uncertainty, Solidarity and Innovation*, ed. D. Held and H. Moore. Oxford: Oneworld.
Yang, Mayfair M.-h. 2020. *Re-enchanting Modernity: Ritual Economy and Society in Wenzhou, China*. Durham: Duke University Press.
Yao, Souchou. 2002. *Confucian Capitalism: Discourse, Practice, and the Myth of Chinese Enterprise*. London/New York: Routledge.
Yu, Yingshi. 2021. *The Religious Ethic and Mercantile Spirit in Early Modern China*. New York: Columbia University Press.
Zelin, Madeleine. 2009. The Firm in Early Modern China. *Journal of Economic Behavior & Organization* 71:623–637.

Carsten Herrmann-Pillath is a transdisciplinary researcher in the human sciences, focusing on economics, the philosophy of economics and China. He is Professor of Economics and Permanent Fellow at the Max Weber Centre for Advanced Cultural and Social Studies; Erfurt University, Germany; and Distinguished Visiting Professor of Beijing Normal University, China. Among his recent books are *China's Economic Culture: The Ritual Order of State and Markets* (2016), *A New Principles of Economics: The Science of Markets* (with Christian Hederer, 2023), *Embodiment, Political Economy and Human Flourishing: An Embodied Cognition Approach to Economic Life* (with Frédéric Basso, 2024) and *Havings. Steps towards a New Economic Philosophy of Property and Beyond* (2024).

Chapter 5
The Dao of Dow Jones: The Confucian Analects, Virtue, and Markets

Mary Szto

Abstract This essay examines texts from the Confucian Analects with respect to virtue and human flourishing. From this worldview, I conclude that virtuous markets promote human flourishing. In contrast, nonvirtuous markets obstruct human flourishing. The Analects first identify the Dao, or the Way, as the guide for human conduct. The Dao embodies joy, filiality, reciprocity, and righteousness. These are cultivated through *li*, or ritual. Therefore, markets are virtuous if they promote these virtues through ritual. Gain should never be an end in itself. In contrast, nonvirtuous markets promote vice through disruption. These vices are greed, disloyalty, disrespect for elders, and despair. Nonvirtuous markets foster disregard for others, especially the vulnerable in society, and promote profit as an aim in itself, including short-term gain.

Keywords Confucianism · Dao · Virtue · Vice · Economic ethics

5.1 Introduction

This essay examines texts from the Confucian Analects with respect to virtue and human flourishing. From this worldview, I conclude that virtuous markets promote human flourishing. In contrast, nonvirtuous markets obstruct human flourishing. The Analects first identify the Dao, or the Way, as the guide for human conduct. The Dao embodies joy, filiality, reciprocity, and righteousness. These are cultivated

---

The Dow Jones Industrial Average, known as the Dow, is perhaps the best known stock market index for stock exchanges in the United States. This essay contrasts the Dao with the Dow.
This is for my father, Paul Szto (1924–2019), who sought God's righteousness ahead of gain.

M. Szto (✉)
Syracuse University College of Law, Syracuse, NY, USA
e-mail: mcszto@syr.edu

G. J. Buijs, J. J. Ballor (eds.), *In Search of the Spirits of Capitalism*, Sophia Studies in Cross-cultural Philosophy of Traditions and Cultures 44,
https://doi.org/10.1007/978-3-032-01137-4_5

through *li*, or ritual. Therefore, markets are virtuous if they promote these virtues through ritual. Gain should never be an end in itself. In contrast, nonvirtuous markets promote vice through disruption. These vices are greed, disloyalty, disrespect for elders, and despair. Nonvirtuous markets foster disregard for others, especially the vulnerable in society, and promote profit as an aim in itself, including short-term gain. First I will discuss the Analects, then the Dao, *li,* virtue, and finally virtuous markets and rituals.

5.2 The Analects

Confucius lived from 551 to 479 BC during China's Spring and Autumn Period, which was part of the East Zhou Dynasty. He was a philosopher and political advisor. Confucius was perturbed by the chaos of his times and sought a return to virtuous government. He had over 3000 disciples.

The Analects are a collection of teachings compiled by Confucius' disciples. They were first delivered as oral teachings. They are believed to have been collected over the course of three centuries (Rosemont 2013). They have undergone many revisions and numerous interpretations. Most notably, after the Song Dynasty (960–1279 AD), knowledge of the Analects was required to pass the Imperial civil service examination, and thus required for all government officials. Even today, after vilification during China's Cultural Revolution (1966–1976), Confucian teachings, including the Analects, have experienced a revival in reading and promotion.

The Analects are composed of 20 books and take the form of conversations with Confucius and others. First we will discuss the Dao. The Dao is the basis of existence and virtue, and ultimately, virtuous markets. The English translation of the Analects used throughout this chapter is by Robert Eno. Eno (2015).

5.3 The Dao

4.8 The Master said, In the morning hear the dao, in the evening die content.

19.7 Zixia said, Artisans of all types dwell in their workshops to master their crafts; the junzi studies to perfect his dao.

7.6 The Master said, Set your heart on the dao, base yourself in virtue, rely on ren, journey in the arts.

6.18 When plain substance prevails over patterned refinement, you have a bumpkin. When patterned refinement prevails over substance, you have a clerk. When substance and pattern are in balance, only then do you have a junzi.

The literal meaning of Dao is the way, or path. The Chinese character for Dao [道] includes the components for movement, 辶[chùo], and head, 首 [shǒu]. Chùo in turn, is composed of 彳 [chì], a person taking a small step, and 止 [zhǐ] stopping. 首

[shǒu] is composed of 川, [chuān], which is a flowing river or hair, above a face (Harbaugh 1999). Therefore, the Analects presuppose an order in the universe called the Dao, that humans can discern and then align themselves to accordingly. As one rises in the morning, one must be attentive to the Dao. During the day one studies the Dao, just as an artisan masters his craft; in fact, we must set our hearts on the Dao. The *junzi* is a sage who cultivates and perfects his Dao. The *junzi* balances substance and pattern. The *junzi* can also be translated as a superior person.

Thus the Dao is both transcendent and immanent. The Dao is both objective and subjective. The Dao is deeply personal. Heeding the Dao involves taking small steps, being attentive, and following a flowing head. The Dao is the balance between substance and pattern. Following the Dao brings contentment, as one seeks the Dao as an artisan.

5.4 Relationship Between Virtue and Dao

19.2 Zizhang said, If a man's grasp on virtue is not broad in practice and his faithfulness to the dao not profound, then his presence or absence in the world counts for nothing.

15.32 The Master said, The junzi makes plans for the sake of the dao, not for the sake of eating. Ploughing: there is a starvation in it. Study: there is a reward in it. The junzi worries about the dao, not about poverty.

Zizhang was a disciple of Confucius. Here he illustrates both the relationship of the Dao and virtue and their core significance to existence. Virtue and the Dao go hand in hand. Without them there is no value in existence. One's virtue must be extensive, and one's faithfulness to the Dao deep.

The Analects often contrast the *junzi, or* superior person, with the petty person. The *junzi* is concerned about the Dao, not about avoiding starvation or poverty. Faithfulness to the Dao is of utmost importance. Therefore, the Dao and virtue are the meaning of life. One must seek them relentlessly.

5.5 Relationship Between Dao and Li

16.2 Confucius said, When the dao prevails in the world, li, music, and punitive military actions proceed on the order of the Son of Heaven. When the dao does not prevail in the world, li, music, and punitive military actions proceed on the orders of the feudal lords. Once they proceed from the feudal lords, it is rare that after ten generations those lords have not lost their power. Once they proceed from grandees, it is rare that after five generations those grandees have not lost their power. Once subordinate officers control the fate of the state, it is rare that after three generations they have not lost their power. When the dao prevails in the world, governance does not lie in the hands of grandees. When the dao prevails in the world, the common people do not discuss governance.

There is also a correlation between Dao and *li*. When the Dao, a supreme force, prevails, ritual, music, and military control will emanate from the Son of Heaven. Also, when the Dao prevails, it is not necessary for the common people to discuss governance. Dao itself reigns. When the Dao does not prevail, governance is in the hands of lesser officials and is lost quickly. Thus, the Dao presumes an order that is cosmic, broad, innate, and lasting. In contrast, when the Dao is absent, *li*, music, and military control are local, external, and temporary. Because governance is externalized, it becomes a matter of concern for the populace.

5.6 The Importance of Li

> *8.2 The Master said, If one is reverent but without li one is burdened; if one is vigilant but without li one is fearful; if one is valorous but without li one causes chaos; if one is straightforward but without li one causes affronts. When the junzi is devoted to his parents, the people rise up as ren; when he does not discard his old comrades, the people are not dishonest.*
>
> *15.18 The Master said, The junzi takes right as his basic substance; he puts it into practice with li, uses compliance to enact it and faithfulness to complete it.*
>
> *14.41 The Master said, When the ruler loves li, the people are easy to employ.*
>
> *6.27 The Master said, Once a junzi has studied broadly in patterns and constrained them with li, indeed he will never turn his back on them.*
>
> *12.1 Yan Yuan asked about ren. The Master said, "Conquer yourself and return to li: that is ren. If a person could conquer himself and return to li for a single day, the world would respond to him with ren. Being ren proceeds from oneself, how could it come from others?" Yan Yuan said, "May I ask for details of this?"*
>
> *The Master said, "If it is not li, don't look at it; if it is not li, don't listen to it; if it is not li, don't say it; if it is not li, don't do it."*
>
> *Yan Yuan said, "Although I am not quick, I ask to apply myself to this."*

Li is necessary for the cultivation of virtue. What is *li*? The character for 禮, which is composed of several components, means obtaining revelation 示 [shì] with a sacrificial vessel 豊 [lǐ]. The sacrificial vessel is in turn composed of a serving container 豆 [dòu] accompanied by music 曲 [qǔ]. Revelation 示 [shì] is composed of three vertical lines, [小] signifying the sun, moon, and stars above [上] written as 二 [èr] (Harbaugh 1999). In other words, revelation comes from the spirit world above. Ritual is accessing revelation from the gods by offering food to them with music. Ritual is a shared meal.

The Chinese character for the human body 體 [tǐ] reveals the close relationship between human existence and ritual as well. 體 is composed of bones 骨 [gǔ] and the ritual vessel 豊. In other words, we are ritual vessels. Our bodies are living sacrifices. The shared meal and engagement with music are critical to our human existence. They not only sustain us physically, but spiritually. Because we are ritual vessels, we can discern the Dao through ritual.

In the Analects *li* tempers reverence, vigilance, valor, and straightforwardness. *Li* prevents heaviness, fear, chaos, and offense. It is the practice of righteousness. *Li* mediates, balances, and protects.

One must restrain oneself and return to *li*. *Li* must also be the content of seeing, hearing, speaking, and doing. To practice *li* is to be human, humane, and righteous. For example, devotion to one's parents results in *ren* [仁], which is love and benevolence. Faithfulness to old friends results in honesty.

Li is also the way of governance. If rulers love *li*, governance flows. It is the way of mutual *ren* [仁], which is love and benevolence. If one does not practice *li*, one cannot be righteous, or govern. Just as the Dao is fundamental to human existence, *li* implements the Dao, and is as well. Therefore virtuous markets must embody *li* as well.

5.7 Relationship Between Spirit and Human Worlds

6.22 Fan Chi asked about knowledge. The Master said, "To concentrate on what is right for the people; to be attentively respectful towards ghosts and spirits but keep them at a distance – this may be called knowledge.

11.12 Ji Lu asked about serving the spirits. The Master said, "While you are yet not able to serve men, how could you be able to serve the spirits?"
"May I ask about death?"
"When you do not yet understand life, how could you understand death?"

Although humans observe ritual and the Dao, we must be attentive to day-to-day interactions with humans. How we interact with humans will determine if we are able to serve spirits. We must do what is right for the general population. Before we can grapple with death, we must grapple with life.

Confucius' emphasis on the primacy of human interaction in the present life seems to be a departure from Daoists who focused on interactions in the spirit world. However, because *li* is essential to human interaction for Confucius, there is always a spiritual element to this human interaction. *Li* is seeking revelation from the spirit world.

5.8 Virtues

I will now discuss further Confucian virtues that emanate from the Dao, and result in *ren*, or human goodness. These virtues are joy, reflection, study, service, filiality, and reciprocity. They also include not seeking profit at the expense of righteousness. They are critical to the Dao of the markets. Confucian virtues must pervade the markets.

5.8.1 Joy/Reflection

6.20 The Master said, Knowing it is not so good as loving it; loving it is not so good as taking joy in it.

19.6 Zixia said, To study broadly and deepen one's resolve, to question closely and reflect on things near at hand, ren lies therein.

19.5 Zixia said, A man who daily assesses what he has yet to understand and who, month by month, does not forget what he has mastered may be said to love learning.

19.13 Zixia said, A man in service who is superior should study; a man who is superior in study should serve.

As mentioned above, one must seek the Dao from morning to evening. This involves delighting in knowledge, studying broadly and deeply. It also involves reflection and questioning on what is near. Knowledge and goodness go hand in hand. One must love learning, daily assess what one must still learn, and monthly, not forget what one has learned. Most of all one must have joy in knowledge. This joy in knowledge results in service. Those who are excellent in service must be informed by knowledge; as those excellent in learning must serve. Therefore the Dao of the markets must include deep and broad knowledge and reflection on goodness.

5.8.2 Filiality and Respect for Spirits and Elders

1.2 The junzi works on the root – once the root is planted, the dao is born. Filiality and respect for elders, are these not the roots of ren?

19.17 Master Zeng said, I have heard it from the Master: A man may have exhausted himself in nothing else, but he must do so in mourning for his parents.

19.14 Ziyou said, In mourning, exhaust grief and then stop.

8.21 The Master said, I can find no fault in Yu. Yu was frugal in his own food and drink, but thoroughly filial towards the spirits; he wore shabby clothes, but ritual robes of the finest beauty; his palace chambers were humble, but he exhausted his strength on the waterways that irrigated the fields. I can find no fault with Yu.

Confucius taught that filiality and respect for elders is the root of *rén* [仁], which is roughly translated as benevolence or human goodness. The character for *rén* [仁] is literally feelings between two [二] people [人] (Harbaugh 1999). Because parents give us life, affection and respect for them is the root of all other human interaction. Therefore, one must mourn deeply for parents when they pass.

We must also be filial to spirits, and zealous about the means that provide sustenance.

Therefore the Dao of the markets must promote filiality and attentiveness to the spirit world. This includes mourning rituals.

5.8.3 Reciprocity

15.24 Zigong asked, "Is there a single saying that one may put into practice all one's life?" The Master said, "That would be 'reciprocity': That which you do not desire, do not do to others."

12.2 Zhonggong asked about ren. The Master said, "When you go out your front gate, continue to treat each person as though receiving an honored guest. When directing the actions of subordinates, do so as though officiating at a great ritual sacrifice. Do not do to others what you would not wish done to you. Then there can be no complaint against you, in your state or in your household." Zhonggong said, "Although I am not quick, I ask to apply myself to this."

Reciprocity sums up what *ren* is. One must not treat others as one would not like to be treated. This is known as the silver rule. But *ren* is not just a prohibition. *Ren* is sometimes lavish acts. One should treat all as an honored guest; and even when working with subordinates, as if part of a great ritual ceremony. This should be in one's family and in one's country. This reiterates the importance of *li* in all actions. The Dao of the markets therefore honors reciprocity and when appropriate, lavish hospitality.

5.8.4 Don't Seek Quick Results/Think Ahead

6.22 He asked about ren. "People who are ren are first to shoulder difficulties and last to reap rewards. This may be called ren."

14.44 A boy from the Que district was acting as a messenger and someone asked about him. "Is he likely to improve?"

The Master said, "I have noticed that he seats himself in company and walks directly alongside his elders. He is not seeking improvement. He's after quick results."

15.12 The Master said, A man who does not think far ahead will have troubles near at hand.

Virtue also involves not seeking short-term gain, but long-term planning. This means first bearing hardship. Virtue also requires respecting elders and guests. This requires humility and deference to others. The Dao of the markets thus promotes long-term planning and gain, humility, and deference to others.

5.8.5 Righteousness Ahead of Gain/Profit/Land/Possessions

19.1 Zizhang said, A gentleman may be deemed satisfactory if he fulfills his orders in the face of mortal danger, bears righteousness in mind when faced with opportunities for gain, bears respect in mind when at sacrifice, and bears grief in mind when at mourning.

4.16 The Master said, The junzi comprehends according to right, the small man comprehends according to profit.

4.11 The Master said, The junzi cherishes virtue, the small man cherishes land. The junzi cherishes the examples men set, the small man cherishes the bounty they bestow. "But for someone to be deemed a complete man nowadays, what need does he have for all this? If, seeing profit, his thoughts turn to what is right, and, seeing danger, he is ready to risk his life, and if he can long endure hardship without forgetting the teachings that have guided his ordinary life, he may indeed be deemed a complete man." 14.12b

8.5 Master Zeng said, To be able, yet to ask advice of those who are not able; to have much, yet to ask advice of those who have little; to view possession as no different than lacking; fullness as no different than emptiness; to be transgressed against yet not to bear a grudge – in past times, I had a friend who worked to master these things.

4.12 The Master said, If one allows oneself to follow profit in one's behavior, there will be many with cause for complaint.

The Analects contrast seeking righteousness and seeking profit. The petty person thinks only of profit, land, or bounty. If profit is one's main goal, then many complaints will follow.

In contrast to merely seeking gain or quick results, a virtuous person seeks righteousness when considering gain. The *junzi* cherishes virtue, whereas the petty person cherishes land. Moreover, the *junzi* is able to possess property as if not owning it. This is because the *junzi's* highest goal is pursuit of the *dao* and virtue.

The Dao of the markets thus promotes righteousness and not mere gain of profit, land, or bounty.

5.8.6 Difference Between Wealth and Virtue

4.5 The Master said, Wealth and high rank are what people desire; if they are attained by not following the dao, do not dwell in them.

16.12 Duke Jing of Qi had a thousand teams of horses, but on the day he died, the people could find no virtue to praise in him. Bo Yi and Shu Qi starved beneath Mount Shou-yang, but the people praise them to this day. The saying, "It is not wealth that matters, but only having this difference," most likely refers to this.

7.16 The Master said, To eat coarse greens, drink water, and crook one's elbow for a pillow – joy also lies therein. Wealth and high rank obtained by unrighteous means are to me like the floating clouds.

Confucius did not eschew wealth and high rank but he argued that they must be obtained by following the Dao. They must be obtained through virtuous means. Otherwise, if obtained by unrighteous means they are like floating clouds. One can have joy with simplicity. It is better to be virtuous and destitute than to be wealthy and immoral. Thus the Dao of the markets does not award mere accumulation and gain. It does not award gain that can vanish such as floating clouds. It awards gain that has been achieved through righteous and virtuous means. This is long lasting gain.

5.8.7 Employment: People Must Be Fit for Their Tasks

13.25 The Master said, The junzi is easy to serve and hard to please. If you do not accord with the dao in pleasing him, he is not pleased; when it comes to employing others, he only puts them to tasks they are fit to manage.

The small man is hard to serve but easy to please. If you do not accord with the dao in pleasing him, he is still pleased; when it comes to employing others, he demands they be able in everything.

19.10 Zixia said, The junzi only labors his people once he has earned their trust. If he has not earned their trust, they will merely see him as demanding. Only after earning trust does he remonstrate with a lord. If he has not yet earned trust, the lord will take it as slander.

In accordance with seeking the *dao*, the *junzi*, or superior person, organizes work that is fit for employees. Moreover, he does not employ them unless he has earned their trust. Those who work for him must work in accordance with the *dao*. In contrast, the petty person does not distinguish tasks among his employees but expects them to do all tasks, regardless of whether or not they are suited for them; those who work for him do not have to work in accordance with the *dao*. The petty person is easy to satisfy because he is not concerned with the *dao*. He is only concerned about what satisfies his need for short-term gain.

Thus the Dao of the markets rewards labor that is suited for the workers. It rewards thoughtful deployment of personnel. It eschews workers who are easily discarded because of short-term gain.

5.8.8 Preventing Litigation

12.13 The Master said, In hearing lawsuits, I am no better than others. What is imperative is to make it so that there are no lawsuits.

Conflict may arise and lead to lawsuits, including at work. How does one prevent lawsuits? Presumably with the *dao*, righteousness, and virtue. This includes filiality, humility, and deference to elders. The Dao of markets thus awards harmony and peace-making.

This brings us to a discussion of governance, taxes, and the markets.

5.9 Governance

12.7 Zigong asked about governance. The Master said, "Provide people with adequate food, provide them with adequate weapons, induce them to have faith in their ruler." Zigong said, "If you had no choice but to dispense with one of those three things, which would it be?" "Dispense with weapons." "If you had no choice but to dispense with one of those two things, which would it be?" "Dispense with food. From ancient times there has always been death. If the people do not have faith, the state cannot stand."

16.1b ...I have heard it said that those who preside over states or family domains do not worry that they will have too few people, they worry that distribution of goods may be uneven; they do not worry about poverty, they worry they will not bring peace. Is it not so that when distribution is even there is no poverty; when there is harmony there is no under-population; when there is peace there is no danger the ruler will topple? It is just in this spirit that if those who are distant do not submit, one must cultivate patterns and virtue to attract them. Once they have come, one must comfort them...

13.17 Zixia served as steward of Jufu and asked about governance. The Master said, "Don't seek quick results; don't attend to matters of minor profit. If you seek quick results, you will not attain success; if you attend to matters of minor profit, you will not succeed in great affairs."

8.13 The Master said, Be devoted to faithfulness and love learning; defend the good dao until death.

Do not enter a state poised in danger; do not remain in a state plunged in chaos.

When the dao prevails in the world, appear; when it does not, hide.

When the dao prevails in a state, to be poor and of low rank is shameful; when the dao does not prevail in a state, to be wealthy and of high rank is shameful.

As individuals must not seek quick results and minor profits, governance must also focus on the Dao and long-term affairs. The state is an enlarged virtuous family. In general, in Chinese culture, government leaders are referred to as parents, and the nation as a family.

How do government leaders rule with virtue? They must ensure that there is equal distribution of resources and peace. If there is equal distribution there will be no poverty. They must also provide security for the populace. However, having the trust of the people is even more critical than food and weapons. Having the trust of the people will lead to sufficient food and security.

When the *dao* prevails, all have opportunity to obtain status and wealth and being poor is a lack of diligence and virtue. When the *dao* does not prevail, then poverty is a result of oppression, and wealth and high rank have been obtained through unrighteous means. And when the *dao* does not prevail, it is best to hide. Thus the Dao of the markets must heed a government that provides peace, security, and sustenance for its people. Such a government promotes status and wealth for all and not a few.

5.10 Taxes

12.9 Duke Ai questioned You Ruo. "In years of famine, when I do not take in enough to meet my expenditures, what should I do?"

You Ruo replied, "Why not set taxes at the rate of one-tenth?"

"At the rate of two-tenths my income is not adequate – how could I manage at one-tenth?" You Ruo replied, "When the people have sufficient means, who will not provide the ruler with what he needs; when the people do not have sufficient means, who will provide the ruler with what he needs?"

A government is concerned about revenue, but it must ensure that the governed have sufficient means. If the populace does not have sufficient income, then taxes will be insufficient. If the populace has sufficient income, then taxes will be sufficient. In other words, the well being of the populace must be of primary concern in assessing taxes. The populace's well being will lead to enough revenue for the state.

Thus the Dao of the markets promotes fair taxation for the income and needs of the populace. Tax practices that deprive the populace of their income and needs is unrighteous.

5.11 Market Rituals

> *9.13 Zigong said, "Let's say I have a precious gemstone; should I place it in a fine box and conceal it, or should I seek out a good merchant and sell it?"*
>
> *The Master said, "Sell it! Sell it! I myself am waiting for a good price."*

A good merchant pays a good price. A good merchant also facilitates circulation of precious items. Virtuous markets promote righteousness with good prices and circulation of precious items. In contrast, artificially inflated prices, and the circulation of bad products are characteristic of destructive markets.

Thus the Dao of the markets promotes good prices and circulation of precious items. Non-virtuous markets create bad prices and products.

5.12 Conclusion

The Confucian Analects teach that humans must pursue the *Dao* with all their hearts. The *Dao* is the order of the universe and the meaning of existence. It is the way of virtue; it is both transcendent and immanent. The *Dao* is personal. We must daily pursue the *Dao*. One seeks the *Dao* through *li*, or ritual. *Li* means to access revelation from the spirit world. In the Chinese worldview, our bodies are ritual vessels.

Virtue seeks and delights in knowledge and righteousness. Virtue honors one's parents, protects the frail, and grieves deeply when necessary. Virtue promotes reciprocity and treating others with lavish hospitality. Virtue requires deep humility and deference to others. If one is virtuous, one holds property lightly, as if not holding property. This is in contrast to seeking short-term profit, property, and gain as ends in themselves.

Virtue also means arranging work that is suitable for the worker. Those who employ others must gain their trust. However, those who seek short-term profit assign any and all types of work to employees, whether suitable for them or not.

Just as individuals must be righteous, those who govern must also be righteous. States should ensure equal distribution so there is no poverty. They should not overtax the populace but ensure that the populace has adequate income. States should provide peace and security for the populace, but the most importance aspect of governance is gaining the trust of the governed, and leading by virtue. When the Dao reigns, the populace does not need to discuss governance.

Can markets lead to human flourishing? Yes, but only if they are virtuous markets guided by virtuous government. Virtuous markets involve good merchants, prices, and the circulation of precious products. Virtuous markets promote filiality, deep learning and reflection, and work that suits workers. They promote deference to elders, harmony, and peace-making. They avoid lawsuits. They lead to sustained wealth obtained through virtue. Virtuous markets are attentive to the spirit world as well as day-to-day interactions with humans. Virtuous markets have rituals that promote flourishing through righteousness. These elevate joy in service.

In contrast, non-virtuous markets obstruct flourishing. They seek short-term profit, property, and gain. They lead to bad prices and bad products. Non-virtuous markets do not promote honoring one's parents or necessary deep grieving. They do not care for the well being of workers, and what is suitable work for them. They promote discarding workers for short-term gain. They do not promote fair taxes but deprive the populace of income and resources. They provide wealth that can vanish like floating clouds.

When the *dao* does not prevail, those who are unrighteous obtain wealth and high rank. Therefore non-virtuous markets promote inequality, poverty, and wrongly obtaining wealth.

Thus, the Dao of markets requires finding measurements for righteousness, and not just short-term profit. The Dao of markets rewards wealth obtained through righteousness. The Dao of markets achieves this through proper ritual. May we heed ancient wisdom. May we seek the Dao of the markets. May we measure the Dao of Jones.

References

Eno, Robert. 2015. The Analects of Confucius: An Online Teaching Translation. https://hdl.handle.net/2022/23420

Harbaugh, Rick. 1999. *Chinese Characters: A Genealogy and Dictionary*. New Haven: Yale University Press.

Rosemont, Henry, Jr. 2013. *A Reader's Companion to the Confucian Analects*. Cham: Springer.

Mary Szto is Teaching Professor at the Syracuse University College of Law, Syracuse, NY, USA. She writes about property issues such as the role of real estate agents and housing discrimination. She also writes on the relationship of ritual and law, both in China and in the USA. Prior to entering teaching, Professor Szto practised law in New York City representing banks in financing matters. She also co-founded a legal aid organization specializing in immigration law. Professor Szto teaches Contracts, Business Associations and Asian Americans and the Law.

Part III
Hinduism

Chapter 6
Free Markets, Hindu Ethics and Human Flourishing

Amitava Krishna Dutt

Abstract This paper examine how market activity and the promotion of free markets contribute to human flourishing and wellbeing from a Hindu perspective. First, it provides an account of the major tenets of Hinduism. Second, it examines Hindu ethics and views on human flourishing. Third, drawing on these ideas, it turns to a discussion of the effects of economic and market activity on ethics and human flourishing from a Hindu perspective, briefly referring to the views of Kautilya and Gandhi, two Hindu exemplars who have discussed the relation between economics, markets and ethics. The paper argues that a Hindu perspective suggests that although there is no necessary contradiction between market activity and systems, ethics, human flourishing and wellbeing, freer markets are likely to have a negative effect on ethics and flourishing.

Keywords Hinduism · Economic ethics · Gandhi · Kautilya · Human flourishing

6.1 Introduction

This paper examines how market activity and the promotion of free markets contribute to human wellbeing and flourishing as viewed from the perspective of Hindu ethics. It main goal is to examine what Hinduism has to contribute to the study of human wellbeing in an era in which the advance of less regulated markets and free market ideology seem to be inexorable.

The paper can be seen as contribution a large literature on the relationship between religion, markets and the economy, ethics and wellbeing. On the relation between religion and the economy, Weber's ideas on both how certain religious values and norms, such as those relating to hard work and thrift that are found in

A. K. Dutt (✉)
Notre Dame University, Notre Dame, IN, USA
e-mail: adutt@nd.edu

G. J. Buijs, J. J. Ballor (eds.), *In Search of the Spirits of Capitalism*, Sophia Studies in Cross-cultural Philosophy of Traditions and Cultures 44,
https://doi.org/10.1007/978-3-032-01137-4_6

Protestantism, promote capitalism and foster economic development (Weber 1905) and human wellbeing, and others—for instance Hinduism—do not particularly do so, although not creating absolute barriers (Weber 1919), and the effect of economic development and modernity based on the idea of rationality (Weber 1916)—the so-called secularization thesis—have been examined and generated heated controversy. Thus, the spread of economic development in different parts of the world has led to the recognition of the weakness of the Protestant ethics claim and of seeing other religions as a barrier to economic development (Kuran 2004; Chang 2007), and the increasing importance of religion in many parts of the world despite economic improvements has weakened support for the secularization thesis (Berger 2014). On the effect of market activity and freer markets on religion and ethics, positive effects are suggested by Adam Smith's argument that free markets rather than state support for religions promote religious competition and religious toleration (Anderson 1988), and the possible effect of market activity in general promoting virtues (McCloskey 2006), and moral values (Storr and Choi 2019), while others have examined the effects of markets in possibly eroding ethical norms (Dutt and Wilber 2010). On the effect of religious norms and ethics in general on markets and the economy, it has been suggested that ethical norms are likely to improve market efficiency by curtailing opportunistic behavior (Dutt and Wilber 2010), although competition between religious groups with strong religious identities can also lead to inequality and violence that can disrupt the economy (Sen 2007).

Some of these ideas have been applied to the case of Hinduism. The social-scientific literature on the relation between the economy, markets and religion has been given some attention to the case of Hinduism (see Morris 1967; Iyer 2018), and attention has been drawn to the rise of Hindu nationalism in recent years. But there has been little discussion of Hindu ethics in this context (aside from the effects of Hindu norms, such as caste and other-worldliness on economic outcomes). While the philosophical literature on the ethics of Hinduism is enormous, its relevance for the economy, markets and wellbeing—on which this paper focuses—has, to the best of my knowledge, not been examined systematically.

The rest of this paper proceeds as follows. Section 6.2 makes some preliminary remarks. Section 6.3 then examines Hindu ethics and the conception of human flourishing. Section 6.4 turns to a discussion of the effects of economic and market activity on ethics, flourishing and wellbeing from a Hindu perspective, referring briefly to the ideas of two exemplars, Kautilya and Gandhi. Section 6.5 provides some concluding comments.

6.2 Some Preliminaries

This section makes some brief remarks on ethics, the market and the economy, and on Hinduism as a religion.

By 'ethics' this paper refers to the study of what is morally good and bad (or better and worse), what is right and wrong. It is concerned with questions like the meaning of the good life (or how to make life better), what are good and bad actions, who is a morally good person, and how society should be organized to be a good society or at least a better one. Ethical ideas can be derived from reasoning, intuition and emotion, or from religious traditions.[1] Western ethics often distinguishes between: virtue ethics, referring to the goodness of people as actors; deontological ethics, on the rightness of actions; and consequentialist ethics, on the goodness of consequences of actions. Well-known Western exemplars of these approaches are, respectively, Aristotle's virtue ethics, the Ten Commandments and Kant's categorical imperative and Jeremy Bentham and John Stuart Mill's utilitarianism. Although it may be argued that the distinction between the three approaches is murky—since a good person is one who mostly does the right things and these generally have good consequences—the division usefully distinguishes between different loci that are the ultimate test of goodness or rightness. Thus, for instance, from a deontological perspective telling the truth is key, and a person who does not do so is not a good person, and the consequences of being truthful or not are irrelevant, while from a virtue perspective a good person can sometimes not tell the truth, for instance, for the sake of kindness, and from the consequentialist perspective, telling the truth is not good if it results in bad consequences. There is no good reason, however, why one approach should be prioritized over the others in every situation.

Turning next to the economy and markets, the economy can be viewed as system in which goods and services are produced, consumed, invested, bought and sold, and distributed among people, and in which assets are held, bought and sold, while markets are the sites in which goods, services and assets are bought and sold. The economy and markets are obviously not the same—since production, need not be for sale in markets but for family consumption, and goods and services may be distributed among people through reciprocal gifts or by the state—but the two are closely identified with each other and becoming more so, since market activity is economic activity by definition, and since production, consumption, investment, and asset holding increasingly involve buying and selling.

It is useful to distinguish between market activity, and market institutions and market systems. Market activity involves buying and selling goods, services, and assets, usually involving money, but can include the other economic activities mentioned, if they are mostly related to buying and selling. Markets as social institutions also involve laws and regulations (such as those that establish property rights and the rules regarding contracts between buyers and sellers), social norms (such as what is generally considered to be appropriate behavior or attitudes), and organizations, both state and non-state, such as the legislators, police, courts, labor unions or private groups (that create, interpret and help to enforce laws and regulations). Market systems include not only institutions, as defined above, but also individual

[1] They can also emerge from social interactions and public discussion, historical evolution, and biological evolution, although these may affect what ethical values people happen to hold, rather than what can reasonably be called morally good.

and group behavior and the motivations behind them, government policies, technology, and widely-shared ideas that can be referred to as ideologies. A related system is the capitalist system. Although these systems are difficult to define precisely, among other things, they include: belief in the efficacy of unregulated markets with minimal state intervention, bringing more and more aspects of the world under the purview of markets, valuing things in terms of the price at which they are or can be bought and sold, viewing labor and essential services as commodities, equating well-being and success to income and wealth; institutions and government policies that promote freer markets with little or no state involvement; and acceptance as the appropriate goal of individuals to be having more for oneself, and the goal of society to be efficiency evaluated in terms of whatever individual preferences happen to be.[2] Market activities do not require the existence of market institutions and systems, but over time, as market activities involve more people and aspects of the society, these quantitative changes give rise to a qualitative change which involve the development of the market system.

On the evaluation of the economy and markets, while generally the emphasis has been on improving human wellbeing, there are different ways of conceptualizing and measuring wellbeing and economic development (see Sen 1999). A popular one is production and income of people, groups and countries, which focusses on average production and income and their growth, and more recently, but to a lesser extent, on the distribution of income and wealth and on poverty. The approach that is dominant in mainstream economics is based on individual preferences and utility. While it was used earlier to justify the focus on real income under the assumption that more of income and consumption is better for people, it is now directly measured by survey results on subjective wellbeing or self-reported happiness. Another approach focuses on the expansion of rights or freedoms including those in political, social and economic domains, but leads to difficulties in terms of possible tradeoffs between those of different people and kinds of them. A final approach, which draws on the earlier basic needs approach, conceptualizes wellbeing and economic development in terms of functionings and capabilities, that is, the extent to which people achieve or have the freedom to achieve those things that they value and have reason to value, such as good health, nutrition and education, and even dignity. These different approaches can be related to different approaches to ethics. The rights and freedoms approach can be seen as a deontological one; income, utility and functionings involve a consequentialist approach; and the functionings and capability approach has been related to an Aristotelian virtue ethics perspective, since they draw attention to things and states that allow human beings to flourish and become virtuous.

Finally, turning to religion and Hinduism, we may start by noting the (Western) definition of a religion, that is "[a]ction or conduct indicating belief in, obedience to, and reverence for a god, gods, or similar superhuman power; the performance of

[2] Not all of these interconnected things are necessary for the system.

religious rites or observances" or a "particular system of faith and worship",[3] applies more to Abrahamic religions, than to Hinduism. The term Hinduism is a later, probably European, invention, the earlier name for it being *sanātana dharma* or the eternal way of life. Hinduism does not have a prophet whose ideas are definitive. It does not have a single holy book with the status of the Bible or the Quran, and some widely-respected exemplars of Hinduism have chosen to reject the ideas from some of its holy books. It has no single organization which can make definitive statements about Hindu doctrine and practice. Hindus can be monotheistic, polytheistic or atheist and can have different conceptions of god.

Although the basic tenets are difficult to summarize, the following are often taken as its core components.[4] First, the individual soul or *ātman*, which is never created or destroyed, is one with the universal soul, or *brahman*, the essence of all of existence, sometimes called the unproduced producer of all existence. Second, according to the process of rebirth and the doctrine of *karma*, the soul passes from body to body through rebirth, which can be human and non-human. Actions in one life, or *karma*, affect the level at which the soul is born in the next life. Third, progress from one life to another requires relinquishing desires, especially worldly ones, humility and detachment and most importantly, the understanding that there is no separate self that is distinct from *brahman*. The full realization of the true nature of the self, that is, its oneness with *brahman*, leads to liberation from this cycle, or *mokṣa*. Fourth, there are many ways of making progress towards liberation. Generally speaking, it requires the following of *dharma*, sometimes interpreted as duty, right conduct, ethical way of life (see the next section). But people can follow different paths depending on their personalities, positions in society, and stage of life. Those taking the worldly path (*pravritti mārga*) are prescribed to undertake meritorious deeds, which help them to be unselfish through prayer aimed at the gods, one's ancestors, the priests, other people (especially those in distress), and even animals. The different duties and virtues do not apply with the same force in the four stages of life, or *āsramas*: *brahmachārya* (when one is a student), *gārhasthya* (householder), *vānaprastha* (forest dweller retired from working for a living), and *sannyāsa* (an ascetic who renounces society). The same is true for the *varṇa* system, with its four castes, the *brāhman* (priests and the learned), *kshatriya* (warriors and political rulers), *vaisya* (merchants and farmers) and *sudra* (residual group of servants and artisans). Even for those who follow the spiritual or otherwordly path (the *nivritti mārga*), there are different paths, or *mārgas* or *yogas*, which people can follow depending on their personalities and proclivities, including *rāja-yoga* (a highly disciplined, intense and sequenced course of physical and mental exercises), *jnāna-yoga* (acquiring knowledge, based on learning and thought), *bhakti-yoga* (divine worship) and *karma-yoga* (good works without attachment and selfishness, especially to help the poor).

---

[3] These definitions are from the Oxford English Dictionary, taken from the web version available at https://www.oed.com/viewdictionaryentry/Entry/161944

[4] This section draws on Dutt (2010). The account does not provide a historical perspective, and is unlikely to be universally accepted.

There are also different traditions of divine worship, including the *Śaiva*, the *Śā kta* and the *Vaiṣṇava* (focusing on the gods Siva, Shakti and Vishnu, respectively). Some Hindus believe in many gods, one god, no god, or are agnostic, sometimes all at the same time, and there is no unique concept of god.

There are several influential philosophical systems within Hinduism, and the list above is an amalgam of these. Different approaches stress different tenets, and some may in fact completely reject one of them. These philosophies include, among others, *Sāmkhya* (which divides the cosmos into different elements and posits a dualism between nature and the self), *Mimāmsa* (the tradition of Vedic exegesis assuming the reality of the many) and *Vedānta* (including the *Dvaita*—dualism and *Advaita* or non-dualism which argues the reality of the one), and the *Chārvaka* (or materialist school that denies the existence of the soul and the karma doctrine). Beyond these, there are Buddhism and Jainism which, though usually treated as separate religions, can be interpreted as reform movements that oppose the domination by the *brāhmans* and their ritualistic excesses, are based on the Hindu ideas of rebirth and liberation and in turn affected elements of Hinduism. Buddhism takes the view that the belief in god is an unnecessary distraction, and is agnostic about god, while Jainism can be called atheistic.

Hindu holy books, or *sāstras*, are classified into the *sruti* (what is heard) and *smriti* (what is remembered). The *sruti* is often considered to be divine revelation, and include the four *Vedas* (the *Rig*, *Sama*, *Yajur* and *Atharva*) and the *Brahmanas*, and the *Upanishads*. The *smriti* are generally attributed to human writers, and include codes or manuals on life and ethics, including the *dharma sāstras*, such as Manu's *Manusmriti*, the *Dharmasutras*, the *Purānas* (histories or mythologies) and the epic poems, *Rāmāyāna* and the *Mahābh ārata*. The most influential texts, aside from the *Vedas*, are the *Bhagavat Gītā* (which, is fact, a part of the *Mahābhārata*) and the major *Upanishads* (which are sometimes considered to be parts of the *Vedas*). There is no unique accepted interpretation of the content of these texts, and major thinkers have interpreted passages in widely different ways, and even rejected some of the ideas contained in them.

Beyond these philosophical tenets and texts, which are of limited direct relevance for the masses, Hinduism can be viewed in terms of the rituals and practices of Hindus, which include the worship of a variety of different gods and goddesses at homes, temples and in temporary structures constructed for *pujas* (ceremonies worshipping gods) once a year; praying for the peace of one's ancestors; going on pilgrimages to holy sites; and the observance of numerous rites, including fasting and having restricted diets on special days, and ritual bathing. There are also social norms that relate to the caste system, which sees society as divided into *varṇas*, mentioned earlier, and *jātis*, which break down society in terms of finer occupational castes that are frequently hierarchical and heritable. These have led to rigid stratification in the past, and still plays a role in promoting inequality, discrimination and oppression. Gender norms, with support from texts like the *Manusmriti*, have also condoned the domination of women (see Dutt 2010).

The absence of clear textual authority makes the views of religious leaders very important. Relatively recent leading figures include Sri Rāmakrishna, Swāmi Vivekānanda and Mohandas Karamchand Gandhi and many lesser-known people have also had influence and some formally declared to be religious teachers or *gurus*. The tenets of Hinduism have permeated the masses through them but, with few restrictions on becoming a *guru*, many are alleged to be charlatans.

This paper will focus mainly on basic tenets of Hinduism based on texts and not on the actual beliefs and behaviors of those who call themselves Hindus. This is because the latter requires an empirical analysis of what these beliefs and behaviors are, and the extent to which they are based on religion rather than other social, economic and political factors, issues which are beyond the scope of this paper. It is also because our interest is in Hindu ethics, since some actual practices and norms, may well be ethically indefensible.

6.3 Hindu Ethics and Human Flourishing

Even if it is accepted that Hinduism refers to a reasonably coherent set of ideas, it is sometimes claimed that there is no such thing as Hindu ethics,[5] a claim based on a number of, sometimes contradictory, arguments. Thus, it is claimed that: while ethics govern what is good and right in motivations and actions in the real world, Hinduism is mainly about liberation from the world for the individual and is otherworldly; Hinduism at best contains a non-systemic discussion of ethical quandaries and religious injunctions, and its scope is limited by the absence of an ethical system based on metaphysical or rational first principles; Hindu ideas are based on religion and not on reason, which ought to be the foundation for ethics; and the ethical injunctions that exist concern people in specific walks of life, distinguished, for instance, by caste, the stage of life of a person, gender, and family relations, and not general ones relating to all people, as ethics should.

These claims, however, are not convincing. Even if the centrality of liberation or *mokṣa* is accepted, real world-ethical concerns are addressed at length in discussions of *dharma* in the *srutis* and *smritis*, and the legitimacy of worldly goals are mentioned in the *puruṣārthas*. To argue that Hindu ethics falls short because of the absence of an ethical 'system' is based on a narrow interpretation of ethics, represented by Kant's categorical imperative or Bentham's utilitarianism, and excludes Hegel's idea of *Sittlichkeit*, a dynamic social ethos, rooted in norms, duties, laws, and virtues prized by texts and community practices and Aristotle's ethics based on different virtues relevant for particular societies (Mohanty 1997). About religion and ethics, religion is a source of ethics even in the West, as illustrated by the virtues and Commandments in Christianity, and Hinduism is not really a religion in the standard sense, there being no sharp distinction drawn between faith and reason as

[5] See, for instance, Bilmoria et al. (2007), and the references cited therein.

in Western Enlightenment (Matilal 2007). On the problem of different ethics for different people, while some duties and injunctions are specific to people and relations, for instance, *varṇadharma* (the *dharma* of members of particular castes) or *kū ladharma* (the dharma of the family), there is a large body of them that pertain to all people, or *sādharanadharma*. Furthermore, having specific ethics for specific groups may be taken as accounting for individual heterogeneities and different situations of people, and need not imply a departure from equal treatment.

A natural place for starting a discussion of Hindu ethics is *dharma*. Literally, the word derives from the Sanskrit verb, *dhri*, which can be translated as 'to support, uphold or sustain'. Beyond the modern usage of the term to mean religion (since the Indian languages do not have another word for it), at least four different definitions in the Hindu classical literature can be distinguished (Mohanty 2007). First, injunctive (or prohibitive) sentences of the *Vedas*, as clarified, expounded and explained in the later *dharmas āstras*, which may be obligatory, occasional or only recommended; they may apply to all people or be specific for members of a *varṇa*, or within the family. Second, that from which prosperity and the highest good results. Third, as the knowledge available to the doer that leads to what is attainable and desirable. Finally, as attainable goals that are described in the *Vedas*. Clearly *dharma* and ethics are closely related.

The Hindu texts provide the major source of *dharma*. The term appears frequently in the *Vedas*, but has different meanings in different contexts (see Nadkarni 2011, 218–9). It is connected closely to *ritam*, the cosmic order or moral law or which sustains the physical and social worlds, and refer to righteousness and *satyam* (truthfulness); to moral ordinances and duties, referring to sins such as cheating, arrogance, violence, cruelty and indolence, and virtues, such as charity, helping others, self-control, chastity, courage, truthfulness, and humility, which, respectively, displease and please the gods, and are considered bad or good for individuals and society; and to ritual obligations. The *Upanishads* retain these basic ethical values, but develop them further, and emphasize study, meditation, reflection and debate rather than the ritualistic elements of the *Vedas*. Most importantly, the highest good is seen as the attainment of *mokṣa*, the realization of unity of the self or *ātman* with the all-pervasive *brahman*, a concept that is not present in the earlier *Vedas*. Distinguishing between wellbeing associated with what leads to self-realization and perennial joy (or *sreyas*) and sensual pleasures and riches, which provide transient happiness and instant gratification (or *preyas*), the *Upanishads* state that "true" happiness, which is chosen by the wise, refers to the former, that is, the realization of a person's oneness with *brahman*, and the liberation from worldly desires. This highest good, however, cannot be attained without controlling selfishness and anger, and having compassion and generosity.

The *Bhagavad Gīta* (or *Gīta*, for brevity) takes the form of a conversation on the battlefield between Lord Krishna and the Pāndava prince Arjuna, who has misgivings about waging war against the Kauravas and their allies, many of whom are their own relatives. It refers to many desirable virtues. For instance, it enumerates the qualities that make humans divine: fearlessness, purity of mind, steadfastness of knowledge, studiousness, charity, self-control, uprightness, austerity, non-violence, truthfulness, tranquility, compassion for all living beings, gentleness, forgiveness, cleanliness, humility, and absence of anger, hatred, covetousness and fickleness (see Nadkarni 2011, 221). Some of these qualities are emphasized for specific *varṇas*, such as serenity, self-control, austerity, fortitude and faith for the *brahman*, and heroism, vigor, resourcefulness, generosity and leadership for the *kshatriya*, while others are universal, including friendliness, compassion, charity, forgiveness and penance (Mohanty 1997, 302). Although many of these qualities are mentioned in earlier texts, the *Gītā* focuses more on the ethics of everyday life, and far less on rituals, contemplation and learning. The *Gītā* stresses the importance of *karma yoga* as unselfish action without attachment to results, but states that self-realization can be attained in different ways, for instance, through *jnāna*, *karma* and *bhakti*, or their combinations, as *mārgas*.

Among the best-known authors of *smritis* is Manu. His *Manusmriti*, which is considered by many to be one of the most authoritative texts on the Hindu code, or *dharmasāstras*, is dated back to around 100 CE. It mentions ten key features of *dharma*, which are especially applicable to the *brāhmaṇa*: fortitude, self-restraint, abstention from wrongly appropriating the property of others, truthfulness, patience, purity, correct discernment, culture, control over the senses, and sweet temper (VI, 91–2). *Ahimsa* (non-injury) is repeatedly praised, which includes pleasant speech and includes that towards animals (although flesh-eating is permitted, but abstention from it is considered meritorious). Although appropriating the property of others is considered unethical, he permits a starving person to take food from wherever he finds it, although not to hoard, and states that someone who takes wealth from the wicked and gives it to the good and needy redeems both (XI, 16–19). Although truth is considered a virtue, nevertheless, "let one say what is true, let one say what is pleasing, let one utter nothing disagreeable, and let one utter no agreeable falsehood: that is the eternal law" (V 109, II 83, IV 138).[6] Manu recognizes that *dharma* or the moral code is not fixed forever, but must be learned in each generation through observation and from good learned people.

There are some additional early works that deal specifically with ethics, such as the *Nīti-shataka* by Bhartrihari (dated somewhere between 100 BCE and the fifth century CE), which states that the noblest people relinquish their self-interest to further the good of others, and the *Tirukkural* by Tiruvalluvar (dated between the second century BCE and eighth century CE) which stresses the avoidance of violence and falsehood and states that greatness and lowness are not inherited traits (Nadkarni 2011).

This brief review of Hindu ethics or *dharma* in some major texts, provides us with a number of qualities, actions, duties and obligations, some of which recur, but as they come from a variety of sources they do not comprise anything like a consistent or ordered set of ideas. Indeed, many scholars have drawn attention to the existence of moral dilemmas in Hindu texts, especially in the epic poems, the *Rāmayāna* and the

[6]Although this quote stated that "agreeable falsehoods" should not be uttered, it also states that "disagreeable" things should not be said, suggesting that one has to balance agreeableness and what one believes to the literal truth.

Mahābhā rata (Matilal 2002), the most famous of which appears in the opening chapter of the *Gītā*, in which Arjuna, is torn between *varṇadharma* according to which, as a *kshatriya* warrior, his duty is to fight against injustice and for righteousness and vanquish evil, and *kuladharma*, which forbids injury to family members, as well as *sādharanadharma* which is against killing and violence. The resolutions of such dilemma are not simple, and may depend on, among other things, the overall context, the specific situation and the characteristics of the people involved, and cannot be prioritized with a simple set of rules. There have been some attempts to provide some order. For instance, according to the *Manusmriti*, *dharma* refers to the ethical code of conduct with sources, in decreasing order of importance, being: the *sruti* (including the Vedas); the tradition and virtuous conduct of those who know and interpret the *Vedas* including the *smriti* (such as the *dharmas āstras*); *sadāchar* (the conduct of good and holy people); and *ātmasruti* (or self-satisfaction). But Shah (1981, 61–2) argues that the relationship between these sources is more complex than this simple hierarchy suggests. In both the *sruti* and *smriti* there are conflicts, even within the same text, ideas are open to different interpretations, and there may be differences in opinion on these issues by good and holy people. Therefore, a person's own judgment may be the deciding factor. Thus, even in the *Gītā* (18, 63), Krishna does not instruct Arjuna to obey him, but says, instead, "[y]ou have heard what I have had to say; now reflect on it fully and critically and do what you want to do". In more recent times, Gandhi, who was a devout Hindu (but also revered aspects of other religions, including Christianity and Islam, as well as Jainism and Buddhism), stated that "Every word of the printed works passing muster as *shastras* is not, in my opinion, a revelation … Nothing in the *shastras* which is manifestly contrary to universal truths and morals can stand … Nothing in the *shastras* which is capable of being reasoned can stand if it is in conflict with reason" (Gandhi 1935; V62, 121–2).[7]

The concept of *mokṣa*, which emerged well after *dharma* in the sense of righteousness or ethics including different qualities and injunctions, refers to liberation or self-realization, that is, the realization that the individual self, or *ātman*, and the indestructible and all-pervasive universal self, or *brahman*, are one and the same. The relation between the two is controversial and a number of different views exist. Arguably the most plausible one is that the concept of *mokṣa* is the over-riding principle, or the ultimate good, of Hindu ethics. People can try to move towards that ideal, the goal of self-realization, through detached and desireless thought and actions (although not without strong commitment), eschewing a focus on the consequences for oneself; this can be taken to be the concept of flourishing, which is dynamic and represent a process towards *mokṣa.* The concept helps people to properly interpret any particular aspect, and to prioritize different elements of *dharma*, that are most consistent with this quest. An example of the proper interpretation, the *Gītā* (Chapter 17, 20–22) distinguishes between three kinds of charity in relation to the three *gunas*: *sātvik*, which is unselfish, giving without the expectation of

[7]Citations to Gandhi refer to its original date, followed by the volume and page number in his Collected Works.

receiving anything in return; *rājasik*, giving with the expectation of receiving something; and *tāmasik*, giving with contempt for the recipient (Nadkarni 2011, 207), and favors charity without selfishness, arrogance and contempt for the recipient. More generally, thoughts and motives for actions is of great importance. Regarding prioritization, the *Gītā* provides the example in which Arjuna has to choose follow his *varṇadharma*, as a warrior, to do his duty and fight, not just to vanquish the foe to benefit himself and his brothers but for a just and righteous cause, since the Kauravas were wrongfully preventing the Pandavas from getting their kingdom back, and his *kuladharma*, that of not killing members of his extended family, or even the universal *dharma* of non-injury. Krishna is not suggesting that there is a rule according to which one kind of *dharma* takes precedence over another, but that Arjuna not be concerned with the *fruits* of *his* actions, but do his just duty with an inner freedom (Mohanty 1997, 299). The concept of *mokṣa* also suggests there is no need to follow all aspects of *dharma*, since some of them can substituted by others by following different paths (for instance, through austerity, devotion to gods, good works or acquiring knowledge) and that aspects can rejected outright: for instance, following practices related to caste (in any case, many of them come from the *smriti*, which is not as authoritative as the *sruti*) and others, such as truthfulness, control over the senses, modesty, and non-violence, are all necessary components in the quest for self-realization, since they are all related to detachment and desirelessness.

The focus on the individual, that is, on *dharma* governing individual behavior and *mokṣa* which relates to the self-realization and liberation of individuals, has been taken to imply that Hindu ethics concerns only individuals and not collective entities such as societies or nations or the world. This view, however, arguably involves a misunderstanding. The idea of *mokṣa* achieves the unity of the individual self with the totality of existence which, not only includes all people, but also the natural world. *Dharma*, in the sense of the moral order, was seen as what holds the world together and ensures the welfare of all, as early as in the *Rig Veda*. Also, allowing the weak to be destroyed by the powerful, as in *matsyanyaya*, or justice in the world of fish in which the big fish eat the little ones, is not in line with *dharma*. The *Mahābhārata* states that "Whatever has its beginning in *nyāyayukta* [justice] that alone is called *dharma*; what is unjust and oppressive is *adharma* [against *dharma*]" (quoted in Nadkarni 2011, 128). It is, however, true that Hindu ethics contains many inegalitarian elements and implications. On caste hierarchies, the *varṇas* are mentioned in the *Rigveda* and the *Gītā*, and later texts, especially the *smriti* establish caste hierarchies by prescribing different duties, obligations, punishments and privileges for members of different *varṇas* and there is also much that points to gender inequality. However, contrary ideas also exist in the Hindu tradition that are geared towards reducing poverty, promote equality of income and gender, and suggest that caste depends not on birth but on virtuous actions. As mentioned earlier, one is free to pick and choose the more egalitarian ideas, especially when the offensive ones come from the *smriti*; this follows the example of many early and modern exemplars, such as Tiruvalluvar, Swami Vivekananda and Gandhi (see Dutt 2010; Nadkarni 2011).

It is interesting to examine which of the three well-known (Western) ethical approaches Hindu ethics fits in with best. A claim can be made for the deontological approach. Sen (2009, 208–214) states that Krishna's instruction to Arjuna in the *Gītā* to do his duty and fight, and problematically ignores the possible devastating consequences of war (which actually came to pass). He argues that this reveals an extreme deontological position of Hindu ethics, since Krishna is seen as an incarnation of god, and because such claims are made frequently in other Hindu texts. This view overemphasizes Krishna's advice on ignoring consequences, missing the fact that—as discussed earlier—Krishna's argument is more about choosing between different duties (of fighting, as a warrior, to promote justice versus practicing non-violence, especially towards one's kith and kin) and not being concerned with the consequences for *oneself*. Thus, the focus of the *Gītā* is not on doing one's duty as such, but to promote the cause of justice and righteousness with detachment in the sense of not aspiring to the fruits of action, especially self-gratification, which relates to the qualities of a person on the path to *mokṣa*. Thus, the actions and rules are less important than the motives for the actions. Indeed, there is no list of simple, inflexible rules, which must be followed. Even regarding the central rules of being truthful and non-violence, there are exceptions. In addition to Manu's statement cited earlier, in the Shantiparva of the *Mahaābhārata* (329, 13), it is stated that "It is good to speak the truth; what does good is still better. What is ultimately good for the welfare of all is what I consider as the truth" (Nadkarni 2011, 226). As we have seen, Krishna recommends that Arjuna engage in violence. Although interpreting this in an allegorical sense to refer to the internal conflict of good versus evil, Gandhi, the apostle of non-violence, states that "where there is only a choice between cowardice and violence, I would advise violence....I would rather have India resort to arms in order to defend her honour than that she should, in a cowardly manner, become or remain a helpless witness to her own dishonor", (Gandhi, 1920, V21, p. 133) and "[l]ife itself involves some kind of violence and we have to choose the path of least violence". (Gandhi, 1934, V65, p. 89).

Regarding consequentialism, *contra* Sen's argument, the *Gitā* does not suggest that consequences of actions should be ignored; indeed, in Chapter 18, verse 25, it denigrates actions taken without regard to consequences or to loss and injury as being *tāmasik*, the lowest of the three *gunas* (Nadkarni 2011, 138). In the *Rāmayāna*, after Rāma—widely considered to be the embodiment of virtue—rescues his wife, Sitā, from imprisonment in Lanka, by her abductor, King Rāvana, sensing that his own kingdom would be in peril because of the unrest that would be created by his subjects who believed that her chastity had been violated, exiled her, despite his firm knowledge that Sitā was pure. In whatever way one evaluates this choice, it is clear that Rāma is very much concerned about the consequences of what he does.

Hindu ethics actually comes closest to virtue ethics, since its emphasis is on human flourishing, in the sense of what kind of person one is or is becoming, in the path towards *mokṣa* and following—albeit selectively, making choices based on context and personality—elements of *dharma*. It is in this sense that Gandhi interprets his experiments with truth (as mentioned in the subtitle to his autobiography) and his pursuit of *swaraj* (or self-rule), which, although it also involves freedom from foreign rule (for India), and freedom from exploitation by the powerful within the country, it refers primarily to the striving within oneself (Gandhi 1920, CW 22, 63). But Gandhi also relates this striving for truth to *dharma* which for him, also emphasizes nonviolence. He states that "[f]or me, 'there was no dharma higher than truth' (*Mahā bhā rata*, Adiparva, ch. xi, 13) and 'no dharma higher than the supreme duty of nonviolence' (Shantiparva, ch. CLXII, 24.) The word dharma, in my opinion has different connotations as used in the two statements. In other words, it means that there cannot be an *ideal* higher than truth and there cannot be any *duty* higher than non-violence. A man can pursue truth only by constantly adhering to this duty. There is no other means for the pursuit of truth." (italics added, Gandhi V 62:224). The truth that Gandhi sought is not simply a matter of not 'uttering falsehoods,' but being completely true to oneself in beliefs, thoughts, speech and deeds, not to the self as whatever it happens to be, but a self which undergoes constant efforts at self-improvement, on the path to *mokṣa*. Thus, the focus of Hindu ethics is on the (virtuous) *person*, not on the *virtues* of the person, and allows flourishing to take different forms. It needs to be emphasized, however, that virtue does not exclude concern for actions and consequences. Whether an action is righteous, according to *dharma*, depends on its motives, its means and its consequences. In terms of consequences, both intended and realized are considered, and *dharma* and *satya* are defined as what achieves the welfare of all (Nadkarni 2011), and not gains for oneself.

6.4 Markets, Virtue and Human Flourishing

To examine the relationship between markets, virtue and human flourishing, it is useful to start from the four *puruṣā rthas*, commonly interpreted as the four 'valid' *goals* of human life, but alternatively representing different *attitudes*.[8] Of these, we have already discussed *dharma*, and *mokṣa*, but there are two others, that is, *artha* (the pursuit of wealth, income or material prosperity, as well as power), and *kā ma* (the enjoyment of the pleasure of the senses including, prominently, sexual activity, but also the pleasure that is obtained from other family relationships, and aesthetic value).[9] Of the four *puruṣā rthas*, *mokṣa* is a later addition, and the other three are referred to as the *trivarga*.

According to the traditional view *dharma* takes precedence over *artha* and *kā ma*. When Vātsyāyana, the author of the *Kā mas ū tra*, the famous treatise on sex,

[8] Potter (1963: 5) recognizes that they refer to 'aims of life' but opts for attitudes or orientations instead of aims because he argues, erroneously, that aims must have a goal, because they can refer to tending towards something that is unspecified. Nevertheless, his interpretation can be considered as well.

[9] For a discussion of some difficulties and controversies concerning these definitions, see Krishna (2007).

discusses the three elements of the *trivarga,* he places *dharma* first, *artha* second and *kāma* last. He also considers the argument that *kāma* can have undesirable features and consequences, such as contact with wicked people, negligence, rashness and distrust, and concludes that it needs to be pursued with adequate caution. The *Manusmriti* (Manu, 2, 224; 4176) states that "[t]o achieve welfare and happiness some declare *dharma* and *artha* are good. Others declare that *artha* and *kāma* are better. Still others declare that *dharma* is the best. There are also persons who declare *artha* alone secures happiness. But the correct view is that the aggregate of *dharma, artha* and *kāma* (*trivarga*) secures welfare and happiness. However, the desire (*kāma*) and material wealth (*artha*) must be rejected if contrary to *dharma*."

The *Arthashāstra*, however, the first surviving treatise on politics and economy, or what can be called political economy, in India and, perhaps the world, is usually attributed to Kautilya (c. 350–275 BCE),[10] who is believed to be the minister and the main advisor of Chandragupta Maurya who established the great Maurya empire. Because of its uniqueness as a detailed study of the economy in early India, it is worthwhile discussing it in some detail. This book flatly states that "*artha* alone is primary; for *dharma* and *kāma* are based in *artha*". While this can be interpreted as an attempt to argue for the importance of its content (which is to provide advice to the king or ruler on how to govern and how to manage the economy), it is also possible that Kautilya is referring to the need for some amount of material wellbeing to fulfill emotional and sensual desires, and to live and practice *dharma,* but does not anywhere take the endless pursuit of *artha* as a legitimate goal. A popular view is that Kautilya is interested only in maintaining the power of the king using unscrupulous and unethical methods opposed to *dharma*, and wants the economy to flourish to extract more tax revenue not out of moral duty, and to make the people contented to obtain their political support, that is, to help the king's self-interest and self-aggrandizement (Johnston 1929: 79). This view finds support from Sen (1987: 4), who distinguishes between two strands of economics, one stressing ethics, which dates back to Aristotle, for which the pursuit of wealth and money-making is not the good which people seek but is only instrumental for human flourishing and leading a life that is ethically good, and the other, engineering, approach which his concerned primarily with logistical issues taking the ends to be fairly straightforwardly given, and takes Kautilya to be an early exemplar of the latter. More recently it has been suggested using philological analysis that the original text, probably written by Kautilya, is more secular-aristocratic and advocates a foreign policy of realpolitik and a domestic politics with a high degree of secrecy of the deliberations of the king's council, the use of spies and assassinations and a pragmatic utilitarian view of religion and ethics, and a later version that was added in the first century CE that is more Brahminical (McClish 2009). This version adds what Misra (2016, 316) calls a "distinctively 'dharmic'" element to the text—that is, one that was both moralistic and justified the hierarchical division of society according to the *varṇa*

[10] Whether or not he is the actual author of this book, is subject to controversy, and it has also been argued that the extant version contains material that was added perhaps a few centuries after the first version (McClish 2009).

system. The *varṇadharma* is included, it is made clear that it is the duty of the king to uphold it, *dharma* takes precedence over *artha*, and Brahmins have special privileges within the state".[11]

Although the issue of dating is relevant for interpreting historical conditions and the ascendancy of Brahmanism and its stress on *varṇa* as a tool to enhance power, the argument that the extant treatise (which may incorporate revisions) deemphasizes *dharma* does not hold water. This is clear that despite claiming the primacy of *artha*, the text views it own subjects—*vārttā* (the science of the means of livelihood, such as agriculture and trade) and *dandanīti* (or the science of politics and power in terms of internal and external security)—as a part of a broader science which also includes *ānvīksikī* (or philosophy, including the samkhya, yoga and lokayata schools), and the *trayī* (the first three *Vedas*). The treatise views the four sciences as interrelated, and if one of them is eliminated as a field, the considerations relevant to it are not, since without the others, none of them will be complete by itself. Making this argument, Shah (1981) argues that "arthashatra lays down a structure to establish political institutions which are in accordance with dharma". The treatise states that "this science (*arthashastr*a) brings into being and preserves spiritual good, material well-being and enjoyment of pleasure; and destroys spiritual evil, material loss and hatred (ill-will)" (Arthashastra, XV, i. 72) and that "when adharma overwhelms dharma, the King himself will be destroyed" (p.180). The importance of ethics is also shown in the recommendations made by the *Arthashāstra* regarding the training, behavior, general approach and specific duties of the ruler. It states that sense of duty needs to be inculcated in the king, first, through a training in all of the four sciences mentioned earlier and second, the control of the senses. It stresses that the *moral* duty of the king is to protect the people from problems and calamities (Sihag 2009), although it also provides an *instrumental* argument for doing so, that is, that enemies would use such problems and calamities to weaken the king's power. It makes many recommendations for reducing the chances of famines, such as building irrigation and other forms of infrastructure, and of mitigating their effects, such as providing food and seed on concessional terms from royal stores, commandeering private stocks of food for public distribution, distributing income from the hoarded wealth of the rich (even using strong language like causing them to vomit their accumulated wealth), food-for-work programs for building

[11] There are other writings that appear to claim the priority of *artha*. I am grateful to an anonymous referee for drawing my attention to Bhartrihari's statement in his *Niti-shataka* (mentioned earlier) that "[o]ur noble birth may go to the lower regions; our virtues may perish; our moral character may fall as if from a lofty mountain; our family may be consumed by fire; a thunderbolt may strike our might as it were an enemy: let us keep our money, for without this all the collected virtues are but a heap of grass" (Bhartrihari 1886 tr., verse 39), where money is the translation of *artha*. However, earlier in the work, he appears to call this into question where he writes, "O kings! cast off your pride before those who have the inward treasure of wisdom: they are not despoiled by robbers, but their treasure, always increasing, grows greater when it is shared with the needy: not even at the end of the world does it perish … Despise not wise men who have attained to knowledge of the truth. They are not held bound by riches, for they count wealth even as grass." (ibid., verses 16, 17). The quotations come from two different sections of the work, the former entitled 'praise of riches' and the latter, 'praise of wisdom', and may be viewed as incommensurable.

forts and irrigation works, and moving people to areas not affected by famines (Book IV, Chapter III or 18th chapter overall, 298). In general, it recommends many programs to help the destitute and especially he infirm.

What then is the relative importance of, and relationship between the four *puruṣā rthas*? Although it may seem that *artha* and *kāma* are what people actually strive for, whereas *dharma* and *mokṣa* is what they ought to pursue, an idea captured by the distinction between *sreyas* (what is morally good) and *preyas* (what is pleasurable), this view is erroneous, since *kāma* and *artha* can be seen as legitimate goals that should be pursued, though not to excess and not in violation of the other two goals, even *mokṣa*, the highest goal, can be seen as the true happiness people actually seek after pursing the first two goals and finding themselves dissatisfied (see Mohanty 1997, 290). What all this implies is that material prosperity and pleasure are not necessarily inconsistent with the pursuit of *dharma* and following Hindu ethics. Indeed, there are some religious practices that seem to emphasize material goals, such as when prayers to deities such as Durga ask for wealth and Ganesha is believed to be the god who removes obstacles and ensures business success and the Lakshmi is worshipped as the goddess of wealth. However, although the prayers ask for wealth (as well as sons, fame and beauty), they also ask for wisdom, and Ganesha is expected to help with the success of only *worth*y ventures. Even *kāma*, interpreted in the narrower sense of sexual activity, has been celebrated in the Hindu tradition (see Doniger 2009). However, if *artha* and *kāma* are pursued in ways that that violate *dharma*, it is problematic, and become an impediment in the path to *mokṣa*.

This brings us to our main topic of interest, the effect of the goal or attitude of *artha*, as reflected in market activity and the free market system, on ethics, virtues and wellbeing according to the Hindu tradition. Although there are numerous references to the use of money in early texts and some celebration of money-making and trading, they are sporadic, since the market system was yet to develop in early India, when the Hindu ideas on ethics first emerged, there is little explicit discussion of this question. However, we may draw on our earlier discussion of Hindu ethics to make some speculative comments on the issue, return to the *Arthashāstra*, and examine the views of Gandhi.

Starting with *dharma*, we saw that several virtues and duties are emphasized as major elements of ethics, some of them are more or less relevant for some people (those in different *ā sramas*) and groups (such as *varṇas*) and *artha* is relevant mainly for the householder and the *Vaishya*, which circumscribes the real of economic and market activity. Some others are universal virtues and duties, including truthfulness, friendliness, compassion, humility and forgiveness apply to all. As we saw earlier, the precise meaning of these terms is not clear and virtues relate not just to actions but also motivations (as discussed in the *Gītā* regarding charity) and attitudes (see Potter 1963). We also saw that the ideal of *mokṣa* provides a way of interpreting and prioritizing different virtues, stressing especially the importance of duty with detachment and unselfishness, that is, without concern for the consequences for oneself. The practice of *dharma* guided by the ideal of *mokṣa* makes a person more virtuous, but also makes it more likely that a person will flourish in the sense of progressing towards the ideal and over time become more virtuous.

Market activity, such as trading, production and consumption, does not necessarily involve motives and actions that are driven by money-making and selfishness. For instance, people engaging in these activities may be motivated by wanting to help others (providing jobs or making necessary goods and services available to people), to fulfil the basic needs of themselves and their families, to obtain money to donate to the less fortunate, or be driven by a creative urge to produce something that results in what has been referred to by Csikszentmihalyi (1990) as flow, an activity that is done for its own sake (rather than for monetary reward) and one forgets oneself. However, motives of actions and attitudes are usually mixed, and what primarily motivates people may not even be known to them. In terms of specific virtues, it can be claimed that market activity can make a person more courageous (by starting new ventures), more prudent (by learning how to be financially responsible), more compassionate (towards people one comes into contact with as workers and buyers, due to interactions with them), and more truthful (since getting a reputation for dishonesty is bad for business and for trust, which is necessary for successful market activities).[12] While some of these effects may exist, market activity and the profit motive can make people less prudent especially if they are protected by lax bankruptcy laws, less compassionate if they are find themselves working against competitors and if they gain at the expense of people they transact with (such as workers and customers), become more dishonest by engaging in deceptive business and trading practices, and become more courageous in promoting dishonest ventures. That both positive and negative effects can occur is not surprising, because there are many differences between the nature of market interactions (face-to-face versus more impersonal, repeated or sporadic), the kinds of goods and service being traded, asymmetries in power between parties involved in the activity, the nature of business organizations and their scale, and institutional aspects of markets including social norms and laws. Moreover, and of great importance for Hindu ethics, there are differences in motives and attitudes: an attitude that emphasizes money-making and selfish motives in market (or, for that matter, any other kind of) activity, can stand in the way of virtue and flourishing, even taking into account possible changes in attitudes and motives caused by engaging in activities.[13] It is likely that the market system, especially if it is relatively unregulated, is more likely to lead to behavior contrary to *dharma* and the pursuit of *mokṣa* than just isolated market activity. This is because unethical norms are more likely to emerge and enter into areas of

[12] McCloskey (2006), makes some of these claims for all of the seven cardinal and theological virtues listed in Christian sources, such as prudence, moderation, courage and fortitude.

[13] These issues are typically ignored by those who argue or try to empirically demonstrate that markets have positive effects on ethical values. For instance, as mentioned earlier, McCloskey (2006), makes one-sided claims without discussing possible negative effects of market activity on virtues. Choi and Storr, 2019, present empirical results suggesting a positive relation between markets and ethics using cross country data on things like charitable donations, trust and materialism to represent ethics (ignoring motivations other than problematic self-reported ones) and taking market versus non-market systems as a binary variable (ignoring differences within market economies and non-market economies) without adequately (and sometimes, not at all) controlling for other influences on ethics. See Dutt and Wilber (2010), for a discussion of some of these complications.

life not previously in the purview of markets in market systems, given the size and importance of market transactions and shared acceptance of commodification and monetary valuation of things and even people.

The relentless pursuit of wealth, status and pleasure is likely to lead to attachment to monetary rewards, selfishness, and loss of self-control. Moreover, performing activities to achieve *artha* or *kāma* may pose stronger challenges compared to other activities, for instance, study and scholarship and in the performing and visual arts, or social (service) work, although these too may eventually involve selfish and goals in terms of glory and financial rewards. These ideas are reflected in the psychological analysis of the *Sāmkhya* school (see Chakkarath 2005) which sees the world in dualistic terms, distinguishing between *prakriti* (nature) and *purusha* (self, pure consciousness, eternal and unchanging). It also focuses on the three *gunas* (qualities although not necessarily in a judgmental sense) that are parts of *prakriti* but do not touch the *purusha,* that is, *sattva* (joy, illumination, balance, purity, virtue), *rajas* (vibrant energy, passion, dynamism, activity, self-centeredness) and *tāmas* (destruction, imbalance, violence, viciousness, anxiety, delusion, sloth) which motivate a person to action. Everyone and, indeed everything, has these qualities, but they do so in different proportions and contexts and may also change over time due to internal and external influences (or the social and natural environment). Physical events involve changes in *prakriti*, or unconscious matter, which includes not only inanimate objects but also the body, intellect, mind and the ego, and each sentient being or (*jiva*) is a fusion of *prakriti* and *purusha.* Consciousness comes when such matter is illuminated by the *purusha*, that is, the self within a person can separate itself from the *prakriti* within it and ultimately identify itself with the universal self or *brahman*. In this quest, it stands to reason that an excessive focus on *artha* and *kāma* guided by selfish and financial motives will increase *rajas* and, eventually, *tāmas* at the expense of *sattva*, creating obstacles on the path to true happiness. Again, as for *dharma*, this is more likely in relatively unregulated market systems than in isolated market activities.

The ideas of *Arthashāstra* discussed earlier not only reveal its engagement with ethics, but also its advocacy of various kinds of state activity in the economy. However, it is clearly not against business, markets and trading activities, which it viewed as not only promoting the wellbeing of the people but also for yielding revenue to support the state's activities. It argues for the encouragement of foreign trade, for instance, by awarding tax rebates to importers of foreign goods to increase their profits (p. 138). However, it also states that "traders, artisans, …, and other idlers who are … thieves, in effect, if not in name, shall be restrained from oppressing the country" (Book IV, Chapter I, p. 290). It points out that traders unite to seek to raise prices for things they sell and reduce them for things they buy (Book VIII, Chapter IV, 458) and recognizes that artisans, craftsmen and merchants try to produce and sell low quality products, adulterate, provide false descriptions in selling, and recommended stiff fines (see Sihag 2009, 90). Sihag argues that these and other statements suggest that Kautilya has a claim to being the true founder of economics and that (or because) he anticipated many of the ideas of modern mainstream or neoclassical economics, including the notion of state intervention to overcome what are now called market failures. While these claims are controversial, not least because Kautilya's ideas focus on ethical failings and distributional issues and not on their consequences for the efficient functioning of markets as in neoclassical economics, Sihag's examples show that Kautilya was well aware of the fact that those who were involved in markets were susceptible to ethical lapses, which has a direct bearing on the question of how market activity affects ethical values. It is worth emphasizing, however, that Kautilya was also quite cognizant of the possibility that government officials misappropriate money and become rich at the expense of the people, and even criticizes decadent kings who fail to protect people from thieves and robs them himself, idolizing the *rājarṣi* or king-sage who has self-control, conquers temptation, and avoids daydreaming, capriciousness, falsehood and extravagance.

Two millennia later, by which time the market system had already emerged, Gandhi's views on economics and markets were based firmly on his ethics. Gandhi (1921, 24:415) wrote that "I do not draw a sharp or any distinction between economics and ethics", and his ethics were related to the concept of *dharma*, which required individuals do their duty to society, and in economic issues this led to his advocacy of *swadeshi* (self-sufficiency), his opposition to a high degree of mechanization and large-scale production when small-scale production with less mechanization are sufficient, the development of villages, employment creation, the reduction of poverty and inequality, including those along gender and caste lines and to *sarvodaya*, or the uplift or welfare of all.

This adherence to ethics made him view of markets with skepticism, leading him to opine that "the law of supply and demand is not a human law, it is a devilish law" (Gandhi 1936, 68:277). Although this may appear to involve hyperbole, his meaning is quite clear from the context in which he says this: that choice based on self-interest, profits, costs and markets will result in the replacement of the bullock cart by the motor car which is cheaper, but this will adversely affect the population of cattle, which for him was a mainstay of the rural economy, which goes against the ethical principle of choosing what is good for society and the village economy as a whole. Elsewhere he argues that market choices based on cost and due to the manipulation of preferences by corporations lead to people buying machine-made cloth rather than that made from home-spun or home-woven cloth or *khādi*, which implies the loss of income and employment for handicraft workers; he recommended that cadres of the Indian National Congress (the party which was at the vanguard of the Indian independence movement, and of which Gandhi, for a long period, was the main leader) become salesmen of *khādi* and he made the *charkha* (spinning wheel) his symbol.[14] The market system has often been praised for generating faster economic growth in terms of average income. However, Gandhi took the view that ever-expanding production is not desirable. He wrote that "if you have one room

[14] It can be argued that the problem here is not with the market itself but with materialism and self-interest. But, as discussed earlier, arguably markets and especially the market system, by shifting the motivations of people towards making profits for themselves and minimizing costs (through competitive forces and changes in social norms), is likely to strengthen these characteristics among people.

you will desire to have two rooms, three rooms, the more the merrier. And similarly, you will have to have much furniture as you can put in your house and go on endlessly" (Gandhi 1931, 53:398). This kind of materialism and self-centeredness is only contrary to human flourishing in the Hindu sense, but is also supported by empirical findings that (at least beyond a point) increases in income do not lead to increases in self-reported happiness and subjective wellbeing (Easterlin 2017). For him, economic growth through mechanization had the danger of not only causing unemployment and increasing inequality, but also of distancing the worker from production, although he recognized the benefits of mechanization for making work less onerous, in improving public health and in the production of goods such as locomotives and steel which needs large scale, mechanized processes.

Gandhi's skepticism regarding markets did not make him a strong advocate of state intervention in the economy, which he viewed as coercive. Gandhi (1934, 65:318) argued that "the State represents violence in a concentrated and organized form. The individual has a soul, but as the State is a soulless machine, it can never be weaned from violence to which it owes its very existence." Thus, his primary focus was on how individuals can change and improve without external coercion. This is illustrated by his view that *khādi* should be promoted not by the use of coercive government policy but "by changing people's sense of values and habits" (Gandhi 1941, 81:41). He also recommended that inequality be addressed not by the confiscation of productive capital by the state, but a system of trusteeship, according to which "the wealthy class was to hold their riches in trust and use them for the service of Society" voluntarily, although if the rich refuse to behave as trustees, sanctions could be imposed, both through nonviolent noncooperation or, if absolutely necessary, through confiscation by the state (Gandhi 1935, 65:318).

6.5 Conclusion

While much has been written about the relation between religion and the economy and some of it is devoted to Hinduism, the discussion of how markets affect wellbeing by affecting ethical values is much more limited. There have been some recent attempts to examine how markets affects ethical values, but to the best of my knowledge the influence of markets on ethics and wellbeing for the case of Hinduism, has not been examined.

This paper has examined the nature of Hinduism as a religion and discussed some of its central ideas, ethics as found in Hinduism, especially its main classical texts, and the effects of markets and economic activity on human wellbeing interpreted as human flourishing. Its main conclusions are as follows.

1. Hinduism is not a religion in the standard Western sense, but an amalgam of different approaches and ideas. However, some key elements within most of the approaches can be identified, which focus on the karma doctrine and *mokṣa*.

2. Although it has been argued that there is no such thing, there actually is a large literature on Hindu ethics in discussions on *dharma* especially seen in conjunction with *mokṣa*, which represents the ultimate good.
3. Hindu ethics comes closest to what is called virtue ethics, but does not ignore deontological and consequentialist perspectives. The concept of *mokṣa* can be seen as referring to human flourishing in a dynamic sense, and represents true happiness and human wellbeing.
4. There is no necessary inconsistency between economic and market activity and Hindu ethics, since such activity is seen as having legitimate goals.
5. However, economic and market activity, when it violates the dictates of *dharma*, is inconsistent with Hindu ethics, and can be particularly problematic in the pursuit of *mokṣa*. The problems are more severe in market systems, especially those with markets relatively unregulated by the state.

The issues raised in the paper are not only of antiquarian interest, but also of great relevance to the broader discussion of the relationship between freer markets and human flourishing, and also of political-economic interest in contemporary India, in which the vast majority of people are counted as followers of Hinduism, and where the role of religion has arguably increased in recent years, especially with the rise of the Bharatiya Janata Party. Paradoxically, however, in this, Hinduism is viewed more in terms of nationalism based on geographical indigeneity and culture, rather than on its approach to ethics. The older divide in Indian political economy was between Western-inspired Enlightenment rationalism and an elitist perspective represented by Jawaharlal Nehru, India's first prime minister, and traditional Indian culture based on religion and morality and a subaltern perspective, as represented by Gandhi. The rise of Hindutva can be interpreted as its replacement by a divide between a materialist, pragmatic and amoral perspective that is—arguably somewhat misleadingly—rooted in the writings of Kautliya and the older moralistic approach shared by both the proponents of the earlier divide (Misra 2016). The question remains whether Hinduism will in the future be interpreted in nationalistic terms or in terms of its ethical ideas.

References

Anderson, Gary M. 1988. Mr. Smith and the Preachers: The Economics of Religion in the Wealth of Nations. *Journal of Political Economy* 96 (5): 1066–1088.

Berger, Peter. 2014. *Many Altars of Modernity*. Boston/Berlin: De Gruyter.

Bhartrihari. 1886. *The Satakas of Bhartrihari*. Translated by B. Hale Wortham. Routledge repr. 2000.

Bilmoria, Purushottam, Joseph Prabhu, and Renuka Sharma. 2007. General Introduction: Thinking Ethics, the West and India. In *Indian Ethics, Classical Traditions and Contemporary Challenges*, ed. P. Bilmoria, J. Prabhu, and R. Sharma, vol. 1, 1–31. Aldershot: Ashgate.

Chakkarath, Pradeep. 2005. What Can Western Psychology Learn from Indigenous Psychologies? Lessons from Hindu Psychology. In *Culture and Human Development: The Importance of Cross-Cultural Research for the Social Sciences*, ed. W. Friedelmeier, P. Chakkarath, and B. Schwartz. Hove: Psychology Press.

Chang, Ha-Joon. 2007. *Bad Samaritans*. London: Bloomsbury Press.
Csikszentmihalyi, Mihaly. 1990. *Flow: The Psychology of Optimal Experience*. London: Harper Collins.
Doniger, Wendy. 2009. *The Hindus: An Alternative History*, Penguin, London and New York
Dutt, Amitava Krishna. 2010. Religion and Development Ethics: The Case of Hinduism. In *New Directions in Development Ethics: Essays in Honor of Denis Goulet*, ed. Charles Wilber and Amitava Dutt, 113–141. Notre Dame: University of Notre Dame Press.
Dutt, Amitava Krishna, and Charles Wilber. 2010. *Economics and Ethics: An Introduction*. Palgrave: Basingstoke/New York.
Easterlin, Richard A. 2017. Paradox Lost? *Review of Behavioral Economics*. 4:311–339.
Gandhi, Mohandas Karamchand. 1999. *The Collected Works of Mahatma Gandhi*, Electronic Book; 98 Volumes. New Delhi: Publications Division Government of India.
Iyer, Sriya. 2018. *The Economics of Religion in India*. Cambridge, MA: The Belknap Press of the Harvard University Press.
Johnston, E. H. 1929. Two Studies in the Arthasastra of Kautilya. *Journal of the Royal Economic Society* 61 (1): 77–102.
Koller, John M. 1968. Purusārthas as Human Aims. *Philosophy East and West* 18 (4): 315–319.
Krishna, Daya. 2007. The Myth ā of the Ethics of *Purusārtha* or Humanity's Life Goals. In *Indian Ethics, Classical Traditions and Contemporary Challenges*, ed. P. Bilmoria, J. Prabhu, and R. Sharma, vol. 1, 103–115. Aldershot: Ashgate.
Kuran, Timur. 2004. Cultural Obstacles to Economic Development: Often Overstated, Usually Transitory. In *Culture and Public Action*, ed. Vijayendra Rao and Michael Walton, 71–90. Stanford Social Science: Stanford.
Manu. (c. 100 CE). *Manusmriti*.
Matilal, Bimal Krishna. 2002. Moral Dilemmas: Insights from Indian Epics. In *The Collected Essays of Bimal Krishna Matilal: Ethics and Epics*, ed. J. Ganeri, 19–35. Oxford: New Delhi.
Matilal, Bimal Krishna. 2007. Dharma and Rationality. In *Indian Ethics, Classical Traditions and Contemporary Challenges*, ed. P. Bilmoria, J. Prabhu, and R. Sharma, vol. 1, 79–102. Aldershot: Ashgate.
McClish, M. R. 2009. *Political Brahmanism and the State: A Cosmopolitan History of the Arthsasatra*. PhD thesis. Austin: University of Texas.
McCloskey, Deirdre. 2006. *The Bourgeois Virtues. Ethics for an Age of Commerce*. Chicago: University of Chicago Press.
Misra, Maria. 2016. The Indian Machiavelli: Pragmatism Versus Morality, and the Reception of the *Arthasastra* in India, 1905-2014. *Modern Asian Studies* 50 (1): 310–344.
Mohanty, J. N. 1997. The Idea of the Good in Indian Thought. In *A Companion to World Philosophies*, ed. Eliot Deutsch and Ron Bontekoe, 290–303. Wiley.
Mohanty, J. N. 2007. *Dharma*, Imperatives, and Tradition: Toward an Indian Theory of Moral Action. In *Indian Ethics, Classical Traditions and Contemporary Challenges*, ed. P. Bilmoria, J. Prabhu, and R. Sharma, vol. 1, 57–78. Aldershot: Ashgate.
Morris, Morris D. 1967. Values as an Obstacle to Economic Growth in South Asia: An Historical Survey. *Journal of Economic History* 27 (4): 588–607.
Nadkarni, M. V. 2011. *Ethics for Our Times. Essays in Gandhian Perspective*. Delhi: Oxford University Press.
Potter, Karl H. 1963. *Presuppositions of India's Philosophies*. Reprinted, Delhi: Motilal Banarasidas, 1991.
Sen, Amartya. 1987. *On Ethics and Economics*. Oxford: Basil Blackwell.
Sen, Amartya. 1999. *Development as Freedom*. New York: Alfred A. Knopf.
Sen, Amartya. 2007. *Identity and Violence: The Illusion of Destiny*. New Delhi: Penguin Books India.
Sen, Amartya. 2009. *The Idea of Justice*. London: Penguin.
Shah, K. J. 1981. Of artha and the *Arthasāstra*. *Contributions to Indian Sociology* 15 (1–2): 55–73.

Sihag, Balbir S. 2009. Kautilya on Moral, Market and Government Failures. *International Journal of Hindu Studies* 18 (1): 83–102.

Storr, Virgil Henry, and Ginny Seung Choi. 2019. *Do Markets Corrupt Our Morals?* Cham: Palgrave Macmillan.

Weber, Max. 1905. *The Protestant Ethic and the Spirit of Capitalism*. Translated and edited by Talcott Parsons. London: Allen and Unwin, 1930.

Weber, Max. 1916. *The Religion of India*. Translated and Edited by Hans H. Gerth and Don Martindale. Glencoe: Free Press, 1958.

Weber, Max. 1919. Science as a Vocation. In *From Max Weber*, ed. C. Wright Mills and H. H. Gerth, 129–156. Oxford/New York: Oxford University Press, 1946.

Amitava Krishna Dutt is professor emeritus of economics and political science at the University of Notre Dame. Professor Dutt's areas of specialization are macroeconomic theory, development economics, international economics, political economy and economics and ethics. His current research focuses on global uneven development and globalization, models of growth and distribution, consumption and happiness and the political economy inequality.

Chapter 7
Weber, Individualism and Hindu Modernity

Victor van Bijlert

Abstract Weber's contribution on the rise of capitalism remains a helpful tool with which to analyze the mentality of (Western) modernity as such. This chapter explores modernity as individual and collective emancipation. Western Protestantism (in different garbs) may have globally instilled a pronounced mentality of individual choice and collective emancipation. Protestantism seems to equal modernity, if we follow the Weberian idea of the latter to its logical conclusion. As a tool it is helpful to understand the emergence of what we may term Hindu modernity. This term is very broad and within the context of nineteenth century colonial India refers to an extremely influential innovation begun by Raja Rammohun Roy (1772–1833). In Rammohun's writings and socio-religious activism we can trace the relative validity of the modernity thesis on Protestantism also for 'reformed and innovated' Hinduism. It is shown how Weber's concept of Protestantism (understood as the strong internalization of a certain religious mentality) can help interpret the process of modernization and innovation in Hinduism of the last one and half centuries.

Keywords Modernity · Economic ethics · Hinduism · Individualism · Protestantism

7.1 Introduction

Weber's thesis on Protestantism and the spirit of capitalism has often been defended and criticized, so much so that many consider it to be finally refuted. This may be partially correct for the specific thesis of Protestantism and modern capitalism, but if we enlarge the scope to encompass the mentality of (Western) modernity as such, Weber's contribution still seems helpful as a tool with which to analyze the latter. In

V. van Bijlert (✉)
Vrije Universiteit, Amsterdam, Netherlands

G. J. Buijs, J. J. Ballor (eds.), *In Search of the Spirits of Capitalism*, Sophia Studies in Cross-cultural Philosophy of Traditions and Cultures 44,
https://doi.org/10.1007/978-3-032-01137-4_7

this chapter we will look at modernity as individual and collective emancipation. Western Protestantism (in different garbs) may have globally instilled a pronounced mentality of individual choice and collective emancipation. Protestantism seems to equal modernity, if we follow the Weberian idea of the latter to its logical conclusion. As a tool it is helpful to understand the emergence of what we may term Hindu modernity. This term is very broad and within the context of nineteenth century colonial India refers to an extremely influential innovation begun by Raja Rammohun Roy (1772–1833).[1] In Rammohun's writings and socio-religious activism we can trace the relative validity of the modernity thesis on Protestantism also for 'reformed and innovated' Hinduism. We will try to show how Weber's concept of Protestantism (understood as the strong internalization of a certain religious mentality) can help interpret the process of modernization and innovation in Hinduism of the last one and half centuries. But in order to do this, we have to first direct our attention to the alleged Christian origins of Western modernity in general and modern Hinduism.

7.2 Modernity as State of Mind

Modernity as a global normative mentality is characterized by respect for the autonomy of the individual person, the physical inviolability of the person's body, and freedom for the individual to develop his or her talents and be able to flourish. All these can also be demanded for groups of individuals, for peoples, and for nations. Thus modernity has an individual and a collective aspect. But the flourishing of the collective is predicated upon the freedom and autonomy of the individual. This presupposes the collective acceptance of the liberty and equality of the individuals that make up the collectivity. Ideally a modern emancipated collectivity (be it region or state) consists of emancipated self-conscious and autonomous individual members of the collectivity and these members have put in place systems of decision-making in which everyone has an equal say. This normative mentality of modernity we may regard as strong moral beliefs held by many. Thus modernity is not primarily about tremendous technological advancements, new architecture, the instalment of rapid forms of transport or the mass production of consumption goods, not even about institutions like the nation-state or general elections. Modernity is primarily a mentality that informs the creation of these visible phenomena. It starts in the human mind, in the mind that is fundamentally changed and opened up to new unprecedented forms of thinking, to imagining novel possibilities of living. Modernity is the moral belief in the equal worth of all human beings, the belief that all human beings must be treated with the same respect and that they all have the right to fully flourish in freedom.

[1] For details about the life of Rammohun see Dobson Collet 1988. On Rammohun's influence on both India and England see Zastoupil 2010.

To many such ideas may seem self-evident truths, but they are by no means held universally and they certainly were not held at all times. That they are widespread is the result of historical processes. Nowadays, these ideas and moral beliefs would be considered to be secular in nature. They are deemed progressive and therefore are probably unrelated to religious traditions, for the latter are often seen as conservative and even oppressive. Secular moral beliefs and practices like treating everyone equally may not be what conservative religions and politics would endorse. Hence, searching for the lineage of modernity one would not in the first place think of religious notions and traditions. And yet this seems precisely the domain where the mentality of modernity originated. Larry Siedentop (2015) has argued this case for what we may term Western modernity. Siedentop traces more in particular how the individual "became the organizing social role in the West," the emergence of civil society and "the characteristic distinction between public and private spheres and its emphasis on the role of conscience and choice" (Siedentop 2015, 2). These were not rediscovered, Siedentop argues, by the Enlightenment in a somewhat spurious return to Greek and Roman Antiquity; rather, they were the outcome of more than one and a half millennium of Christianity. Siedentop's historical sketch leaves out Weber. However, we might say that Weber's spirit hovers over Siedentop's idea: Christianity fundamentally influenced and altered European culture, and accomplished this through the power of (religious) ideas and doctrines.

Those with postmodern and postcolonial leanings could object to the thesis that modernity owes many of its characteristics to Western Christianity. For it seems to suggest that values of modernity such as individual autonomy, and individual and collective emancipation from oppressive forms of tradition or alien rule are of European origin and did not emerge in any other culture but the Western Christian one. This certainly sounds Eurocentric. Furthermore, Western Christianity was often the handmaid of various forms of oppression from the medieval crusades to the Western colonial expansion from the fifteenth century onwards until quite recently. Thus, to suggest that Western Christianity produced emancipatory values and no-one else is uninformed and hypocritical to say the least, it may even reveal a spirit of white colonial feeling of superiority. The criticism is valid. As the Indian social theorist Partha Chatterjee once remarked in connection with Benedict Anderson's thesis on the imagined community that is the modern nation-state:

> History, it would seem, has decreed that we in the postcolonial world shall only be perpetual consumers of modernity. Europe and the Americas, the only true subjects of history, have thought out on our behalf not only the script of colonial enlightenment and exploitation, but also that of our anticolonial resistance … Even our imaginations must remain forever colonized. (Chatterjee 1993, 5)

This criticism was levelled against historical interpretations of anticolonial nationalism, thus it addresses Western ideas of historiography; but it could be levelled against any theoretical interpretation of non-Western modernity (granted such a phenomenon exists).

Within the context of Siedentop's thesis about the origins of the idea of the autonomous individual, we could critique this by pointing out that the values of modernity which Siedentop extracts from Christianity can be extracted from other religions as well. In other words, the idea that modernity is of Western origin should be falsified, and it can be falsified. Indian Hinduism of the early nineteenth century offers interesting examples of this. The outcome of this Hinduism is not the perpetuation of some pure, regional tradition unsullied by Western influences but an interesting case of Hindu self-realization that has led to modernity in a mode different from the Western one in details but similar in overall effect. What the Indian Hindu case also shows, is the religious origin of this modernity, in much the same way as Siedentop has traced the origins of Western modernity in Christianity. In order to trace the genealogy of parts of Indian modernity, one has to look at the particulars of the Hindu reform movement that started in the early nineteenth century. It reveals a condensed and shortened trajectory that is comparable to the Western trajectory to modernity via the Reformation in the sixteenth century and the Enlightenment in the late seventeenth and the eighteenth centuries. What took Western Europe almost three centuries was accomplished in India in less than a century. Or to put it differently: Europe needed four centuries to modernize itself, India did this in less than a century with comparable outcomes. Europe ended up with independent nation-states, many of them constitutional republics by the end of Word War I, India ended up a secular constitutional republic after World War II.

7.3 "Protestantization" of Hinduism

Terms like *religion*, *scripture*, *Hinduism*, even *Protestantization*, are useful terminological tools to denote certain phenomena which we know exist somehow, even if not in an exact definable way. We could probably use these terms while constantly keeping in mind that in connection with Indian religious traditions summarized under the heading *Hinduism* they designate phenomena which look like religion, or like a scripture, or like Protestantism. These terms act mostly metaphorically, not literally. They are not exact but seem to work and convey some meaning. Of course, it would be unscientific dogmatism to claim these terms denote precisely definable facts with an exactly matching counterpart in Christianity (or Islam for that matter). Protestantization in relation to Hinduism does not designate exactly the same historical given as the rise of Protestantism in Western Europe in the early sixteenth century. Protestantism in Hinduism refers to something akin to the Western Christian Reformation in some important ways and seems to have led to somewhat similar outcomes as Protestantism has led to in Europe. But there are differences as well, and these must not be ignored or overlooked.

In Hinduism there is no counterpart of the Roman Catholic Church with an ecclesiastical hierarchy and a centralized network of churches. Hinduism is difficult to define, as can be gathered also from Amitava Dutts' contribution in this volume, but to anyone who has lived with Hindus for some time it is clear that ritual, conformity to certain patterns of ritual behavior, adherence to rules of maintaining ritual purity, taboos on what to touch with what part of the body, vegetarianism or no vegetarianism, showing respect to images of Hindu gods are all components of everyday Hindu life. Being Hindu is mostly about adhering to local customs, local rituals, local deities, local holy places, local temples. All these are recognizable as belonging to Hinduism in a very vague way but the local details and numerous variations give the impression that there is no unity in Hinduism. Some things may be quite similar everywhere, like *caste*, *gotra*, *varna*, and the Brahmin *pandit*. Still Hinduism looks like fragmented local and regional forms of orthopraxis and 'ortho-conformity.' There is no thing like 'orthodoxy' because the latter indicates right doctrine and right belief, but lived day-to-day Hinduism is not characterized by explicit beliefs or creeds but by conformity (often without knowing and without asking questions) to ritual practices. Most Hindus do not and need not cognitively 'know' about doctrines or Hindu 'scriptures.' There are some narratives that bind Hindus together, like the epics Mahabharata and Ramayana. However, their stories are widely known but not directly through widespread knowledge of their Sanskrit 'originals.' Rather, the narratives are known often only orally in vernacular versions that are not exact translations of the Sanskrit versions. This shows that Hinduism has defining narratives like these two epics, but no fixed scriptures to which one could always return and that are universal. Basically Hinduism is what local communities and families think it is and what they have always practiced by way of family rituals, public festivals and pilgrimages. But there is no fixed set of pan-Hindu doctrines or a pan-Hindu creed. Taking all these facts into consideration, Hinduism doesn't resemble the Christianity of for instance the Roman Catholic Church. If this is granted, then what is Hindu Protestantism and how can we meaningfully use this term?

We can trace the origin of Hindu 'Protestantism' to the Bengali Brahmin thinker Rammohun Roy who set the tone for what was to become Hindu Protestantism.[2] It is perhaps more accurate to call Rammohun's intervention a form of limited Hindu innovation, rather than a reformation of all of Hinduism practiced throughout the Indian Subcontinent. This is for several reasons. First, because he limited his Hinduism to Vedanta spirituality.[3] He did not reform Hinduism from a degenerated form back to a pristine original form. Vedanta never was the original Hinduism but a special form of ancient Hinduism, a special stream within it. Second, Rammohun propagated the study of the main texts of Vedanta by publishing his own vernacular translations of some of the Upanishads, the oldest sources of Vedanta. This may look Protestant but at the same time, these texts did not represent the bible of Hinduism. Rammohun made them into the bible of his brand of new Vedanta

[2] In the sequel we will refer to Rammohun Roy simply as Rammohun, thus following a custom in Indian writing in English to refer to such well-known figures by their first name.

[3] The term Vedanta is used in a perhaps somewhat loose way, referring to the ideas found primarily in the Upanishads, in the Bhagavad Gita, and in the Brahma Sutra. Vedanta is not meant to refer strictly to a particular Hindu theological school. Even though Rammohun based his interpretations of these texts on the commentaries of Shankara, he also took some distance to the Hindu sociological implications of Shankara's writings. Throughout the nineteenth and the twentieth century it is not wrong to refer to Vedanta as the loosely designated ideology/theology/soteriology derived from the above-mentioned texts.

Hinduism. Third, Rammohun copied the Protestant church model to organize his Vedanta innovation in a congregational form. This part of the innovation was not very successful as far as attracting voluntary membership to his Vedantic church. The first and second innovations met with greater success because that mode has in fact determined the popular perception of modern Hinduism as a whole. It is well to stress once more that Rammohun propagated Vedanta, that is, the Upanishads, as Hindu scriptures *par excellence*; and that his idea of real Hinduism was a religion based on the teachings of the Upanishads and thus relatively free from all kinds of elaborate Hindu rituals. Vedanta could be adhered to voluntarily by anyone who felt attraction for its teaching and spirituality. For more than a century this perception has persisted of Vedanta as the pinnacle of Hinduism (free from ritual and inhuman customs but full of high philosophy and spirituality) and it is around even to this day. It was Rammohun and his followers who thought that Hinduism ought to be founded—anew in a way—on the Upanishads, and that Vedanta constituted the paramount meta-theology of Hinduism as a whole. Hence the propagation of the Upanishads to which later on the Bhagavad Gita was added, as the scriptures of Hinduism.

7.4 A Modern Hindu Canon

An important step in the direction of renewal of Hinduism along Vedantic lines was the dissemination in printed form of its basic texts, that is, the Upanishads and the Bhagavad Gita. Most editions (to this day) were bilingual in that the original Sanskrit was added to the vernacular translation. These printed editions of Upanishads and Bhagavad Gita were the Hindu answer to the Christian missionaries' promoting the bible in Indian languages. Hindu Protestantism really boils down to propagating among practicing upper-caste urbanized Hindus the study and spirituality of classical Vedantic texts, texts with which such Hindus were not at all familiar. Yet the texts were also reinterpreted to meet the social challenges of the times. One could call the Hindu Protestantization perhaps with equal validity a modernizing revival of Vedanta philosophy, theology and spirituality, an amalgam of ancient and modern that was distinctly different from and alien to the everyday practice of lived Hinduism (especially in the rural areas into which this Vedantist revival cum reform never reached).

Rammohun was the first to have an idea of a Hindu canon of limited size and somewhat comparable to the New Testament or the Qur'an. His demand of a Hindu canon was that it would promulgate a monotheistic theology, be free from elaborate ritual, and emphasize personal spiritual growth. An extra benefit of an ideal Hindu canon would also be that it should be free from specific narratives highlighting specific Hindu gods or divine heroes. The texts should be of high antiquity, bear great cultural and religious authority and be appropriate to showcase to outsiders as well, for also outsiders should be able to admire these texts. Rammohun propagated Vedantic texts as the Hindu canon, precisely because they more or less fulfilled these exigencies.[4] The Vedantic texts had some added benefits. They were already commented upon by the great Hindu theologian Shankara in the eight century CE, and their ideas could be recognized within a wealth of later Hindu texts such as the epics Mahabharata and Ramayana, and the numerous Puranas. Moreover, the Upanishads were regarded as part of the Vedas, the oldest Hindu texts in Sanskrit. The choice for the Upanishads was further animated by the fact that Europeans (and even the Moghul prince Dara Shikoh before them) admired the philosophy and theology of the Upanishads. With hindsight Rammohun's rediscovery and promotion of the Upanishads (and in its wake the promulgation of the Bhagavad Gita as well) seems to have been a natural and most obvious choice for an innovation of Hinduism. The ideas of Vedantic texts indeed lend themselves very well to modernizing interpretations without having to use a hermeneutical sledge-hammer to make these texts say the things a modern reformer wants them to say. Some of the ideas of the Upanishads seem to coincide very well with modernity as a state of mind.

An important issue that Rammohun and those that came after him faced was: how to mobilize people behind this newly found Vedantist/Hindu modern state of mind? There was no Hindu church and thus organizing reformed Hindus in a Hindu church was an innovation unparallelled in traditional Hinduism. Hinduism was not and largely still is not organized in church-like congregational form. Traditional Hinduism is practiced at home, in temples, in large public festivals and pilgrimages to sacred places (including famous temples). But there is nothing like a Hindu church, neither along the Roman Catholic centralized model, nor along the more decentralized and autonomous Protestant models. There is no centrally trained and directed clergy in Hinduism. Rammohun's invention of the Brahmo Samaj (founded in 1828) was a model that later Hindu reformers emulated widely though. Yet the formal membership of these congregations or societies (samajes) was always extremely small, a few thousand nationwide at the most. The church model was not the most effective way to disseminate modernity even if the Hindu reform church, like the Brahmo Samaj attracted wide attention, sympathy and criticism far beyond the actual number of real members. The reform movements were certainly widely talked about. One might say that the Brahmo Samaj and its successor movements exerted a great social charismatic influence without attracting many actual followers. This influence can be attributed more to the movements' publishing of booklets, pamphlets, and magazines, rather than to active recruitment of members.

[4] One might say that Rammohun knew beforehand what his reformed religion ideally should look like and was searching for a proper scripture that would fulfil his needs. This is very much the opposite of Christian Protestantism where the bible is the basis of belief. Here in Rammohun's Hindu Protestantism we have belief in search of a suitable bible.

7.5 World-Renunciation

The unity behind Hinduism—at least that which make people (insiders and outsiders alike) recognize the amalgam of local, regional or supranational practices, rituals, festivals, Gods, sacred texts, social structuring, as forming part of Hinduism—this unity is found in the sociology of Hinduism, not in the accidentals of local traditions.[5] The social hierarchy and the notion of ritual purity belong to the main features of the sociological architecture of Hinduism. Next to this hierarchical notion of Hindu society stands its complement: the total rejection and renunciation of this social structure. To put it succinctly: Hinduism is the binary model of sacred hierarchical social order on the one hand, and the sphere of world-renunciation on the other. Rituals and social order, caste, class, hierarchy, the cults of the different Hindu Gods and Goddesses, these are all the domain of the social moiety of Hinduism.

Spirituality, self-realization, release from suffering, these are the domain of world-renunciation. The world-renouncer is the one who strives for final insight, supreme devotion to God, realization of the Self, intuitive insight in supreme truth, release from rebirth and suffering. The renouncer can only realize such goals by retreating from all social and family ties, obligations and all else that binds him or her to caste, class, gender and concomitant duties. World-renunciation is the sphere in which Hinduism develops its wide variety of philosophies, theologies, soteriologies, private devotions, personal mysticism, religious virtuosity.

World-renunciation for many means the sphere of Hindu monkhood. When renouncers gather as a group they could be regarded as a band of Hindu monks (or nuns as the case may be). Hindu monastic orders are many and as an institution monasticism traces its origins back almost to the times of Buddha. World-renunciation could and still does appear in two modalities: either as solitary world-renouncing ascetics are as initiated members of monastic orders. All great Indian religious leaders from the times of the Upanishads and Buddha onwards were mostly world-renouncers or used the idiom of world-renunciation.[6] Thus renunciation in whatever modality, is the sphere from which spirituality emerges and to which individual seekers after truth and religious meaning can turn. Importantly, one cannot choose one's station in the Hindu social hierarchical order, but one can opt voluntarily for renouncing this order, in other words, to renounce the (Hindu social) world.

---

[5] The problem of real multiplicity and our imposition of unity on it is behind much debate on how to define Hinduism. Louis Dumont has actually proposed this sociological reading of Hinduism, Dumont 1980, 267–286, 425–439. In spite of all the criticism it invited, it seems the theory had got something right, see Michaels 2004, 10–13. For a large collection of Indian critiques of Dumont's approach, cf. Khare 2006.

[6] I am aware that these generalizations are extremely broad and would probably be regarded as undue homogenization of the multiplicity of real life Hinduism. The binary scheme is no more than a helpful instrument to try and make sense of the multiplicity and to provide some context for the Hindu/Vedantic innovation that began with Rammohun.

It is not without significance that Rammohun chose the Upanishads as his new bible of Hinduism. The Upanishads are the earliest texts in which world-renunciation is mentioned as spiritual practice and goal, the sphere in which ultimate truths are revealed.[7] Traditionally it was mostly (Brahmin) world-renouncers who studied and transmitted the Upanishads.[8] Thus the emphasis on the classical Upanishads in the early nineteenth century not only helped innovations of Hinduism, it also implicitly pointed to the sphere of world-renunciation as the sphere from which renewal, private spirituality and innovation should emerge. Since the first millennium in India renunciation had been a dominant element in Hindu religious life. In the words of Olivelle: "In most Hindu sects the renouncer was considered the paradigmatic holy man. These sects were for the most part founded and led by renouncers" (Olivelle 1993, 170).

The Hindu sects were the places or institutions to which one could turn for personal Hindu religious quests, precisely the motivation that drew Rammohun to the Upanishads. But evidently the church model did not provide the answers to personal religious quests. If the dissemination of Upanishadic thought and inspiration was to be successful, it had to return to the model of the traditional Hindu renunciatory sect. Some important figures who followed in Rammohun's ideological innovation were Debendranath Tagore (1817–1905), Bankim Chandra Chatterjee (1838–1894), Swami Vivekananda (1863–1902), Rabindranath Tagore (1861–1941), Sri Aurobindo (1872–1950) and later in the twentieth century even Mahatma Gandhi (1869–1948). In their writings these Hindu thinkers and socio-political activists followed the Vedantic texts that Rammohun had begun to promote and they all utilize the notion of world-renunciation in an informal (non-sectarian) way. This is understandable because (traditional) world-renunciation represents the final break with worldly Hindu social tradition, the break with the past, and it opens up space for renewal and innovation of Hinduism.

There is however a division between these authors. Broadly speaking, those who stressed collective Hindu modernity on the basis of the Bhagavad Gita—especially Bankim Chandra Chatterjee and Sri Aurobindo—became icons of later Hindu communalists.[9] Those who stressed the Upanishads—mainly Rammohun and

[7] The famous Katha Upanishad is a case in point. In its first two chapters it is already made clear that the Vedic rituals do not suffice for ultimate salvation: one needs to renounce worldly pleasures and life in order to realise one's true immortal Self, cf. Olivelle 1996, 232–238. As to the probable date of this Upanishad, Olivelle assigns it to the last few centuries BCE, Olivelle 1996, xxxvii. The Brihad Aranyaka Upanishad, probably the earliest Upanishad and predating the Katha by several centuries, has a passage that already seems to point to world-renunciation. The famous dialogue between Maitreyi and Yajnavalkya occurs twice in it (Brihad Aranyaka Upanishad 2.4 and 4.5). In both versions of the dialogue Yajnavalkya announces his departure and leaves Maitreyi with his wisdom (cf. Olivelle 1996, 28–30, 69–71).

[8] An historical overview of world-renunciation in relation to the later Upanishads is found in Olivelle 1992, 11–97.

[9] Communalism is a typically Indian English word designating the often aggressive struggle of religious majorities against religious minorities. Concretely it concerns the struggle of Hindus against Muslims or vice-versa. Enlightened liberal Indians regard communalism as the religious

Rabindranath Tagore—are icons of Indian individualist liberalism and the struggle against Hindu chauvinism and jingoism. Indian liberals nowadays, like Sagarika Ghose, insist that their notions of individual freedom and equality of opportunity and equality of all human beings derives from Vedantic philosophy (cf. Ghose 2018, 88ff). Some attribute the origin of modern Hindu communalism to Bankim Chandra Chatterjee, whereas Rabindranath Tagore is greatly revered as the leading light of secularism and humanism, both in India and in Muslim majority Bangladesh (in spite of the fact that Rabindranath Tagore was not a Muslim and seldom refers to Islam in his religious writings).[10] Many Indians (intellectuals, some of them convinced Marxists) regard Rabindranath Tagore as a pillar of Indian secularism even though many of his writings breathe an atmosphere of indefinable Vedantic religiosity. In the writings of Bankim Chandra Chatterjee, and in the writings and practices of Swami Vivekananda and Sri Aurobindo, world-renunciation is real and physical. Bankim describes Hindu monks while Swami Vivekananda was an actual initiated Hindu monk, and Sri Aurobindo was a yogi living like a world renouncing Hindu sage. In the writings of Rabindranath Tagore the renunciation is individual and psychological: the person living in society abandons traditional practices and ideas and thus modernizes himself or herself. Rabindranath Tagore did not endorse monkhood or retreating from the world. His renunciation is internal, not factual.

In sum we could say that all forms of Hindu modernity are Vedantic in nature and consist in bringing traditional Hindu world-renunciation into the Hindu social world in order to fundamentally change the latter. This is possible because those who are renouncers, have practically and psychologically rejected traditional society. They filled their minds with the Vedantic idea of self-realization. The latter does not mean freedom from constant rebirth (as is the goal of traditional world-renunciation) but freedom from social peer pressure and traditional social constraints like caste, social hierarchy, rules concerning untouchability, and similar taboos. This is precisely how the Vedantic texts could replace traditional orthopractic Hinduism with the internalization of the idea of individual autonomy and personal freedom. The traditional binary sociological model of Hinduism as outlined earlier now seems to have collapsed into a single new system of Hindu modernity in which individual emancipation led to the idea of citizenship, and collective emancipation inspired progressive anti-colonial nationalism but also Hindu communalism.

bane of both colonial and independent India. Secular-minded Pakistanis and Bangladeshis are of very similar opinions.

[10] Rabindranath wrote mostly in his native Bengali, a language that is also the national language of Bangladesh.

7.6 Weber's Theory Revisited

Now what about Max Weber and the influence of Protestantism on the development of European modernity? And what about the relationship of Weber with what we have seen so far of Indian religious modernity? Ever since Max Weber first published his *The Protestant Ethic and the Spirit of Capitalism*, the main ideas defended in it never ceased to generate controversy. Weber's contemporaries in Germany probably misunderstood him without having fully digested what he was trying to argue. 'But the so-called Weber thesis' only gained more advocates and opponents when Talcott Parsons published his English translation of the book in 1930. Debates on Weber still continue.[11]

Leaving aside the details of the controversy that Weber's *Protestant Ethic* has sparked, its importance for Indian modernity lies in the links it establishes between an eminently physical/social phenomenon (modern capitalism) and a profoundly religious ethic. Applying Weber's ideas to Indian modernity we will not look at the way modern capitalism was influenced by Protestantism but rather how Western modernity as a state of mind was influenced by Protestantism. This amounts to a specification of the broader idea introduced by Siedentop on the Christian origins of Western individualism. What precisely did Weber argue in his *Protestant Ethic*? From the outset Weber is very careful about the claims he is going to make:

> If any inner relationship between certain expressions of the old Protestant spirit and modern capitalistic culture is to be found, we must attempt to find it … in its purely religious characteristics. (Weber 2001, 11)

In Weber's view capitalism in general is an "attitude which seeks profit rationally and systematically" (2001, 27). But this attitude is not based on economic considerations, but religious ones. In order to show the spirit behind "modern capitalistic culture," Weber quotes from two writings by Benjamin Franklin (1706–1790): *Advice to a Young Tradesman* and *Necessary Hints to Those That would Be Rich*. Some of the most representative maxims of Franklin are, in summary:

- Time is money.
- Credit is money.
- Money can beget money.
- The good paymaster is lord of another man's purse.
- Be mindful of what you owe.
- Honesty increases your credit.
- He that idly loses five shillings' worth of time, loses five shillings, and might as prudently throw five shillings into the sea. (Weber 2001, 14–16)

This business advice constitutes an ethos (Weber 2001, 17). Weber explains that the "earning of money within the modern economic order, is, so long as it is done

[11] See for instance Lash and Whimster 1987; Lehmann and Ouédraogo 2003; and Schluchter and Graf 2005.

legally, the result and the expression of virtue and proficiency in a calling" (Weber 2001, 19). Weber's thematic is to "form a contribution to the understanding of the manner in which ideas become effective forces in history" (Weber 2001, 48) and "to ascertain whether and to what extent religious forces have taken part in the qualitative formation and the quantitative expansion of that spirit [ie of capitalism] over the world" (Weber 2001, 49). This can only be done "by investigating whether and at what points certain correlations between forms of religious belief and *practical ethics* can be worked out" (Weber 2001, 49 [emphasis added]). Investigating the religious forces that furthered the ethics of capitalism leads Weber to an even wider thematic, namely "to what extent the historical development of *modern culture* can be attributed to those religious forces" (Weber 2001, 50 [emphasis added]). These carefully worded sentences suggest that Protestant religiosity inculcated in its conscious and willing followers a strong ethic fostering modern capitalism and modernity itself in Europe. If ideas "become effective forces in history," then in order to find the origins of (Western) modernity we have to investigate more closely certain strongly held ideas and assumptions. Contrary to popular Marxism, Weber believed in the primacy of human motivation and culture over the economy.[12]

Weber does not discuss these many diverse aspects of Protestantism but instead concentrates on its Calvinist form. It was the Calvinist, and subsequent Puritan, doctrine of predestination that Weber identifies as an essential motivation of the capitalist spirit. Predestination meant that no religious merit can be attached to personal worth or virtue, but salvation rests entirely on the sovereign will of God. God elects some to be saved and others to be doomed. This left the believer completely alone with no external help. Rituals, priests and personal ethical merit are of no avail (cf. Weber 2001, 59–61). Weber sums up the consequent attitude to life as negative to "all the sensuous and emotional elements in culture and in religion, because they are of no use toward salvation and promote sentimental illusions and idolatrous superstitions" (Weber 2001, 62). Exclusive "trust in God" is all there is for the Calvinist Puritan. Some are elected by God, others are not. But no one knows whether he is elected or not to eternal salvation. This doubt did not act as a brake on social organization but rather fostered it. In a closely-knit passage Weber explains this:

The world exists to serve the glorification of God and for that purpose alone. The elected Christian is in the world only to increase this glory of God by fulfilling His commandments to the best of his ability. But God requires social achievements of the Christian because He wills that social life shall be organized according to His commandments, in accordance with that purpose. The social activity of the Christian in the world is solely activity *in majorem gloriam Dei* [for the greater glory of God]. This character is hence shared by labor in a calling which serves the mundane life of the community.

[12] This point is stressed by Weber again and again; see Weber (2001, 48–50; 139). But Karl Marx also had a high opinion of human agency. See Habib in Karat ed. 2001, 49–50. Habib shows that Marx was not a materialist determinist. Thus agency and will were important. A similar point is made by Ahmad 2001, 42–43. Discussing Marx, Henry 2019, 44–45, argues along similar lines.

> Brotherly love ... only practiced for the glory of God ... is expressed in the first place in the fulfilment of the daily tasks ... in the interest of the rational organization of our social environment. (Weber 2001, 64)

To further the glory of God and not one's own greatness or even self-interest is the motivation towards a rational organization of the social environment. In concrete terms: improving the material infrastructure of society and building a comfortable society means promoting God's greatness. The doctrine of predestination taught that God has from the beginning of the world only elected some to salvation. As nothing concerning ultimate salvation rests on human merit, one must simply live and act for God's glory. Whether one is really elected or not does not make any difference. It is "an absolute duty to consider oneself chosen, and to combat all doubts as temptations of the devil, since lack of self-confidence is the result of insufficient faith" (Weber 2001, 66). For faith and self-confidence are the signs of possible future Divine grace:

> The community of the elect with their God could only take place and be perceptible to them in that God worked ... through them and that they were conscious of it. That is, their action originated from the faith caused by God's grace, and this faith in turn justified itself by the quality of that action. (Weber 2001, 68)

> In practice this means that God helps those who help themselves. Thus the Calvinist ... himself creates his own salvation, or, as would be more correct, the conviction of it ... is a systematic self-control which at every moment stands before the inexorable alternative, chosen or damned. (Weber 2001, 69–70)

This constant prodding faith and self-control in order to achieve a rational organization of the social world is what Weber famously calls the "worldly asceticism" of Calvinist Protestantism. In a way this asceticism also answers the question why the "horrendous doctrine" of predestination did not lead to total fatalism but rather its opposite. But Calvinists themselves subsume the "worldly asceticism" and its impact on the social world under the head of "sanctification of daily life" or "sanctification of the world" (Berkhof 1990, 494–498; Van den Brink and Van der Kooi 2012, 611–613). Weber, however, regards the "combination of [Calvinist Puritan] faith in absolutely valid norms with absolute determinism and the complete transcendentality of God" to be a "product of great genius" and "much more modern than the milder doctrine" of among others the Lutherans, "making greater concessions to the feelings which subjected God to the moral law" (Weber 2001, 78). God, in Weber's reading of Calvinism, is almost a symbol of the impersonality of the universe itself. The total absence of any human emotion or human characteristic in the Calvinist God makes Him in Weber's view a profound token of modernity itself. Calvinist Protestant religious ethics thus released a tremendous creative energy that transformed the traditional Western world into the modern world. This transformation is visible among others in the universalization of the concept of the nation-state, but it also clearly had darker aspects such as the erasure of traditional cultures in the areas that Western expansionism colonized. The thesis of Western modernization being equal to Calvinism is of course an oversimplification. Yet is seems to retain some of its explanatory value.

7.6.1 Social Activism

In a study on the origins of modern Western politics Hancock (1989, 162) argues that John Calvin (1509–1564) himself had laid the foundation of this-worldly social activism. Supporting Weber's thesis, Hancock maintains that the reason for this activism lies within Calvin's double doctrine that "without knowledge of self there is no knowledge of God" and "without knowledge of God there is no knowledge of self." God's glory has one direction:

> the thriving of the creation, particularly of the rational instincts of innocent human nature … Man must not even attempt to cultivate consciousness of God's power as an inward feeling … for this is … to obstruct God's sheer activity. Consciousness of [God's] power is not a benefit to the [human] soul but a spur to action. To be conscious of God's power, to contemplate God's will …, is to continually enact it. (Hancock 1989, 162)

> Man "lives and moves" in God, because the Spirit lives and moves in man … The relationship between man and God is the governing instance of union without fusion. … It is … the ground on which Calvin radically distinguishes politics and religion in order to unify them in worldly activity for the prosperous preservation of man-kind and the glory of God. (Hancock 1989, 163)

The knowledge of God and self and self and God is the point at which God's will on earth can be enacted. Although God is totally transcendent, he works through men. In fact, everything owes its existence wholly to God alone. This point is emphasized in the very beginning of Calvin's main work the *Institutes of the Christian Religion*, to which Hancock is referring. Calvin writes about God's creation:

> [God's] essence, indeed, is incomprehensible, utterly transcending all human thought; but on each of his works his glory is engraven in characters so bright, so distinct, and so illustrious, that none, however dull and illiterate, can plead ignorance … wherever you turn your eyes, there is no portion of the world, however minute, that does not exhibit at least some sparks of beauty; while it is impossible to contemplate the vast and beautiful fabric as it extends around, without being overwhelmed by the immense weight of glory. (Calvin 1953, 1.5.1)

7.6.2 The Privateness of Conscience

An important component of Calvinist ideology with revolutionary consequences was the doctrine of the freedom of conscience. The concept of "conscience" itself is a term occurring often in the New Testament.[13] The Greek word is *syneidèsis.* The Latin *conscientia* from which "conscience" is derived, is found also in the writings of the Roman statesman and philosopher Cicero (especially in *Tusc. Disp.* 2.64, 4.45 and *De natura deorum* 3.85). In earlier and contemporary non-Christian Greek texts *syneidèsis* meant either "knowledge," "consciousness," "awareness," or

[13] Acts 23:1; 24:16; Rom 2:15; 9:1; 13:5; 1 Cor. 8:7; 10:9; 10:25, 27–8; 2 Cor. 4:2; 5:11; 1 Tim 1:5, 19; 3:9; 2 Tim 1:3; Tit 1:15; Hebr. 9:9,14; 10: 2,22; 1 Petr. 3:16, 21.

"consciousness of right and wrong." Both meanings are also implied in Paul's epistles, which are the earliest source of the Christian doctrine of conscience. Both meanings are relevant for the Calvinist doctrine: the soul as inner witness is also the inner guide towards the knowledge of what is good. Thus one needs no elaborate external regulations to govern one's life. All one needs to do is learning to listen to the inner voice of conscience. Calvin maintains that the definition of conscience

> must be sought in the etymology of the word. For as men, when they apprehend the knowledge or *science*, so when they have a sense of the divine justice added as a witness which allows them not to conceal their sins, but drags them forward as culprits to the bar of God, that sense is called *conscience*. For it stands as it were between God and man, not suffering man to suppress what he knows himself. (Calvin 1953, 3.19.15)

Conscience, in other words, is a faculty by which every person is able to understand right and wrong, good and evil. This faculty follows upon and is superior to mind and intellect which only generate scientific knowledge. Conscience generates moral knowledge. Calvin discusses the obedience a person owes to human laws, and whether a person is obliged to obey any laws whatsoever:

> If they [ie human laws] are imposed for the purpose of forming a religious obligation, as if the observance of them was in itself necessary, we say that the restraint thus laid on the conscience is unlawful. Our consciences have not to do with men but with God only. (Calvin 1953, 4.10.5)

Obedience to authority, both worldly and ecclesiastical is enjoined here, but only in general terms. Laws that step in between man and God and thus try to bind conscience, need not be obeyed. Such laws are unlawful. Stretched to its logical conclusion, Calvin's interpretation of the New Testament concept of conscience, opened the possibility of political revolution: it inculcated obedience to God's will alone, which implies the potential disobedience to worldly political rulers. The obedience or non-obedience to rulers is thus left to the individual's own choice.[14]

The concept of conscience goes a long way to explain Siedentop's claims about the Christian origins of individual freedom. For the inner voice of conscience is basically the mental locus where the individual person exerts the greatest amount of autonomy over him or herself, not to do as he or she pleases but to contemplate what it is right to do and what is wrong. One could do the wrong thing as well, but one is free to choose, free either to listen to the voice of one's conscience or choose to ignore it. Especially in relation to obedience to an external power like a ruler or a magistrate, the doctrine of the freedom of private conscience defines the freedom of private judgment, a freedom which only fully makes sense within a social context.

[14] Edmund Leites in his volume on conscience and casuistry in early modern Europe claims that the idea of the freedom of conscience emerged gradually as a practice in Europe and did not all of a sudden come fully upon the scene due to the Reformation (1988, 11). Conscience in other world religions is the theme of the volume edited by Amaladass (1999). But this book only proves how little the doctrine of conscience has been theorised in for instance modern Hindu thought. See for example Amaladass (1999, 38). Even nowadays the Protestant doctrine of conscience attracts theological attention as may be seen from the study by Staten (1988). Staten discusses among others the theology of Gerhard Ebeling and Bultmann.

One acts always with regard to other persons. When one is totally isolated one does not act within a social context. Any act is only morally relevant or meaningful when there are those who may be affected by the act, good or bad. The voice of conscience would tell the person before the action whether it is a good or a bad action. It also tells the person when to obey external rules and when not to obey them.

7.6.3 Calvinism and Revolutions

The social changes that Western capitalism is supposed to have caused are huge. Probably no one has 'glorified' the global transformative power of capitalism—the ideology of the bourgeoisie—more than Karl Marx and Friederich Engels in their *Manifesto of the Communist Party* published first in 1848:

> The need of a constantly expanding market for its products chases the bourgeoisie over the whole of the globe ... The bourgeoisie has through its exploitation of the world market given a cosmopolitan character to its production and consumption in every country...
>
> The bourgeoisie, during its rule of scarce one hundred years, has created more massive and more colossal productive forces than have all preceding generations together. Subjection of Nature's forces to man, machinery, application of chemistry to industry and agriculture, steam-navigation, railways, electric telegraphs, clearing of whole continents for cultivation ... what earlier century had even a presentiment that such productive forces slumbered in the lap of social labor? (McLellan 2011, 248–249)

We have here a fitting description of the material aspects of Western expansionist modernity. Read together with Weber's arguments on the origins of the bourgeois capitalist mentality, we can appreciate the enormous global impact that Calvinist Protestantism is ultimately credited with. What Marx and Engels emphasize here is the great organizational energy of the bourgeoisie and of course they do not attribute this to Calvinism. Ultimately the huge profits made by capitalists were extracted from the labor force. Marx may have admired the acumen of eighteenth- and nineteenth-century businessmen, but otherwise he had nothing but disdain for their religious hypocrisy. Emancipatory politics, in Marx's opinion, was the only answer to the plight of the proletariat. But in this respect, Marx did not deviate from another aspect attributed to Calvinism, namely modern democratic politics.

Can we locate the origins of modern political institutions also in Calvinist Protestantism? Some scholars after Weber have asked themselves this question, and, after the fashion of Weber, tried to unravel the Calvinist origins of modern politics (Walzer 1965; Gorski 2003). The ideas of the modern nation-state, of citizens' rights, of democratic procedures and of the republican form of government, in the end derive from the same Calvinist ethos that brought forth the capitalist spirit. The emergence of the modern nation state is the result of more than three centuries of violent political struggle and revolutions, most of which took place in Europe. Revolution was subsequently exported to North America. Calvinist Protestantism was an important ideological factor in these revolutions. This fact makes the socio-political aspects of Calvinism relevant with regard to anti-colonial struggles and the

Indian Freedom struggle in particular. Indian modernity and anti-colonial notions partly emerged from the Protestantization of Hinduism as we have tried to show in the beginning of this chapter. As we are trying to argue, this Hindu 'Protestantism' based on a novel interpretation of Vedantic texts, provided a mobilizing ideology in the late nineteenth century in East India, comparable to Calvinism in North Western Europe in the sixteenth and seventeenth centuries. In other words: what Weber and Weberians had shown for European Protestantism, also seems valid for non-Christian Protestantism, in our case Hinduism. So it is to Rammohun and the reformed Vedanta that we turn once more in order to show the extent to which the Weberian approach to Protestantism can be fruitfully applied to Vedantic reform of Hinduism.

7.7 Concluding Remarks

Weber's analysis of Calvinism focuses on the emergence of the capitalist mindset, not so much on the mindset of modernity in a broader sense. Rammohun's Vedantic reformation of Hinduism did not aim at instilling a mindset of capitalism in his Hindu audience; rather his intentions were more social and humanistic. He does indicate the reason for his reformation. In his endeavor to acquaint his fellow Hindus with the liberating ideas of the Vedanta Rammohun introduces a new modern concept, namely "public use." In his opinion a large public—anonymous and evidently not limited by caste or religious affiliations—has to be informed of the teachings contained in the original Hindu scriptures. The public, thus defined, would benefit by this knowledge. Rammohun elaborates upon the idea of "public use" in a letter written in 1827 to John Digby. Rammohun sums up his reasons for translating and disseminating the 'original' scriptures of Hinduism.[15]

> I ... with a view of making them [i.e., the Hindus] happy and comfortable both here and hereafter, not only employed verbal arguments against the absurdities of the idolatry practiced by them, but also translated this most revered theological work, namely, Vedant, into Bengali and Hindustani[16] and also several chapters of the Ved, in order to convince them that the unity, of God, and absurdity of idolatry are evidently pointed out by their own scriptures. (Rāmmohan Racanāvalī 1973, 461)

The argument of providing comfort to Hindus in general by acquainting them with the true meaning of the ancient scriptures of Hinduism also occurs in Rammohun's

[15] As already stated before, I do not intend here to debate the actual validity or wrongness of Rammohun's claim that the Vedas and the Upanishads are the original scriptures of Hinduism. One could perhaps say that he was wrong because Hinduism never evolved from a limited written canon, and that he was right because the Upanishads constitute an important ancient textual source for later Hindu theology.

[16] This Hindustani translation seems to be lost. Rammohun's Bengali translation of the Brahma Sutra has been in print to this day.

introduction to the translation of the Kena Upanishad (1823). There he explains the idea of "comfort" in more detail:

> I trust, by explaining to my countrymen the real spirit of the Hindoo Scriptures, which is but the declaration of the unity of God, tend ... to correct the erroneous conceptions ... with regard to the doctrines they inculcate. It will also, I hope, tend to discriminate those parts of the Vedas which are to be interpreted in an allegorical sense, and consequently to correct those exceptionable practices, which not only deprive Hindoos in general of the common comforts of society, but also lead them frequently to self-destruction, or to the sacrifice of the lives of their friends and relations. (Rammohun Roy 1995, 13)

In connection with "self-destruction" Rammohun adds a note on the same page: "As at Prayaga, Ganga Sagar, and under the wheels of the car of Jagannath."[17] About 'sacrifice' Rammohun adds another note on the same page: 'As, for instance, persons whose recovery from sickness is supposed to be doubtful, are carried to die on the banks of the Ganges. This is practiced by the Hindoos of Bengal only, the cruelty of which affects even Hindoos of Behar, Ilahabad, and all the upper provinces'.

Yet the main thrust behind Rammohun's interest in disseminating the Upanishads was his conviction that these texts teach monotheism and a simple but high morality. For Rammohun

> ... the Vedanta by declaring that "God is everywhere, and everything is in God," means that nothing is absent from God, and nothing bears real existence except by the volition of God, whose existence is the sole support of the conceived existence of the universe... (Rammohun Roy 1995, 47)

These quotations amply show that Rammohun wanted to enlighten his compatriots about what he regarded as true Hinduism. This included high morality, stressing the unity of God, rejection of the ritual worship of the later Hindu gods and goddesses, and it implied that every Hindu should get personally acquainted with the content of the most holy parts of the Hindu religious literature of the ages, namely the Upanishads, the basic texts of the Vedanta. These intentions compare well with how the sixteenth century European Reformation saw itself. What it amounts to in both cases is the internalization of a doctrine/theology that is supposed to be well studied and well understood. Hence the emphasis on translation of the sacred writ. Studying scripture is a religious activity that is done in the inner space of one's own consciousness (also the seat of one's conscience). Thus the study of scripture is eminently a form of most private devotion. In the case of Protestantism this is done through the study of the Bible, in the case of Vedantic Hinduism it is the study of scriptures like the Upanishads and the Bhagavad Gita. This emphasis on private study as religious devotion also means a phasing out or rejection of the externalities of Hindu rituals, or the rejection of the paraphernalia of the Roman Catholic Church.

[17] This refers to an old practice: devotees of Lord Jagannath in Puri in Orissa sometimes used to let themselves be crushed by the giant wooden wheels of procession cars that were drawn into the streets of Puri during the festival of Rathayatra. On top of this car (often as high as a large house) was an image of Krishna in his form of Jagannatha (Lord of the World). In English the name Jagannatha turned into "Juggernaut," a huge thing that crushes people.

In the way Weber has stressed the internalization of a new doctrine of Christianity as the source of the economic activities known as capitalism, similarly it seems reasonable to assert that Rammohun's Vedantic reform has produced a mentality in certain members among the urbanized Hindu middle classes leading to radical social change.[18] It is the great merit of Weber's approach to have drawn attention to the importance of a strongly internalized doctrine or set of ideas, reinforced by constant repetition and great self-discipline, motivating people to radically alter their life-style and outlook on society and politics. Weber has set the research agenda for linking certain forms of religion to certain mentalities that change the world fundamentally. Weber has pointed to the connection between modernity as a state of mind and its genetic links to religions with a Book or Books. We have tried to show the relevance of Weber's thesis on Calvinism by comparing a similar tendency in early nineteenth century Hindu India. Rammohun Roy emulated the idea of a religion of the Book. In his case the Book were the Upanishads and the Vedanta. From further developments in the course of nineteenth century in India it is clear that Rammohun's Vedantic reformation did unleash spiritual forces of modernization, individual choices and later in the nineteenth century also became an important ideological component of nascent anti-colonial nationalism.[19]

References

Amaladass, Anand S. J., ed. 1999. *A Crosscultural Look at Conscience*. Chennai: Satya Nilayam Publications.

Calvin, John. 1953. *Institutes of the Christian Religion*. A New Translation by Henry Beveridge. Volumes 1 and 2. London: James Clarke and Co.

Chatterjee, Partha. 1993. *The Nation and Its Fragments: Colonial and Postcolonial Histories*. Princeton/New Jersey: Princeton University Press.

Dumont, Louis. 1980. *Homo Hierarchicus: The Caste System and Its Implications*. Complete Revised English Edition. Translated by Mark Sainsbury, Louis Dumont, and Basia Gulati. Chicago: The University of Chicago Press.

Ghose, Sagarika. 2018. *Why I Am a Liberal: A Manifesto for Indians Who Believe in Individual Freedom*. Gurgaon: Penguin Viking.

Hancock, Ralph C. 1989. *Calvin and the Foundations of Modern Politics*. Ithaca/London: Cornell University Press.

Henry, Michel. 2019. *Marx: An Introduction. Foreword by Frédéric Seyler, Translated by Kristien Justaert*. London/New York/Oxford/New Delhi/Sydney: Bloomsbury Academic.

Karat, Prakash, ed. 2001. *A World to Win: Essays on the Communist Manifesto*. Delhi: LeftWord Books.

Khare, R. S., ed. 2006. *Caste, Hierarchy, and Individualism: Indian Critiques of Louis Dumont's Contributions*. New Delhi: Oxford University Press.

Kopf, David. (original 1979) 1996. *The Brahmo Samaj and the Shaping of the Modern Indian Mind*. New Delhi: Atlantic.

[18] The still classic study of the social impact of Rammohun's followers organised in the Brahmo Samaj (society of believers in the One God) is Kopf (1996).

[19] For a detailed analysis of this development: see van Bijlert 2021.

Leites, Edmund, ed. 1988. *Conscience and Casuistry in Early Modern Europe*. Paris: Cambridge: Cambridge University Press. Editions de la Maison des Sciences de l'Homme.
McLellan, David, ed. 2011. *Karl Marx: Selected Writings*. New York: Oxford University Press.
Michaels, Axel. 2004. *Hinduism: Past and Present*. Translated by Barbara Harshav. Princeton/ Oxford: Princeton University Press.
Olivelle, Patrick. 1992. *Saṃnyāsa Upaniṣads: Hindu Scriptures on Asceticism and Renunciation*. Translated with Introduction and Notes by Patrick Olivelle. New York/Oxford: Oxford University Press.
Olivelle, Patrick. 1993. *The Āśrama System: The History and Hermeneutics of a Religious Institution*. New York/Oxford: Oxford University Press.
Olivelle, Patrick. 1996. *Upaniṣads: Translated from the Original Sanskrit*. Oxford/New York: Oxford University Press.
Racanāvalī, Rāmmohan. 1973. *Pradhān sampādak Dr. Ajitkumar Ghosh*. Calcutta: Haraph Prakashani.
Roy, Rammohun. 1995. In *The English Works of Raja Rammohun Roy*. Parts I to VII in One Volume, ed. Kalidas Nag and Debajyoti Burman. Calcutta: Sadharan Brahmo Samaj.
Siedentop, Larry. 2015. *Inventing the Individual: The Origins of Western Liberalism*. New YorK: Penguin Books.
van Bijlert, Victor A. 2021. *Vedantic Hinduism in Colonial Bengal: Reformed Hinduism and Western Protestantism*. London/New York: Routledge.
Weber, Max. 2001. *The Protestant Ethic and the Spirit of Capitalism*. Translated by Talcott Parsons. With an introduction by Anthony Giddens. London/New York: Routledge.
Dobson Collet, Sophia. 1988. *The Life and Letters of Raja Rammohun Roy*. Edited by Dilip Kumar Biswas and Prabhat Chandra Ganguli. 4th edition. Calcutta: Sadharan Brahmo Samaj.
Zastoupil, Lynn. 2010. *Rammohun Roy and the Making of Victorian Britain*. New York: Palgrave Macmillan.
Lash, Scott and Sam Whimster eds. 1987. *Max Weber, Rationality and Modernity*. London: Allen and Unwin.
Lehmann, Hartmut and Jean Martin Ouédraogo eds. 2003. *Max Webers Religionssoziologie in interkultureller Perspektive*. Göttingen: Vandenhoeck & Ruprecht.
Schluchter, Wolfgang and Friederich Wilhelm Graf eds. 2005. *Asketischer Protestantismus und der 'Geist'des Modernen Kapitalismus*. Tübingen: Mohr Siebeck.
Staten, John C. 1988. *Conscience and the Reality of God: An Essay on the Experiential Foundations of Religious Knowledge*. Berlin, New York, Amsterdam: Mouton de Gruyter.
Walzer, Michael. 1965. *The Revolution of the Saints: A Study in the Origins of Radical Politics*. Cambridge, Mass: Harvard University Press.
Gorski, Philip S. 2003. *The Disciplinary Revolution: Calvinism and the Rise of the State in Early Modern Europe*. Chicago and London: The University of Chicago Press.

Victor van Bijlert studied Indology at Leiden University, with a PhD in 1987 on Buddhist epistemology and logic. He writes and teaches on Indian religions and culture. His main specialities are Vedānta, Nyāya, Yoga darśana, Mahāyāna Sūtras and śāstras, Hindu religious reform, Bengali literature and modern Indian history. His special interest is Rabindranath Tagore, some of whose Bengali writings he translated into Dutch. He has held teaching positions at Leiden University; the Nordic Institute of Asian Studies, Copenhagen; and the Vrije Universiteit Amsterdam, now retired. From 2000 to 2003, he taught Indian values at the Indian Institute of Management and the National Institute of Human Development in Calcutta. His most recent publication is *Nyāya Sūtra – On Philosophical Method: Sanskrit Text, Translation, and Commentary*. London and New York: Routledge, 2024.

Part IV
Buddhism

Chapter 8
An Introduction to Socially Engaged Buddhist Economics

Joel Magnuson

Abstract The chapter is an introduction to a branch of socially engaged Buddhism that focuses on economics. The work presented here is centered on the core teachings of the Buddha including the middle way, the four noble truths, and the noble eightfold path, all of which provide a foundation for Buddhist economics. Although Buddhism originated in the East and has a global presence today, the ideas presented here on social engagement and economics are Western in orientation. Socially engaged Buddhist economics specifically is a heterodox approach to economics, non-individualistic, and draws from research on the social phenomenon of institutionalized greed, hatred, and delusion.

8.1 Introduction

The human race is drifting into a perfect storm of pathology. Climate change, mass species extinction, extreme polarization of wealth and income distribution, the ascent of violently reactionary politics and divisiveness, and grand episodes of economic instability are all on a path of convergence. The common element among these pathological conditions is that they are anthropogenic. They are self-inflicted. Many of us are becoming numb to our self-inflicted wounds and burying our heads in the sands of cognitive dissonance as a way of avoiding the pain. People find it easier to look at these conditions as abstractions or crises in the future rather than exigencies that need to be dealt with head-on now. By doing so, we become like so many mythological "boiling frogs" who avoid taking corrective action until they become so numb to the troubles that they eventually become consumed by them. As this goes on, finding solutions and ways to heal becomes increasingly difficult.

Socially engaged Buddhist economics is about taking corrective action in a way that is inspired by the philosophy and practice of Buddhism, with a focus on

J. Magnuson (✉)
Independent scholar, Portland, OR, USA

G. J. Buijs, J. J. Ballor (eds.), *In Search of the Spirits of Capitalism*, Sophia Studies in Cross-cultural Philosophy of Traditions and Cultures 44,
https://doi.org/10.1007/978-3-032-01137-4_8

economics. A central theme developed here is that Buddhism can help us make positive changes in our personal lives as well as our social surroundings and thereby help address at least some aspects of these anthropogenic crises. Specifically, it provides a philosophical basis for a dual process of transformation. One part of the process is to look deeply inward into ourselves and our minds and work toward dissolving the personal vexations that make us suffer—the inner work. The other is to extend from this place of personal liberation to work toward liberating our social structures from the same vexations—the outer work. This dual process of inner and outer work becomes the basis for the transformation of our economic lives for a healthier and more stable way of living. Hopefully, a useful first step in this work is to explore some of the concepts underlying Buddhist economics as part of that inner-outer work of change. Buddhism, of course, originated and evolved over thousands of years in the East, and only in the last fifty years did the idea of something called Buddhist economics become known in the West.[1]

8.2 E.F. Schumacher and Buddhist Economics

For most Westerners, the idea of Buddhist economics was introduced by economist E.F. Schumacher in his enormously influential collection of essays, *Small is Beautiful: Economics as if People Mattered* (1973). Schumacher was among the most prominent intellectuals of the post-Great Depression era. As Chief Economic Advisor to Britain's National Coal Board between 1950 and 1970, he had an inside view of the troubling prospects of ongoing economic growth powered by fossil fuels. He anticipated that economic expansion would eventually ebb from energy scarcities and high prices and openly challenged the typical economist's infatuation with technology and their assumption that technology will solve every problem of scarcity.[2]

Schumacher also challenged the core philosophical foundation underlying mainstream economics. In the late 1950s he was working in Myanmar as an advisor to the government and while he was there, he spent time with Buddhist monks. He became fascinated with their religion and wrote a short essay titled, "Buddhist Economics," which was subsequently published in *Small Is Beautiful*. His essay was not intended to convey a comprehensive picture of Buddhist economics. Rather, it simply explored a sampling of the differences between the Buddhist's view and the views of Western economics.

Schumacher discovered that in the Buddhist system of ethics known as the *noble eightfold path* contains a provision called "right livelihood" and concluded that it

[1] What is presented in this chapter is partly based on earlier contributions to this development, Magnuson 2008, Magnuson 2016, and most recently Magnuson 2022.

[2] It is worthwhile to note that Schumacher's book appeared just after the famous 'Limits to Growth'-report of the Club of Rome. See Donella Meadows et al., 2004. *Limits to Growth: The 30-Year Update.*

"is clear, therefore, that there must be such a thing as Buddhist economics" (Schumacher, 53). From that point on, Buddhist economics grew into a lively but very small corner of the economics profession. It is considered a heterodox approach as it is distinctively at odds with many of the core assumptions in standard economics, particularly the theoretical assertion that self-interest, egoism, and greed are useful as motivating forces for economic development. Schumacher, echoing the Buddhist view, questioned the veracity of this assertion. He argued that if we accept the idea that we can benefit from rampant self-interest, economic society will be fashioned into a culture of plunder based on "...greed and envy, which destroy intelligence, happiness, serenity, and thereby the peacefulness of man." (Schumacher, 31). Foul cannot be fair as it leads to a general collapse of intelligence, a loss of wisdom, people become blinded by their own rapacity, and it eventually strips bare all that has meaning. Schumacher laments that it is nonetheless deftly rationalized by economists in the simple stroke of a pen—vice leads to virtue. He writes, "If whole societies become infected by these vices, they may indeed achieve astonishing things, but they become increasingly incapable of solving the most elementary problems of everyday existence." (Schumacher, 31). Perhaps one of the most outstanding examples of the destructiveness of greed is the financial and economic instabilities that come from the boom-bust volatilities in markets that are rationalized by a "greed is good" ideology.

8.3 "Greed Is Good" Economics

Shortly after the 2008 banking crisis exploded across the planet, former Goldman Sachs executive, Greg Smith, publicly announced his resignation in a *New York Times* editorial. Smith had worked for Goldman Sachs in New York for about a decade before he transferred to its operations in London where he managed equity derivatives, and then soon after resigned in protest. The reason he gave for his departure was that he felt that the elite investment bank had become "toxic and destructive" and increasingly focused on its own profits at the expense of its clients. According to Smith, greed rather than client trust was Goldman Sachs's primary operating principle. In a blog response to Smith's letter, American economist and former labor secretary, Robert Reich, posted, "The problem isn't excessive greed," he asserted, "If you took the greed out of Wall Street all you'd have left is pavement." He went on to argue that the problem with banking establishments in New York and London is rampant abuse of power and trust, and his solution for better and more responsible banking should be better government regulation.[3]

It is not surprising that a former government official would advocate for better regulation, but it is remarkable that he would claim that excessive greed is not a

[3] Robert Reich, "If You Took the Greed Out of Wall Street, All You'd Have Left is Pavement: Why Greg Smith's Critique is Way Too Narrow," March 16, 2012. http://robertreich.org; Greg Smith, "Why I am Leaving Goldman Sachs," *The New York Times*, Op Ed., March 14, 2012.

problem. Even more remarkable is that he is dismissive of a widespread condition of institutionalized greed on Wall Street, the heart of America's financial system. Greed, according to Reich, is so ubiquitous that the entire structure of Wall Street institutions would vanish without it. Yet to say that this is not a problem when seen against the backdrop of the famous greed-inspired banking calamity that spread economic ruin around the globe like the Covid pandemic is evidence of an even deeper problem: an inability to recognize that greed permeating essential and powerful institutions of finance is a serious problem.

Reich was not the first economist to see greed as a benign social condition. There is a long-standing belief in standard economics that greed—an obsession with accumulating more and more as if there could never be enough—is an essential source of human industriousness, and such industriousness leads to overall economic development. This view holds that craving and self-interest are necessary because they are the only viable motivating forces that lead to economic action.

In keeping with this line of thought, economists have for centuries been spinning elaborate theories about how greed is a special kind of vice that renders benefits for societies overall. From eighteenth-century philosophers such as Bernard De Mandeville and Adam Smith, to the utilitarian philosophers of the nineteenth century and on, mainstream economics in the West has been centered around a core axiom that greed may be seen as an individual vice, but the vice leads to the social virtue of prosperity.

By the twentieth century, the eloquent liberal economist, John Maynard Keynes, was also captured by the alluring notion that greed is a good thing. Keynes writes, "The love of money as a possession … will be recognized for what it is, a somewhat disgusting morbidity, one of those semi-criminal, semi-pathological propensities which one hands over with a shudder to the specialists in mental disease." (Keynes 1971, 329–331). Though Keynes sounds moralizing, he nonetheless holds on to the idea that societies need to embrace greed for another century in order to be set free from economic depressions and insecurity. "For at least another hundred years," Keynes writes, "we must pretend to ourselves and to everyone that fair is foul and foul is fair; for foul is useful and fair is not. Avarice and usury and precaution must be our gods for a little longer still. For only they can lead us out of the tunnel of economic necessity into daylight." (Keynes 1971, ibid.). Thus elevated to Godlike status, it should not come as a surprise that greed and self-interest have become idealized in Western culture and mindset. Reflecting on this, economic historian, Dirk Philipsen writes, "If greed is culturally dominant, and … that it leads people to what our culture considers success, we are likely to emulate it as a model for ourselves." (Philipsen, 2015**, 44). When something becomes culturally dominant in this way, it typically escapes critical examination and becomes easy for all of us to fall under its control. Philipsen completes the circle between the individual and society.** Greed is a human emotion felt by an individual, but as Philipsen argues, it has become culturally normalized so that the individual is socialized to accept being under its control.

Socially engaged Buddhist economics upends Reich's argument that greed is not the problem. The problem is not a lack of government regulation, the problem is greed. And if you took the greed out of Wall Street and everywhere else, this would be a liberating step forward in human evolution. By doing so, we would eliminate the need for layers of government regulations in the first place.

Much of what stands as Buddhist economics today deals with how Buddhist philosophy and practice can offer insights into our motivations—unhealthy or healthy—and sharpen our abilities to see into them deeply and perhaps change them for healthier ways of living. These insights can eventually lead to a profound sense of liberation and self-awareness that stem from a gradual process of dissolving the confusion between what is harmful economic activity and what is truly beneficial. Such insights provide a foundation for a paradigm of lived ethics. The concept of lived ethics holds particular importance in Buddhist thought as it resonates with the Buddha's own dramatic life change as part of a personal journey to discover the truth of human suffering.

8.4 The Buddha's Early Discourses

The root narrative of Buddhist philosophy and practice originates with the personal story of Siddhartha Gautama, the man who became the Buddha about two and half millennia ago. Siddartha was born into wealth and privilege and the chosen son to become the head of the Shakya dynasty that was sovereign over a vast territory in a border region between what is now India and Nepal. As a boy and young man, he lived in splendid luxury with all the comforts imaginable in his time. Yet Siddartha was discontented and felt compelled to find more meaning to life outside the cloister of aristocratic privilege. He occasionally wandered outside of his palace into nearby villages, where he saw masses of people trapped in a vortex of poverty and disease. In his home, he also saw that the wealthy and powerful were captured by anxiety, jealousy, fear, and an insatiable desire for more wealth. Siddhartha realized that people everywhere, wealthy or poor, young or old, were experiencing some degree of unease, vexation, and misery. Siddartha came to understand by observation that suffering is a universal but not necessarily inescapable human condition. He wanted to find an answer to the problem of how people can liberate themselves from this condition. Siddartha also realized that to do this he would have to live his life differently. True insights into the human condition needed to come from experience outside the opulence of his home and away from his family of origin. He resolved to let go of his own wealth, the status of his house, and even his own family and set off to become a mendicant wanderer in an arduous quest for truth, and to uncover the way to alleviate suffering. For a time, he experienced homelessness and serious poverty and survived largely by begging for food. He drifted from one place to another seeking instruction from various masters on yoga, meditation, and every other form of practice he could find. Throughout these experiences he remained frustrated as these practices did not provide him with the deeper insights he was seeking. Intuitively he knew that these truths and insights existed, but he could not define them. He was like a blind man who understood sight but was unable to see.

Further on his journey Siddhartha joined a group of ascetics who were committed to a spiritual practice that was predicated on self-denial and extended periods of fasting. They believed this practice would purify the spirit from the corruption of sense-pleasures. With the ascetics, Siddhartha subjected himself to long periods of starvation with the hope that such physical stress would bring him closer to the spiritual purity promised by the ascetics. But again, frustrated he eventually concluded that asceticism was ultimately self-defeating as it brought him to the very precipice of death. He came to understand that such a weakened physical condition would make it impossible for him to achieve the breakthrough to enlightenment that he intuitively knew was there. Later he told his followers,

> Because I ate so little, my buttocks became like a camel's hoof, my backbone protruded like a line of spindles, my ribs corroded and collapsed like the rafters of an old and rotten shed, the gleams of the pupils in my eye sockets appeared deeply sunken, my scalp became wrinkled and shrunken... Though I have undergone severe ascetic practice, I cannot reach the special and wonderful knowledge and insight transcending the affairs of human beings. Could there be another way of enlightenment?[4]

He left the ascetic community and ended his long sessions of extreme fasting and self-denial. After regaining his strength, he set out once again to wander alone. He eventually settled in Bodhgaya in the northeastern part of modern-day India. It was at Bodhgaya that Siddhartha experienced a profound turning point. He realized that he was not going to find what he was seeking outwardly in the world and redirected his journey inwardly to the inherent potential of the mind. Siddhartha sat in deep inward meditation under a pipal tree, a large fig with heavy branches that span outward to provide shade like an elm. He remained resolute to stay in meditation until he experienced true wisdom or enlightenment, a state to which he knew he was coming close.[5]

As Siddartha meditated, he was reminded of a pleasant childhood memory of resting in the shade of a similar tree in one of his father's fields. He had let his mind wander freely, without attachments. His mind became quite still and in a state of perfect serenity and equanimity. Siddartha remained in this state for a stretch of time, completely unattached to his thoughts or feelings, with the pure calm he once knew in his childhood and a breakthrough finally came in a deep and sudden flash. In that moment, he realized that the truth he had been searching for all this time was something that he had known all along, but it had become clouded over by a deluded state of mind. This was his enlightenment, his nirvana, and he was momentously liberated from what seemed up to that point an inescapable state of suffering and despair (Thich Thien An 1975, 3, 11).

His discovery was simple but profound: the end to human suffering is to liberate ourselves from the defilements of our minds. From that point on, Siddhartha came

[4] Combined quotes from Bhikku Nanamoli, 2001. *The Middle Length Discourses of the Buddha*, 175 and 329.

[5] In Bodhgaya today there is a shrine at the Mahabodhi temple that built around a pipal tree that is believed to be a descendant through a succession of replantations from the original tree under which Siddhartha experienced his enlightenment.

to be known as Shakyamuni Buddha, meaning "the enlightened one from the Shakya dynasty" or simply, the Buddha. The Buddha devoted the rest of his life to teaching, like Socrates, by way of oral tradition the things he had learned and understood about the way of enlightenment, or *the dharma*. What he taught was not conventional religious doctrine as understood in the West, nor was it metaphysical discourse on divinity, heaven, and hell, nor the wrath of deities. His teachings were a series of discourses on his experiences, the mind, and a kind of spiritual psychology with guidelines for living a liberated life. These early discourses became the doctrinal foundation of Buddhist philosophy and practice.

In many of his early teachings, the Buddha emphasized practical matters of living. He made it clear to his followers that meeting the foundational needs of a person must be met as a necessary condition before attaining spiritual enlightenment. Contemporary Buddhist scholar Peter Hershock emphasizes the idea that basic economic production, distribution, and consumption of goods and services constitute the structural basis for meeting what he identifies as the foundational needs of human security: reasonable environmental quality, healthcare, adequate food, clothing, shelter, etc. Failing to meet these needs makes it virtually impossible to develop the higher-level capacities for human development such as advanced technology, literacy, civic participation, environmental stability, or social justice. At the same time the Buddha taught moderation as greedily chasing after mountains of wealth is as much of an encumbrance to enlightenment as poverty.

As an alternative to poverty and lavishness, the Buddha taught the *middle way*. What he designated as the middle way is a standard of living that is above the deprivation he experienced as an ascetic yet free from the feverish clamor for wealth he knew as the privileged progeny of the powerful Shakya clan. He experienced both and rejected both. He realized that the life of asceticism and self-emaciation leads to enormous suffering and little good can be expected to come from that. He also noted that suffering is not brought to an end by relentlessly pursuing great wealth; the pursuit itself only leads to being consumed by chronic dissatisfaction and insatiable greed. The Buddha taught that "There are these two extremes… giving oneself up to indulgence in sensual pleasures; this is base, common, vulgar, unholy, unprofitable…[or] giving oneself up to self-torment; this is painful, unholy (and also) unprofitable."[6] To be clear, the idea of something being unprofitable is not in the business sense of profit or loss but rather implies self-destructiveness and spiritual malaise.

The notion of the middle way is not a compromise between the extremes of intensifying frustration caused by insatiable greed, or the pain and humiliation caused by poverty. A positive cannot be found between two negatives. Rather, it is a mode of departure from two pathways that lead to the same place of suffering. The Buddha taught that to be liberated is to neither subject ourselves or those in our community to damaging poverty, nor should we become blindly enslaved by

[6]Quote to be found in Samyutta Nikaya, 2000. Translation of *The Connected Discourses of the Buddha*, by Bhikku Bodhi, p. 1843.

delusions of endless accumulation of power, possessions, and money. The former is a humiliating trap, and the latter is an addiction from which no amount of material wealth can provide liberation. The middle way is to take a different path altogether. He also recognized that along the way people need guidance and understanding to arrive at the destination which is true liberation. From his own experience he was aware that the process of achieving true deliverance from suffering is difficult and requires much hard work. To make it easier for his followers to carry on the Buddha taught the *four noble truths* of suffering and liberation in his early discourses.

The first is to know the truth that suffering exists, the second is to know the truth about the causes of suffering, the third is to know the truth that changes need to be made to free ourselves from suffering, and the fourth is to know the truth that we need a system of ethics and guidelines that chart a course for these changes for more healthful living that puts an end to suffering. The fourth noble truth is coupled with a broader framework for guiding healthy action. This framework is the *noble eightfold path* as set forth by the Buddha, "And what, friends, is the noble truth of the way leading to the cessation of suffering? It is just this Noble Eightfold Path; that is, Right View, Right Intention [Thinking], Right Speech, Right Action, Right Livelihood, Right Effort, Right Mindfulness, and Right Concentration" (Kramer, 77). These four noble truths and the noble eightfold path lie at the doctrinal heart of Buddhist philosophy and practice.

8.5 The Four Noble Truths of Buddhist Economics

The first of the four noble truths is to acknowledge the truth that suffering exists. This is a reality check, avoiding denial and coming to terms with the spectrum of disagreeable conditions in which we find ourselves. This is not to say that human life is nothing but suffering from beginning to end, as some have interpreted (Walpola S. Rahula, 16). It is merely acknowledging that aspects of life can lead to suffering to some degree or another. Sometimes the troubles we encounter are relatively mild such as a winter cold, a bee sting, a flat tire, or a scratch across the arm while gardening. Or we might experience suffering more severely from physical trauma, incurable disease, chronic hunger, or the death of a loved one. It should be noted here also that we acknowledge the existence of suffering we acknowledge the existence of joy. There is joy to be found in a skilled craft, repairing things, growing food, helping others, or making the perfect mousetrap. In a way, the first noble truth is seeing two faces of the same coin in a dialectical sense. Through the lens of an awakened mind, seeing the existence of suffering and also seeing the existence of joy. The Buddha taught both the truth of suffering, and the truth of joyful living in seeing things as they are. This begins with developing an awareness that certain disagreeable conditions do exist so that we can take the next steps of transforming those conditions into authentic wellbeing. Such awareness takes work as it requires liberating our minds from the fog of confusion by way of meditation.

In terms of Buddhist economics, somewhere on the spectrum of different degrees of suffering are those we experience in our daily lives: stress at work, job or financial insecurity, unemployment, bankruptcy, foreclosure, or poverty. To recognize these for what they truly are is to come to terms with the reality that there is much malaise that we have brought on ourselves by our own actions.

As an example, in January 2025 the world witnessed a large section of the city of Los Angeles burn to the ground. It was the most devastating wildfire in Los Angeles history. Shortly after the fires were put out the region was further decimated by landslides caused by torrential rainfall. The fires were triggered by drought conditions and the landslides were triggered by massive atmospheric rivers, both conditions are considered by scientists to be symptomatic of climate change. Climate change is brought about by anthropogenic global warming, which is something that we as consumers and producers have brought upon ourselves. Echoing the first noble truth in sentiment, climate activist and author Greta Thunberg writes, "The first step in solving a crisis is not evaluating the full situation or taking immediate action. That comes later. The first step in solving a crisis is to realize that you are in one" (Thunberg, 2023**, 278). In terms of the first noble truth, there is no question that** suffering in Los Angeles exists, and this points to the second noble truth of its cause.

The second noble truth is more challenging as it requires that we not only see through the fog, but also to know its root cause. It is coming to know the root causes and origins of our suffering. In the case of Los Angeles, the causes of the suffering were the fires and landslides, but the root cause is climate change stemming from our own economic activity, specifically those involving burning fossil fuels. There are perhaps as many root causes as there are different varieties of dislikable conditions of life, but for the project of developing Buddhist economics, our focus is on the forms of suffering that arise from our actions and our societal conditions.

In Buddhist economics, the root causes of suffering are seen within a holistic frame of observation. In this view, we see that everything is connected to everything else, and within this holistic frame, we also see that the existence of suffering is connected to a deeper existential defilement. This is to say, certain pathological conditions that are creating troubling conditions in ourselves as well as in our society. As Zen teacher David Loy shows us "an extraordinary parallel between our usual individual predicament and our present collective situation." (Loy 2020, 53). The collective situation being social and environmental malaise: global warming, social injustice, human rights violations, social and economic inequality, and conflict. The vexations we find in ourselves are also found in our social milieu—a collective sense of alienation and a collective attempt to react to this alienation in destructive and even violent ways (Loy, id., 56–57). Yet at the same time there is the possibility of a collective realization and a collective movement toward liberation. If we collectively get ourselves into social and environmental trouble, we must collectively get ourselves out.

To find the root causes of suffering in economic society, we have to look for truth both inwardly and deeply into ourselves as well as outwardly and expansively to the conditions of our surroundings. There is much suffering that originates from the troubled conditions wrapped up in our individual sense of self, and from the same defiled conditions embodied in our social institutions. As we will see shortly, what the Buddha called "the three fires" of greed, hatred, and delusion are root causes of much trouble in us individually, and parallel to these are society conditions defiled by the same greed, hatred, and delusion.

Taking the second noble truth a step further, this inner-and-outer holistic view is part of what Buddhists call *dependent origination*. This is the ontology or state of being of all things in which their existence depends on the existence of all other things. Nothing exists as a distinct entity in isolation. Everything is contingent. A tomato plant, for example, is something that arises from the coexistence of sunshine, rainfall, seeds, soil, and minerals. The human body arises from the existence of blood, skin, organs, and bones, which are all aggregations of cells, which are the aggregation of biochemicals and molecules. And the people who plant tomatoes form farming communities, which arise from human bodies, life and social organization and so on. One exists because of the other, and without the other one does not exist.

In this view, the individual self or person is something that does not exist as a distinct, discrete thing.[7] Buddhists call this the "non-self" which is something that has no real being on its own. It arises and passes away according to surrounding causal conditions, which means it is dependent on other things that also arise and pass away (Loy 2008, 48). Everything, including the very core of our sense of self, exists contingently through the interaction with other things. Without deeper insight and wisdom this can be unsettling. A deeply rooted existential fear often arises when we come face to face with such an ephemeral conception of ourselves as a non-self or a kind of nonexistence. Nothingness. In the Buddhist view, such fear of nothingness gives rise to attachments, particularly to a constructed self, or ego, and from these deep existential attachments so many of our troubles stemming from greed or hatred or fear originate.

The first and second noble truths are about learning the existence of suffering along with its root causes. But identifying the source of our suffering has little meaning unless we are prepared to do something about it. The third and fourth noble truths are about the processes of making changes to end this suffering. As we look deeply into the causes of our suffering, we cannot help but make discoveries, one of which is that we would inevitably have to change our ways of thinking and acting in the world, particularly those locked together with self-attachment.

The third noble truth emphasizes simultaneously ceasing the patterns that have engendered our suffering by dissolving away the habits of thought and action that

[7] In the Pali Canon and other Buddhist literature there are widespread references to the "Three Dharma Seals." Metaphorically, these seals are markers or stamps that are found on all things signifying that they are conditioned phenomena and therefore are characterized by (1) impermanence, (2) without a separate self or non-self, and (3) nirvana or perfectly tranquil; See Thich Nhat Hanh, *The Heart of the Buddha's Teaching* pp. 131–145. Notwithstanding, there is contention as to whether the last seal is nirvana or suffering. I'll leave this debate to Buddhist scholars and chose the former as it is consistent with the notion that not all of life is about suffering.

are part of the root cause. By dissolving these habits, we can allow the development of new ways of life to emerge. With time, effort, and practice, the suffering we create by the ways we live our lives can be transformed into an authentic existence that is joyful, creative, and free from vexation. The process of transformation takes place by stepping aside from the conditioning and habits that make it impossible to pursue livelihoods with a genuine sense of peace or dignity. If we cannot or will not take this step, we remain trapped in economic business as usual, wheezing on the hamster wheel of consumerism, acquisitiveness, and malcontent. To make these changes real, however, we need to identify pathways that can guide us toward healthy habits and healthy living.

The fourth noble truth is the truth of how the process of transforming suffering into wellbeing is made possible and accessible with some guidelines. As mentioned above, it is the connection between the truths of suffering, causes, and changes and the ethical system of the noble eightfold path. Before we explore the eightfold path, another of the core teachings of the Buddha needs to be mentioned: the three fires of greed, hatred, and delusion. These fires extend from self-attachment and are together the root cause of a galaxy of human suffering.

8.6 Greed, Hatred, and Delusion

According to the second noble truth, the task is to identify the root causes of suffering. The Buddha taught his followers that the three fires of greed, hatred, and delusion lie just beneath the surface of a whole spectrum of human suffering. Buddhists are not alone in seeing the destructiveness of these mental conditions. All the great spiritual traditions have a set of ethical principles or precepts to guide individual behavior away from the traps of destructive emotions, and societies everywhere would be much healthier if each of us were to skillfully follow such ethical guidelines. But establishing the do-and-don't guidelines for individual behavior is only part of the story. There is also much to be said about how our social institutions and cultures play a potent role in how we act in the world. Social institutions can forge certain habits of thought and action that are in the opposite direction of ethical or healthful living.

Social institutions are powerful forces in every society. They shape our values, worldviews, and ideologies. They influence how we consume and produce things, how we think about value, and use our time and energy. For this reason, Buddhist economics needs to have a vision for social change alongside providing guidelines for individual behavior. It needs to extend and reflect on the behavior patterns of individual producers, investors, and consumers within the purview that such patterns are heavily, if not entirely, structured by corporate, financial, and government institutions. What we will address here is the existence of large and powerful economic institutions that have been growing in power and influence for over a century. We also submit that these institutions fan the flames of what the Buddha called the "three fires" of greed, hatred, and delusion, with their drive to conquer markets, celebrate cunning in financial markets, and foster the cult of consumerism.

The power of corporate media and advertising to propagandize a certain obsessive-compulsive lifestyle is obvious to anyone who cares to take a critical look. But most of us choose not to think about it. There is comfort in surrendering to a kind of sleepy acceptance of corporate influence and not bothering with seeking the truth outside of what we are told. This acquiescence stems in part from the fact that corporate society has created its own systems for modulating social behavior. Engaged Buddhist Sulak Sivaraksa reflects on this, "We have to see the relationships between social structures, self-surveillance, and self-censorship. To enforce social constructions, institutions intimidate us… The media—almost all are for-profit corporations—are expert in legitimizing the actions of those in power." (Sulak Sivarksa, 15). David Loy (2008, 89) also draws the conclusion that "…the problem is not only that the three poisons [three fires] operate collectively but that they have taken a life of their own." The social construction of greed, hatred, and delusion, is itself a powerful force and needs to be addressed by any serious socially engaged Buddhist movements.

Before we get to that, however, the starting place for Buddhism is always with the mind. Zen teacher Philip Kapleau teaches us that the process of changing society always begins with work on the self, but remaining mindfully present with affecting social change, "To help people without hurting them at the same time, or hurting yourself, means that we must first work on ourselves." (Kapleau, 2000, 243). In this Buddhist view, the mind is something that needs training. Training the mind in this sense is not just about education, though that is a part of the practice. Buddhists make no distinction between the conscious mind and the spiritual essence of one's being, which ultimately is pure emptiness. Training the mind in a Buddhist practice, therefore, is a process of dissolving the figments, vexations, obsessions, and other things that crowd into mental space and give rise to a troubled consciousness. A troubled consciousness leads to troubled motivations, intentions, and eventually troubling behavior. Without such training—mindfulness training specifically—the mind is vulnerable to be crowded with an array of mental states that can be destructive.

In a society where people's minds are captured by craving or obsessive acquisitiveness, it is as if we all have an internal voice in our heads that is continuously compelling us to gain more, consume more, and make more. This opens the starting gates in a race to accumulate more and more in a process that has no end or finish line. With each lap there builds a deepening sense of dissatisfaction, which crowds out a mind condition of authentic wellbeing. As Thich Nhat Hanh, reminds us, "you probably have a notion that there's some as yet unrealized condition that has to be attained before you can be happy… a promotion or income level. But that notion may be the very thing that prevents you from being happy." For Nhat Hanh, the first step toward liberating ourselves from this is to begin fostering mindful awareness, "To release that notion and make space for true happiness to manifest, you first have to experience the truth that entertaining your current ideas is making you suffer." (Nhat Hanh 2015, 71). Craving makes one see things in a way that they are not.

One's perception of reality becomes warped, which then ties greed with delusion, which combined with aggression or hatred, leads to a heightened feeling of anxiety.

Language rarely captures an essence with precision, and it is helpful to see these as generic categories for a multitude of destructive mind conditions summarized in the figure below. We refer to these mind conditions as destructive for the simple reason that they cause harm to ourselves and others. Seen in a broader context, these conditions can fester, spread, and ultimately lead to ill-fated results at the societal level, yet somehow being accepted as normal in corporate, consumerist culture. Strangely, when pathology is writ large at the societal level and has become socialized, it tends to be treated as normal. Pyromania is classified as an impulse control disorder. It is a type of psychopathy in which the afflicted cannot control their impulse to set things on fire. The act of starting fires provides a sense of relief, instant gratification, or euphoria to which the person becomes addicted. But when we look at our economic activity that underlies anthropogenic global warming, the results are the same and even more severe wildfires. As this activity is shared and habituated through our economic institutions, it becomes difficult for many to care as they seem beyond individual control (Fig. 8.1).

What is key here for Buddhist economics is to trace these destructive mental states to their fundamental origin of self-attachment. Self-attachment is a deeply ingrained grasping to an entity that has taken form as ego. When we are self-attached, the ego-self is believed to be an unchanging noumenon in the Kantian sense that it exists independently of sense, perception, or experience. The ego-self forms a delusion that its own existence is permanent, which is the paramount delusion in the Buddhist view of things.

In Buddhism, the existence of the ego-self is an illusion or mental figment. It is a construction to which we attach names but cannot be found in either body or consciousness. The figment originates at the point of contact between the conscious mind and the surrounding world. It is an emergent entity that is created uniquely in

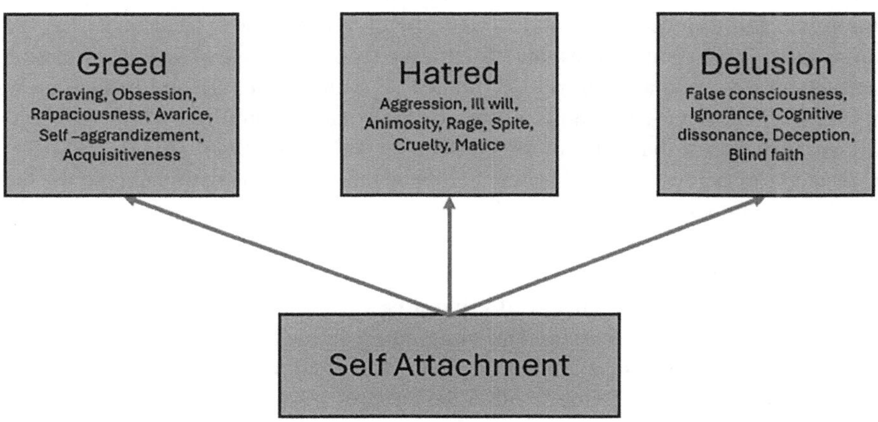

Fig. 8.1 Traits and Emotions Arising From Self-Attachment

this place but has no substance or tangible existence. It cannot be located in space or time, nor can it be perceived by any of our senses. Rather, it is an illusory construct reified through an underlying interface between physical and cognitive processes. In the Buddhist view, the physical body and the consciousness that give shape and form to the illusion are ultimately formless and empty. The body is a swarm of molecules and atoms that come and go in the otherwise completely empty space-time dimensions. The chatter stream of mind activity is either something that was thought and passed or is something that has not yet become manifest. The space between that which has passed and that which is not yet manifest can be reduced to infinitesimally smaller and smaller dimensions until it vanishes completely. In other words, it is nothing.

Self-attachment is forged out of a cauldron of fear of this nothingness, which is felt existentially as death. Consequently, the ego-self is a construct created out of a cauldron of fear, sometimes monumentally so. There is a powerful tendency for us to create the ego-self as an abstraction and then become attached to it as if life depends on it. The ego-self suffers from an existential vulnerability as if it is under constant threat and needs to be protected and pampered. As such, we form a white-knuckled attachment, and this ego-self attachment is the taproot from which greed, hatred, and delusion are subsidiaries.

As we become self-attached in this way, we are grasping onto a figment of our imagination like identifying with a character in a movie. A deep sense of dissatisfaction and frustration looms as we try to constantly affirm a fabricated self. It is like trying to fill a void that cannot be filled yet feeling eternally frustrated because the more we try to fill the imagined hole, the more we realize the futility of trying to fill an endless chasm. Paradoxically, as we try to feel more alive, we go out of our way to mask who we really are. We cling and grasp onto impermanent, illusory things, feelings, and sensations that we believe will affirm our ego. This can only make us feel even more vulnerable and thus strengthen a resolve to reject anything that seems to pose a threat. All of this begins to take on a life of its own and a sense of vulnerability builds; we cling, grasp, and covet out of worry that if we stop, everything will fall to pieces. It is almost as if the clinging itself is what makes us feel alive. On this Ken Jones notes that "Liberation from our sense of lack is impossible as long as we evade accepting its ultimately ego-created nature and instead go on trying to fill the imagined hole by top-loading our lives and the world with ego-affirming behavior that is needless, ineffective, and destructive." (Jones, 2003, 32). Our need for such security is insatiable; that is, until we come to understand the fact that it is the grasping neediness itself that is the problem.

In the Buddhist view, this attachment to the fabricated ego-self is the most fundamental affliction in the human psyche as it leads to a painful, unsatisfactory, even pathological state of existence. Suffering arises from an inability to experience a broader sense of pure goodness and clinging to things that only serve immediate ego-gratification. In this way, we slide into a vicious circle of pathology and deeper into a state of delusion formed with a desire to possess or acquire things that we believe will shelter us from the abyss of nothingness. The emptier we feel, the more we wrap ourselves with inauthentic accouterments of materialism and consumerism until we become mummified. The result from chronic dissatisfaction is an ersatz life that, given societal norms of corporate and consumerist standards, appears to be thriving. Coveting and grasping naturally leads to aggression as we start getting in each other's way. In time, we create the disagreeable social conditions that are passed on as karma from one generation to the next. And because we normalize these conditions collectively, there is a general condition that is often depicted in Buddhist literature as the "Realm of Hungry Ghosts."

In some interpretations, the Realm of Hungry Ghosts is a mythological place where people languish in a kind of hellish world of discontent. In this realm, each is trapped in a state of escalating cravings that will never be satisfied. Here people are captured by their compulsions to chase after what seems to be an illusory "good life," only to experience these fleeting moments of joy that are soon overshadowed by the heavy feelings that things are never good enough. Physician and author, Gabor Maté refers to this realm as the domain of addiction, "where we constantly seek something outside ourselves to curb an insatiable yearning for relief or fulfillment." (Maté, 2008, 1–3). Maté sees contemporary Western culture, particularly in the United States, as awash with addictions: to drugs, alcohol, food, cell phones, computers, sex, and not least of which to consuming, shopping, gambling, and of course money.

Jungian psychologist and financial analyst, Deborah Gregory, looks at these questions from the point of view of modern psychology and draws the conclusion that they are partially driven by the cultural fascination with money. She writes, "...when examined on the unconscious level from a psychoanalytic perspective... [greed] is being driven by an inner need to accumulate money... the compulsion to amass wealth is akin to an empty hole that will need continual filling." (Gregory, 2014, 40). Compulsions lead to craving and hoarding and chronic dissatisfaction, which leads to jealousy, prejudiced hostility toward others, and aggression.

The more people are motivated by the three fires, the more they feel they must manipulate their surroundings to get what they want. Manipulative behavior inevitably leads to feelings of alienation as each begins to see how they are being manipulated by others. Society becomes awash in mutual distrust and anxiety (Loy 2008, 63). The anxiety, in part, stems from a condition of living conceptualized as a free market survival of the fittest. Each individual is pitted against all other individuals in a combative market environment in which survival is never assured. In a commodity-producing system, such suffering is said to be ameliorated by consumer spending and gratification in consumption. The more people feel anxiety in this system, the more there is a felt need to improve the consumers' material standard of living, which ironically leads to more competitive acquisition and more anxiety.

Producers are also driven to exhaustion by acquisitive and combative market competition. Capitalism has always been characterized as a system of competitors struggling against one another in a gladiatorial combat for market share and profits. In this endless struggle, the power of any given capitalist depends on the amount of capital he or she controls. If one acquires more capital, then they will grow, have technical advantages, and build their economic strength with the advantages gained as such, making them more fiercely competitive and eventually driving others out of the market. In the Spencerian struggle for survival of the fittest, aggression thus abounds along with heightened anxiety about facing market extinction. Capitalism has always been characterized by the frantic effort of capitalists to make more profits and to convert these profits into more capital. Thus, acquisitiveness and combativeness, and market aggression fall into the clusters of kinship of greed, hatred, and abound with pathological system conditions.

Recent studies in psychological pathology indicate that societies everywhere are moving in the direction of permitting, reinforcing, and valuing some of the traits listed in the "psychopathy checklist" including traits such as impulsivity, irresponsibility, and lack of remorse (Hare, 1993, 177). The pathology arising from greed and hatred is evident not just in the harm we do but also from our distorted perception of reality. This causes harm, too, but in more subtle ways. A destructive emotion can be seen as an obscuring phenomenon such that it prevents the mind from ascertaining reality as it is. Without training, the mind is susceptible to self-attachment that is the sinkhole into which we can fall into obsessive-compulsive behavior.

Greed, hatred, and delusion are destructive emotions stemming from self-attachment, but they also exist alongside a multitude of other emotions, including compassion, trust, and a desire to make life joyful. None of us is impervious to being captured by destructive emotions, yet none of us is also without the potential for living with healthy emotions. On this Thich Nhat Hanh provides an important metaphor. He sees the potential to be overtaken by greed is like a seed lying dormant in a garden bed along with seeds of hatred, aggression, or despair. When the seeds are watered through experience, they become mental narratives that eventually drive behavior. Nhat Hanh writes, "Store consciousness is like the land, the ground, with many seeds preserved in it. In our store consciousness there are seeds of joy… also seeds of anger, hate, despair… One of the functions of the store consciousness is to maintain these seeds… When a seed is watered in our store consciousness, it manifests as an energy in our mind consciousness and becomes a mental formation." (Nhat Hanh 2007, 17–18). These seeds are sown by our own experience as well as the experiences of our families, our societies, and our histories and are drivers of behavior. The human potential for greed-inspired behavior is thus like a seed in our store consciousness waiting to sprout along with a multitude of many other seeds. This is a profound understanding as it points to the importance of social context. In other words, social context and institutional priorities determine which seeds receive the water and nutrients they need to thrive while others remain dormant. In socially engaged Buddhism, we must look both inwardly, deeply into ourselves, and outwardly to the conditions of our surroundings. This is the inner and outer work.

For the inner work, we can see this as the existential origins of the greed of self-attachment, though the word greed carries judgmental connotations. The intention here is not to indict humanity for such afflictions but rather to understand their social origins and to map out a program for change. For the outer work, we must take a step back and see that greed extends beyond the individual and is part of the cultural fabric of capitalist society. The existence of suffering is connected to the fearful ego as well as societal conditioning. There is much suffering that originates from the troubled conditions wrapped up in our individual sense of self, the ego, and just the same from the defiled conditions embodied in our social structures, our institutions. In socially engaged Buddhist economics, changing our economic institutions rests on the foundation of the four noble truths of understanding troubling conditions and changing them. Zen teacher, Philip Kapleau, writes about the widespread suffering that is created in corporate capitalism, "Capitalist industrial society has created conditions of extreme impermanence, terrifying insubstantiality, and a struggling dissatisfaction and frustration. It would be difficult to imagine any social order for which Buddhism was more relevant and needed." (Kapleau, 2000, 244).

8.7 The Corporation and the Institutionalization of Greed

Nearly a century ago, legendary economist Thorstein Veblen looked to the future and was troubled. In one of his very last pieces of writing he outlined what he called "The Secular Trend" (Veblen [1923] 1997, 398–445). He examined past trends, present conditions, and extrapolated to the future of economic society in America that is certain to tear itself apart into a state of antagonism among our economic institutions. What he predicted for America's future was a nation deeply divided between healthy, well-adjusted institutions and those that are maladjusted and imbecilic. On the well-adjusted side, Veblen identified habitual ways of behaving that are grounded in science, problem-solving, and creativity and are useful to the human life process. They guide our work in ways that are useful to people, not because there are fortunes to be made, but because of the historically rich craft traditions in which humans are fascinated with the idea of doing things better. These stand on the side of progress, appropriately implemented technology, stability, and the provision for the general wellbeing of the population.

At the same time, he was vexed by what he observed as such traditions being canceled out and replaced by powerful corporate institutions. Veblen saw the consolidation of corporate power as no less than a raw, maladaptive, myopic pursuit of wealth accumulation and a strategic seizing of control of all the major industries "through shrewd investments and coalitions with other business men" with disregard for the legitimate and pragmatic purposes for which the industries were originally created (Veblen [1904] 1975, 24). Veblen also attested to the rise of the corporation as a dominant institution and not merely a business model or form of business enterprise as characterized in mainstream economics. For Veblen, the Interests represent the principal shareholders and the corporate class of professionals that work at the top of the corporate hierarchy. Paper wealth accumulation became the economic priority and was pursued at all costs. He saw the members of this class positioning themselves to take control of the economy with a patent indifference to economic stability, industrial progress, or anything else that might contribute to social wellbeing beyond financial gain. He also saw a system emerging in which the entire economy would eventually succumb to predatory impulses in which taking profits and conquering become more important than actual productive work or social provisioning. Veblen's secular trend came to be a kind of structural drift in which the entire system was moving toward a system condition of maladjustment which he described as "systematic retardation and derangement." (Veblen [1904] 1975, 421).

As he saw things, Wall Street and giant corporations are the maladjusted institutions that exist to accumulate ostentatious fortunes, status, and conquests for a class of the wealthy and powerful "absentee owners." Rather than contribute to progress, they smother the economy with greed, corruption, and stagnation. By their own mandate, corporate institutions are fashioned to be indifferent to social provisioning and are governed by the narrowest of objectives—to make money for vested owners. Veblen writes, "The effective control of the economic situation, in business, industry, and civil life, rests on the on the control of credit [finance]. Therefore, the effectual exercise of initiative, discretion, and authority is perforce vested in those massive aggregations of absentee ownership that make the Interests." (Veblen [1904] 1975, 398–399). He attested to an evolutionary drift toward corporate hegemony in which all other major institutions were becoming increasingly pressed under the boot of corporate power. He described the formation of an emergent system as, "One Big Union made up of partners, auxiliaries, subsidiaries, extensions and purveyors of traffic." (Veblen [1904] 1975, 399). In other words, what Veblen was describing was an evolutionary trend toward corporate hegemony, which, like so many other creations of capitalism, has developed a kind of mind of its own. What was most troubling for Veblen was that he saw a future in which the corporate world would push all else aside and the entire economic system would cease to be concerned about providing for the needs of people and only about financial gain—a pathological end game.

Veblen paraphrased what contemporary engaged Buddhists see now as a global problem of the institutionalization of greed, aggression or hatred, and delusion. With its emphasis on aggregating financial capital, buying, selling, and taking profits wherever they can be found, the corporation rose to prominence with a singularity of purpose: to ceaselessly maximize and compound shareholder returns without limit. Financial wealth accumulation became an economic priority, and along with this came an addiction to economic growth and consumerism. Zen teacher and scholar, David Loy, has often pointed out that greed—which in this case is the boundless compulsion to accumulate financial and material wealth—is not just a human emotion; it is an institutionalized force within the capitalist world, "our economic system institutionalizes greed in at least two ways: corporations are never profitable enough and people never consume enough." (Loy 2008, 89). In his book, *The Wisdom of Sustainability*, Sulak Sivaraksa, argues that capitalism encourages greed and consumerism and reinforces delusion with media advertising. He also points out that the message from the media is that happiness is something that can be gained from consuming endless quantities of stuff (Sivaraksa 2010, 8). Loy emphasizes that media companies never question the delusions spawned by their manipulative advertising, which are specifically designed to foster consumerist impulses to buy things. Zen master Thich Nhat Hanh also tells us how corporate media is a source of mental and spiritual pollution that encourages greed, violence, and anxiety.

The large publicly traded corporation is unquestionably the dominant economic institution in the United States economy. Emboldened by federal government subsidies, patent protections, the effective removal of state controls of corporate charters, and the constitutional protections provided by corporate personhood, the corporation now towers over American society. The corporation continues to defy most attempts to bring it under democratic control or regulate it in the public interest. And although it routinely defies accountability to a democratically elected government, the corporation is nonetheless able to exert enormous influence on local and national government. As the corporation became the dominant institution, its agenda of endless accumulation of wealth accumulation became the *raison d'etre* for all economic activity.

Thus, from the point of view of socially engaged Buddhist economics, greed and other destructive habits of thought are not just defilements of an individual's mind, they are deeply rooted in our dominant economic institutions and in our collective psyche. Socially engaged Buddhist economics is aimed at helping not only the individual worker, consumer, or investor to move away from the three fires, but to create and evolve our social institutions in the same way.

As we look around us and see the raging pathologies of global warming, resource depletion, and massive economic instabilities, we can see the need for considering a new and very different approach to economics. David Loy makes this case succinctly, "Buddhism can provide what the modern world most needs: the spiritual message that may yet awaken us to who we are and why we as a species have such a penchant for making ourselves unhappy" (Loy 2008, 3). And the modern world needs practical things that people can do and see the results of their efforts. In the fourth noble truth, which includes the noble eightfold path, the Buddha outlined a system of ethics that can help guide us to such a way of life.

8.8 The Noble Eightfold Path

The *noble eightfold path* is a set of strategies that can help us cultivate wholesome action stemming from wholesome potentialities that lie within us all. Each strategy is designated "right," but what is considered right here is not a set of moral commandments or judgments but one that leads to liberation from suffering and more beneficial living. Each strategy is inseparable from all the others, like eight legs supporting a table, and all are wide open for interpretation depending on need and context. The interpretation here is for the purposes of crafting socially engaged Buddhist economics.

Right View comes from a clear mind and the ability to comprehend the truth of things as they are without mental embellishment. As we free ourselves from the fog of greed, hatred and delusion, we become more capable of viewing things as they really are. With right view there is no need for reality checks or reassurances in moments of paranoid speculation. Reality simply comes to us calmly in plain sight and we are able to see which kinds of economic behaviors are wholesome and which are not, which actions lead to wellbeing and which do not.

Right Intention also sometimes interpreted as Right Thinking, is the practice of keeping the mind clear and focused on healthy things with a sense of good will rather than ill will, with a sense of good health rather than ill health. By staying focused and diligent on healthy activities, we can train ourselves on how to prevent being lured toward destructive behavior. With right concentration and thinking, we can see more deeply into the purpose or end results of our work. We can benefit from reminding ourselves why we are doing what we are doing or asking ourselves whether there is another way. Staying focused on healthy purposes makes it easier to dissolve unhealthy motivations that originate in the three fires. This also serves to develop an awareness of the impact what we do has on everything and everyone around us.

Right Speech is a practice of working against tendencies of expression that spill out from a mind fraught with greed, hatred, and delusion. As long as people remain captured by these fires, they will express themselves caustically toward one another and in ways that are intended to offend, manipulate, and deceive. Right speech is the opposite of the all-too-familiar venomous gossip at the workplace and deceitful marketing strategies.

Right Action is being observant of the relationship between habits of mind and habits of action. A mind swallowed up in greed, hatred, and delusion motivates economic actions prone to destructiveness—trashing the environment, depleting resources, exploiting people, or creating a toxic and unstable culture of greed. When we talk of right action, we are not trying to place judgment or blame on others, but rather to illuminate cause-and-effect relationships. Stepping away from the "greed is good" ideology, an entrepreneur blinded by greed and the compulsion to take ever-expanding profits might be compelled to produce things without regard to the potential damage they cause, such as violent video games targeted specifically for children. If violent games foster violent sensibilities in children during early development, they may develop deeply ingrained habits toward violence for the remainder of their lives. Without a strong sense of right action, the entrepreneur is perhaps unwittingly worsening cultural conditions of violence and aggression. With right action, we can cultivate a deeper sense of the implications of our economic behavior.

Right Livelihood, as E. F. Schumacher observed, is part of the Buddhist way. Originally, right livelihood was conceived as a process of earning a living without violence, slaughter, deceit or trickery, usury, narcotics or alcohol, slave trade, weapons, or prostitution.[56] In a modern interpretation, perhaps this can be generalized to simply say earning a living without causing harm to others, to the environment or habitat, or culture. Narrowing this down to specific provisions would have to be defined differently in different cultures.

Right Effort is diligence or conscientiousness in all aspects of life and maintaining vigilance against unwholesome motivations. Being diligent and working hard is often heralded as a virtue in itself. But can we really say that without also knowing toward all this work is for? If the entrepreneur who produces violent video games is working hard, the effort is wasted as it does not lead to anything beneficial. We would be delusional or cynical to think that our hard work constitutes healthy diligence even though the work ultimately leads toward unhealthy results.

Right Concentration is staying focused and giving our task at hand our full concentration. As we will see, this is closely related to mindfulness in that it involves a kind of total immersion or absorption. It is a true skill to be impervious to distractions when most of us live in societies that are full of faddishness and lacking in clarity of purpose aside from profit-making. Right concentration is the living verification of Right View of things as they are without distortion or delusion.

Right Mindfulness is the most powerful of the eight strategies and is at the very heart of the Buddha's teachings.[57] Right mindfulness is a state of mind in which people become aware of their thoughts and actions and are fully occupied in the present moment. To be mindful is to be fully and calmly engaged in the here and now. It is a state in which our minds are not cluttered with a running mental commentary or the noise and confusion that hums with the millions of things that can capture our thoughts. It enables us to be openly and directly engaged in the activities before us. It is thoughtfulness without superfluous mental baggage, and the thoughts are clear, open and directly focused and lucid.

Mindfulness is centrally important for socially engaged Buddhist economics and is something that we will explore in much more detail further on. The four noble truths and the noble eightfold path would be hollow doctrines without mindfulness that brings it all to life in practice. It is the tool that we use to chip away the layers of junk that delude our minds and compel us to act in ways that cause suffering and damage, particularly the actions that arise from greed, hatred, and delusion. Mindfulness can help us gradually disentangle ourselves from all kinds of ego-based attachments, including those things that reside nowhere else but in our own minds.

It is presence of mind and being wholly in the moment with a clear, attentive awareness. The mind is deliberately kept at the level of bare attention, a detached observation of what is happening within us and around us in the present moment. All judgments and interpretations must be suspended, or if they occur, just registered and dropped. A delusive mind captured by defilements and clouded by mental formations that create distortions in thought. These distortions in thought lead to actions that are at odds with the reality of actual situations or circumstances.

Without mindfulness, we can easily be prone to sinking into a deluded and troubling state, like finding ourselves drowning, yet for no other reason than we stumbled into water without the ability to swim. Mindfulness is the way toward wisdom as sought by Schumacher with his vision for an economic life based on a spiritually informed way of being that transcends the specific aspects of daily living. Informed wisdom helps us see clearly which life actions lead to true wellbeing and which do not. In this sense, mindfulness perhaps is the closest approximation to Schumacher's eye of the heart and is the very substance of Buddhist economics.

Mindfully dissolving the old and leaving it behind, kicking the habits of thought and action that make us suffer, and seeking a path away from all this suffering toward true, genuine wellbeing is the key to realizing genuine socially engaged Buddhist economics. Meditation is a key part of this process of unclouding the mind. The process is fairly simple to understand, but the practice takes time and effort. Try for a moment to simply sit on a cushion or chair, breathe, ungrasp, and dissolve all that occupies your mind. It is not as easy as it sounds. In time, and if practiced well and diligently, we can dissolve the attachments that give rise to so much anguish and become free. From this liberation comes the spontaneity, true sense of joy, and authenticity that springs naturally from the very nothingness that we need not fear.

If all of us were to strive to make our living in a way that follows some or all of the guidelines in the noble eightfold path, our economic systems would transform, and we would change the momentum of history. We would not only change the kinds of goods and services people enjoy, but transform the collective mindset as we would do things and think about economics in a different way. Habits of thought and habits of action are inseparable. With mindfulness practice, we can develop a greater awareness of our state of mind with some measure of objectivity. If we can be in the moment, recognize aggression or greed as agitated states of mind when they arise, and become more adept at not becoming so possessed by them that they maintain control over our lives. When we change our minds, we change our actions, and when we change our actions, we are actively changing society even though we may not even be aware of it.

8.9 Conclusion

Most of the contemporary literature in socially engaged Buddhism that branches into economics focuses on the inner work of individual conduct without the outer work of changing social structures. Focusing on such conduct is consistent with Buddhist philosophy and practice, though the attention is largely on building skillful means or livelihoods for individuals. It is fair to say that if a critical mass of the population were to pay attention to the middle way, the four noble truths, and practice the ethics taught in the noble eightfold path, the population and the planet would both be in much healthier shape than they are now. But notably absent from this work is an emphasis on making change at the institutional level. It is arguable that societies will never get to the other side of global, social, economic, and environmental crises we face unless we address these crises at the institutional level as well as the emphasis on personal practice. Engaged Buddhism must broaden its scope beyond individualism and address specific crises sourced from socially constructed human behavior patterns embedded in social structures and institutions. Mindfulness is an awareness of things as they truly are without judgment. This clarity of perception applies to seeing not only our own behavior, but to an awareness of the social forces around us as well. This awareness is crucial, particularly in economics. We will never be able to understand how economies function if we do not understand the institutions that comprise them and how they influence our daily lives. Doing the outer work of rebuilding our economic institutions that lead toward systemic change is a long-term, evolutionary process that will be fraught with conflict. This is the part of Buddhist economics that often gets overlooked. On this Ken Jones shares his insights,

> If the existential roots of greed are to be exposed, why the consumerism that fuels greed and feeds on existential anxiety? If we are to ameliorate personal truculence and rancor then why not the 'up front,' 'in your face' culture-with-attitude that stokes it up. Conversely, why does modern Western society so rarely support the kinds of political and economic conditions that encourage compassion and generosity? Is it really possible to believe that modern society is no more than a collection of individuals, so that if enough try to behave decently to one another, oppressive regimes will cease to oppress and transnational corporations will cease to exploit? Lifestyle change is a good start, but it can never be enough without a commitment to radical structural and institutional change. The Buddhist teaching, if it is to be sustained into the next millennium of our crisis-ridden planet, must be socially and ecologically engaged. (Jones, 2003, 39)

In the fall of 2018, just as Hurricane Michael was trampling the southeast part of the U.S. the Intergovernmental Panel on Climate Change (IPCC) issued a new report titled, "Special Report on Global Warming of 1.5 °C: Summary for Policymakers." The report urges that immediate and comprehensive action needs to be taken to reduce concentrations of carbon dioxide and other greenhouse gases from the atmosphere. The goal would be to limit the warming trend in global ambient temperatures down to 1.5 °C or less over the next decade. The IPCC notes that this effort "would require rapid and far-reaching transitions in energy, land, urban and rural infrastructure (including transport and buildings), and industrial systems."[8]

This may seem daunting, but it is no less daunting than doing the self-work of liberating something as complex and mysterious as our own minds.

References

Gregory, Deborah. 2014. *Unmasking Financial Psychopaths: Inside the Minds of Investors in the Twenty-First Century. NY: Palgrave Macmillan.*

Hare, Robert D. 1993. *Without Conscience: The Disturbing World of the Psychopaths Among Us*. NY: Pocket Books.

Intergovernmental Panel on Climate Change. Special Report on Global Warming of 1.5°C: Summary for Policymakers. October 2018. https://www.ipcc.ch/sr15/chapter/spm/

Jones, Ken. 2003. *The New Social Face of Buddhism: An Alternative Sociopolitical Perspective*. Boston: Wisdom Publications.

Kapleau, Philip. 2000. Responsibility and Social Action. In *Dharma Rain: Sources of Buddhist Environmentalism*, ed. Stephanie Kaza and Kenneth Kraft. Boston: Shambala.

Keynes, John M. 1971. In *Collected Writings*, ed. Donald E. Moggridge, vol. IX. London: Macmillan.

Kramer, Gregory. 2007. *Insight Dialogue: The Interpersonal Path to Freedom*. Boston: Shambhala.

Loy, David. 2008. *Money, Sex, War, Karma: Notes for a Buddhist Revolution*. Boston: Wisdom Publications.

[8] Intergovernmental Panel on Climate Change, "Special Report on Global Warming of 1.5 °C: Summary for Policymakers," October 2018. https://www.ipcc.ch/sr15/chapter/spm/

Loy, David. 2020. Ecodharma: A New Buddhist Path? *Canadian Journal of Buddhist Studies*, pp 52–73.
Magnuson, Joel. 2008. *Mindful Economics: How the U.S. Economy Works, why it Matters, and how it Could be Different*. New York: Seven Stories Press.
Magnuson, Joel. 2016. *From Greed to Wellbeing: A Buddhist Approach to Resolving our Economic and Financial Crises*. Bristol: Policy Press.
Magnuson, Joel. 2022. *The Dharma and Socially Engaged Buddhist Economics*. Cham: Springer Nature/Palgrave Macmillan.
Maté, Gabor. 2008. *In the Realm of Hungry Ghosts: Close Encounters with Addiction*. Berkely: North Atlantic Books.
Meadows, D., J. Randers, and D. Meadows. 2004. *Limits to Growth: The 30-Year Update*. White River Junction: Chelsea Green Publishing.
Nanamoli, Bhikku. 2001. *The Middle Length Discourses of the Buddha*. 2nd ed. Boston: Wisdom Publications.
Nhat Hanh, Thich. 1998. *The Heart of the Buddha's Teaching: Transforming Suffering into Peace, Joy, and Liberation*. New York: Broadway Books.
Nhat Hanh, Thich. 2007. *The Art of Power*. New York: Harper One.
Nhat Hanh, Thich. 2015. *Silence: The Power of Quiet in a World Full of Noise*, 2015. NY: Harper Collins.
Nikaya, Samyutta. 2000. *The Connected Discourses of the Buddha*. Translated by Bhikku Bodhi. Boston: Wisdom Publications.
Philipsen, Dirk. 2015. *The Little Big Number: How GDP Came to Rule the World and What To Do About It*. Princeton/New Jersey: Princeton University Press.
Rahula, Walpola S. The Noble Eightfold Path: The Buddha's Practical Instructions to Reach the End of Suffering. *Tricycle Magazine*. https://tricycle.org/magazine/noble-eightfold-path/
Rahula, Walpola S. [1959] rev. 1974. *What the Buddha Taught*, New York: Grove Press.
Reich, Robert. 2012. If You Took the Greed Out of Wall Street, All You'd Have Left Is Pavement: Why Greg Smith's Critique Is Way Too Narrow. March 16, 2012. http://robertreich.org
Schumacher, E. F. 1973. *Small Is Beautiful: Economics as if People Mattered*. New York: Harper and Row.
Sivaraksa, Sulak. 2010. *The Wisdom of Sustainability: Buddhist Economics for the 21st Century*. Kihei: Koa Books.
Smith, Greg. 2012. Why I am Leaving Goldman Sachs. *The New York Times*, Op ed., March 14, 2012.
Thien An, Thich. 1975. *Zen Philosophy, Zen Practice*. Berkeley: Dharma Publishing.
Thunberg, Greta, ed. 2023. *The Climate Book*. New York: The Penguin Press.
Veblen, Thorstein. [1904] 1975. *The Theory of Business Enterprise*. Clifton: Augustus Kelly.
Veblen, Thorstein. [1923] 1997. *Absentee Ownership: Business Enterprise in Recent Times: The Case of America*. New Brunswick: Transaction Publishers, 1992, pp. 398–445.

Joel Magnuson is an independent economist based in the USA. He is the author of several books on economics, philosophy and history, including *The Dharma and Socially Engaged Buddhist Economics* (Springer/Palgrave Macmillan 2022). His forthcoming book *Self, Society, and Economy* (2026) explores the development of the American schools of philosophical pragmatism and institutional economics at the turn of the twentieth century.

Chapter 9
Buddhism and Economic Ethics: Perspectives on Theravada, Mahayana, and Modern Applications

Candauda Arachchige Saliya

Abstract This chapter explores the intersection of Buddhist economic thought, ethics, and contemporary economic systems, with a focus on Theravada and Mahayana Buddhism. Both traditions emphasize ethical behavior, compassion, and non-attachment to material wealth, yet their philosophical differences yield distinct approaches to economic activity. Theravada Buddhism, prevalent in countries like Sri Lanka and Thailand, advocates for personal responsibility, mindful consumption, and the ethical use of wealth. In contrast, Mahayana Buddhism, influential in East Asia, encourages collective action, wealth for social welfare, and societal transformation. Drawing from texts such as the *Sigalovada Sutta* and Buddhist economic teachings, this chapter critically compares the application of these principles in modern contexts, particularly in Sri Lanka. The study assesses how Theravada's conservative economic ideals adapt to the capitalist, globalized economy, while Mahayana's flexible interpretations align with philanthropy and modern economic policies. The findings suggest that both traditions offer valuable ethical frameworks, but adapting these ancient principles to contemporary global economies poses significant challenges.

Keywords Buddhist economics · Theravada Buddhism · Mahayana Buddhism · Wealth ethics · Right livelihood · *Sigalovada Sutta* · Globalization · Capitalism · Sri Lanka · Buddhist ethics · Socio-economic development

C. A. Saliya (✉)
Sri Lanka Institute of Information Technology, Malabe, Sri Lanka
e-mail: saliya.a@sliit.lk

G. J. Buijs, J. J. Ballor (eds.), *In Search of the Spirits of Capitalism*, Sophia Studies in Cross-cultural Philosophy of Traditions and Cultures 44,
https://doi.org/10.1007/978-3-032-01137-4_9

9.1 Introduction

Buddhism, as both a spiritual and philosophical tradition, has profoundly influenced the socio-economic landscape of Asia. This literature review is developed using a flexible integrated research method, as outlined by Saliya (2022, 2023a, b, c). This approach allows for the combination of various research perspectives and methodologies, integrating qualitative and quantitative data, historical analysis, and interdisciplinary insights to provide a comprehensive understanding of the subject. By adopting this method, the review remains adaptable to emerging themes and evolving research questions, ensuring a thorough and multi-faceted examination of Buddhist economics, ethics, and their socio-economic implications in contemporary contexts. Central to Buddhist teachings is the principle of ethical conduct, not only in personal spiritual practice but also in broader societal interactions, including economics. This intersection of Buddhism and economics has led to the development of what some scholars refer to as "Buddhist economics," an approach that integrates ethical values, compassion, and mindfulness into economic life (Payutto 1994; Saliya 2024). In an era of rapid technological advancement, globalization, and growing income inequality, many traditional Buddhists, particularly in Sri Lanka, emphasize the enduring relevance of Theravada Buddhist values in addressing these modern challenges (Gombrich 2016).

Theravada Buddhism, predominant in South and Southeast Asia, emphasizes personal responsibility, frugality, and the ethical use of wealth. It promotes the ideal of "right livelihood" and advocates for mindful consumption, where wealth is not pursued for its own sake but rather for virtuous purposes such as supporting family, charity, and religious institutions (De Silva 2006). In contrast, Mahayana Buddhism, which has a strong presence in East Asia, embraces a more collective approach to both spiritual practice and economic activity. It encourages individuals to use wealth for the benefit of society, aligning with the Bodhisattva ideal of working toward the welfare of all beings (Suzuki 1993). These differing perspectives on wealth and economic activity reveal important insights into how Buddhist ethics influence economic thought and practices across the region.

This chapter seeks to explore the foundational concepts of Theravada and Mahayana economic thought, comparing their approaches to wealth accumulation, ethical consumption, and societal roles. It examines the ways in which these two branches of Buddhism address modern economic challenges, particularly in the context of globalization and capitalism. Using Sri Lanka as a case study, where Theravada Buddhism is deeply embedded in the cultural and political fabric, the chapter explores how Buddhist principles have shaped the country's economic policies and how these principles are being adapted in response to contemporary economic realities. By examining the ethical framework outlined in key Buddhist texts, such as the *Sigalovada Sutta*, the study will assess the applicability of these ancient teachings in today's globalized world.

In doing so, the chapter highlights the challenges of integrating Buddhist ethical principles into modern economic systems, particularly in countries like Sri Lanka, where the tension between traditional values and capitalist practices is becoming increasingly pronounced. While both Theravada and Mahayana Buddhism offer valuable insights into ethical economic behavior, their differing interpretations of wealth and societal responsibility provide distinct responses to the complex economic issues of the twenty-first century.

Many traditional Buddhists in Sri Lanka emphasize the relevance of Theravada Buddhism in addressing the challenges posed by a rapidly evolving world driven by science and technology. They stress the need to preserve the core values of Theravada Buddhism while sharing its wisdom globally (Gombrich 2016). Beyond its spiritual teachings, Buddhism has deeply influenced socio-economic life across Asia, with Theravada and Mahayana—the two main branches of Buddhism—offering differing views not only on religious practice but also on economic principles. Both schools emphasize ethical behavior, compassion, and non-attachment to material possessions, but their philosophical differences lead to varying interpretations of economic activity, wealth accumulation, and societal roles (Payutto 1994).

9.2 Foundations of Economic Thought in Buddhism: Theravada Versus Mahayana

The core teachings of Buddhism focus on the Middle Path, balancing indulgence and asceticism, with the ultimate goal of reducing suffering (*dukkha*) (Saliya 2008). These teachings shape both Theravada and Mahayana views on wealth and economics. Central to this framework is the Buddhist view of interdependence and the moral consequences of actions (*karma*). Economic activities, according to Buddhism, should align with ethical principles that promote collective well-being rather than personal greed (Piyasīlo 1992).

Theravada Economic Concepts—Theravada Buddhism, often regarded as more conservative and focused on individual liberation, emphasizes personal responsibility in the accumulation and use of wealth. It is predominant in countries like Sri Lanka, Thailand, Myanmar, and Cambodia, where economic behaviors reflect the ethical values promoted by the teachings (De Silva 2006). Theravada stresses the mindful use of resources, encouraging individuals to practice "right livelihood" and use wealth for virtuous purposes such as supporting family, charity, and religious institutions. The practice of *dāna* (generosity) reflects the belief that acts of giving purify the mind and contribute to spiritual growth (Gombrich and Obeyesekere 1988). Additionally, Theravada economics promotes social stability through the relationship between the laity and the monastic community (*Sangha*), which fosters economic interdependence (Swearer 2010).

Mahayana Economic Concepts—Mahayana Buddhism, prominent in East Asia, offers a broader interpretation of spiritual practice with an emphasis on the Bodhisattva ideal, which encourages individuals to work not only for their own enlightenment but also for the liberation of others (Suzuki 1993). This collective outlook affects how economic activity is perceived, promoting a more expansive view of wealth and social responsibility. Mahayana encourages wealth to be used for the greater good, promoting large-scale philanthropy and social welfare (Jones 2017). The Bodhisattva ideal motivates individuals to extend beyond acts of charity and address the root causes of poverty and inequality (Harvey 2013).

Wealth, Ethics, and Capitalism—In both Theravada and Mahayana traditions, the acquisition of wealth is viewed through an ethical lens. Mahayana's broader focus on social responsibility creates a somewhat more compatible outlook with modern economic systems like capitalism, where wealth creation can be seen as an opportunity for the greater good if aligned with ethical goals (Jones 2017). Mahayana Buddhism's emphasis on compassionate economic systems has also influenced the development of socially conscious enterprises in East Asia, promoting environmental sustainability and fair labor practices (Harvey 2013).

Theravada, on the other hand, maintains a more cautious approach to wealth, advocating a simpler lifestyle and warning against the dangers of material accumulation. The monastic community in Theravada societies acts as a moral check on economic inequality, providing spiritual guidance and fostering a counterbalance to capitalism (Swearer 2010).

Comparative Critique—While both Theravada and Mahayana Buddhism emphasize ethical behavior and compassion, their distinct perspectives on wealth accumulation offer different responses to economic challenges. Theravada focuses on personal morality, frugality, and mindful consumption as antidotes to consumerism, but its individualistic approach may be less equipped to address systemic inequality (De Silva 2006). In contrast, Mahayana's collective outlook promotes social responsibility and motivates efforts to reduce poverty and inequality, aligning better with modern economic systems that prioritize societal transformation (Suzuki 1993).

Sri Lanka's Economic Policies: Theravada and Mahayana Influences—As a predominantly Theravada Buddhist country, Sri Lanka has historically intertwined religious principles with governance and economic policies. However, globalization and capitalism have increasingly shaped the country's modern economic structure, which seems more aligned with Mahayana's flexible economic interpretations (Gombrich 2016). Post-independence, Sri Lanka has embraced capitalist policies, particularly following economic liberalization in 1977, resulting in urbanization, tourism expansion, and growing wealth inequality (De Silva 2006).

While traditional Theravada values emphasize simplicity and non-attachment, Mahayana's more flexible view on wealth accumulation and its focus on altruistic use of wealth seem to resonate with Sri Lanka's current economic model. Large corporations and wealthy individuals are seen contributing to charity and religious institutions, reflecting Mahayana's emphasis on using wealth for societal benefit (Harvey 2013).

9.3 Consumerism and Buddhist Values

The rise of consumer culture in Sri Lanka highlights the tension between traditional Theravada values and modern capitalism. This trend mirrors what is seen in other Mahayana Buddhist countries like Japan and China, where Buddhism adapts to modern economic realities while maintaining an emphasis on charitable giving and social responsibility (Jones 2017). As Sri Lanka's economic policies shift towards wealth accumulation and international trade, the tension between Buddhist principles and consumerism continues to grow (Gombrich 2016).

Overall, both Theravada and Mahayana offer valuable frameworks for ethical economic behavior, but the increasing influence of capitalist ideals in Sri Lanka suggests a closer alignment with Mahayana's more flexible interpretation of wealth. Although the core principles of Buddhism continue to shape economic thought in Sri Lanka, the practical realities of globalization and capitalism are leading to adaptations that mirror Mahayana approaches in other parts of Asia.

Sri Lanka, while identifying as a Theravada Buddhist country, displays economic policies and societal trends that suggest a growing alignment with Mahayana Buddhist concepts, particularly in its flexibility toward wealth accumulation and the use of wealth for social and religious causes. The capitalist structure that dominates Sri Lanka's economy promotes wealth creation, material consumption, and global integration, which contrasts with the traditional Theravada ideals of simplicity and non-attachment. This shift reflects the broader philosophical differences between Theravada and Mahayana Buddhism.

Theravada Buddhism's focus on individual enlightenment results in a cautious, ethically-driven view of wealth, emphasizing personal responsibility and mindful consumption. In contrast, Mahayana Buddhism encourages collective action, using wealth for societal transformation and broader social welfare. Sri Lanka's hybrid model blends Theravada ethical teachings at the individual and religious levels with a capitalist economic framework that aligns more closely with Mahayana's adaptable approach to wealth and societal responsibility.

This integration of Theravada and Mahayana economic concepts offers valuable insights into how Buddhist ethics can shape modern economic systems. The challenge for Sri Lanka, and other Buddhist-majority countries, lies in maintaining spiritual principles within a capitalist framework. By drawing from both traditions, there is potential to develop an economic system that is not only productive but also compassionate, equitable, and sustainable in a rapidly globalizing world.

The rules of income distribution as outlined in the *Sigalovada Sutta*, often referred to as the "householder's discipline" or the "layperson's code of conduct," provide a framework for ethical financial management in Buddhist thought. As part of the *Digha Nikaya* of the Pali Canon, this sutta offers guidance on how a layperson should conduct their life in relation to family, friends, and community, particularly focusing on the responsible use of wealth (Harvey 2013). The sutta prescribes a fourfold division of wealth, designed to promote personal security, family care, social responsibility, and spiritual well-being (Swearer 2010).

1. *One Portion for Daily Needs:* This portion refers to spending on livelihood, ensuring that basic needs such as food, shelter, and clothing are met without excess. The Sigalovada Sutta emphasizes mindful consumption and avoiding material excess (Jones 2017).
2. *Two Portions for Investment:* The sutta advises using two portions of wealth for investment, which could include business ventures, savings, or other means of increasing wealth. This principle reflects the Buddhist value of planning for the future with mindfulness and ensuring long-term financial stability (De Silva 2006).
3. *One Portion for Charity:* The final portion should be allocated to charitable giving, supporting religious institutions such as monks and temples, and contributing to social welfare. This reflects the Buddhist principle of dana (generosity) and reinforces the moral responsibility to support those in need (Payutto 1994).

9.4 Validity and Relevance of the Sigalovada Sutta in the Modern Economic Context

While the rules of income distribution in the *Sigalovada Sutta* offer a sound ethical foundation, their direct applicability in modern economic systems faces challenges. In many developing countries, wealth inequality is stark, with 10% of the population controlling 90% of the wealth. This disparity raises concerns about the feasibility of adhering to such a balanced approach to income distribution in a globalized economy (Gombrich 2016).

1. *Balance Between Consumption and Savings*: The sutta's advocacy for balanced spending, saving, and investing aligns with modern financial principles, especially in advanced economies. In these societies, a significant portion of income is often allocated to investments like home loans or retirement funds, consistent with the sutta's advice to invest wealth for future security (Piyasīlo 1992).
2. *Investment for the Future*: The emphasis on reinvesting wealth highlights the importance of sustainable wealth accumulation. While the sutta does not specify the types of investments, modern interpretations of "right livelihood" (*samma ajiva*) can guide individuals to make ethical investment choices, ensuring their investments do not harm others (Harvey 2013).
3. *Charity and Social Responsibility*: The Sigalovada Sutta places significant importance on charitable giving, a principle echoed in modern concepts of philanthropy and corporate social responsibility (CSR). However, unlike occasional charitable acts in modern society, the sutta frames charity as an integral and regular part of one's financial life (Jones 2017).
4. *Moderation and Non-Attachment*: The sutta encourages wealth management without attachment, a message relevant to today's consumer-driven societies. The Buddhist focus on moderate consumption and wealth-sharing offers a

counter-narrative to modern materialism and emphasizes well-being over material accumulation (Swearer 2010).

Challenges and Limitations—While the *Sigalovada Sutta* provides a robust ethical framework, there are some challenges in applying its principles in a globalized economy:

- *Changing Economic Systems*: The economy during the Buddha's time was simpler, with agrarian and barter systems. Today's complex financial systems, with varied forms of income (salary, investments, passive income), require a reinterpretation of the sutta's guidelines to fit modern financial arrangements (De Silva 2006).
- *Wealth Disparity*: The sutta assumes a relatively equitable distribution of wealth. In modern economies, vast differences in income levels challenge the practical application of its principles, especially for those in lower-income brackets (Gombrich 2016; Saliya and Hooper 2020).

Comparison of Application Between Theravada and Mahayana. The *Sigalovada Sutta* holds significant importance in both Theravada and Mahayana Buddhism, but its application and interpretation differ between the two traditions.

Theravada Buddhism emphasizes personal ethical conduct and moderation in wealth accumulation. The *sutta*'s teachings on income distribution—allocating portions for daily needs, savings, and charity—are seen as part of leading an ethical and balanced life (Swearer 2010). In this tradition, wealth is viewed as a tool for securing basic needs and performing acts of generosity towards the monastic Sangha and the community (Gombrich 2016).

Mahayana Buddhism, with its emphasis on the Bodhisattva ideal, interprets the sutta more broadly, focusing on using wealth for societal transformation. The portion of wealth allocated to charity is seen as a tool for large-scale social initiatives, such as education and healthcare. This reflects the Mahayana ethos of compassion and collective welfare (Suzuki 1993).

Key differences concern the following issues:

- *Scope of Charity:* In Theravada, charity focuses on local communities and the monastic *Sangha*, while Mahayana extends charity to benefit all beings, reflecting its broader vision of interconnectedness and social transformation (Harvey 2013).
- *Moderation vs. Social Transformation:* Theravada emphasizes moderation and caution in wealth accumulation, whereas Mahayana allows for more significant wealth accumulation if it serves altruistic goals (Swearer 2010).

Overall, The *Sigalovada Sutta* provides valuable guidelines for ethical financial management. However, its direct application in modern economies, especially those marked by inequality, requires adaptation. While Theravada focuses on individual responsibility and moderation, Mahayana's interpretation expands to include social transformation, making the sutta's teachings relevant in different cultural and economic contexts.

9.5 Conclusion

The *Sigalovada Sutta* offers timeless and valid principles for the distribution of income, grounded in ethics, balance, and social responsibility. Its focus on moderation, investment, and charity provides an ethical framework that remains relevant even in today's complex economic systems. However, adapting these principles to modern financial realities—where global capitalism, income inequality, and consumerism dominate—requires careful interpretation.

At its core, the *Sutta* challenges individuals and societies to rethink their relationship with wealth, encouraging a balance between material needs and spiritual well-being. By integrating these teachings into modern financial systems, there is potential for a more equitable and compassionate approach to wealth distribution, one that supports both individual security and the common good.

The application of the *Sigalovada Sutta* varies between Theravada and Mahayana Buddhism due to their differing philosophical orientations. In Theravada, the focus remains on individual ethical conduct, personal moderation, and responsibility toward family and community. In Mahayana, the focus expands to include collective welfare, with wealth seen as a tool for societal transformation and broader altruistic efforts. While both traditions uphold the ethical management of wealth, Theravada emphasizes moderation and personal merit, whereas Mahayana allows for a more expansive, flexible use of wealth in service of others. Together, these approaches offer complementary perspectives on how Buddhist ethical teachings can inform income distribution and the role of wealth in society.

References

De Silva, Padmasiri. 2006. Buddhist Economics in Practice: Perspectives from Southeast Asia. *Journal of Buddhist Ethics* 13:45–62.

Gombrich, Richard F. 2016. *Theravada Buddhism: A Social History from Ancient Benares to Modern Colombo*. London: Routledge.

Gombrich, Richard, and G. Obeyesekere. 1988. *Buddhism Transformed: Religious Change in Sri Lanka*. Princeton: Princeton University Press.

Harvey, Peter. 2013. *An Introduction to Buddhist Ethics: Foundations, Values, and Issues*. Cambridge: Cambridge University Press.

Jones, Charles. 2017. *Buddhism and Modern Economics: A Comparative Study of Mahayana and Theravada Economic Ideals*. Oxford: Oxford University Press.

Payutto, P. A. 1994. *Buddhist Economics: A Middle Way for the Market Place*. Thailand: Buddhadhamma Foundation.

Piyasīlo, K. 1992. *The Buddhist Perspective on Economic Ethics*. Singapore: Dharma Publishing.

Saliya, Candauda A. 2008. Bad Buddhists, Good Buddhists and True Buddhists. *Philosophy of Religion eJournal* 11 (22): Jun 29, 2018. https://papers.ssrn.com/sol3/papers.cfm?abstract_id=3193913

Saliya, Candauda A. 2022. *Doing Social Research and Publishing Results: A Guide to Non-native English Speakers*. Spring https://doi.org/10.1007/978-981-19-3780-4

Saliya, Candauda A. 2023a. Integrated-Flexible Research Methodology: An Alternative Approach. In *Social Research Methodology and Publishing Results: A Guide to Non-Native English Speakers*, ed. Candauda A. Saliya. https://doi.org/10.4018/978-1-6684-6859-3.ch001

Saliya, Candauda A. 2023b. Research Philosophy: Paradigms, World Views, Perspectives, and Theories. In *Social Research Methodology and Publishing Results: A Guide to Non-Native English Speakers*, ed. Candauda A. Saliya.. https://doi.org/10.4018/978-1-6684-6859-3.ch004

Saliya, Candauda A. 2023c. *Social Research Methodology and Publishing Results: A Guide to Non-Native English Speakers*. IGI Global. https://doi.org/10.4018/978-1-6684-6859-3.

Saliya, Candauda A. 2024. *Navigating the Complex Landscape of Religious Beliefs: A Multidimensional Exploration*. ResearchGate. December. https://doi.org/10.13140/RG.2.2.26380.01925

Saliya, Candauda A., and K. Hooper. 2020. The Role of Credit Weapon and Income/Wealth Inequality: A Sri Lankan Case Study. *Journal of Applied Economic Sciences (JAES)*. ASERS Publishing. https://www.ceeol.com/search/article-detail?id=894704

Suzuki, Daisetz T. 1993. *The Essence of Mahayana Buddhism*. London: Buddhist Society/Shambhala Publications.

Swearer, Donald K. 2010. *The Buddhist World of Southeast Asia*. New York: State University of New York Press.

Candauda Arachchige Saliya is a Professor at the SLIIT Business School of the Sri Lanka Institute of Information Technology (SLIIT). He is a Senior Fellow Chartered Accountant, a CPA (Australia), a Professional Banker and holds a PhD from Auckland University of Technology (AUT) in New Zealand. He has served as a Director and the CEO of multiple companies listed on the Colombo Stock Exchange. He has numerous publications in premier indexed journals and has authored three books including *Doing Social Research and Publishing Results: A Guide to Non-Native English Speakers* (Springer), and he also writes the weekly column '*Out of the Box*' for The Island, a leading national newspaper in Sri Lanka.

Part V
Judaism

Chapter 10
The Impact of Jewish Values on Marketing and Business Practices

Hershey H. Friedman

Abstract Judaism, which relies on the Torah for its written law, has had a great impact on marketing and business. The Torah is replete with precepts dealing with business, and the Talmud, the source of Jewish oral law, elaborates and expands Torah law. The process is ongoing and rabbinical authorities today build on the decisions of their predecessors to apply Jewish law to modern problems. Some of the issues examined in this paper include: honesty in the marketplace, fair pricing, employer-employee relations, and environmental issues. Jewish law is not only concerned with practical legal advice but also with encouraging individuals to go beyond the requirements of the law and practice the "way of the pious." Judaism does not have a negative attitude towards business and wealth—indeed, most of the Talmudic sages had occupations and some were quite wealthy—but riches must be acquired honestly and used to help the poor, the needy, and the stranger.

Keywords Torah · Talmud · Business ethics · Honesty · Fair price · Environment · Responsibility

10.1 Introduction

Jewish culture, values, and ideas have permeated many aspects of modern life including the modern marketplace. This impact of Judaism on marketing and business is manifested not only in such areas as business ethics, but also in the organization's perceived social responsibility, and in a positive attitude towards business and

This article has been published before as Friedman, H. H. 2001. The Impact of Jewish Values on Marketing and Business Practices. *Journal of Macromarketing. 21*(1), 74–80. It has been cited often and is still of great value which justifies a reprint. Reprinted with permission from SAGE Publications Inc.

H. H. Friedman (✉)
Brooklyn College, New York, NY, USA

G. J. Buijs, J. J. Ballor (eds.), *In Search of the Spirits of Capitalism*, Sophia Studies in Cross-cultural Philosophy of Traditions and Cultures 44,
https://doi.org/10.1007/978-3-032-01137-4_10

wealth (when obtained and used in a proper manner). Numerous articles and books have been written describing applications of Jewish law from antiquity to the modern era and their continued relevance to the business problems of contemporary society (see, *e.g.*, Elon 1975; Friedman 2000; Jung and Levine 1987; Levine 1980, 1987; Levine and Pava 1999; Tamari 1987, 1991; Wagschal 1991; Warhaftig 1987). To understand this impact, one must first examine Jewish law, tradition, and culture, especially those principles relevant to the marketplace.

10.2 Going to the Sources

The Hebrew Bible, particularly the Pentateuch (*i.e.*, the Torah), contains the written law and, to the believer, is the word of God. The precepts in the Torah are the foundations of Jewish law and are cited by rabbinical authorities as a kind of constitution to this very day. According to Jewish tradition, the Torah contains 613 precepts, many of which deal with business practices. The Torah is revered by other religions; the Talmud and the Midrash, however, are distinctly Jewish. Thus, to understand the impact of Judaism on marketing and business one must examine the Talmud and Midrash, as well as the Torah.

The Talmud, which is the compilation of Jewish oral law, expounds on the Hebrew Bible and consists of the *Mishna* and *Gemara*. The *Mishna*, originally an ancient oral tradition, was compiled and edited in written form about 1800 years ago by Rabbi Judah the *Nasi* (President of the Sanhedrin). The *Gemara*, which was completed about 1500 years ago, consists mainly of commentaries on the *Mishna*. There were two academies, in Israel and Babylon, independently studying the *Mishna*. Thus, there are two versions of the Talmud: the Jerusalem Talmud, a product of the academies in Israel, and the Babylonian Talmud, a product of the academies in Babylon. The Babylonian Talmud is considerably larger than that of the Jerusalem Talmud, and it is more authoritative.

The Talmud is primarily concerned with *halacha* (Jewish law) but also provides a detailed record of the beliefs of the Jewish people, their philosophy, traditions, culture, and folklore, i.e., the *aggadah* (homiletics). The *Midrash*, a separate scripture which records the views of the Talmudic sages, is mainly devoted to the exposition of Biblical verses but is also rich in philosophy, folklore, and legends. It should be noted that, other than the few individuals who headed academies, the overwhelming majority of the scholars referred to in the Talmud had secular occupations, such as beer brewer, farmer, farm worker, peddler, physician, wood chopper, merchant, blacksmith, gravedigger. Indeed, some were known by their occupations, for example, Rabbi Yochanan the Shoemaker (*haSandlar*). Even in later times, many of the great Jewish Biblical and Talmudic commentators had ordinary occupations, *e.g.*: Rabbi Shlomo ben Yitchak (1040–1105), known as Rashi, was a vintner in France; Rabbi Abraham ibn Ezra (1089–1164) was a poet and astronomer from Spain; Rabbi Moshe ben Maimon (1134–1204), known as Maimonides, was a physician and philosopher in Egypt; and Rabbi Ovadiah Sforno (1470–1550) was a physician in Italy.

Maimonides wrote *Mishneh Torah*, in which he arranged and codified the laws without the Talmudic debate and homiletics. Later, Rabbi Joseph Karo (1488–1575), relying on the works of Maimonides and other scholars, wrote the *Shulchan Aruch*, the authoritative code of law for observant Jewry. The Torah, Talmud, *Mishneh Torah*, *Shulchan Aruch*, and thousands of responsa (legal decisions handed down by Jewish authorities) are major sources for the rules and regulations governing Jewish law today. Even in the secular arena, Rakover (1992) demonstrates that hundreds of decisions handed down by secular courts in Israel today refer to Jewish law. For instance, in one case, Maimonides' ruling that "It is prohibited to deceive people in transactions or to mislead them" (*Mishneh Torah*, Laws of Selling 18:1) was quoted to demonstrate the obligations of sellers (Rakover 1992, 755). Friedman (1980, 1984, 2000) shows how many current business laws and practices and numerous concerns of business ethicists today have their antecedents in the Hebrew Bible and the Talmud.

10.3 Law Versus Ethics: 'The way of the pious'

Friedman (1980) notes that the Talmud often resorts to ethical principles in order to improve upon the law. Following the strict letter of the law is not sufficient. In fact, the Talmud (T. Bava Metzia 30b)[1] claims that Jerusalem was destroyed because judgments were based strictly on the law and did not go beyond the strict line of justice. This principle of Jewish law, that demands that one be ethical and even go beyond the legal requirement, is derived from the verse (Deuteronomy 6:18): "You shall do that which is fair and good in the sight of the Lord." The Talmud (T. Bava Metzia 108a) uses this verse to establish the right of pre-emption, *i.e.*, when one sells a field the adjoining neighbors are given the right of first refusal. In addition, individuals who go beyond the requirements of the law will return found objects even if the object was lost in a place where it is clear that the owner gave up any hope of recovery (*e.g.*, if it fell into the sea), and there is thus no legal obligation to return it (T. Bava Metzia 24b).

Another indication that one must do more than simply obey the letter of the law is that "one may be (legally) compelled not to act in the manner of Sodom." In some situations where one party benefits and the other party loses absolutely nothing, the courts can compel an individual to do the right thing (e.g., T. Bava Bathra 12b). Spiteful selfishness of this type is considered a behavior characteristic of Sodom and is not tolerated by Jewish law.

[1] T. denotes Talmud. References to the Talmud without qualification are to the Babylonian Talmud. The Babylonian Talmud contains sixty0three tractates, of which Bava Metzia is one.

Friedman (1985) demonstrates that the Talmudic sages believed that there is an ethics hierarchy and that individuals should strive to reach the summit. He notes that the highest level of ethics described in the Talmud is "the way of the pious." Businesspeople leading their lives according to this principle go beyond the letter of the law and are willing to lose money rather than take advantage of another person's misfortunes. Gifter (2000) uses the following case discussed in the Talmud (T. Bava Metzia 83a) to prove that the purpose of the Torah and Talmud is not solely to provide precise answers to legal questions but to develop the morals and ethics of individuals.

Some porters negligently broke a barrel of wine belonging to Rabbah bar Bar-Chana who then confiscated the porters' property as restitution. Rav, the judge, advised Rabbah to return the property belonging to the porters. Rabbah asked Rav whether this was indeed the law and was quoted the following verse from Proverbs (2:20): "In order that you may walk in the way of the good ..." The porters then complained to Rav that they were poor, had worked all day without earning anything, and were in need. Rav told Rabbah to pay them. Rabbah again asked whether this was the law. Rav responded with the conclusion of the verse from Proverbs: "... and keep the paths of the righteous."

Because the Talmud is concerned with improving the ethics of the individual, cases are discussed in which the courts cannot legally prosecute the defendant. This is not surprising given that, in Jewish law, the legal content of the law is totally conjoined with ethics, religion, and morality (Silberg 1973, 83). It is interesting to note that the Ten Commandments (Exodus 20:2–14; Deuteronomy 5: 6–18) mixes laws that are the foundations of every legal system (*e.g.*, those dealing with murder, theft, and bearing false witness) with laws that are religious (*e.g.*, against idolatry and observing the Sabbath), and with the Tenth Commandment dealing with "coveting" and "desiring." Legislation against desiring is not part of any legal system and relates more to ethics and morality than to practical jurisprudence. These very different types of laws are combined to demonstrate that crimes against people are also crimes against God and that individuals have an obligation to go beyond the letter of the law and elevate themselves spiritually and ethically. Indeed one wonders whether advertising whose sole purpose is to arouse envy and desire on the part of those that do not possess a certain product is inconsistent with the spirit of the Tenth Commandment.

Friedman (1985) describes cases in which the Talmud rules that the offender is "liable under the laws of Heaven," is described as "wicked," as having "behaved with deceit," "acted in the manner of Sodom," "lacking in honesty," and engaged in a behavior "that is not pleasing to the spirit of the sages." Whether or not a defendant can or cannot be prosecuted for an action may be less important than knowing about whether it is the "right" thing to do. Rabbi Moshe ben Nachman (1194–1270), Nachmanides, a major commentator on the Torah (and also a physician), notes that one can follow the letter of the law and still be considered a "vile person within the permissible realm of the Torah" (Nachmanides, Leviticus 19:2).

There are gradations of unethical behavior and the objective is to motivate individuals to move up the ethics hierarchy. Not everyone is capable of reaching the level of Rabbi Safra who is described in the Talmud (T. Maakoth 24a) as an individual who abided by the verse (Psalms 15:2) "who speaks truth in the heart." One day, while Rabbi Safra was praying, a man offered to buy some merchandise from him. He made an offer, but Rabbi Safra did not want to respond in the middle of a prayer. The prospective buyer assumed that Rabbi Safra was holding out for more and kept increasing the bid. After Rabbi Safra concluded his prayer, he informed the buyer that he would sell the merchandise at the first price because he had "agreed in his heart" to this price. Legally, one is not required to do as Rabbi Safra; this is the "way of the pious." On the other hand, if two parties have concluded negotiations leading to a sale and are in the process of closing the deal, and a third party jumps in and makes the purchase, the interloper cannot be prosecuted legally but is described by the Talmud (T. Kiddushin 59a) as a "wicked person."

The Talmud (T. Maakoth 24a) enumerates 11 ethical principles (based on Psalm 15) that underlie the 613 precepts of the Torah. These include such virtues as "speaks the truth from his heart," like Rabbi Safra; "deals righteously," like Abba Chilkiyahu, who would not even greet people while working as a day laborer since he did not want to waste time—even a few moments—that was not his; and "who has done his fellow human no evil," referring to one who does not infringe on his fellow craftsman's business. Opening a store next door to a store selling the same merchandise is something a pious person does not do (Wagschal 1991, 25).

10.4 Honesty in the Marketplace

The prohibition against stealing is the eighth commandment of the Ten Commandments (Exodus 20:13; Deuteronomy 5:17) and is interpreted by several of the classic Jewish commentaries to include every kind of dishonesty and deception (*e.g.*, Sforno and ibn Ezra). One ancient commentary (Targum Yonathan) translates this commandment to include being a partner or friend of unscrupulous individuals. It is also stated in Leviticus (19:11–13): "Do not steal, do not deny falsely, and do not lie to one another. Do not swear falsely by My name…Do not cheat your fellow and you shall not rob." Any type of deceptive act or practice, including deceptive advertisements and deceptive packaging, would also be a violation of the Biblical principle (Exodus 23:7), "Distance yourself from a false matter." Moreover, the Torah's injunction against "placing a stumbling block before the blind" (Leviticus 19:14) is interpreted by the Talmud and Midrash to include proffering bad advice to unsuspecting people or causing others to sin (Sifra Leviticus 35; T. Bava Metzia 75b). Thus, Jewish law would consider deceptive advertising and misleading labeling as placing a stumbling block before the blind and a violation of Torah law. Even the advertising agency that created the deceptive advertisement would be guilty of transgressing this law.

Adulteration of products was a problem even in ancient times as can be seen from Isaiah's criticism (1:22) of the Israelites: "Your silver has become dross, your wine diluted with water." According to most commentaries, this is not a metaphor but refers to actual deceptive practices in ancient Judah and Jerusalem that angered the Lord.

Merchants were prohibited from falsifying weights and measures by the Torah or even owning a dishonest weight (Leviticus 19:35–36; Deuteronomy 25:13–15). The prophet Amos (8:5) reproached the Jews for "making the *ephah* (a dry measure) smaller and the *shekel* larger and falsifying the scales of deceit." After all, "Deceitful scales are an abomination of the Lord" (Proverbs 11:1). In fact, any deception or dishonest business practice is "an abomination unto the Lord, your God" (Deuteronomy 25:16). To ensure honest weights and measures, the Talmud (T. Bava Bathra 88a) required merchants to wipe their weights once a week and clean their scales after every weighing. Market commissioners were appointed to ensure that businesses used honest weights and measures (T. Bava Bathra 89a). Vendors were prohibited from rapidly pouring liquids from great heights (T. Bava Bathra 89b), which was done by retailers to generate foam thereby ensuring that the customer would end up with less product.

Included in the Torah law against theft and deception is the requirement that vendors must be honest in selling. Hiding faults from the buyer is not permitted and such a sale is null and void. The Talmud (T. Bava Metzia 59b-60a) prohibits such deceptions as: mixing your own produce with that of other farmers when the agreement was to provide produce from your field; painting animals or utensils in order to fool prospective buyers into thinking they are younger or newer; deceiving potential customers by placing the better quality merchandise on top of the bin (and the lower quality merchandise on the bottom) in order to make it appear that the merchandise is of uniformly high quality throughout; selling wine that has become adulterated with water in your store without informing the customers. The laws dealing with transactions under mistaken assumptions are relevant even in marriage, *i.e.*, the discovery of a bodily defect in a spouse can nullify the marriage (T. Kethubos 11b, 57b).

Clearly, firms must be aggressive in ensuring that all their advertisements and communications are honest, straightforward, and unlikely to deceive the public.

10.5 Fair Pricing

The Torah states (Leviticus 25:14): "If you sell something to your neighbor or buy something from your neighbor's hand, you shall not wrong one another." The Talmud interprets this verse to refer to overcharges and undercharges. The Talmud (T. Bava Metzia 50b) ruled that if the overcharge is more than one-sixth—i.e., the retailer sells an item for a price that is one-sixth higher than what is generally accepted as a fair price—the sale is null and void. Similarly, if an individual is unaware of the true value of an item and wishes to sell it, one must not take advantage of the seller's ignorance and underpay.

The law against overcharging was extended by the Talmud to include excessive markups on necessities (T. Bava Bathra 90a). Profits from the sale of staples such as wheat, oil, or wine was not to exceed one-sixth.

Price stability was of great concern to the Talmud, and the Talmudic sages considered causing prices to rise by hoarding or other means a violation of Torah law similar to usury or tampering with weights and measures (T. Bava Bathra 90b). Leaders such as Rabbi Shimon b. Gamliel, the head of the Sanhedrin, threatened to revise laws concerning sacrifices when he heard that the price of doves used for certain sacrifices had increased to a golden dinar (T. Krithoth 8a). He was successful and the price dropped to one-quarter of a silver dinar.

Shmuel was another Talmudic sage that used his legislative powers to keep the prices of myrtles, used during the holiday of Tabernacles, and of pots, purchased before the holiday of Passover, from rising prior to the holidays (T. Sukkah 34b; T. Pesachim 30a). Shmuel and his father were known to purchase and subsequently sell produce in such a way as to keep the market price stable and low throughout the year (T. Bava Bathra 90b).

Firms have an obligation to engage in fair pricing and not overcharge or hoard products in order to make excessive profits, especially for necessities and drugs.

10.6 The Appearance of Propriety Is Important Too

The Torah states (Numbers 32:22): "and you shall be innocent before God and Israel." The Talmud uses this verse to derive the principle that one must behave in a manner that does not give rise to suspicions on the part of others. The Torah (Exodus 38:21–31) provides a detailed list of the amounts of gold, silver, and copper used in the construction of the Tabernacle. This was done to demonstrate the importance of keeping clear records and behaving in a way that does not cause the public to suspect one's veracity. The Torah states (Exodus 38:21): "These are the accounts of the Tabernacle, the Tabernacle of the Testimony, as they were calculated according to the commandment of Moses…" Moses wanted to make it evident that he and the builders of the Tabernacle did not divert any of the precious metals for their own personal use and he therefore used others to audit the records. The Midrash (Exodus Rabbah 51:1) comments: "though Moses was the sole treasurer, yet he called others to audit the accounts with him."

The Talmud (T. Pesachim 13a) states that the overseers in charge of the soup kitchen were not allowed to purchase surplus food when there were no poor people to whom to distribute it. Surpluses were only allowed to be sold to others so as not to arouse suspicion that the charity overseers were profiting from public funds. For the same reason, children in the family of Garmu, that made the showbread for the Temple, were never seen with fine bread; brides from the family of Abtimas, the Temple's incense manufacturers, never wore perfume (T. Yuma 38a). Those who entered the Temple chamber to collect the money (for the sacrifices) wore clothing with no pockets or other receptacles so that people should not suspect them of stealing money (T. Shekalim 3:2).

Organizations have the same obligation as individuals to act in a manner that does not arouse suspicion and to use outside auditors that are truly objective.

10.7 Employer-Employee Relations

In an agrarian society, the laborers who worked the fields were usually slaves. Regarding the treatment of slaves, the Bible states: "You shall not rule over him through rigorous labor" (Leviticus 25:43). The Midrash (Sifra, Leviticus 86; Midrash Hagadol, Leviticus 25:39) explains this to mean that one is not permitted to make a servant engage in degrading work (e.g., removing his master's shoes), perform work that has no purpose (i.e., "busy" work), or carry out a task without a defined limit (e.g., "hoe until I return" when the servant does not know when the master will return). Employers are required to pay employees on time. The Torah states (Leviticus 19:13): "You shall not oppress your fellow and you shall not rob; the wages of a worker shall not remain with you overnight until morning."

The concept of fringe benefits is alluded to in the Torah. Field workers are given the right to eat of the produce while they work. The Torah states (Deuteronomy 23:25–26): "When you come [as a worker] into your neighbor's vineyard, you may eat as many grapes as is your desire, to your fill, but you may not put any into a receptacle. When you come into your neighbor's standing corn, you may pluck ears with your hand, but you should not lift a sickle on your neighbor's standing corn." When their servitude ended, the master was required to give the slave a severance gift know as *hanakah*. The Torah states (Deuteronomy 15:13–14): "Do not send him away empty-handed. You shall give him a severance gift from your flocks, from your threshing floor, and from your wine cellar …".

Wagschal (1991, 37) states that employees must be treated with respect and describes various obligations of employers. He concludes: "Is an employee worse than a slave?"

10.8 Social Responsibility

An organization should try to achieve its goals (*e.g.*, profit) but must also care for others. Hillel's simple rule summarizes this philosophy of business ethics as well as anyone can (T. Avot 1:14): "If I am not for myself, who will be for me? And if I only care for myself, what am I?"

The Torah makes it quite clear that the landowner has a responsibility to help the indigent. Landowners were obligated to help the poor by leaving the corners of the field for them; during the harvesting, individual stalks that unintentionally fell from the sickle also became the property of the "stranger, orphan, and widow" (Leviticus

19:9). Similarly, vines and olive trees were not to be picked clean: gleanings of the vine and olive tree were left for the destitute (Deuteronomy 24: 20–21). A sheaf of grain that was inadvertently left in the field during the harvest had to be left behind for the indigent (Deuteronomy 24:19). The landowner was obligated to provide a tithe for the priests and the Levites (Numbers 18:21–32) and a special tithe for the poor (Deuteronomy 14:28–29). There is also an obligation to "open one's hand" for the impecunious and lend them money (Deuteronomy 15:7–8).

The Torah is very concerned with the welfare of the stranger, an individual that often can be easily taken advantage of. Indeed, the stranger is often mentioned together with the destitute, widows, and orphans. The Talmud (T. Bava Metzia 59b) notes that the precept of not mistreating a stranger is alluded to 36 times in the Torah. For instance, the Scripture states: "You shall strengthen him, whether he is a stranger or a native, so that he can live with you" (Leviticus 25:35). Abusing, taunting, wronging, or oppressing the stranger is forbidden (Exodus 22:20; Exodus 23:9); in fact, the Bible obligates one to love the stranger (Leviticus 19:34; Deuteronomy 10:19). Jerusalem was destroyed for wronging the poor, the needy, and the stranger (Ezekiel 22:29), and Sodom was annihilated for not using its wealth to help the poor and needy (Ezekiel 16:49). The Torah (Numbers 15:16) insists that: "One law and one ordinance shall be both for you and for the stranger who sojourns with you." Individuals, organizations, and government must ensure that all ethnic and religious groups are treated equitably; special efforts should be made to help the poor and the handicapped get jobs—the highest form of charity (Maimonides, *Mishneh Torah*, Laws of Gifts to the Poor 10:7).

Deuteronomy (22:8) states "when you build a new house you must place a guardrail around your roof, so that you will not place blood in your house." The Talmud extends this law to apply to any dangerous situation, for example, keeping a defective ladder (T. Kethuboth 41b). Certainly, selling a broken ladder would be no better. One may infer from this that any product with the potential for harming the user is prohibited by Talmud and, by extension, the Torah. In addition, employers must be extremely careful to make certain that the workplace environment is safe and not deleterious to employees' health.

10.9 A Responsibility for the Environment

Wasteful consumption is proscribed by the Torah. Soldiers are not permitted to cut down fruit trees even when besieging an enemy's city (Deuteronomy 20:19). The Talmud (T. Shabbos 129a; T. Bava Kama 91b) extends the prohibition of not destroying fruit trees to any type of wasteful destruction; thus, wanton destruction of any kind is a violation of Torah law. This is known as the principle of *bal tashchit* (literally meaning "do not destroy"), a prohibition against unnecessary destruction or waste. Schwartz (1997) shows how more recent rabbinical authorities have applied the principle of *bal tashchit*.

Some questions discussed in the Talmud include how far to locate a tannery (which emits bad odors) from a city (T. Bava Bathra 25a). Noise pollution resulting from an individual opening up a store in a courtyard shared by several families is also discussed in the Talmud (T. Bava Bathra 20b). Turkel (1991) applies many of the Talmudic laws and responsa dealing with relations between neighbors to modern questions dealing with pollution.

The Torah requires that the land be given a complete rest in the seventh year, known as Shemitah (Leviticus 25: 1–7). One purpose of the Sabbatical year may have been to protect the land from depletion. During the Jubilee (50th) year, the land was also rested and reverted back to former owners.[2]

The obligation to care for the environment and minimize pollution and waste is one that falls on individuals as well as companies. The Talmud (T. Bava Kama 30a) notes that one who wishes to be pious must be extremely scrupulous in matters that may cause harm to others, *e.g.*, in the disposal of glass and thorns.

10.10 Attitude Towards Business and Wealth

The Jewish attitude towards business is quite positive. In fact, wealth, peace, and/or long life are rewards from God for obeying God's laws (Leviticus 26: 3–13; Deuteronomy 11: 13–16; Deuteronomy 25:15; Proverbs 22:4). The Bible makes it clear that one who helps the poor will be blessed by God (Deuteronomy 15:10; Isaiah 1:17–19; Proverbs 19:17); those that mistreat the stranger, widow, or orphan will be punished by God (Exodus 22:20–23; Isaiah 1: 23–25). There is nothing wrong with being wealthy as long as the rich do not forget that wealth comes from God and that there is an obligation to help the needy. The danger of wealth and its true purpose is explicitly stated in the Bible (Deuteronomy 8: 11–18): One should not believe that "my power and the might of my hand has made me all this wealth"; rather, one should remember that God gives wealth to individuals in order that they may do His will.

It is clear that Judaism sees nothing wrong with wealth as long as it is obtained honestly and used to help the poor. The Talmud also reinforces this idea: In a wordplay on the verse (Deuteronomy 14: 22): "You shall surely tithe," the Talmud (T. Taanis 9a) advises that one should tithe in order to become rich (the Hebrew word that means to tithe is very similar to the word that means to become rich). The verse (Proverbs 11:24), "There is one who scatters and yet is given more" is interpreted by many of the commentators (*e.g.*, Rashi and ibn Ezra) as referring to one who spends his money on the needy. The question of what a person should do to

[2] This may be an appropriate point to note that the Shemita years are still continuing in the Jewish calendar, e.g. 2000–2001 (5761), 2007–2008 (5768), 2014–2015 (5775) and 2021–2022 (5782), and there is a great deal of controversy in the state of Israel regarding how to apply these laws today. A legal loophole that was used in the past when farmers were very poor (i.e. temporarily selling the field to a non-Jew) is now being rejected by many religious authorities.

become rich is discussed in the Talmud; one answer is to engage in much business and deal honestly (T. Niddah 70b). Wealth is seen as "comely to the righteous and comely to the world" (T. Avot 6:8), and affluent people who used their possessions to help others were respected by the Talmudic sages (T. Eruvin 86a).

Similarly, the Talmud has a favorable attitude towards working. The ideal is to combine the study of Torah with an occupation. Some statements about work include: "Whoever does not teach his son a trade, it is as though he taught him to commit robbery" (T. Kiddushin 29a); "All Torah that is not combined with work will eventually cease and lead to sin" (T. Avot 2:2); "A person should love work and not hate it; for just as the Torah was given with a covenant, so too was work given with a covenant" (T. Avot D'Rabbi Noson 11:1); "Even God did not let His presence rest upon Israel until they had performed some work" (T. Avot D'Rabbi Noson 11:1); "Skin a carcass in the street and receive wages and do not say I am an important person and this type of work is beneath my dignity (T. Pesachim 113a)." As noted above, the Talmudists practiced what they preached and also had occupations.

The Talmud (T. Pesachim 113a) records Rav's business advice to his son Aibu, which included the idea to "sell your wares while the sand is still on your feet" (i.e., do not procrastinate, and sell as soon as possible). The idea of diversification—i.e., dividing one's assets into thirds: 1/3 in land, 1/3 in business, and 1/3 kept liquid—is also mentioned in the Talmud (T. Bava Metzia 42a). Advice is provided as to the ideal occupation, which, according to Rabbi Chisda, is needle work (T. Berachos 63a). Another sage believed that investing in business was better than being a farmer (T. Yevamos 63a). Rabbi Papa claimed that he became wealthy by being a beer brewer and recommended this occupation since it allowed one to become affluent and to be charitable (T. Pesachim 113a). Rabbi Yochanan's opinion was that raising small cattle would make one wealthy (T. Chullin 84b).

Judaism sees nothing wrong with business and making a profit as long as the firm realizes that it has other responsibilities as well. Jeremiah (9:23) stressed that God demands that people practice "lovingkindness, justice, and righteousness." The same can be asked of any organization.

10.11 Conclusion

The Psalmist (Psalms 15) describes some of the attributes of a virtuous individual. We cannot help but notice that these same attributes are just as important for an organization: "One who walks in total integrity, deals righteously, and speaks the truth from his heart. One who has no slander on his tongue, who has done his fellow human no evil nor cast disgrace upon his close one… Whoever does these things shall never falter." Achieving the highest level of ethical behavior in the marketplace and practicing the social responsibility that must accompany success in business are the hallmarks of the 'way of the pious.'

Indeed, business ethics occupies such an important place in Jewish law, culture, and tradition that the Talmud (T. Shabbos 31a) has as the very first question an individual is asked in the next world at the final judgment: "Were you honest in your business dealings?"

References

Elon, Menachem, ed. 1975. *The Principles of Jewish Law*. Jerusalem: Keter Publishing House.

Friedman, Hershey H. 1980. Talmudic Business Ethics: An Historical Perspective. *Akron Business and Economic Review* 11 (Winter): 45–49.

Friedman, Hershey H. 1984. Ancient Marketing Practices: The View from Talmudic Times. *Journal of Public Policy & Marketing* 3 (Spring): 194–204.

Friedman, Hershey H. 1985. Ethical Behavior in Business: A Hierarchical Approach from the Talmud. *Journal of Business Ethics* 4:117–129.

Friedman, Hershey H. 2000. Biblical Foundations of Business Ethics. *Journal of Markets and Morality* 3 (Spring): 43–57.

Gifter, Mordechai. 2000. Human Law and Torah Law. In *The Ethical Imperative: Torah Perspectives on Ethics and Values*, ed. Nisson Wolpin, 243–251. Brooklyn: Mesorah Publications.

Jung, Leo, and Aaron Levine. 1987. *Business Ethics in Jewish Law*. New York: Hebrew Publishing Company.

Levine, Aaron. 1980. *Free Enterprise and Jewish Law: Aspects of Jewish Business Ethics*. New York: Yeshiva University Press.

Levine, Aaron. 1987. *Economics and Jewish Law: Halakhic Perspectives*. New York: Yeshiva University Press.

Levine, Aaron, and Moses Pava, eds. 1999. *Jewish Business Ethics: The Firm and its Stakeholders*. Northvale: Jason Aronson Inc.

Rakover, Nahum. 1992. *Modern Applications of Jewish Law*. Jerusalem: The Library of Jewish Law.

Schwartz, Eilon. 1997. Bal Tashchit: A Jewish Environmental Precept. *Environmental Ethics* 18 (Winter): 355–374.

Silberg, Moshe. 1973. *Talmudic Law and the Modern State*. New York: The Burning Bush Press.

Tamari, Meir. 1987. *'With All Your Possessions:' Jewish Ethics and Economic Life*. New York: The Free Press.

Tamari, Meir. 1991. *In the Marketplace: Jewish Business Ethics*. Southfield: Targum Press.

Turkel, Eli. 1991. Judaism and the Environment. *Journal of Halacha and Contemporary Society* 22 (Fall): 44–61.

Wagschal, Shaul. 1991. *Torah Guide for the Businessman*. New York: Feldheim Publishers.

Warhaftig, Itamar. 1987. Consumer Protection: Price and Wage Levels. In *Crossroads: Halacha and the Modern World*, ed. Yisrael Rozen, vol. 1, 49–77. Jerusalem: Zomet. Original article can be found here: http://www.jlaw.com/Articles/impactjewish.html

Hershey H. Friedman is Professor of Business in the Department of Management, Marketing, and Entrepreneurship at Brooklyn College of the City University of New York. He holds a PhD from the Graduate Center of the City University of New York. He has published more than 400 articles in scholarly journals, including the *Journal of Business Ethics*, *Decision Sciences*, *Journal of Statistical Computation and Simulation*, *International Journal of Market Research*, *Journal of Marketing Management*, *Simulation*, *Journal of Systems and Software* and the *Journal of Applied Psychology*. He has co-authored a book with Dr. Linda W. Friedman, *God Laughed: The Origins of Jewish Humor* (Routledge, 2014).

Chapter 11
Creative Economy in Judaism

Joseph Isaac Lifshitz

Abstract Just as according to Max Weber the particular teachings of Puritanism imbued capitalism with a distinctive ethos, so too does Jewish doctrine have significant implications for understanding such significant economic phenomena as labor, creativity, and trade. The teaching that human beings are created in the image of God involves human beings as creative, which ultimately results in a creative economy. The history of Jews in seventeenth- and eighteenth-century Poland provides evidence for the salience of this self-understanding as it worked out in concrete circumstances, as they sought new ways of thriving economically amid various social challenges. A creative theology generates a creative economy—an economy that like God, creates a new world.

Keywords Judaism · Markets · Trade · Creative economy

11.1 Introduction

Economic theology is an evolving field of thought, and it includes a variety of subjects, from ethics to law, from theology to management. The wide range of the subjects of economic theology may be criticized, but management, at least, is actually one of the oldest subjects of economic theology. Economy, *oikonomia* (οἰκονομία) in Greek, is managing a household, which was applied in Christian theolgy to describe the hierarchy within the Trinity. Thus, for many years, designating the three different figures in the Trinity and their interrelationships was considered under the rubric of the economy of religion. But religious economy included a subject that is much more connected to our intuition of what we will call economic theology, that is, the economic relationship between man and God. Man is able to

J. I. Lifshitz (✉)
Shalem College, Jerusalem, Israel
e-mail: isaacl@shalem.ac.il

G. J. Buijs, J. J. Ballor (eds.), *In Search of the Spirits of Capitalism*, Sophia Studies in Cross-cultural Philosophy of Traditions and Cultures 44,
https://doi.org/10.1007/978-3-032-01137-4_11

improve his relationship to God through payments. These can be sacrifices or *indulgentia*, and they are ways of commercial negotiations with God. This sort of an economic theology is that of Max Weber, articulated in his understanding of the relationship between capitalism and Protestantism. According to Weber, Calvin's theology of predestination does not give its believers any way to know to whom God had extended the grace of salvation. The Puritans looked for the profit of hard labor as a sign from God that grace is bestowed upon them. Benefits from their capital thus received religious importance.

Economic theology in Judaism does not have a similar history. *Oikonomia* and its effects on God's dispositions on man have very little resonance in Judaism. Commercial negotiations with God do exist but they are perceived with vulgar connotations. A pious person will not seek personal gain for obeying God.[1] Yet even though a Weberian theology may not exist in Judaism, a similar approach to Weber may be found, not as Weber pointed out in the Puritan theology, not a theology of hard labor, but a theology of creativity. As I am going to show, God demands from man creativity and not only obedience. Man is expected to be a creator as an expression of *imitatio Dei*. It is true that man was cursed after the fall to eat in pain, and to "eat the plants of the field, by the sweat of your face" (Genesis 3:19). But hard labor itself will not suffice.

Max Weber investigated the history of the Puritans and gave a theological explanation for their economic ethic. I would like to examine the history of the Jews in Poland in a similar way, and claim that they had a theology that encouraged them to choose trade and management instead of farming, money lending, and industry, as did their peers.

The history of the Jews in Poland is as old as the second millennium. Jews immigrated to Poland from Germany along with their neighbor Germans to seek better sources of income. European Jews are known to be involved with money lending and trade, but this assumption is heavily criticized (Mell 2017, 1:155–236; Mell 2012). While the tendency of historians these days is to claim that many Jews in Western Europe and much more in Eastern Europe were indeed involved in farming and craft, the fact is that many lived from trade and management and not from production. There were of course historical reasons for this effect. The guilds prevented the Jews in the Middle Ages from entering into artisanship. In Poland, where the power of the guilds was not as strong, and many Jews started working in textile and fur, when the opportunity opened for them to manage the estate of the Szlachta, the Polish nobility, it was the Jews who jumped on the opportunity. As we estimate now, the percentage of Jews in Poland who were farmers is around twenty percent, and thirty percent were artisans. All the rest were working in management, trade, and services—teachers, rabbis and students. Of course there is a historical reason for the choice of profession that Jews made, but I contend that there was also a theological explanation. It was imitating the creative God that drew them to seek for creative solutions, and to reinvent their economics.

---

[1] Mishna 1:3: "Don't be like slaves who serve their master for a price."

11.2 Creativity

The Jewish sages saw work as intimately related to the religious ideal of adherence (*deveikut*), that is, of man's attempt to draw close, or "cling," to God.[2] Now, such a demand poses a serious theological difficulty for the Jew: Given the unbridgeable gulf between the Creator and his creatures, how can man "adhere" to the Eternal? The *midrash* suggests one possible answer: Adherence can be achieved through imitation.

R. Yehuda, son of R. Simon, began: "Walk after the Eternal your God."[3] But can a flesh-and-blood creature walk after the Holy One? Rather, from the very beginning of his creation of the world, the Holy One was engaged first of all in planting, as it is written, "The Eternal God planted a garden in Eden."[4] So should you, too, engage first of all in planting when you enter into the land.[5]

Since one can never bridge the gap between the finite and the infinite, the sages taught that one may instead adhere to God by simulating divine activity through earthly human labor (Soloveitchik 1979, 180). According to this view, the human being is blessed with a unique element that distinguishes him from other creatures and draws him nearer to God: The desire and ability to create. R. Haim of Volozhin, a leading rabbinical authority of the early nineteenth century, drew a connection between man's imitation of God and his ability to create and to influence whole worlds: "Man is seen as the heart and soul of a hundred million worlds...and to him alone is given the rule of choice, to turn himself and the worlds in whatever direction he chooses."[6] R. Joseph B. Soloveitchik makes the point more explicitly: "There is no doubt that the term 'image of God'...refers to man's inner charismatic endowment as a creative being. Man's likeness to God expresses itself in man's striving and ability to become a creator" (Soloveitchik 1997, 12). When man makes bold changes in his world to make it meet his needs and plans, his actions are a reflection of the original model of all work: The divine act of Creation. Appreciating creativity in the Jewish world is revealed in many ways. One of them is the myth of the Golem. The idea that man can create man exists already in the Talmud,[7] but was preserved throughout Jewish history (Idel 1989).

When it first appeared, this idea of human creativity—that is, of an analogy between productive human effort and the divine act of Creation—was, in all likelihood, completely new. The pagan worldview understood human culture to be an integral part of a larger complex of nature, with its eternal rhythms, and was therefore ill-suited for anyone who saw innovation, the effort to create something that has not previously existed, as a positive ideal. Thus, for example, the Greek language

[2] This section rehearses material to be found in Lifshitz (2020).

[3] Deuteronomy 13:5.

[4] Genesis 2:8.

[5] Leviticus Rabba 25:3.

[6] R. Haim of Volozhin, Nfesh Hahaim 1:7.

[7] BT Sanhedrin 65b.

lacks any verb meaning "to create." Instead, it suffices with the verb "to make" (*poi'ein*). This approach is also reflected in the way the Greeks understood the ideal of imitation, or *mimesis*. Like the Hebrews, the Greeks believed in imitation as necessary for proper thought and conduct; yet the object of their imitation was not God, but nature. In this spirit, the philosopher Democritus wrote that "in the most important things, we have learned from [animals], spinning and mending from the spider, housebuilding from the swallow, and singing by imitation from songbirds, the swan and the nightingale" (Plutarch 1999, 147). The Greeks believed that man must find his place in the cosmos while merging, via *mimesis*, with the eternal, objective order of the phenomenal world (Ferry 1994, 136). For them, the gods were merely limited entities, themselves incapable of violating the cosmic law; they certainly did not constitute a perfect model for identification and imitation. Even the gods at times engaged in mimetic activity; for example, the creation narrative cited by Plato in the *Timaeus* depicts the image of a godly but limited demiurge who unsuccessfully attempts to imitate the eternal ideas, which are beyond his grasp (Plato 1961).

The biblical approach is altogether different. As against the pagan longing for union with the natural order, the Torah depicts the idea of a sovereign, active, and dynamic will, which is creative at its core. The idea of creation *ex nihilo* attests to the unlimited power and freedom of the Holy One. God is not part of a preexisting cosmos, but rather is its creator and author. The laws of nature are upstaged by the will of the divine legislator, who can break them at any time. It is the will of God, and not its derivatives, which is of foremost concern to the religious person. By imitating the Creator rather than nature, man, through acts of creativity, introduces innovations into his world, breaking free from the predetermined cycle of nature, and gaining thereby a taste of the divine freedom.

This doctrine was alien to the spirit of classical culture, the latter's impressive artistic and technical achievements notwithstanding. Even when, with the rise of Christianity, Western culture accepted the idea of *creatio ex nihilo*, creativity was still widely perceived as an exclusively divine privilege, beyond human ability. As the sixth-century Christian philosopher Cassiodorus wrote, "Things made and created differ, for we, who cannot create, make" (Tatarkiewicz 1980, 247).

The idea of liberating the human spirit from its subordination to the "natural forms" began to take hold in the West only with the Renaissance. The philosophers of that period, such as Nicolaus Cusanus and Giordano Bruno, drew a distinction between created nature (*natura naturata*) and artificial nature (*natura naturans*), regarding the latter as the field in which man's creative potential would be realized, through his deliberate efforts to imitate God (Tatarkiewicz 1980). Nature no longer symbolized the limits of human ability, but its point of departure, from which nearly anything was possible. Creative labor, wrote Leonardo da Vinci, "surpasses nature in dealing with things that are simply natural and finite, for the works which our hands do at the command of our eyes are infinite" (da Vinci 1956, 23).

The debt owed by Western culture to Jewish theology is difficult to measure. Still, it would seem that inherent in the belief that God created the world from nothing, and that man's role is to imitate the Creator through willful works, there was always a promise of bringing to fruition those qualities which make the human race unique. This redemptive promise, with the rejection of fatalistic naturalism that it implies, is one of the underlying assumptions of Western civilization since the Renaissance—an assumption which has played no small part in the great material and spiritual achievements of the West.

11.3 Creativity in Trade

Creativity is a human virtue, an expression of God's portion. Man is therefore ordered in the Torah to labor. Unlike other creatures that live out of nature, and do not change nature but benefit from the fruit of the earth, man changes nature and makes a living from his own creation. That is why the forefathers worked as shepherds and so did the prophets.[8] Others worked as farmers.[9] Labor is appreciated in Talmudic literature as well.[10] Man creates but also eats the plants of the field, by the sweat of his face (as in Genesis 3:19). Commerce are, on the other hand, criticized in Talmudic literature: "you will not find [the knowledge of Torah] among traders."[11] Knowledge of Torah demands a peace of mind that is lacking among traders. The Sages thought that trade leads to wealth, but respected "a man who is not involved in trades but instead labors his field, [only] he will be satisfied and is called a king."[12] It may be that the Talmudic Sages adopted Hellenistic virtues of autarky, but on the other hand, one cannot suspect that there is an intrinsic theological criticism against trades and commerce.

Yet the idea of labor as valuable went through a change. What was a virtue in a closed economy lost its value when markets started to open up. Later Talmudic Sages advise whoever wants to be wealthy to involve himself with trade.[13] Wealth became a virtue.[14] Man was not asked anymore to labor, to sweat. Efficient acts of commerce, of trade, is better than needless labor. The Sages even go as far as characterizing labor as punishment. The future will promise a good fate for the Israelites where they will enjoy labor of others so their heart will be open and free for Torah learning. A better off person is the one who is not working but the one who is able to manage others to work.[15]

The question is how was labor transformed into commerce? If labor is a virtue, why was it replaced so easily with trade? As mentioned above, *imitatio dei*, imitating the creator, is the supreme achievement. If labor is appreciated as a healthy,

[8] As did Abraham, Jacob and Moses. Midrash Tanaim. See Deuteronomy 5.

[9] As did Isaac and Jeremiah.

[10] "Great is labor." Gitin 67b, BT Nedarim 49b.

[11] BT Eruvin 55a.

[12] Psikta Zuta, Kohelet 5.

[13] BT Nisa 70b.

[14] BT Eruvin 86a.

[15] BT Berakhot 35b.

virtuous life, imitating His creativity is considered the highest achievement. To be creative is to be like God. That is why creativity is restrained, according to the Torah, and it is forbidden one day a week, on the Sabbath, because it is that which makes a person to be like God. Being like God could be too dangerous, because of loss of hierarchy between him and God. But at the same time, this virtue of man enables him to relate to God as an ally, in a way of covenant, and not like an obedient agent.

Creativity is about changing nature to fit to human life. Instead of adapting to nature, a creative man changes nature so it will adopt itself to him. In other words, creativity is adding human values to nature. In the world of the artisan, shaping a piece of raw wood into a table or chair is adding values of human behavior such as seating or eating to the wood, which ends up as a furniture. For a builder, materials like stone, iron, and wood are shaped into a building, while adding to them a value, an affordance for human living.

Adding human values applies to simple production like carpentry and construction, but also to commerce and trade. The market is indeed a human artifact, or rather a social artifact, but it does not have to be fixed. Adapting it to one's needs is a creative act, and organizing and reorganizing is a creative act. The organizer adds his own values into the social raw material.

Being creative in trades demands an individualistic perspective. Instead of following his old habits, the way of life that he is accustomed to living by, he is able to interpret reality anew. In the life of commerce, a creative person sizes up a situation and arranges it to fit to his benefit. Such a trait is especially useful in times of economic change. When economic life runs smoothly, when the economy is stable, maintaining an old profession is a good source of income. But in times of change, in economic revolution, many sources of income change. In such times, the one that gets ahead of the game is the one who is not statically fixed in his way of relating to life.

As I mentioned, creativity is tightly connected to theology. The demand to create in this world, as *imitatio Dei*, is a demand to add value to reality. But the ability to change, to size up any situation anew, is not only about adding value, but also about a change in perspective. Instead of seeing reality from within, a creative person is able to see reality from above. Such a perspective is common among those who believe in God. Faith in God generates a godly perspective. Christianity as well as Judaism enables such perspective, though the weight that is given in Christianity to the fall, an event that defined the limits of man, prevents Christians from thinking so positively about change. The fall in Judaism does not denote limits of creativity but is rather a demand for ethical responsibility (Maimonides 1906, 14–16). Adam himself was created with a soul that is above nature, which gives him an ability to correct nature. This soul was not taken away from him because of the fall. It is this soul that gives man a perspective from above, and not to be taken by the serfdom of his old occupation and habits. That may well be why so many Jews were able to reinvent themselves anew, as we are going to see in the economic history of the Jews in Poland.

11.4 The Jewish Economic History in Poland in the Seventeenth and Eight Centuries

The case of the Jews in Poland in the seventeenth and eighteenth centuries, and their effect on the Polish economy is an example of successful creative thinking. The history of the Jews in Poland is probably as old as the Polish state. Immigration of Jews to Poland started in the twelfth century, but accelerated during the thirteenth when in 1264 the Status of Kalisz or the General Charter of Jewish Liberties introduced numerous rights for the Jews in Poland, leading to a nearly autonomous "nation within a nation." Jewish immigration from the west of Germany to east Germany started earlier, but the opportunities that were available for them in Bohemia and Poland enhanced their immigration. Jews settled mainly in cities as merchants and money lenders, but competed successfully with the city guildsman on crafts as well. Jews started gaining economic power as managers of the magnates (*szhlacta*), managing their estate (Rosman 1992; Teller 2016; see also Young 2010). As Moshe Rosman called it a marriage of convenience, the relationship between the magnates and the Jews was convenient for both. The Jewish financial talent together with their lack of will to compete politically, joined with the interest of the magnates' need for managers and therefore led them to choosing the Jews and not their non-Jewish city dwellers. From the sixteenth century, Jews moved more and more from their attachments to the majestic estates into estates of the magnates. The result was that during the eighteenth century, nearly half of the Jews lived in cities and villages of the magnates. The power of the magnates was generated by their estate. After the wars of the seventeenth century, the magnates had to adapt their estates to the new conditions, and it was under the management of the Jews that it turned to be successful. The Jews for their part experienced a population explosion, and were desperate for new sources of income. Despite the huge losses of lives during the massacres of Bohdan Chmielnicki in the years 1648–49, they soon reached a population of 750,000.

During the eighteenth century Poland underwent a political division and towards the end of the century Poland was divided three times, and large parts of Poland were taken by Prussia, Austria, and the Russian empire. The political division led to an economic decline which affected its monetary system. Jews who were hitherto involved in lending money changed positions, becoming borrowers instead of lenders. They took credit that lost its value and thus lost less from the decline of the value of the Zloty, the Polish coin. One of the characteristics of the economic declines was the export of wheat and barley. After a long history of being the European source of these cereals, Poland failed to sell its produce. The superfluous cereals were used for producing alcohol. Taverns were opened all over Poland, and the rights to sell alcohol and to run these taverns were bought by Jews.

The ability to adjust to economic change, or economic mobility, is unique to Jews. Throughout their occupation in Poland, Jews moved from trade and loans to crafts, to management and to selling alcohol. After almost a millennium in Poland, Jews reinvented themselves anew, time after time. Unlike their neighbors, who many times emigrated like them from Germany to Poland in the thirteenth century, but maintained the same sources of income, for the Jews, economic changes were an opportunity to get ahead.

11.5 Summary

The connection between theology and economy may seem artificial. Religion is concerned with the spiritual, with higher areas in life, as some speculate. Economic theology may seem an oxymoron. But the history of theology does show a tight connection between religion and economics. From the *oikonomia* of the Trinity, to *indulgentia* in Catholicism, to the accumulation of wealth, as the Puritans believed according to Max Weber, economics plays an important role in Christian theology. In Judaism, man may not negotiate with God regarding his religious state, but his application of his Godly spirit may enhance his ability to succeed financially.

Man is created with a portion of God within him. If man uses his portion of God, he becomes like God, and he becomes a creator. He not only enjoys the world, benefits from nature and eats from its fruits, but man also changes the world and improves it. He invents new ways of benefiting from the world, easier ways to make a living, and is no longer in serfdom to the world. He controls and re-invents nature. The more man develops his soul to be God like, the more he is able to perceive nature through the eye of the inventor or of the entrepreneur. To see reality through a creative eye is to change it anew.

As I have shown, Jews in Poland, throughout the last millennium, and especially in the seventeenth and eighteenth centuries, were entrepreneurs. They managed to re-invent themselves like the phoenix, and created new occupations and new sources of income, and they thrived and increased in population regardless of wars and pogroms. In my view, the economic behavior of the Jews in Poland expresses an exceptional relationship between theology and economics. I claim that it is their Jewish theology that helped to generate their economic behavior.

The case of the Jews in Poland is unique as a case study because of their size as a distinct group within the Polish society and their large percentage within the urban society. But it is certainly not unique as an economic behavior in comparison to other Jewish communities. The Jewish community in the U.S. and that of the state of Israel, as a "startup nation," are good examples of the creative economy. Yet after all, what is unique is not the economic case, but the theology. A society for which creativity is a central value in its religion will easily apply creativity in its economic affairs.[16] Their perception will be ready for new ways, and their habits will be less fixed, or as I defined it, they will not be attached to the road of serfdom of old ways

[16] Of course, faith alone does not help creativity. The only condition for enhancing creativity is when religion speaks for creativity and not merely obedience. See Illes, K. and Zsolnai, L. "Spiritually Inspired Creativity in Business", A paper presented at the World Congress on Spirituality and Creativity in Management, Barcelona, 23–25 Apr 2015, pp. 1–19.

of economics, but will forever seek for solutions and improvements. A creative theology generates a creative economy—an economy that like God, creates a new world.

References

da Vinci, Leonardo. 1956. *Treatise on Painting*. Vol. 1, Translated by A. Philip McMahon. Princeton: Princeton University Press.

Ferry, Jean-Marc. 1994. Ancient, Modern, and Contemporary. In *New French Thought: Political Philosophy*, ed. Mark Lilla. Princeton: Princeton University Press.

Idel, Moshe. 1989. *Golem: Jewish Magical and Mystical Traditions on the Artificial Anthropoid*. New York: Sunny.

Lifshitz, Yosef Yitzhak. 2020. Secret of the Sabbath. In *Tikvah Daily: A Shabbat Reader*. New York: Tikvah Fund.

Maimonides, Moses. 1906. *A Guide for the Perplexed*. 4th ed. New York: E.P. Dutton.

Mell, Julie. 2012. Hybridity in a Medieval Key: The Paradox of Jewish Participation in Self-Representative Political Processes. *Jewish Historical Studies* 44:127–138.

Mell, Julie. 2017. *The Myth of the Medieval Jewish Moneylender*. 2 vols. New York: Palgrave Macmillan.

Plato. 1961. Timaeus. In *The Collected Dialogues of Plato*, ed. E. Hamilton and H. Cairns, Translated by A.E. Taylor. Princeton: Princeton University Press.

Plutarch. 1999. On the Rationality of Animals. In *The Atomists: Leucippus and Democritus*. Toronto: University of Toronto.

Rosman, Moshe. 1992. *The Lord's Jews: Magnate-Jewish Relations in the Polish-Lithuanian Commonwealth During the Eighteenth Century*. Cambridge, MA: Harvard University Center for Jewish Studies.

Soloveitchik, Joseph B. 1979. And You Shall Search From There. In *Halachik Man: Revealed and Hidden*. Jerusalem: World Zionist Organization.

Soloveitchik, Joseph B. 1997. *The Lonely Man of Faith*. New York: Doubleday.

Tatarkiewicz, Wladyslaw. 1980. *A History of Six Ideas: An Essay in Aesthetics*, Translated by Christopher Kasparek. Warsaw: Polish Scientific Publishers.

Teller, Adam. 2016. *Money, Power, and Influence in Eighteenth-Century Lithuania: The Jews on the Radziwiłł Estates*. Stanford: Stanford University Press.

Young, John D. 2010. *The Naturalization Debate of the Twelfth Century: Jews in Monastic Thought and Experience*. Virginia Tech, November: *Southeastern Medieval Association Conference*.

Joseph Isaac Lifshitz is Professor of Philosophy and Jewish Thought at Shalem College (Jerusalem, Israel) and is an expert on Jewish philosophy and history, with an emphasis on the philosophy of Ashkenaz in the high Middle Ages. He earned his PhD in Jewish Thought from Tel Aviv University, and holds an MA in Jewish history from Touro College.

Luk Bouckaert and Laszlo Zsolnai, "Spirituality and Business: A Systemic Overview", Society and Economy 201234(3), pp. 489-514https://www.researchgate.net/publication/ 270531458_Spirituality_and_business_An_interdisciplinary_overview

Part VI
Islam

Chapter 12
Being Virtuous in Markets: An Islamic View

Ayman Reda

Abstract Traditions reported in the *hadith* on the vicious or virtuous character of merchants and traders do not contradict one another, but instead convey a common theme, and that is: that the moral disposition of a merchant is the determining factor for one's eternal salvation (or damnation). It is a simple and straightforward message, yet of the utmost gravity and consequence. Whereas an impious and profligate merchant is forewarned of the utmost punishment, a pious and virtuous merchant is promised the greatest of rewards. As much as the former is a strict caution against immoral market behavior, the latter is an active call to virtuous market conduct. The Prophet's traditions are in no way a condemnation of markets or market activity, but a most profound summon to merchants to don their market behavior with the cloak of piety and virtue. Far from being censured, such virtuous markets are commended and encouraged.

Keywords Virtue · Islam · Economic ethics · Markets

12.1 Introduction

A *hadith* reports that the Prophet once passed by a group of merchants,[1] who were then called middlemen or brokers, and said unto them: "I will not call you brokers, but instead will call you traders, and a trader is profligate, and the profligate go to

[1] *Hadith* (plural *ahadith*) is a report of a saying of the Prophet Muhammad transmitted over time by narrators. The collection of the Prophet's *ahadith* and deeds together constitute the *sunna*. After the Qur'an, the *sunna* represents a major source of Islamic law and doctrine. Some have even argued that such sayings and deeds, if ascertained, possess a divine status, as suggested by these

A. Reda (✉)
University of Michigan-Dearborn, Dearborn, MI, USA
e-mail: areda@umich.edu

G. J. Buijs, J. J. Ballor (eds.), *In Search of the Spirits of Capitalism*, Sophia Studies in Cross-cultural Philosophy of Traditions and Cultures 44,
https://doi.org/10.1007/978-3-032-01137-4_12

hell."[2] The Arabic word for a broker is *semsar*, a label that for a long time was imbued with negative connotations, on the suspicion that such 'facilitators' of market transactions were largely unscrupulous and superfluous. This is supported by another *hadith* in which a merchant observed, "We used to be called *semsars*, and then the Prophet gave us a more amicable title, [that of traders]" (Qahf & Al-Muballaghi (2007) 2007, 2:437). But if brokers or *semsars* were regarded as such, why did the Prophet assign them the superior label of 'traders,' only to later condemn them as doomed to hell? Clearly, there is no greater admonition than being condemned by the Messenger of God to the eternal fires of hell (*Jahannam*). We may begin to answer this question by looking more closely at the two cited *ahadith*.

According to the first *hadith*, upon hearing the Prophet's declaration, the traders stopped trading and closed their shops. The next day, the Prophet inquires as to the traders' whereabouts and was told, "O Messenger of God, they heard what you said and so ceased their activities." He replied, "And I say it again today, save those who receive and give justly." And in the second *hadith*, the Prophet said, "O traders, your trade is teeming with loquacity, deception and false oaths. Instead, blend it with charity and sincerity." A third *hadith* reiterates this meaning, in which the Prophet stated, "Traders will be resurrected on judgment day as profligate, save those who are pious, benevolent and honest" (NI 2007, 2:434). Such proclamations would surely disturb the most benumbed of consciences, causing one to question every market act or movement. The effect is no less than the angst that Matthew 19:24 (where Jesus says: it is easier for a camel to go through the eye of a needle than for someone who is rich to enter the kingdom of God) produces in the poor souls of rich men and women, who desperately seek to reconcile their wealth with the demands of salvation. But a few more *ahadith* may get us closer to the Prophet's intended meaning. In one tradition, the Prophet states, "On the day of judgment, the truthful and trustworthy Muslim merchant will stand side by side with the martyrs," and in another, "The truthful and trustworthy merchant is [on the day of judgment] with the prophets, the righteous, and the martyrs" (NI 2007, 2:431).

Clearly, the traditions cited above do not contradict one another, but instead convey a common theme, and that is: that the *moral disposition* of a merchant is the

---

Qur'anic verses: "[N]or does he speak out of caprice. It is naught but a revelation revealed, taught him by one of awesome power" (53:3–5).

[2] *Al-Nusus Al-Iqtisadiyya* (NI) 2007, 2:436. Nasr et al. (2015, 1486) translates *fujjar* (sing. *fajir*) in the Qur'an as "the profligate," while Arberry (1964, 634) translates it as "libertines." According to Nasr (2015, 1486), the word derives from "the verb *fajara*, meaning, 'to break open,' and implying that those who do evil break open what should be left closed." The term is meant to signify that such extravagance and abuse of resources is characteristic of human corruption and wickedness, or, as the following verses suggest, impiety:

> Or shall We make those who believe and perform righteous deeds like those who work corruption upon the earth? Or shall We make the reverent like the profligate? (38:28)

> Truly the pious shall be in bliss; and truly the profligate shall be in Hellfire. (82:13–14)

determining factor for one's eternal salvation (or damnation). It is a simple and straightforward message, yet of the utmost gravity and consequence. To be sure, however, such a message is meaningful only to those who believe in the divine authority of the message itself, and its messenger. And this only serves to accentuate the significance of the traditions (*ahadith*) and their conveyed message. To a Muslim merchant, such proclamations confer an immense responsibility that cannot be discounted on account of market practicality or expediency. The stakes are just too high. But they are all too clear as well: while a market career of profligacy and impiety would lead one to hell, that of virtue and piety would grant a merchant not just entry to heaven, but a place amongst the distinctive group of "the prophets, the righteous, and the martyrs." The extremity of either ending is quite suggestive, for whereas an impious and profligate merchant is forewarned of the utmost punishment, a pious and virtuous merchant is promised the greatest of rewards. As much as the former is a strict caution against immoral market behavior, the latter is an active call to virtuous market conduct. To be clear, therefore, the Prophet's traditions are in no way a condemnation of markets or market activity, but a most profound summon to merchants to don their market behavior with the cloak of piety and virtue. Far from being censured, such *virtuous* markets are commended and encouraged.

But if a market imbued with virtue is granted such reverence and sanctity, and its participants promised such heavenly standing, what are the features or characteristics of such a market? What virtues are considered essential for such a market to exist? Are such virtues accessible to all religions and ideologies, or do they require a distinctive way of life that is predicated on a particular worldview and set of principles? Moreover, is the need for virtue confined to the moral character of market participants, or extends as well to the institutional structure of markets and public policy? In short, what would such a market *really* look like?

To be sure, these are not questions for which the answers are readily available; in fact, it is not at all clear that they can all be answered. The question as to "what would such a market *really* look like" is especially problematic, because it leads us into the realm of the hypothetical. Even more, such an exercise in conjectural thinking can be easily branded as utopian, and therefore risks the possibility of being intellectually ridiculed, or at the very least, ignored. As a case in point, it may be relatively easier to identify and elucidate the specific virtues conducive to virtuous market behavior than to describe the manifest form and content of such behavior in an economic domain. What is more difficult would be an attempt to draw any necessary connection between such behavior and human flourishing. Such a connection presupposes that we have a clear notion of what constitutes human flourishing, and even more, that such an aim is universally acknowledged and sought. To a pious believer, for example, one's flourishing is simultaneously material and spiritual, manifest and immanent, of this world and the next. And the relationship between the two, that is, virtues and human flourishing, is neither mutually exclusive, nor exactly complementary. It is a relationship that is largely impervious to any dualistic conception or scientific precision.

For example, though the grueling trials of Prophet Job would not correspond, even remotely, to any modern interpretation of human flourishing, it is perfectly consistent with the view of divine justice presented in the Old Testament and the Qur'an. That such a "blameless and upright" man, "one who feared God, and turned away from evil" (Job 1:1) was yet subjected to an extraordinary ordeal is merely one sample of countless human experiences that are incomprehensible to the modern conception of human flourishing that is fundamentally secular and materialistic. For though he was eventually rewarded with more family and property, it is the flourishing of his heart and soul, effected by his unflinching virtues of piety and forbearance, that ultimately mattered to Job. And as such, he was to become "a reminder for possessors of intellect,"

> And remember Our servant Job, when he called upon his Lord, "Truly Satan has afflicted me with weariness and punishment." "Strike with thy foot; this is cool water wherewith to wash and to drink." And We bestowed upon him his family and their like along with them as a mercy from Us and a reminder for possessors of intellect. (38:41–43)

According to *The Study Quran* (Nasr et al. 2015, 1111), "'possessors of the intellect' indicates those who possess true knowledge of the inner essence and meaning of things," a quality that Job, as a prophet of God, possessed and exemplified. It is inconceivable that any human would accept and endure, and for so long, such "weariness and punishment," unless he or she possesses "true knowledge of the inner essence and meaning" of such tribulations. And yet such "knowledge," whether complete or partial, would grant its holders an economic outlook that is fundamentally at odds with modern economic theory and practice. For while such believers are convinced of the sanctity and utility of virtues, they are under no illusions that such virtues would guarantee them even a minimal state of material well-being. They live in constant anticipation of being subject to daily trials of their bodies and souls, and 'see' in the events that transpire 'signs' of divine knowledge and wisdom: "Truly in that are signs for a people who believe" (6:99). In their commentary, Nasr et al. state that, "those who believe are the real beneficiaries of these *signs*, for they alone are able to see in these signs the proofs of Divine Power and Oneness, whereas those who disbelieve have hearts that are 'sealed' against such understanding" (Nasr et al. 2015, 377). It follows, that "those who believe" do not perceive any strict causality between virtues and virtuous behavior on the one hand, and human flourishing, understood in a material sense, on the other. Yet such conviction in no way diminishes the intensity or sincerity of their faith, whose reward they believe is beyond this finite and fleeting world. And it is precisely the absence of such conviction by "those who disbelieve," whose "hearts are 'sealed' against such understanding," that explains their tentative and shifting approach to virtues in markets. Such market participants, having thrust aside any belief in the divine authority and sanctity of virtues, eventually lose faith in their utility as well, as they repeatedly fail to see in the application of such virtues a secure and steady return. Absent any appeal to a transcendental moral authority, and faced with a quite often frustrating relationship between virtues and profit, it becomes increasingly difficult for 'disbelievers' to develop a sustainable case, ethical or practical, for virtues within markets. This, more than anything else, explains the rather deplorable state of virtues in today's markets.

Any justification for the exercise of virtues in markets must be based on theoretical grounds that transcend markets, otherwise such virtues are doomed to nothingness. The argument that markets can or will *miraculously* (or, using conventional terminology, *endogenously*) develop the morality that ensures human flourishing is both naïve and contradictory. Any ensuing 'morality' will inescapably be mutable, transitory, and pliable. Moreover, the very notion of human flourishing will become arbitrary and evanescent, endlessly adapting to fit the narrative that is in vogue. Unless a moral authority that is exogenous to markets is adopted, markets will succumb to the most banal and least charitable of ends, namely, profit. And markets whose sole end is the maximization of profits will scarcely allow virtues any noticeable significance or relevance, insofar as virtues refuse to serve profit, the last god standing. It goes without saying, therefore, that the nature and role of virtues is ultimately derivative of the end or purpose of human thought and action. More specifically, unless the notion of human flourishing is defined in accordance with the nature and role of virtues, we are bound to fall into the contradictions that ultimately ostracize virtues in the marketplace. To put bluntly and unapologetically, human flourishing defined in strictly materialistic or utilitarian terms is simply incompatible with virtues and virtuous behavior. The exercise of virtues is only meaningful and valuable if predicated on an understanding of human flourishing that transcends the material, to encompass the spiritual and religious. Only when human flourishing is understood as transcending this finite and temporal world, will humans truly appreciate the nature and role of virtues in markets, and thus discern the *real* relationship between virtues and profits. Then, and only then, will we realize the true meaning and purpose of Job's torment, what it meant for him, and what it means for us.

In this chapter, we seek to address the issues raised above, concerning the relationship between virtues and human flourishing within markets, from an Islamic perspective. The Islamic viewpoint we adopt is inspired by two letters written by Imam Ali, the last of the four Rightly Guided Caliphs and the first of the 12 Shi'a Imams. The first letter was addressed to his son, Hasan, upon Ali's return from the Battle of Siffin in Syria (657 AD), while the second letter (658 AD) was addressed to Malik al-Ashtar, whom Ali had appointed as the Governor of Egypt and its surrounding areas. Our selection of these two letters may seem like an odd juxtaposition, given the apparent contrast of the letters in terms of their respective recipients, purpose, and background. But a careful reading of the letters reveals a striking complementarity, even harmony, of substance and spirit.[3] The letters, separately and together, present us with a treasure of intellectual and practical wisdom suitable for all aspects of human life. Specifically, they provide us with an ethical model that can

[3] We should mention that the Battle of Siffin was a war that Imam Ali felt ultimately compelled to undertake, despite his many efforts for a peaceful settlement through persuasion and negotiation. It was in response to a rebellion by Mu'awiya, the governor of Damascus, who refused to accept Ali's position as Caliphate. See Madelung (1997) and Chirri (1998).

serve as a practical guide to all human affairs, a model that does not suffer from any discontinuity of theory and practice, but is itself based on the Imam's personal life. It follows, that such a model can be especially instructive to us with respect to the nature and role of virtues in markets, and their connection to the desired goal of human flourishing.

In the next section, we carefully develop this ethical model from the Imam's two letters, highlighting the crucial Islamic concepts that together form this moral construct. In the third section of the essay, we engage in a comparative study of the Imam's ethical model in relation to that of Adam Smith, as it was developed in his *Theory of the Moral Sentiments*. While some interesting parallels will be examined between the two models, the essay argues for the superiority of the Imam's model, both in theory and practice. We conclude in the final section.

12.2 The Imam's Ethical Model

Humanity has never suffered for want of wisdom, but for the lack of commitment. And if the life of any one person is a testament to this truth, it is that of Imam Ali, who had imparted to us all the wisdom that we may ever need, and some more. The Imam spared no effort in educating and instructing others, and is forever remembered by his famous utterance: "O people! Ask me before you lose me …." Yet with all the answers he presented to us, we continue to lose our way, even as we plainly profess our loyalty to his life and wisdom. This wisdom is especially conspicuous in the two letters we intend to examine, as ideal specimens of the ethics proper to a life of virtue.

Widely regarded as "an ideal constitution for Islamic governance," the Imam's letter to Malik al-Ashtar is also believed to contain "universally applicable ethical principles and is therefore as relevant to those ruled as to those who rule" (Shah-Kazemi 2006, 61–62). The "most fundamental" of such principles is that of justice, and the Imam presents us with a "sacred conception of justice" that "is consciously linked to the spiritual precepts of the Islamic faith" (Shah-Kazemi 2006, 61–62). It is this "sacred" notion of justice that will form the basis for the ethical model we believe is most conducive to virtuous behavior in markets. As such, it is necessary that we start with the definition of justice provided by the Imam himself.

According to the Imam, "Justice puts everything in its right place" (Shah-Kazemi 2006, 65). This definition is reminiscent of that presented by Plato, in which he states that "we have laid down, as a universal principle, that everyone ought to perform the one function in the community for which his nature best suited him … that principle, or some form of it, is justice" (Shah-Kazemi 2006, 65). It also evokes Confucius' "definition of 'the art of government' as consisting in 'making things right, or putting things in their right places" (Lakhani 2006, 27). Expounding on this definition of justice, Sayyed Hossein Nasr writes,

> To be fully human is to have an innate sense of justice and a yearning for justice.... When we speak of justice, we have the intuitive sense of putting things aright and in their appropriate place, of re-establishing a lost harmony and equilibrium, of remaining true to the nature of things, of giving each his due. (Nasr 2006, xi)

Granted the important parallels between the definitions, the Imam's conception of justice is distinguished by its intrinsically sacred or religious essence, being predicated on a metaphysical view of the world, or the 'order of creation.'

The divine 'order of creation,' as presented in the Qur'an, maintains that humanity was appointed to the special role of vicegerency or stewardship upon the earth (2:30; 6:165; 33:72; 35:39). The bounties of creation were offered as a gift to humanity, and humans were thereby entrusted with the making of a just society, based on the proper conservation and fair administration of God's bounties. The responsibility of good stewardship requires that humans exhibit gratitude for such bounties (2:283; 27:73), through preservation (17:28), sharing (4:32), and moderation (7:31). Humanity, however, was not abandoned to its fate, forsaken and untended, but was blessed with divine guidance over time, in the form of prophets and revelation. Through the ages, the function of prophecy was to offer divine counsel to humanity, and especially when societies were rampant with corruption and injustice (2:37–8; 2:213; 62:2; 16:89). By exemplifying the role of vicegerency, prophets sought to instill in communities a life of faith and piety, the spiritual foundation essential to a moral and just society (49:13; 51:56).

As a form of divine intervention, prophecy aimed at tapping into the 'hearts' of believers and connecting with their "'inner prophet', or inmost degree of consciousness," otherwise known as the 'intellect' (Shah-Kazemi 2006, 27). The 'intellect' *(al-aql)* refers to the human faculty that "is capable of a direct contemplative vision of transcendent realities," and is unlike reason, which is of "an indirect, discursive nature." While reason "works with logic and arrives at mental concepts, only, of those [transcendent] realities, [the intellect] is able to contemplate or 'see' the Absolute; with the reason, one can only think about it" (Shah-Kazemi 2006, 22–23). The 'intellect' is generally associated with the 'heart', as verse 22:24 suggests: "Have they not journeyed upon the earth, that they might have hearts by which to understand or ears by which to hear? Truly it is not the eyes that go blind, but it is hearts within breasts that go blind." In their commentary, Nasr et al. remark that "the heart is the seat of knowledge and the organ of spiritual understanding. This is further explicated in the *hadith*: 'In the body there is a lump of flesh: when it is healthy, the whole body is healthy, and when it is rotten, the whole body is rotten. Yea, it is the heart'" (Nasr et al. 2015, 841). This view is also emphasized by M. Ali Lakhani in his essay, *The Metaphysics of Human Governance*,

> That faculty which is capable of discerning reality in its most subtle nature – bearing in mind that the merely human is not privileged to know the Divine – is not the human faculty of the common senses or of the discursive reason, but the transcendent faculty of the supra-rational Intellect, the core of our discerning self, which is sometimes labeled the 'Heart'. (Lakhani 2006, 6).

It follows that the 'intellect' reflects a deeper sense of conviction, while allowing for a more penetrating view of reality and one's responsibility vis-à-vis the divinely appointed role of vicegerent. The 'intellect', however, can only attain such a comprehension or 'vision' of reality if it achieves an "inner assimilation of the substance [of revelation]" (Shah-Kazemi 2006, 11). According to Shah-Kazemi,

> [R]evelation is a clarion call to the spiritual depths of the intellect; it cultivates and brings to fruition the seeds of consciousness planted therein by God.... From this perspective, the revealed text is not to be seen as some extraneous source opposed to the intelligence, but as the objective, outward expression of the very principles that the intellect itself yields to the 'inner prophet' – understanding by 'intellect' not simply the faculty of reasoning but the source of consciousness articulating the human spirit. (Shah-Kazemi 2006, 28)

Reason, therefore, "should be perceived as one of the modes of the intellect," and not a separate or mutually exclusive entity (Shah-Kazemi 2006, 28). The 'intellect' allows for a quality of comprehension that goes "beyond the limits imposed by [rationality], something more than reason is necessary; *and this 'something more' is that which makes the ethos we are considering a spiritual one, not a rationalistic one*" (Shah-Kazemi 2006, 29–30, emphasis added). And it is precisely this "supra-rational mode of awareness" that can comprehend the divine order of creation and thus realize, in theory and practice, the justice befitting humanity's role as God's vicegerents on earth. When asked to characterize the intelligent, the Imam responded, "That is the one who puts things in their proper places" (Cleary 1995, 44). Thus, it is only the 'intellect,' with its supra-rational and spiritual qualities, that possesses the ability to integrate divine prophecy and realize earthly justice. Lacking a spiritual dimension in thought and practice, reason alone is incapable of discerning the essence or appreciating the gravity of the role of vicegerency, and will thus fail to accomplish the justice that such a role demands. The primary purpose of the Imam's letters is to outline the conditions necessary for believers, in their respective positions and vocations, to realize this notion of 'sacred justice.'

In the opening sentence of his letter to Malik al-Ashtar, the Imam writes,

> This is that with which Ali, the servant of God and Commander of the Faithful, charged Malik ibn al-Harith al-Ashtar in his instructions to him when he appointed him governor of Egypt ... (Chittick 1980, 68).

The Imam, in his usual practice of putting everything in its proper place, describes himself first as "the servant of God," and second as "Commander of the Faithful." He then continues:

> He charged him to fear God, to prefer obedience to Him (over all else) and to follow what He has directed in His Book – both the acts He has made obligatory and those He recommends – for none attains felicity but he who follows His directions, and none is overcome by wretchedness but he who denies them and lets them slip by. (He charged him) to support the cause of God with his heart, his hand and his tongue, for He – majestic is His Name – has promised to help him who exalts Him. And he charged him to break the passions of his soul and restrain it in its recalcitrance, for the soul incites to evil, except inasmuch as God has mercy. (Chittick 1980, 68)

In a letter primarily concerned with matters of governance and society, the Imam begins with a call to piety and virtue. It is a call to set one's priorities in their proper order, with "obedience" to God transcending all else. This *just* ordering of one's life is perfectly captured in the following saying attributed to the Imam:

> For those who put in order
> what is between them and God,
> God will put in order
> what is between them and other people.
> And for those who put in order
> their task for the Hereafter,
> God puts in order
> their business in this world.
> And those who have caution from themselves
> have protection from God. (Lakhani 2006, 38)

Piety, informed by prophecy, is thus "a prerequisite for justice" (Lakhani 2006, 38). Justice, as the conscious effort to "put [everything] in order," would be meaningless if it were to exclude our relationship with God, as Ibn Miskawayh so lucidly puts it:

> Since justice consists indeed giving to the right person what ought to be given in the right way, it would be inconceivable that we should not owe God, exalted is He, who granted us all these immense goods, an obligation which they should fulfill (Kalin 2012, 56).

This "obligation," fulfilled through a life of piety and virtue, becomes the very embodiment of justice. This is even more so if we consider that one of God's 99 names is *Al-Adl* (The Utterly Just), and the Imam had once said, "I bear witness that He is Justice and He acts justly" (Shah-Kazemi 2006, 111). It follows, that if God's 'order of creation' is predicated on humanity's role of vicegerency, then the principle that should govern our conduct as vicegerents must be the same principle that governs His 'order of creation,' and that is justice. Created in His image, we are thus expected to emulate Him, as the hadith by the Prophet clearly states: "Assume the virtues of God, for most people enter paradise because of their piety and virtue." 'Sacred justice,' therefore, is to be distinguished from other notions of justice because it distinctly presupposes a metaphysical view of the world that becomes manifested in a life of piety and virtue. As explained earlier, this view of the world is realized through the evolving interaction of prophecy and our intellect. Together, they signify the theoretical dimension of religion, while piety and virtue represent its practical element; neither part is feasible without the other. Morality, as such, consists of thought, which is derivative of prophecy and intellect, and action, that is informed by piety and virtue. The crucial implication is that any ethical framework that may be derived is simultaneously exogenous and endogenous, with the former corresponding to prophecy and scripture, and the latter to the interaction between prophecy on the one hand, and our intellect on the other. Such an ethical setting is necessary for any ensuing moral conduct to be characterized as pious and virtuous. And it is in this spirit that we will attempt to understand the Imam's model for moral conduct and its implications for markets. In the letter to his son Hasan, the Imam begins by saying,

> From the father who is (shortly) to die, who acknowledges the hardships of times, who has turned away from life, who has submitted himself to the (calamities of) time, who realizes the evils of the world, who is living in the abodes of the dead and is due to depart from them any day … to the son who yearns for what is not to be achieved, who is treading the paths of those who have died, who is the victim of ailments, …. (Ibn Abi Talib 2009, 749)

These opening statements describe the state of mind of the Imam as he writes the letter to his son. It is that of a father who knows that there is but little time left to share with his son the account of a lifetime summarized in the best possible way. This account, however eloquent or instructive it may be, would be of little use to his son and to us if not augmented with words of wisdom and counsel. And in this regard, the Imam is more than generous. Such generosity seems to emanate from a profound sense of compassion to his son, and to all those he hoped that one day will get to read this letter. In the second paragraph, he writes,

> [W]hen I confined myself to my own worries, leaving aside the worries of others, my intelligence saved me and protected me from my own desires. It clarified to me my affairs and let me to seriousness wherein there was no trickery and truth which was not tarnished by falsehood. Here, I found you a part of myself, rather I found you my whole, so much so that if anything befell you, it was as though it befell me, and if death came to you, it was as though it came to me. (Ibn Abi Talib 2009, 749)

This deep awareness of his impending encounter with death urged him to concentrate all his thoughts on himself and his life. And in doing so, his attention was centered on his son, whom he came to equate with himself. In a few words, the Imam presents us with one of the most striking depictions of the relationship that bonds a parent and a child. This relationship has evolved such that he no longer recognizes any essential distinctions between himself and his son, but rather sees his image in his son, and his son's image in him. This superior ability to envisage himself in his son's position, and vice versa, allows the Imam to share, freely and fully, his vast treasure of thought and practice. Only by relating to his son as such, is he able to impart to him the best of his knowledge and experience. And it is precisely this manner of human interaction that will form the basis of the Imam's ethical model that he later describes to his son in the letter. And the Imam, ever so true to his words, begins by applying this model to the relationship with his son, thereby instructing and leading by example.

Several paragraphs later, the Imam presents to his son the rule that ought to govern all one's thought and action:

> My dear son, so far as your behavior with other human beings is concerned, let your 'self' act as scales [mizan] to judge its goodness or wickedness. Do unto others as you wish others to do unto you. Whatever you like for yourself, like for others, and whatever you dislike to happen to you, spare others from such happenings. Do not oppress and tyrannize anybody because you surely do not like to be oppressed and tyrannized. Be kind and sympathetic to others as you certainly desire others to treat you kindly and sympathetically. If you find objectionable and disgusting habits in others, abstain from developing those traits of character in yourself. If you are satisfied or feel happy in receiving a certain kind of behavior from others, you may behave with others in exactly the same way. Do not speak (negatively) about them in the same way that you do not like others to speak (negatively) about you. Do not speak on a subject about which you know little or nothing, and if you at all want

> to speak on anything or about anyone of whom you are fully aware, then avoid gossip, defamation and accusation as you do not like yourself to be scandalized and scorned in the same manner. (Quoted in Mohseni-Cheraglou 2015, 23)

Clearly, the Imam is putting forward a nuanced version of the golden rule, which he believes is the proper maxim to guide moral behavior. What is especially important is his depiction of the self as the "scales" or "balance" by which all such behavior must be evaluated. It is only by placing one's "self" in the position of others that we can determine whether our forthcoming decision or action is morally good or bad. And the "self" that the Imam is referring to is not the "self" that is the product of a largely secular culture, lacking in definitive substance and purpose. In other words, this is not a "self" that is merely the empirical outcome of human social spontaneity, bereft of any moral direction or destination. Instead, it is a "self" that is fully aware of the divine order of creation, and its moral responsibility in establishing justice in accordance with this order of creation. The Imam's golden rule is not simply a moral rule of thumb that can be instrumentally used in any social context. It signifies a practical code of conduct that is derivative of a metaphysical worldview, directly informed by prophecy and piety. It is therefore characterized by absoluteness and verticality, as opposed to arbitrariness and horizontality.

In his letter, and prior to introducing his golden rule, the Imam counsels his son to lead a life of utter and complete devotion to God:

> I advise you my son to fear God and abide by His commandments. Fill your heart with His remembrance and hold tight to His rope.
>
> Enliven your heart with morality, mortify its desires with renunciation, strengthen it with certitude, enlighten it with wisdom, …
>
> Resign yourself to God's will in all your affairs.
>
> Promote good deeds and you will be a doer of good. Resist injustice by word and by action …
>
> Acquire insight into religious law. (Ibn Abi Talib 2009, 750)

It is clear from the above statements that the Imam's golden rule presupposes a personal life that is deeply and thoroughly informed by religious prophecy and piety; it is a moral code of conduct that can only flourish amidst hearts and minds that gravitate naturally towards the Absolute. According to M. Ali Lakhani, this demonstrates the "dependence and derivation of the 'horizontal' ordering of creaturely relations on the 'vertical' ordering of man's relationship to God." In other words, "to know and love God (i.e., to properly order oneself in relation to Truth) means to know and love 'other people.' As the traditionalist Marco Pallis puts it, 'the love of God contains the love of neighbors 'eminently', as cause contains effect'" (Lakhani 2006, 38–39). Of singular relevance to us, is the fact that this divine quality of the Imam's golden rule imbues it with moral substance that is evidently lacking in the secular versions, an argument that we will develop in the following section. Our discussion of the Imam's golden rule and its divine quality, however, remains incomplete if we do not examine another depiction of the golden rule that has been used extensively in the literature, and that is, the concept of the self as a 'mirror.'

According to Cyrus A. Zargar, "the polished mirror is an image that unites two ethical traditions, philosophy and Sufism. One finds it mentioned repeatedly as a way to describe a *receptive* self-perfection, whether that be the perfection of the human intellect, heart, or soul" (Zargar 2017, 18). Ibn Arabi employs the concept in "comparing Adam's capacity for reflecting all of God's attributes to a 'polished mirror,'" while Ghazali uses it to describe one's capacity in understanding the Qur'an:

> The heart is like a mirror; desires are like rust; and the meanings of the Qur'an are like forms that appear in that mirror, so that ascetic practice, by extirpating the lower desires, does for the heart what polishing does for a mirror (Zargar 2017, 19).

It follows that both piety and prophecy (the Qur'an and *Sunna*) can together 'polish' our 'mirrors' from the "diseases of the heart" (Zargar 2017, 93). Or, as Zargar puts it, "religion, in its scripture, practice, injunction, and divine aid, gave a person all he or she would need to polish the heart's mirror" (Zargar 2017, 238). But these depictions of the heart or soul as a mirror focus primarily on the self, and say little so far about the relationship of the self to others and, consequently, its practice of virtues. This connection is made in the following hadith by the Prophet: "A believer is the mirror of his brother. When he sees a fault in it, he should correct it" (Abbasi and Raj 2021, 59). A similar statement was uttered by Imam Ali: "O Kumail! A believer is the mirror of his fellow believer. A believer will help identify a fellow believer's weaknesses and he will help rectify them" (Al-Tabari. 2005, 60).

The 'self' that is a 'mirror' to others is itself that which "acts as 'scales' (*mizan*)" to judge moral behavior as good or bad. In the very act of considering one's self as the standard or measure by which moral conduct is evaluated, one necessarily presents himself or herself as a mirror that reflects the moral quality of such conduct. It follows, that a pious and virtuous 'self' is as effective in assuming the role of a moral scale of judgment as a polished mirror is in reflecting the moral state of others. What is more, such evaluation or reflection must go beyond the simple act of conveying information to others, by taking the extra step of offering counsel and guidance. The golden rule thus presented is characterized by the fundamental Islamic obligation of "enjoining right and forbidding wrong," stated in the Qur'an: "Let there be among you a community calling to the good, enjoining right, and forbidding wrong. It is they who shall prosper" (3:104). A believer has a moral obligation in not only highlighting the observed errors of his or her fellow believers, but in offering pertinent and proper advice. Such advice, however, must remain "gentle" and "merciful":

> Then [it was] by a mercy from God that thou wert gentle with them. Hadst thou been severe [and] hard-hearted they would have scattered from about thee. So pardon them, ask forgiveness for them, and consult them in affairs. (3:159)
>
> A Messenger has indeed come unto you from among your own. Troubled is he by what you suffer, solicitous of you, kind and merciful unto the believers. (9:128)

This proactive property of the golden rule, exemplified in the images of "scales" and "mirror," is best captured by the Quranic notion of believers as "witnesses for mankind": "Thus did We make you a middle community, that you may be witnesses for mankind and that the Messenger may be a witness for you" (2:143). The Arabic word for "middle" is *wasat*, which the Prophet is reported to have explained as meaning "just," and in another *hadith*, "The best of things is their middlemost [*wasat*]." "To be a *witness*," argues Nasr et al., "means one has a consequential role in the judging of a thing through one's knowledge of that thing" (Nasr et al. 2015, 64). A believer who possesses a profound comprehension of the "knowledge" inherent in prophecy and scripture on the one hand, and an unfaltering degree of piety on the other, is best suited for assuming the "middle" role of "scales" or "mirror" or "witness." Such a person is in the ideal position to practice the golden rule, and is therefore most apt at being just. It follows, that the Imam's golden rule is comprehensible only in the context of his notion of "sacred justice," defined as giving every person or thing its due. The golden rule thus becomes a prerequisite for justice, because it is only by imagining ourselves in the position of others that we can suitably give to each person or thing its proper due. When we do imagine ourselves in their position, however, we do so from the perspective of a "witness" imbued with divine knowledge and profound piety, and not merely a "spectator" whose knowledge and experience are largely derivative of "secular, human, empirical matter" (Samuels and John 1986, 16). Or rather, it is a "witness" who is deeply and utterly religious, and one who does not avoid the responsibility of offering kind, goodly advice when needed. In the next section, we compare and contrast the Imam's golden rule with Adam Smith's concept of the 'impartial spectator,' in an attempt to highlight the significance and consequence of a religious conception of the golden rule as opposed to a secular one.

12.3 The 'Witness' and the 'Spectator'

In his *Theory of Moral Sentiments*, Adam Smith introduces one of his most important ethical concepts: the impartial spectator. He does so in the context of developing a general view of social morality based on the human sentiment of sympathy. This concept is arguably a restatement of the golden rule, albeit in a slightly different form: "As we have no immediate experience of what other men feel, we can form no idea of the manner in which they are affected, but by conceiving what we ourselves should feel in the like situation" (Smith 1976, 9). To experience sympathy for others, therefore, is very much a personal matter:

> Every faculty in one man is the measure by which he judges of the like faculty in another. I judge of your sight by my sight, of your ear by my ear, of your reason by my reason, of your resentment by my resentment, of your love by my love. I neither have, nor can have, any other way of judging about them. (Smith 1976, 19)

And yet, the wise and virtuous among us firmly believe that such sentiments, whether with regards to their origin or purpose, do possess an element that transcends the human or the personal:

> A wise man never complains of the destiny of Providence, nor thinks the universe in confusion when he is out of order. He does not look upon "himself" as a whole, separated and

> detached from every other part of nature, to be taken care by itself and for itself. He regards himself in the light in which he imagines the great genius of human nature, and of the world, regards him. He enters, if I may say so, into the sentiments of that divine Being, and considers himself as an atom, a particle, of an immense and infinite system, which must and ought to be disposed of, according to the conveniency of the whole. (Smith 1976, 276)

This capacity to consider oneself as part "of the whole" has the desirable effect of encouraging us to "sacrifice" for the sake of the whole, and to regard such "sacrifice" as in "conformity with reason" (Smith 1976, 275). More importantly, such a capacity, argues Smith, has its roots in our very nature, as fashioned by the

> The all-wise Author of Nature, who has, in this manner, taught man to respect the sentiments and judgments of his brethren; to be more or less pleased when they approve of his conduct, and to be more or less hurt when they disapprove of it. He has made man, if I may say so, the immediate judge of mankind; and has, in this respect, as in many others, created him after his own image, and appointed him his vicegerent upon earth, to superintend the behavior of his brethren. They are taught by nature, to acknowledge that power and jurisdiction which has thus been conferred upon him, to be more or less humbled and mortified when they have incurred his censure, and to be more or less elated when they have obtained his applause. (Smith 1976, 128–130)

But in *being* the "immediate judge of mankind" or "the jurisdiction of the man without," one must have recourse to "the jurisdiction of the man within," or the "impartial spectator":

But though man has, in this manner, been rendered the immediate judge of mankind, he has been rendered so only in the first instance; and an appeal lies from his sentence to a much higher tribunal, to the tribunal of their own consciences, to that of the supposed impartial and well-informed spectator, to that of the man within the breast, the great judge and arbiter of their conduct. (Smith 1976, 130).

With all this in mind, it is not unreasonable to argue that Smith's notion of the 'impartial spectator' bears much resemblance to the notion of the self as 'scales' (*mizan*) introduced by Imam Ali. This is even more so if we consider that Smith's rhetoric frequently invokes Providence or the divine:

> When by natural principles we are led to advance those ends, which a refined and enlightened reason would recommend to us, we are very apt … to imagine that to be the wisdom of man, which in reality is the wisdom of God (Smith 1976, 87).

Nevertheless, a careful reading of Smith's text reveals that his references to the divine are largely superficial and inconsequential. To begin with, the text clearly conforms to the prevalent view that Smith's religious views were consistent with Deism, where the divine is given little or no influence beyond the initial act of creation; hence, his use of the "watch-maker" analogy (Smith 1976, 87). We should note, however, that others have argued that Smith was an atheist, and not a deist, as in the case of Kennedy (2011). Either way, it is evident to us that Smith's moral framework, represented by the concepts of 'sympathy' and the 'impartial spectator,' is devoid of any religious or spiritual substance. And it is precisely in this regard that his moral framework lacks the purposefulness and definitiveness that are characteristic of Imam Ali's ethical model.

Amartya Sen had argued that Smith's moral system is based on the notion that morality is fundamentally derivative of the social forces of approbation and disapprobation. As such, the system is "open rather than closed, and confined to the perspectives and understandings of the local community only" (Sen 2010, 125–126). This opinion is shared by Viviane Brown, who argues that the "moral judge" depicted by Smith in his *Moral Sentiments* renders all "truly moral outcomes … open; they are not rule-bound or obligatory but are the result of an open process of debate between the moral agent and the impartial spectator, in which the final outcome is neither predetermined nor legislated upon by a theological determinism." This, she continues, is mainly due to the "deeply problematic" nature of the model that "requires that a person should be both judge and judged." The requirement that we "assume a double identity" invalidates our capacity for "imagination to provide a reliable basis for moral judgments" (Brown 1994, 66–69). Hence, the 'impartial spectator' fails to provide us with a definite moral framework for thought and action, and both "imagination and sympathy fail in achieving complete moral wholeness for the moral agent, even for the wisest and firmest of all" (Brown 1994, 75). Warren Samuels, in his impressive work on Smith's concept of the 'invisible hand,' provides a similar assessment of the impartial spectator,

> Smith charts the operation of individual conscience (the impartial spectator plus the sense of propriety) and of social conscience (the general rules of conduct) that interact and together constitute the formation and internalization of social control. Individual choice and rationality exist within collective choice and rationality, which are in turn influenced by individual choice and rationality. The operation of the principles of approbation and disapprobation applied to the actions of oneself and others both govern and are influenced by the sense of propriety and the substance of moral rules. The impartial-spectator principle helps build up the moral rules and customs that serve as social cement, yet the principle depends for its content on already internalized social control. It is truly a process of cumulative causation or general interdependence and not one in which particular rules or particular patterns of socialized behavior may be taken as given once and for all time. Interdependence signifies endogenous change. (Samuels 2011, 50)

It is clear that the notion of the 'impartial spectator' fails to provide any objective or absolute moral substance, and thus offers no moral compass that can guide human thought and action. Morality is basically a "secular, human, empirical matter," and lacks any transcendental or divine quality (Samuels and John 1986, 18). It is a morality symptomatic of contending political, economic and social interests, where winners dictate the dominant ethics, and losers settle for hope or despair. It is no surprise that such a reality should result in feelings of absurdity, forlornness, and fatalism. Dostoevsky in *The Brothers Karamazov* envisions a similar reality, where "everything would be lawful" in the absence of God (quoted in Brague 2007, 91). The tragedy that would befall an atheistic world where everything is permitted is that nothing is cherished or loved, for love cannot thrive in a world devoid of meaning and purpose. In comparing Karamazov's statement to that of Paul in First Corinthians, Rémi Brague argues that while Paul is affirming the sanctity of liberty in the commandments, he "retain[s] the notion of the law in what he announces. There is a 'law of Christ,' and Paul declares himself subject to it." More importantly, continues Brague, is the fact that the "law is accomplished by love (Gal. 5:14). Here

Paul reiterates a statement made by Jesus himself (Matt. 22:40) … who summarized the Law as 'you will love your neighbor as yourself,' everything else being simply commentary" (Brague 2007, 92). This brings us back to the golden rule, without which there is no morality. But this rule, in the absence of God, would lack the essential agency and urgency: "The necessity for love is thus not the dream of an exalted leap outside the moral domain; to the contrary, it implies an entire program of work for the human subject, turned back to his own responsibility" (Brague 2007, 93). It is this sense of responsibility (an intrinsic element of human vicegerency) that characterizes the divine order of creation, and that is exemplified by the Imam's notion of the golden rule.

In contrast to Smith and his concept of the 'impartial spectator,' the golden rule presented by Imam Ali evokes moral substance and permanence. Though the Imam's golden rule suggests a universal mode of human interaction, it does so under the presumption that humans a priori subscribe to a view of justice that is necessarily congruent with the rule's moral requirements. In other words, the golden rule is the exclusive practical manifestation of the sacred notion of justice; to give each person his or her due, one must first envision himself or herself in their position. Moreover, the 'self' that theoretically assumes the position of the other is a deeply pious one, and considers that such justice towards others is incomplete if not preceded by justice towards God. Such piety consists of achieving a state of constant remembrance of God, through worship, prayer, meditation, supplication, and charity. It refers to "those who believe and whose hearts are at peace in the remembrance of God" (13:28). It follows, that piety is a prerequisite for justice and the golden rule, as the following *hadith* indicate:

> Ye will not enter Paradise until ye have faith, and ye will not complete your faith until ye love one another.
>
> No man hath believed perfectly, until he wishes for his brother that which he wishes for himself. (Al-Suhrawardy 2001, 64)

Piety provides an agent with moral substance and permanence, allowing him or her to be the "mirror" or "scales" by which the actions of others are viewed and weighed. The agent's appraisal of the behavior of others is not entirely subjective or "endogenous," but is also derivative of an objective or exogenous moral root. This rootedness in an objective moral standard grants the agent a keen sense of justice that transcends private desires, interests, and prejudices, and he or she becomes a true "witness" unto others:

> O you who believe! Be steadfast maintainers of justice, witnesses for God, though it be against yourselves, or your parents and kinsfolk, and whether it be someone rich or poor, for God is nearer unto both. So follow not your caprice, that you may act justly (4:135).

As "witnesses for God," those "who believe" retain constant access to a moral authority that is above and beyond the horizontality of human interaction. Such access grants believers a capacity for comprehension and thought that transcends the "process of cumulative causation or general interdependence" that Samuels highlights. Believers thus have recourse to a moral vocabulary that is relatively exogenous and independent of the status quo that defines social morality.

The "endogenous change" that is characteristic of Smith's moral system frustrates any attempt at profound social reform, because the very system that may be in need of reform is itself the sociopolitical source that defines problems and proposes solutions. This traps the members of society in an endless cycle, with little hope of escaping the predominant forms of "social control." In fact, a moral system that defines morality strictly as the product of "endogenous change" is incapable of radical or drastic change. And even if such change were possible, it lacks the moral authority for social implementation, since there is no established or objective standard by which society can make such a choice. Charles L. Griswold Jr. (1999, 146) offers a similar assessment of the 'impartial spectator,' observing that the "impartial spectator may work up several different standards of evaluation and then judge that one or the other is appropriate in the context. His or her determination and use of these standards is definitive; there is in principle no higher court of appeal above the impartial spectator."

A case in point is the issue of interest and usury in contemporary societies. Today, it is inconceivable to imagine an interest-free economy that regards all interest as usury, and therefore must be prohibited. By having lost the moral vocabulary that equates interest with usury, we are no longer in a position to institute such reform. Only a valiant recourse to an earlier worldview can offer such hope, a feat that only the likes of a biblical prophet can accomplish.

In contrast, a religious society whose members are "witnesses for God" possesses the capacity for instituting substantial social reform. This is because its members subscribe to a moral authority that is independent of human thought and social interaction. Granted that such moral authority, in the form of religious scripture, is subject to human interpretation, there remains a moral core that cannot be overlooked, ignored or transgressed. This moral core, and regardless of numerous human attempts at altering the original message of revelation, will, at the very least, endure as the spirit of a collective conscience persistently disturbing our secular 'peace.' Despite being quarantined within a reclusive part of our shared memory, the sin of usury occasionally resurfaces in our public discourse in times of economic crisis and social hardship, only to re-disappear amidst the carefully planned clatter and chaos.

In addition to the substantive advantage that an absolute moral authority contributes to a practical morality, a crucial aspect of the role of a "witness" (or "mirror" or "*mizan*") is its corresponding obligation to "enjoin good and forbid evil." There exists a moral responsibility beyond that of doing good unto others: we are expected to encourage others to do good unto others. This encouragement, however, must remain "gentle" and non-coercive:

> There is no coercion in religion. (2:256)

> Then [it was] by a mercy from God that thou wert gentle with them. (3:159)

Thus, the 'self' that Imam Ali alludes to in his golden rule is one that is more than a spectator, but less than a judge: it plays a more active role than that of a passive observer who is reluctant to highlight errors (or sins) and offer advice, but is nevertheless careful not to assume the position of arbiter or enforcer, powers that exclusively belong to God: "Then they are returned unto God, their true Master. Surely judgment belongs to Him, and He is the swiftest of reckoners" (6:62). Such a proactive approach to practical morality, embodied in the golden rule, is far more likely to effect meaningful social reform, than a moral system that promotes impartiality and appeasement, both of which result in an obsessive conformity with the status quo. The golden rule's proactive approach is nowhere more visible than in markets, where 'being virtuous' is much more than a useful business strategy, but is a complete way of life.

12.4 Being Virtuous in Markets

To be virtuous in a market is to be just, and to be just one must practice the golden rule. By consciously envisioning oneself in the position of another, one can therefore give each person his or her due. But the act of assuming the position of another is more than just a polite display of understanding or empathy, a brief moment of humanity that rarely translates thought into meaningful action. To be just is to have an adequate understanding of what constitutes justice, and to possess the requisite courage and willingness to do what must be done. In other words, concomitant to the requirement that we place ourselves in the positions of others, is the moral obligation to correct any form of injustice that such a reciprocal conceptualization reveals to us. If it so happens that the injustice was caused by us, then only by personally attending to such wrongs can we then claim to have been truly just: "O you who believe! Be steadfast maintainers of justice, witnesses for God, though it be against yourselves …" (4:135). If the injustice is caused by others, we still have a moral responsibility to assist in alleviating any wrongdoing, as the following *hadith* confirms:

> Whosoever of you sees an evil, let him change it with his hand; and if he is not able to do so, then [let him change it] with his tongue; and if he is not able to do so, then with his heart — and that is the weakest of faith (Sidani 2022, 46).

As explained earlier, this moral obligation to be just develops in a person as a consequence of his or her belief in a divine order of creation, and that humans have been entrusted with enacting justice as God's vicegerents. Being virtuous, therefore, is synonymous with being pious, which simply means that one sincerely and adequately fulfills his or her responsibility as God's vicegerent. And it is with such mindset and spirit that pious believers are expected to approach markets, and certainly not as impartial spectators, or utility and profit maximizers.

When they do enter markets, pious or virtuous participants share a common purpose: to behave as responsible vicegerents and be just in all market dealings. This calls for a devoted and profound measure of spiritual awareness and moral deportment, as the following verses and *ahadith* emphasize:

> O believers, fulfill your legal obligations. (5:1)

> God commands you to return trusts to their owners and, when you judge between people, to judge with fairness. (4:58)

> By men whom neither commerce nor trade distracts from the remembrance of God, from constant prayer, and from giving alms. They fear a Day when hearts and eyes will turn and turn again, when God shall reward them for their best deeds, and multiply His favors upon them. And God bestows His bounty, uncountable, upon whomsoever He wills. (24:37–8)

> O believers, when the call is made for prayer on Congregation Day, hasten to the remembrance of God, and leave your commerce aside; this is best for you, if only you knew. When prayer is ended, disperse in the land and seek the bounty of God, and mention God often—perhaps you will prosper. When they spot some commerce or frivolity, they rush towards it and leave you standing. Say: "What is with God is better that frivolity or commerce, and God is the best of providers." (62:9–11)

> Be trustworthy to whoever trusted you, and do not betray whoever betrayed you.
> The believer is one whom the people entrust with their money and lives. (NI 2007, 2:493)

And as they engage in market transactions, practicing the golden rule allows participants to realize private virtue and public benefit, as the following verse and *ahadith* clearly suggest:

> O you who believe! Consume not each other's wealth falsely, but trade by mutual consent, and slay not yourselves. Truly God is Merciful unto you. (4:29)

> Trade is by mutual consent unless they differ; if they are honest and clear their trade is blessed, but if they are untruthful and unclear the blessing is removed. (NI 2007, 2:499)

> God blesses one who is generous when he sells, buys, and solicits.
> God forgives one who is merciful when he sells, buys, and solicits. (NI 2007, 2:468–469)

The potential benefit and harm to the public from trade and markets is highlighted by the Imam in his letter to Malik,

> Then make merchants and craftsmen – those who are permanently fixed, those move about with their wares and those who profit from (the labor of) their own body – your own concern, and urge others to do so, for they are the basis of benefits and the means of attaining conveniences… Examine their affairs in your presence and in every corner of your land. But know, nevertheless, that in many of them is shameful miserliness, detestable avarice, hoarding of benefits and arbitrariness in sales. (Chittick 1980, 77)

It is important to reiterate that this virtuous behavior in markets is but a social revelation of inner properties, the practical symptoms of religious piety. It follows that such behavior is not primarily oriented towards the realization of given worldly ends, such as human flourishing or happiness. It is behavior aimed at a specific path and for a single end, God. These are hearts and minds incessantly preoccupied with achieving salvation for their souls, and are exceptionally mindful of the rough road ahead. They seldom concern themselves with material outcomes, never demand assurances of this world, and are always careful to extinguish any anxiety that may creep into their thoughts and dreams. Their singular thought is God, and in Him alone lies their faith: "But (the threat of danger) increased them in faith, and they said, 'God suffices us! Most Excellent is He in Whom we trust!'" (3:173). This is market behavior that is indifferent to maximization and efficiency principles, trusting that the sincere and universal application of the golden rule will give each person or thing its proper due; it is behavior that seeks justice, not sympathy. This approach to markets is best illustrated in the following *hadith*: "Benevolence is one aspect of profit" (Chittick 1980, 77).

Yet precisely because most of us do not view this world and the next as such that explains why the golden rule is shunned and abandoned. In *What's Wrong with the World* G. K. Chesterton remarked that, "The Christian ideal has not been tried and found wanting. It has been found difficult; and left untried" (Chesterton 1987, 61). Wendell Berry in *A Continuous Harmony* utters a similar sentiment, "The peculiarity of our condition would appear to be that the implementation of *any* truth would ruin the economy. If the Golden rule were generally observed among us, the economy would not last a week" (Berry 2019, 169). It is not only the case that we have severed ties with the tradition that prepares us to practice the golden rule, but that the markets we have fashioned frustrate any individual effort to live according to the rule. Karl Polanyi offers an insightful account of how modern markets actually do this:

> The market acts like an invisible boundary isolating all individuals in their day-to-day activities, as producers and consumers. They produce for the market, they are supplied from the market. Beyond it they cannot reach, however eagerly they may wish to serve their fellows. Any attempt to be helpful on their part is instantly frustrated by the market mechanism. Giving your goods away at less than the market price will benefit somebody for a short time, but it would also drive your neighbor out of business, and finally ruin your own, with consequent losses of employment for those dependent on your own factory or enterprise. Doing more than your due as a working man will make the conditions of work for your comrades worse. By refusing to spend on luxuries you will be throwing some people out of work, by refusing to save you will be doing the same to others. As long as you follow the rules of the market, buying at the lowest and selling at the highest price whatever you happen to be dealing in, you are comparatively safe. The damage you are doing to your fellows in order to serve your own interest is, then, unavoidable. The more completely, therefore, one discards the idea of serving one's fellows, the more successfully one can reduce one's responsibility for harm done to others. Under such a system, human beings are not allowed to be good, even though they wish to be so. (Polanyi 2014, 19).

'Free' markets today proscribe our freedom to be virtuous. A market that cannot tolerate the golden rule is one that is inimical to virtue and morality. By forgetting God, we have abandoned the golden rule, without which no meaningful human flourishing is possible. Instead, Berry adds, "we have made our false economy a false god" (Berry 2019, 169). But alas, the "false god" of profit has little or no patience for virtuous behavior, when such behavior is not deemed 'rational.' It would seem that being virtuous in our world is utterly 'irrational,' a virtue that few dare to embrace.

References

Abbasi, Abdus Sattar, and Razaq Raj. 2021. *Principles of Islamic Ethics for Contemporary Workplaces*. Hershey: IGI Global.

Al-Suhrawardy, Abdullah Al-Mamun. 2001. *The Wisdom of Muhammad*. London: Citadel Press.

Al-Tabari. 2005. *Glad Tidings of Mustafa for the Shia of Murtaza*. Richmond Hill: Shia Books.

Berry, Wendell. 2019. A Continuous Harmony. In *Wendell Berry: Essays: 1969–1990*. New York: The Library of America.

Brague, Remi. 2007. *The Law of God: The Philosophical History of an Idea*. Chicago: The University of Chicago Press.

Brown, Viviane. 1994. *Adam Smith's Discourse: Canonicity, Commerce and Conscience*. London: Routledge.

Chesterton, G. K. 1987. What's Wrong with the World. In *The Collected Works of G. K. Chesterton*. San Francisco: Ignatius Press.

Chirri, Mohamad Jawad. 1998. *The Brother of the Prophet Muhammad (the Imam Ali)*. London: Imam Ali (A.S.) Foundation.

Chittick, William C., ed. 1980. *A Shi'ite Anthology*. Beirut: Imam Ali Foundation.

Cleary, Thomas. 1995. *Living and Dying with Grace: Counsels of Hadrat Ali*. London: Shambala.

Griswold Jr, Charles L. 1999. *Adam Smith and the Virtues of Enlightenment*. Cambridge: Cambridge University Press.

Ibn Abi Talib, Ali. 1996. *Nahjul Balagha*. Potomac: Ahlul-Bayt Assembly of America.

Kalin, Ibrahim. 2012. *Reason and Rationality in the Quran*. Amman: Jordanian Press.

Kennedy, Gavin. 2011. The Hidden Adam Smith in his Alleged Theology. *Journal of the History of Economic Thought* 33 (3): 385–402.

Lakhani, M. Ali. 2006. The Metaphysics of Human Governance: Imam Ali, Truth and Justice. In *The Sacred Foundations of Justice in Islam: The Teachings of Ali ibn Abi Taleb*, ed. M. Ali Lakhani. Vancouver: World Wisdom.

Madelung, Wilfred. 1997. *The Succession to Muhammad: A Study of the Early Caliphate*. Cambridge: Cambridge University Press.

Mohseni-Cheraglou, Amin. 2015. Socio-economic Justice and Poverty in Nahj Al-Balagha. *International Journal of Islamic and Middle Eastern Finance and Management* 8 (1): 20–35.

Nasr, Seyyed Hossein. 2006. Introduction. In *The Sacred Foundations of Justice in Islam: The Teacings of Ali Ibn Abi Taleb*, ed. M. Ali Lakhani. Vancouver: World Wisdom.

Nasr, Seyyed Hossein, Caner K. Dagli, Maria Massi Dakake, Joseph E. B. Lumbard, and Mohamme Rustom, eds. 2015. *The Study Quran: A New Translation and Commentary*. New York: HarperOne.

Polanyi, Karl. 2014. *For a New West*. Edited by Giorgio Resta and Mariavittoria Catanzariti. Cambridge: Polity.

Qahf, M. M., and M. R. Al-Muballaghi. 2007. *Al-Nusus Al-Iqtisadiyya*. Tehran: The World Forum for Proximity of Islamic Schools.

Samuels, Warren J. 2011. *Erasing the Invisible Hand: Essays on an Elusive and Misused Concept in Economics*. Cambridge: Cambridge University Press.

Samuels, Warren J., and Henderson P. John. 1986. *Introduction to Thomas Robert Malthus, an Essay on the Principle of Population*. Unpublished Manuscript.

Sen, Amartya. 2010. *The Idea of Justice*. London: Penguin Books.

Shah-Kazemi, Reza. 2006. A Sacred Conception of Justice: Imam Ali's Letter to Malik al-Ashtar. In *The Scared Foundations of Justice in Islam: The Teachings of Ali Ibn Abi Taleb*, ed. M. Ali Lakhani. Vancouver: World Wisdom.

Sidani, Yusuf M. 2022. *Responsible Management in Theory and Practice in Muslim Societies*. Bingley: Emerald.

Smith, Adam. 1976. *The Theory of Moral Sentiments*. Indianapolis: Liberty Fund.

Talib, Ali Ibn Abi. 2009. *Peak of Eloquence. Nahjul al-Balagha*. New York: Tahrike Tarsile Qur'an.

Zargar, Cyrus A. 2017. *The Polished Mirror: Storytelling and the Pursuit of Virtue in Islamic Philosophy and Sufism*. London: OneWorld Academic.

Ayman Reda is a lecturer in economics at the University of Michigan-Dearborn and the author of *Prophecy, Piety and Profits: A Conceptual and Comparative History of Islamic Economic Thought* (Palgrave Macmillan, 2018). He has a PhD in Economics from Michigan State University, and specializes in the history of Islamic economic thought.

Chapter 13
An Islamic Theology of Work and Vocational Occupation: Implications for Islamic Economic Theory and Practice

Waleed El-Ansary

Abstract Most Muslim economists limit their attention to Islamic economic law, which sets the outward conditions of work, but fail to engage the Islamic wisdom tradition for understanding the spiritual significance of nature, with all this implies for Islamic art and the making of things. According to this tradition, the natural world reflects God's Perfect Names and Qualities and manifests His blessings and bounties. The beauty, symbolism, and corporeal utility of nature thus fulfills a hierarchy of spiritual, physical, and other human needs that define "holistic" work. From this point of view, what man makes, or man's art, should communicate a spiritual truth and presence analogous to nature, or God's art. This position is in stark contrast to the "disenchantment of the world" that has brought about "deformed" work, work defined by its failure to satisfy a hierarchy of spiritual and other needs and its resulting implications for the environmental crisis. This chapter clarifies the intimate but currently neglected connection between traditional Islamic cosmological sciences and an Islamic theology of work. Economic theory cannot be value-free, for every theory presupposes a view of man and nature (whether implicit or explicit). The Islamic intellectual and esoteric heritage is therefore central to the foundation of Islamic economic theory and praxis.

Keywords Islam · Theology of work · Vocation · Economic ethics

13.1 Introduction

Islam provides a clear theology of work by declaring that to struggle for a living is tantamount to defending the faith (Abdul-Rauf 1984, 5). The Prophet Muhammad stressed this fact before the battle of Badr, the first attack which threatened the

W. El-Ansary (✉)
Xavier University, Cincinnati, OH, USA
e-mail: elansaryw@xavier.edu

G. J. Buijs, J. J. Ballor (eds.), *In Search of the Spirits of Capitalism*, Sophia Studies in Cross-cultural Philosophy of Traditions and Cultures 44,
https://doi.org/10.1007/978-3-032-01137-4_13

existence of the nascent Muslim community, when a young man with a strong physique was running to his shop through the area where the Prophet was marshalling his men. Someone remarked that he wished the youth would use his body and health to run in the way of God by enlisting to defend the faith. The Prophet responded, "If this young man runs with the intention of not depending on others and refraining from begging, he is in the way of God. If he strives for the livelihood of his weak parents or weak children, he is in the way of God. If he tries to show his health out of pride, he is in the way of the devil" (Al-Ghazzali 1982, 2:54). In fact, the Divine Law in Islam gives religious meaning to all acts that are necessary for human life (Nasr 2012, 55).

According to this view, every aspect of life is sacred, for nothing is outside of the Absolute, and no aspect of life is profane, for everything humans do in life (or fail to do) pertains to their relationship with God. What would appear to be the most mundane of activities has religious significance. Far from merely serving to maintain one's physical and material wellbeing, work for pious Muslims involves the edification of human nature in all its fullness, requiring that right actions in economic activity be combined with right intentions in order to actualize its spiritual dimension, thus following the "Straight Path" (*al-s:ira¯ t:al-mustaqīm*). Acting with right intentions is the most important because of the fact that one and the same action, although not every action, may be good or bad according to the intention, whereas the opposite is not true: an intention is not good or bad according to the action. Accordingly, work should be performed as "an act of worship as if [one] were praying" (Nasr 1994, 98).

If work could not fulfill a hierarchy of spiritual and other needs, one would have to face the awkward question of why the Creator would oblige men and women to follow a course of physical action that seems to prevent them from fulfilling the deepest need of their nature. Did God make some ghastly error in making our survival dependent upon pursuing the opposite of what is necessary to attain happiness, peace, and the highest aspirations of our nature? If not, we must conclude that work must somehow support us in attaining those aspirations rather than prevent us from realizing them by engaging in degrading work that is beneath our human dignity.

The division of labor and coordination of economic activity required by Islamic (and many other religions') economic systems therefore must have a spiritual and not simply a corporeal significance. On one hand, Islamic law requires a minimum division of labor to provide society with its necessary and useful goods and services, requiring that some members of the community practice each of the tasks, functions, and professions necessary to fulfill the needs of society. The division of labor is thus analogous to other collective and civic duties, such as building orphanages and hospitals. If no members in the community fulfill these needs, each member of the community is held spiritually accountable. Such division of labor is conceived of as a *duty*, not simply a pragmatic possibility.

On the other hand, the division of labor must leave ample room for human creativity, intrinsic meaning, and personal satisfaction in production, to use and thereby perfect our God-given gifts so that we may be good stewards of the vitality and heritage of our communities, as well as the whole of nature. As Adam Smith noted, an extremely high or overspecialized division of labor that employs too few of man's faculties could have serious social costs by reducing or constraining the proper development of human talents and skills that could richly benefit the individual workers, their families, and society as a whole. He states,

> The understandings of the greater part of men are necessarily formed by their ordinary employments. The man whose life is spent in performing a few simple operations… has no occasion to exert his understanding… He naturally loses, therefore, the habit of such exertion and generally becomes as stupid and ignorant as it is possible for a human creature to become. … But in every improved and civilised society this is the state into which the labouring poor, that is, the great body of the people, must necessarily fall, unless government takes some pains to prevent it. (Smith 1812, V.1.3.2.)

While Adam Smith recognized that work was not homogeneous and the relationship between work and welfare was multifaceted, other figures such as David Ricardo and James Mill, the father of John Stuart Mill, opposed this view, denying the existence of such harmful effects by claiming that all types of work were homogeneous.[1] Moreover, even Smith was unwilling to address the root cause of these problems, only encouraging the government to take "some pains to prevent" these effects after the fact, not to avoid them in the first place. More recently, contemporary mainstream, or "neoclassical," economists generally adopt what appears to be a "compromise" position between Smith and Mill on work and welfare by claiming that different types of work might be *quantitatively* different in terms of desirability, but not *qualitatively* different.[2]

None of these positions is acceptable from an Islamic point of view according to which qualitative differences between work are not reducible to quantitative ones, trade-offs between the qualitative and quantitative objectives of work are unsustainable in the long-term, and new analytical tools are necessary to properly conceptualize the relationship between work and welfare in an Islamic context. All this has sobering implications for one's assessment of industrial (and post-industrial) capitalism and communism, as we shall see. As Seyyed Hossein Nasr states, "Equilibrium on the socio-economic plane is impossible to realize without reaching that inner equilibrium which cannot be attained save through surrender to the One and living a life according to the dictum of Heaven" (Nasr 1982, 89).

Unfortunately, most Muslim economists limit their attention to Islamic economic law (e.g., Khan 2013), which sets the outward conditions of work, but fail to engage the Islamic wisdom tradition for understanding the spiritual significance of nature, with all this implies for Islamic art and the making of things. According to this view, the natural world (*āyāt Allāh*) reflects God's Perfect Names and Qualities and manifests His blessings and bounties (*faḍl*). The beauty, symbolism, and corporeal utility of nature thus fulfills a hierarchy of spiritual, physical, and other human needs simultaneously. From this point of view, what man makes, or man's art, should communicate a spiritual truth and presence analogous to nature, or God's art.

[1] For an excellent survey of classical and neoclassical approaches to work in the history of economic thought, see Pagano (1985).

[2] Some economists adopt this position implicitly by acknowledging the validity of religious beliefs while employing the neoclassical approach to work as "forgone leisure." See, for instance, Pagano (1985, 11–115).

Recognizing fully the spiritual significance of nature is thus a necessary condition for spiritually meaningful work and vocational occupations, all of which are ultimately also gifts from God. Indeed, man is able "to build, write poetry, paint, or compose music" only because "God is "Grand Architect of the Universe" as well as "the Poet, the Painter, the Musician" (Nasr 1989, 224). The arts and crafts have therefore "never been regarded as different forms of activity in Islam" (Nasr 2010, 58).

This chapter therefore clarifies the intimate but currently neglected connection between traditional Islamic cosmological sciences and an Islamic theology of work. Section 13.2 examines the application of these principles to Islamic production processes and their implications for vocational occupations and exchange processes. Section 13.3 applies these principles to critique industrial (and post-industrial) capitalism and communism. In Weberian terms, the modern industrial world has moved from an "enchanted" world full of spiritual meaning to a "disenchanted" one devoid of it (Weber 2004). Section 13.4 draws the implications of this for understanding the differences between modern mainstream, or "neoclassical," economic and Islamic economic theories.

13.2 Moral Cosmology and an Islamic Theology of Work

Surat al-Iqtiṣād[3] more than any other chapter of the Qur'an emphasizes the beauty and wonder of the natural world as signs of God, or *āyāt Allāh*, as fulfilling our spiritual needs while simultaneously highlighting its material benefits as fulfilling our corporeal needs. For example, verses 5–7 state:

> And cattle has He created for you, in which there is warmth and [other] uses, and whereof you eat.
>
> And in them there is beauty for you, when you bring them home, and when you take them out to pasture.
>
> And they bear your burdens to a land you would never reach, save with great hardship to yourselves. Truly your Lord is Kind, Merciful.[4]

Maria Massi-Dakake comments on these verses as follows:

> In the Qur'an cattle is used to designate four types of grazing animals: sheep, goats, camels, and oxen. … The manifold benefits of cattle for human beings… include their service as riding animals and beasts of burden, their provision of milk and meat, and the use of their skin and wool for making dwellings and furnishings. … [and] their beauty (*jamāl*) is invoked… as one of their benefits for humanity, indicating that the natural world should be seen as a source of beauty and wonder, not just of material benefits. (Nasr et al. 2015, 657)

The same applies to horses, mules, and other riding animals in the next verse, which describes them as "adornment" in addition to highlighting the many other services they provide in fulfilling corporeal needs (Nasr et al. 2015, 657). The Quranic

[3] This surah is more commonly known as *Surat al-Naḥl*, chapter 16 of the Qur'ān.

[4] Unless otherwise specified, all translations of the Qur'ān are from Nasr et al. (2015).

emphasis on the beauty of nature as conveying signs "for people who understand" and "who reflect" clearly demonstrates that nature reveals a spiritual truth and presence (Nasr et al. 2015, 660). Subsequent verses express similar principles regarding a hierarchy of spiritual and other needs in different contexts such as the sea, streams, and stars, which are dazzling in beauty while making it possible for human beings to seek God's Bounty by acquiring goods through distant trade by land or sea.[5]

From this perspective, the cosmos itself is there to be read as if it were a boundless book revealing multi-faceted meanings and purpose placed therein by its Author. It is the relation between the cosmos, the Qur'an, and humankind that is central in Islam. In a sense it can be said that there are two Qur'ans: the written Qur'an, *al-qur'ān al-tadwīnī*, and the cosmic Qur'an, *al-qur'ān al-takwīnī*, the second of which speaks to us in *āyāt* or signs and symbols. The Qur'an itself refers to these signs in the verse, "We shall show them our signs upon the horizons [*āfāq*] and within themselves [*anfusihim*] till it becomes clear to them that it is the truth" (41:53). The words and letters of the Qur'an, the elements of the macrocosmic creation surrounding us, and the microcosmic world within us, that is, our faculties of intelligence and of the heart—all these signs and symbols exist that we may perceive within them the Divine message they reveal.

Titus Burckhardt explains the interconnections between art, beauty, and work as follows:

> God is beautiful and he loves beauty (*Allāhu jamīlun yuḥibbu'l-jamāl*): this saying of the Prophet opens up limitless perspectives, not only for the inner life, where the beauty loved by God is above all that of the soul, but also for art, whose real purpose, understood in light of this prophetic teaching, is to support the contemplation of God. For beauty is God's radiance in the universe, and every beautiful work is a reflection of it….
>
> According to (another) saying from the Prophet, "God prescribes perfection in everything" (*Inna-Llāha kataba-l iḥsāna 'alā kulli shay'*); the word *iḥsān* which we translate as "perfection" also has the meanings of "beauty" and "virtue." It is thus a duty of the Muslim to seek perfection in every work, this perfection implying beauty in its turn. The traditional practice of the arts refers to this maxim, and one will immediately understand that on this basis there could be no schism between craftsmanship and art. (Burckhardt, quoted in Michon 1999, 117–119).

Thus, the production process is conceived as a spiritual discipline in which what one makes is not only a means of livelihood but also a product of devotion. As Coomaraswamy asserts, "Every man is a special kind of artist" in this perspective; the artist is not "a special kind of man" (Coomaraswamy 2004, 124).

Thus, there is a necessary connection between beauty and spiritual realization. Beauty has its source in the Ultimate Reality and as such it radiates throughout all levels of existence. As human beings we find an inner resonance with beauty, for it reminds us of our celestial origin, that origin whose memory we carry deep within our being and in which we recognize our true nature. By reading the signs and symbols, the *āyāt Allāh*, throughout creation, we gain in spiritual wisdom, ultimately realizing our potential as beings made in God's image.

---

[5] See, for instance, 16:14–16.

This ideal approach to the making of things has always been closely wed to the spiritual practices of Islam, because the necessary condition for this approach is consciousness of one's mortality and complete dependence on the Absolute, or "spiritual poverty" (*faqr*).[6] Significant spiritual preparation involving prayers, meditation, and spiritual contemplation were an integral part of the creative process for traditional Muslim craftsmen and craftswomen, at the end of which a beautiful design would emerge combining utility with spiritual truth and presence (Ibish 1999, 6). Purity of soul and nobility of character were obviously indispensable for such works. The aesthetic aspect of work is thus fundamentally linked to the ethical production of products.

While it reflects principial knowledge and grace, traditional Islamic art can be functional and fulfill the spiritual and material needs of both maker and user in its interweaving of beauty and utility. Living traditional civilizations generate art at all levels, including the utilitarian, in the knowledge that to create something for people's use is ultimately to create that object for God since each person is capable of being God's vicegerent on earth.

In traditional civilizations, high quality and beautiful products also reflected the love the maker had for his or her work. The product made with such awareness enhanced the life of its owner through its beauty and significance as a manifestation of devoted artistry. One need only think of the harmonious patterns and colors of a Persian carpet to understand that its makers put much more than the goal of economic gain into its weaving; its production elevated the soul of both maker and user.

The human being is created in God's image (*'alā ṣurātihī*) and is, therefore, a work of art par excellence as a reflection of His Divine Names and Qualities. When the spiritually realized individual participates consciously in the act of creating any object or art form such as music or poetry, that person is fulfilling his or her potential as God's vicegerent by imitating His aspect of Creator. Through the individual's creative act, carried out in harmony with the laws of the cosmos and drawing upon the cosmic archetypes, he or she expresses his or her essence as a being whose existence is itself a work of Divine art. By creating a work that has meaning across a hierarchy of levels, the maker finds equilibrium with his or her true nature. However, when art is not intended to express the rightful place of theomorphic man in the cosmos, but is meant instead to express the artist's base ego separated from God, the end result is a march toward forgetfulness of the human being's true nature as one capable of knowing and making in God's image.

There is thus a profound resonance between knowledge and the creative act in the traditional Islamic perspective, and this is rooted both in man's role as a reflection of Divine Attributes as well as in the inverse relation that exists between the creative act of God and that of man. God's creative act or "art" results in the

[6] For the man who has acquired *faqr*, its immediate consequence is "detachment with regard to all manifested things, for the being knows from then on that these things, like himself, are nothing, and that they have no importance whatsoever compared with the absolute Reality." This detachment implies "indifference with regard to the fruits of action… which enables the being to escape from the unending chain of consequence which follows from this action." See Guénon (1973, 16–20).

manifested order; it is an externalization whereas the art of man is an internalization. The act of Divine creation brings into existence that which is made by God. The creative act of the human is in a sense a process that returns the maker to his or her inner essence wherein spiritual knowledge is realized.

Ideally, every member of society engages in a vocational occupation corresponding to one's spiritual and psychological needs. This would allow every individual not only to best serve the society to which one belongs, but also to best realize one's perfections. As the Qur'an states, "To each is a goal to which God turns him. Then strive as in a race towards all that is good, and wherever you are, God will bring you together" (2:148).[7]

Moreover, Islamic law gives the social division of labor *itself* spiritual significance based on the principle of *farḍ kifāyah*. As mentioned in the introduction, this principle requires that some members of the community must practice each profession to discharge collective obligations to provide private and public goods for the rest of the community, including the building of orphanages and hospitals (Nasr 2004a, 126).[8] If no members in the community fulfill such needs, each member of the community is held spiritually accountable. Similarly, if *some* members of the community practice *each* profession that fulfill everyone else's needs, then each individual is absolved of that spiritual obligation. In this regard, the Qur'an states,

> But it is not for the believers all to go forth. And why should not a party from each group go forth to gain understanding in religion, and to warn their people when they return to them, that haply they will beware? (9:122).

Caner Dagli summarizes several interpretations of this verse concerning the social division of labor, one of which follows:

> In the final years of the Prophet's life, tribes would sometimes embrace Islam as a group. Some interpret this verse to be saying that when a tribe accepted Islam, its members should not all come at the same time to Madinah and overwhelm the accommodations of the city; rather, some should come to learn from the Prophet and then return to teach their fellow believers the doctrines and practices of the religion (IK, R, Ṭ). This is what Islamic Law would later call a collective obligation (*farḍ kifāyah*) as opposed to an individual obligation (*farḍ ʿayn*), since it only requires that there be some members of the community who seek knowledge in this way (Q). Al-Rāzī reflects on the fact that, in the time of the Prophet, journeying to find spiritual wisdom and religious knowledge was a nearly universal necessity, whereas in his own time, because the spiritual and intellectual tradition had become strong and well established, the necessity for such travel was diminished. (Nasr et al. 2015, 540).

---

[7] This verse has multiple interpretations, the most common of which concerns the direction of prayer. But the verse also bears a vocational meaning, since every verse in the Qur'an has multiple levels of meaning that are legitimate so long as they do not violate the literal meaning of the text. Henri Corbin summarizes this Islamic doctrine by noting that, "The Quran possesses an external appearance and a hidden depth, an exoteric meaning and an esoteric meaning. This esoteric meaning in turn conceals an esoteric meaning so it goes on for seven esoteric meanings (seven depths of hidden depth)" (Corbin 1993, 7).

[8] *Farḍ kifā'ī* is in contrast to *farḍ 'aynī*, an individual duty such as prayer, rather than a collective duty.

Scholars of Islamic law have expanded the application of this verse to the practice of diverse vocations by analogy, making the social division of labor *itself* a spiritual duty, not simply a right. The principle of *farḍ kifāyah* therefore has tremendous implications for mutual respect, appreciation, the spirit of reciprocity, and economic justice, since *homo Islamicus* recognizes that everyone is involved in freeing the community from a particular responsibility before God. The diversity of vocations in the context of the social division of labor on one hand and the spiritual significance of production processes on the other are thus necessary to provide what one might call "existential justice" in an ideal Islamic economy.

A living religious *intellectual* heritage is therefore necessary to achieve existential justice. Only a functioning and intact orthodox tradition can produce enduring works of art, science, and metaphysics that contain within themselves the dimension of knowledge that is intrinsic to that tradition. Such knowledge is expressed symbolically by those who have learned their craft in accordance with cosmic laws and have been taught within a system that aims to perfect the soul of the maker while at the same time training the maker in the technique needed to achieve its highest expression. This combination of spiritual, moral, and technical training results in human beings capable of mirroring the Creator in their works, thus fulfilling their role as God's vicegerent while providing objects or other works that ennoble the beholder.

In traditional Islamic society, the guilds transmitted the Islamic doctrines and practices on the division of labor, production, and market exchange that allowed man to live in harmony with himself, his community, and nature. We are not suggesting a restoration of the specific practices of historic Islamic economic models. But this history can serve as a source of inspiration for understanding how Islamic economic principles were previously applied, and how we can apply them today to strengthen the ethics of contemporary economic practices. Nasr maintains that although the values resulting from the application of these traditional economic principles are no longer as pervasive or strictly manifested in many parts of the Islamic world, that is due for the most part to the penetration of Western secular modes of thought and practice in these lands (Nasr 2012, ch. 3). For example, prior to the colonization of Egypt by the UK in the late nineteenth century, nearly the entire gainfully occupied population of towns were members of the guilds (Baer 1964).[9] The guilds themselves highlighted their religious origins with important implications for interreligious cooperation:

[9] In the case of Cairo, Baer explains: Not only were all the artisans and merchants organized in guilds according to their crafts and trades, but also people engaged in transport (such as donkey-drivers) and in services (such as story-tellers and other types of entertainers). The guild system embraced owners of shops …, owners of workshops such as starchworkers, makers of wax and candles, makers of dyes, bottles, carpets, etc.; owners of large stores such as salt-merchants, corn-merchants, iron-merchants, etc. There were also guilds of people who worked in their own houses, such as painters and those who worked with sulphur ('because of the bad smell'), as well as of salaried workers (e.g. in the building trade) and government employees, such as employees of the mint … . Both rich and poor had their guilds: corn-merchants as well as sewermen, saddlers as well as makers of rope. (Baer 1964, 5–6)

> ...practically every guild identified a particular Prophet or saint as being the patron of its particular craft, thus endowing the craft with something of the sacred character of the personage.... For example, the carpenters took as their patron the Prophet Noah: having built the ark, he stands forth as the exemplary master carpenter. The Virgin Mary was adopted by the weavers as their patroness: it was she who wove the swaddling clothes for the child Jesus. The Persian companion of the Prophet, Salman al-Farisi, having been the Prophet's barber, was the patron of the barbers' guild.... The Caliph ʿUmar was reputed to have said that he would have adopted perfume-making as his profession: if he made no profit, he would at least have with him always a beautiful scent—hence his adoption by the perfumers as their patron. (Ibish 1999, 6–7).

Ibish adds that, "material work and holy significance were in this manner never allowed to diverge, the sacred was manifested outwardly in the work, and the work was ennobled by the inward presence of the sacred" (Ibish 1999, 7). In fact, the common recognition of many of the monotheistic prophets of the Abrahamic family of religions encouraged the existence of inter-faith guilds (with Muslim, Christian, and Jewish members) and fostered harmony among many different intra-faith guilds in traditional Islamic civilization (Lewis 1937). There were thus links and cooperative arrangements among members within a particular guild as well as among various guilds, where they all shared a common interest in the work they did, as well as the spiritual and economic benefits of performing such work with excellence.

This approach to production and social organization entailed a system of personal exchange in which coordination between members was quite manageable. In fact, traditional craftsmen accepted the duty to supply their goods at just and stable prices, since the division of labor was a duty, not just a right.[10] To avoid over- or under-supply of the market at a particular time, for example, a master craftsman could postpone or accelerate taking on extra apprentices while another qualified craftsman had insufficient or excess work, respectively. In short, equilibrium in Islamic economies was critical not only for meeting physical needs through reliable employment and steady income but also satisfying the guildsmen's spiritual needs by their pride in the deeper dimensions of work. All this is lost with the "disenchantment" of the world to use Weber's apt terminology, the economic implications of which I now turn to.

Even the *ʿulamāʾ*, or religious scholars, had their own organization that was not dissimilar to the guilds (Baer 1964, 47).

[10] See for instance Volumes 17 to 19 on prices (*al-asʿār*; sing. *siʿr*) in Gomaʿa (1997).

13.3 Understanding the Root Causes of the Environmental Crisis and Economic Instability

Economists generally view the environmental crisis in terms of "market failures," as results of the overuse (or underuse) of goods relative to their "true" costs—and most particularly the fact that natural resources (clean air, water, and a stable climate) that should have a "price" are considered "free," or are drastically underpriced (we shall return to industrial communism in which prices are allegedly "correct" shortly).[11] A classic example illustrating this price discrepancy is that of a factory polluting a nearby neighborhood, imposing costs on its neighbors that are "external" to the polluter who ignores its social and environmental responsibilities. In situations involving such "negative" externalities, economists maintain that goods such as clean air are "underpriced." The cumulative effect of this is "market failure"—the pollution of clean air without paying the cost of that pollution's harm to others. According to Gus Speth,

> We live in a market economy where prices are a principal signal for guiding economic activity. When prices reflect environmental values as poorly as today's prices do, the system is running without essential controls....Today's market is a strange place indeed. At the core of the economy is a mechanism that does not recognize the most fundamental thing of all, the living, evolving, sustaining natural world in which the economy is operating. Unaided, the market lacks the sensory organs that would allow it to understand and adjust to this natural world. It's flying blind. (Speth 2008, 54)

Accordingly, markets can fail to account for myriad environmental threats, including marine losses, deforestation, desertification, freshwater system decline, loss of biodiversity, proliferation of toxic pollutants, acid rain, nitrogen excess in fertilization, and so forth (see, e.g., Charles 2010, ch. 2). The increasing scarcity of unpolluted natural resources, most of which have been used or damaged by their use in production processes without costs to the exploiting enterprise, reverses Adam Smith's well-known claim that an individual pursuing his own interest might be

> led by an *invisible hand* to promote an end which was no part of his intention. Nor is it always the worse for the society that it was not part of it. By pursuing his own interest, he frequently promotes that of the society more effectually than when he really intends to promote it. (Smith 1812, IV.2.9, emphasis added).

However, this "free" exploitation of unspoiled nature converts the benign "invisible hand" into a malevolent "invisible foot," in which each person pursuing only their own good:

> ... will automatically, and most efficiently, do his part in maximizing the general public misery.... To paraphrase [Adam Smith's] well-known precursor of this theory: Every individual necessarily labors to render the annual external costs of the society as great as he can. He generally, indeed, neither intends to promote the public misery nor knows how much he is promoting it. He intends only his own gain, and he is in this, as in many other cases, led by an invisible foot to promote an end which was no part of his intention. Nor is it any better

[11] Parts of this section draw on El-Ansary (2017, 314–316).

> for society that it was no part of it. By pursuing his own interest, he frequently promotes social misery more effectually than when he really intends to promote it. (Hunt and Lautzenheiser 2011, xiii)

Market failure and the invisible foot put a blinding spotlight on the need for reasonable regulation of markets and commerce, particularly in response to the heedlessness that treats environmental and "social" capital (the latter including social networks marked by reciprocity, trust, and cooperation) as though they were disposable income. But the political process necessary for proper regulation can also fail due to the corrupting influence of special interests. From this perspective, the indispensability of effective regulation in the public interest, and the integrity and impartiality of its administration depends on lawyers, judges, policy-makers, and public servants at all levels of government being trained to truly and impartially administer justice, and to maintain their integrity in carrying out those duties. This is a particularly daunting challenge for politicians and regulators facing powerful, well-financed special interests.

Such special interests arise because small groups with mutual interests have a greater incentive to organize and lobby than larger groups do, since one's share in the goods thereby procured diminishes as the number of stakeholders increases (see, e.g., Buchanan and Tollison 1984).[12] And if these narrowly defined and unregulated interests are allowed to proliferate willy-nilly, the danger increases of the "death of our *just* economy by a thousand cuts." As Speth explains,

> Political failure perpetuates, indeed magnifies, this market failure. Government policies could be implemented to correct market failure and make the market work for the environment rather than against it. But powerful economic and political interests typically stand to gain by not making those corrections, so they are not made or the correction is only partial. (Speth 2008, 53)

The problem of special interests tends to worsen over time, since the longer economic disorders remain unremedied, the more special interests amass wealth and organize more effectively to protect their advantages (see, e.g., Sandler 1992). Moreover, special interest groups spread disinformation to deflect public recognition of the major role these groups play in causing the environmental crisis (see, e.g., Franta 2021).

In short, the ethical orientation and commitment necessary to prevent the degradation of both people and the environment is generally *absent* from both the economic and political domains in modern industrial countries where nature is "disenchanted" and work is depleted of spiritual meaning, or "deformed." This is because:

> The moment nature became secularized, the moment the Hands of God were cut off from nature… man no longer felt any responsibility for nature. Nature served only as a source of materials; it could be dominated and used for whatever purpose, and in which ever way without having any rights of its own (Nasr 2007, 125).

[12] Public choice theory refers to the application of economic theory to the problems of political science, particularly collective choice processes.

From this point of view, efforts to remedy economic and environmental disorders are thus "too little, and too late."

It is necessary here to highlight the radical difference between science as organized knowledge, which can provide a theology of work through reference to multiple levels of reality, and scientism, which claims that modern science, defined as a strictly empirical or sensory means of knowing the material world, has a monopoly on knowledge—that is, that anything beyond the sensory world is unreal, impossible to prove, or purely fanciful. Whereas the holistic worldview discussed in the first section of this chapter studies nature in the light of metaphysical principles, a mechanistic worldview studies nature as an independent or autonomous reality in which qualitative differences are reducible to quantitative ones and there is an irreducible gulf between the subject that knows and the object that is known. Accordingly, scientism is an ideological construct that effectively supplants a metaphysical view of the universe, eliminating any possibility for a theology of work, vocational occupation, and religious ethics as regards the environment through its reductionism. If religion and science are to join together in a lasting recognition of the role of the human being vis-à-vis the natural world, with a consequential cooperation that results in the protection of nature, then scientism, which is inherently hostile to religion, must not be allowed to usurp the role of science. In fact, scientism is "bad philosophy," not "good science." It is self-refuting—because it is impossible to prove that "the *only way* to know *anything* truly is by using your physical senses" (Cutsinger n.d., 6). Moreover, the discoveries of physics over the course of the last centuries have proven beyond a shadow of a doubt that a strictly mechanistic conception of the universe is false, a crucial point we shall return to in the final section of this chapter. It is then a scientistic (not a scientific) worldview which generates materialistic technological, political, economic, and other social structures, that does injustice to man and threatens nature by treating both as resources rather than as the sacred creations they are from a theological perspective.

Moreover, if it is true that complete fulfillment is only found in the unlimited reality of God (whether approached in personal or supra-personal terms), as all the world's major religions assert, then it follows that to seek the *Infinite* in finite goods can only result in profound disappointment, pain, and even despair. Indeed, a misdirected search for the Infinite has stoked appetites that now insatiably devour the beauty of the natural world. But since sensible beauties are situated outside the soul, their meeting with it are generally accidental. Thus, the only way for the soul to be happy in an unconditional and permanent manner is to carry the beautiful within itself. To fill the void created by the absence of inward beauty with heedless consumption can therefore be likened to drinking saltwater—it will only make us thirstier. Schumacher describes this cycle in the context of modern economies:

> The basic aim of modern industrialism is not to make work satisfying but to raise productivity; its proudest achievement is labor saving, whereby labor is stamped with the mark of undesirability. But what is undesirable cannot confer dignity; so the working life of a laborer is a life without dignity. The result, not surprisingly, is a spirit of sullen irresponsibility which refuses to be mollified by higher wage awards but is often only stimulated by them. (Schumacher 1979, 27–28)

It is precisely such a cycle—the endless need for more—that is destroying our natural world.

One might think that a socioeconomic system based on central command explicitly appealing to cooperative ideals, or the "visible hand" of the state rather than the "invisible" hand of the market, would be better equipped to neutralize the negative externalities than systems lacking these characteristics. But in fact the opposite is arguably true, as evidenced by the dismal environmental record of communist countries—in addition to its many other life and freedom-crushing effects. Joseph Dellapenna, in fact, goes so far as to argue that the ultimate cause of the collapse of communism was not the commonly cited yearning for democracy, human rights, and a higher standard of living—all of which existed before—rather it was communism's dismal record on the environment that was the final catalyst of the public consensus that the Soviet Union had to be dismantled and purged of communism (Dellapenna 2010). And as Speth avers, "Its [communism's] authoritarian political system and highly centralized economic planning produced one environmental disaster after another" (Speth 2008, 58).

Regardless of how accurate this account may be, communism did attempt to achieve economy-wide cooperation through central planning, but undermined the basis for such cooperation by its approach to work based on its atheistic, mechanistic worldview that ignored the intrinsic connections between meaningful work and spiritually productive cooperation. Moreover, special interests can take on even more corrupt and dysfunctional forms in industrial communism than in capitalism, since "bureaucrats tend to confuse their own interests, and the interests of their bureaucracy, with the interests of society as a whole" (Médaille 2014). From this point of view, the complete lack of any spiritual dimension in communist political theory is bound to result in both massive market and political failure when put into practice. It is as though communism purports to achieve a sort of "Christian" charity without reliance on the inspiration of Christ, or any other revelation.[13] As Schumacher explains,

> *[E]ither* you believe in God, then you will pursue politics 'mindful of the eternal destiny of man and of the truths of the Gospel'; or you believe that there are no higher obligations, then you cannot resist the appeal of Machiavellianism—politics as the art of gaining and

[13] For a brilliant analysis of how Marx's anti-theological critique of industrial capitalism actually depends upon a theological critique despite his disavowal of it, see Hughes (2007). With regard to economic cooperation, Alisdair MacIntyre maintains that philosophical ethics is ultimately reducible to one of two options: the "way of Aristotle" involving objective values based on the nature of things, which is consistent with a religious approach to law and ethics, and the "way of Nietzsche" involving a subjective "will to power" that denies any nature to things. MacIntyre argues that no middle position is intellectually sustainable (MacIntyre 1984, especially ch. 9). Although some commentators have argued that Marx refrained from discussing political realities in the light of ethical ideals because of his materialist reading of history, others have disputed this position (see Wolff and Leopold 2021). As Bertell Ollman has written, "Another major characteristic of communist society is the high degree of cooperation and mutual concern which is discernable in most human activities" (Ollman 1979, 71). Such cooperation and mutual concern are intellectually and practically unsustainable in communist society according to Hughes and MacIntyre.

> maintaining power so that you and your friends can order the world as *they like it*. There is no supportable middle position. Those who want the Good Society, without believing in God, cannot face the temptations of Machiavellianism; they become either disheartened or muddleheaded, fabulating about the goodness of human nature and the vileness of one or another adversary. (Everything is the fault of Khrushchev, Nasser or Gaitskell.) Optimistic 'Humanism' by 'concentrating sin on a few people' instead of admitting its universal presence throughout the human race, leads to the utmost cruelty. (Wood 1984, 264)

Communism and industrial capitalism therefore have *much* more in common than their proponents admit: both neglect the loss of intrinsic meaning in production and exchange processes based on the "disenchantment" of nature, thereby promoting *conflict* rather than *cooperation* between workers, owners (whether individuals, corporations, or the state), and consumers (see, e.g., Putterman 1990). Although communism opposes spiritual values much more directly than industrial capitalism, they both undermine spiritual values. Personal reform *within* a system is then rendered powerless to reform the system itself:

> This is of decisive importance. It shows that appeals for good behavior and the teaching of ethical or spiritual principles, necessary as they always are, invariably stay, as it were, *inside* the system and are powerless to alter it: unless and until the preaching leads to significant new types of work in the physical world. (Schumacher 1974, 12)

Unfortunately, the Muslim world is also contributing to the environmental crisis, which has gone from bad to worse in Muslim countries. But this is despite Islamic teachings, not because of them. As Nasr explains,

> When one studies the Islamic view of nature and humankind's relation to the natural environment, as well as the way classical Islamic civilization created a society and especially an urban settmg in harmony with nature, and when one compares these realities with the situation in tbe Islamic world today, it becomes obvious that neither governments nor most people in Muslim countries are following Islamic principles in their treatment of the natural environment. Nor are most of the '*ulamā*' teaching and preaching the Islamic view of this subject to the public. (Nasr 2007, 15)

In short, contemporary Muslim economies are not essentially different from their industrial capitalist or socialist counterparts when compared to a classical Islamic economy. Significant change is therefore also necessary within the contemporary Muslim world itself.

If competing forms of modern social organization cannot address the root causes of the crises related to the environment, the depletion of non-renewable resources, and social escapism, can new technologies provide the necessary solutions? Indeed, there is no question that current technologies must change. The only question is whether or not the scientific paradigm within which the technology is developed must also change (Nasr 1997; Bakar 1991; Bakar 2014). From an Islamic perspective, any new paradigm must be able to integrate the findings of modern science into higher orders of knowledge if it is to develop spiritually meaningful production and exchange processes for environmental and socio-economic stability. From this point of view, modern science can at best postpone crises and at worst lead to a vicious downward cycle of technologies, with each "cure" leading to more and more adverse (and even catastrophic) "side effects."

The latter possibility can be illustrated with the *true* story of a man who, having a spot of arthritis in his finger joints, was given tablets by his doctor that resulted in a stomach ulcer (Mishan 1986, 174–175). A subsequent operation for the ulcer in conjunction with strong antibiotics interfered with his cardiovascular system to the extent that the doctor felt an obligation to carry out two more minor operations. Complications from these operations then required treatment by a heart specialist; but in the patient's weakened condition, he contracted a lung infection. The patient died within 2 weeks of the operations despite the continuous care of three doctors and the hospital staff. Such an example of the inadequacies of allopathic medicine (a philosophy and practice of medicine that largely ignores the well-being of its patients' psycho-spiritual dimensions, or at least abandons holism through compartmentalization) is not put forward for the purpose of denying the merits of all modern medical technologies. It aims to point out that such advances constitute a very relative progress when taken in their greater context and considered in the light of their costs. In any regard, the reductionism and hyper-specialization in the medical profession are known to cause unforeseen and detrimental effects on our immediate and long-term physical health; this reductionism and hyper-specialization also prevail in the agricultural methods and dietary habits of modern societies, which in fact are largely responsible for many of the health-related issues that modern medicine is in turn credited (rightly or wrongly) with being adept in addressing (Campbell 2013, 17).

Finally, even from a purely reductionist point of view, nature is an open, complex system that modern science is incapable of modeling in a comprehensive way. For example, while it is easy to calculate the force of gravitation between two objects in isolation in a hypothetical world, it is immensely complicated to do so with three objects, and is practically impossible with four objects. Tarik Quadir concludes that, "If modern science cannot identify the actual interrelationships among the innumerable variables in nature, we have no reason to believe that there could be a technological solution [for our technologically ravished environment] even in the remote future" (Quadir 2013, 16).

In short, because the reductionist paradigm of modern science excludes the integration of the findings of modern science into higher orders of knowledge, both man and nature have suffered a plethora of unintended adverse consequences. The solution is to recognize the erroneous presuppositions in this distorted and fragmented view of man and nature, correct them, and begin drawing the correct conclusions about a path to a healthy society (Nasr 2001, 4).

From this point of view, those who hope for a technological fix within the current reductionist paradigm are substituting a *secular* faith for a traditional faith. The history of the notion of progress is grounded in the secular belief that modern science is leading humanity, step by step, to some future utopia, where mankind will live in a virtual paradise.[14] The point here is that these issues involve questions that

[14] For example, the positivist cult of Saint-Simon, who "envisaged an assembly of 'the 21 elect of humanity' to be called the Council of Newton," acquired "all the paraphernalia of the Church—hymns, altars, priests in their vestments and its own calendar, with the months named after

economists *cannot* answer *qua* economists. Any possibility of dealing effectively with these perilous issues requires economists to elevate this debate to the philosophical and theological level where it belongs.

Here, it is important to respond to environmentalists who criticize the Abrahamic traditions for elevating humanity to the crown of creation, thereby promoting an "anthropocentric" approach to the environment similar to that of industrial capitalism and communism, and hence blame them all for the current environmental crisis. Deep ecology, for example, espouses the equality of man and other creatures, or an "eco-centric" or "bio-centric" approach in place of an "anthropocentric" one (Nasr 1997, 218). But such a critique misunderstands Abrahamic teachings, which instill a theocentric, rather than purely anthropocentric, approach. Indeed, the Abrahamic traditions conceive of humans not as owners of the earth, but in the dual role of God's servants and vicegerents on earth. As Nasr explains,

> The danger of anthropomorphism lies, however, in the fact that it is false not because it is substituted for bio-centrism but because it takes the place of theocentrism, which accords with the true nature of things and which is also found in traditional Christianity as in other theistic religions with corresponding doctrines to be found in nontheistic religions. God is the center of our being as well as the Origin and End of all Creation. Our center is not in the biological world, certainly not if we view man from a spiritual and theological point of view. To introduce simply the prevalent and fashionable idea of democracy into the whole of Creation is to overlook both biological and cosmological realities and the hierarchy of existence. If we were equal to other creatures, there would in fact be no environmental crisis. Moreover, to propose such a view of equating man with the biological world in a quantitative sense and of seeking our center in a world perceived solely through the external senses is to remove from man his great responsibility as not only the custodian of the Earth but also the channel of grace for all beings. Moreover, it is to destroy further man's true center within himself, the center that is ultimately the Center, the Center of us and of all beings. It would thus bring about even further disequilibrium in a chaotic world already suffering from the loss of the Center. (Nasr 1997, 218)

Before concluding this section, we must note that in addition to the pernicious effects of special interest groups on environmental economic policy, they also capture an increasing share of the income from production within industrial capitalism, leading to economic injustice and instability. Indeed, although worker productivity in the United States has approximately doubled since 1979, real income adjusted for inflation has remained relatively stagnant, creating a situation in which productivity has grown nearly three times more than pay (Economic Policy Institute 2024). Indeed, wages as a percentage of gross domestic product (GDP) are near record lows, whereas corporate profits are near record highs (Watts 2025). This gap is due to what is sometimes called the "pre-distribution of income" by special interest groups lobbying to change the "rules of the [economic] game" in their favor.

Archimedes, Gutenberg, Descartes, and other rationalist saints." See Gray (2003, 30–34). Contemporary writers and film-makers, however, seem to envision, almost unanimously, a dystopic future, where the most inferior possibilities are frighteningly realized, with "happy endings," where such endings can be imagined, only provided by "superheroes" who somehow transcend the limitations of ordinary human beings. Even some contemporary politicians take this view: Only a super-heroic "strong man" can save humanity from the catastrophic future that looms before us.

Insufficient demand is the inevitable result of such an uneven distribution of income, making a more reasonable distribution of income crucial for economic stability. But the accelerating financial success of special interest groups results in an increasing "pre-distribution of income," once again leading to an economic "death by a thousand cuts" (Sandler 1992) due to the "disenchantment" of nature and therefore of work.

From this point of view, recurring socio-economic instability in the short-term and environmental unsustainability in the long-term are intrinsic to industrial capitalism. The same principles apply to industrial communism where special interests can take on even more corrupt and dysfunctional forms *mutatis mutandis*. Rather than blindly following industrial capitalist or socialist models of economic development that are increasingly speeding toward the edge of a cliff, the Islamic world must recover its own intellectual heritage and, on the basis of that heritage, integrate the findings of modern science into higher orders of knowledge. Such recovery and integration is necessary to provide a new paradigm within which to develop new, holistic technologies that will inform Islamic economic practice.

13.4 Implications for the Critique of Economic Theory

The Islamic theology of work outlined in Sect. 13.2 along with the critique of industrial capitalism and communism outlined in Sect. 13.3 have serious implications for economic theory. This is because Adam Smith

> consolidated, even if he did not initiate, a way of looking at modern society as made up of two spheres: an economic sphere of individual initiative and interaction, governed by impersonal laws that assure a beneficent outcome by pursuit of self-interest; and the rest of social life, including political, religious, and moral interactions that require the conscious balancing of self-interest with social considerations (Foley 2006, 1).

I refer to this as the "separate domain" argument, namely, that the motivations of the "actors," whether ethical or not, have nothing to do with whether a market economy generates "beneficent" outcomes. But as we have seen, externalities leading to market and government failures quickly convert the benign "invisible hand" of economic theory into a malevolent "invisible foot." And since classical Islamic markets, which are only on the periphery of contemporary Muslim economies, achieved environmental sustainability and socio-economic equilibrium because they were thickly "embedded" in spiritually based non-market institutions, the separate domain argument applies neither to a classical Islamic economy based on holistic work nor to industrial capitalism based on deformed work. Moreover, since disequilibrium is only intelligible in terms of equilibrium, economic theory cannot dispense with a theology of work and ethics, nor with an environmental theology, as the starting point of economic analysis, completely inverting the separate domain argument. Although economists may reply that the "invisible hand" is central whereas the "invisible foot" is peripheral, the reverse is the case according to Islamic metaphysics and cosmological sciences in which the unicity or interrelatedness of creation reflects the unity of the Divine Principle. Islamic and modern mainstream economic thought are, therefore, essentially competing approaches to economic theory based on different worldviews, although aspects of mainstream economic thought can be incorporated into Islamic economic thought to model market failures (as well as political failures to correct them because of lobbying by special interest groups) and other symptoms of disequilibrium within industrial capitalism and communism.

Another major problem in modern mainstream, or "neoclassical," economic theory is that it reduces values to tastes while erroneously claiming to provide a theory of choice that can accommodate spiritual values, making spiritual values appear to be irrelevant. For example, economists routinely claim that

> The desires (of *Homo economicus*) can be 'good,' 'bad,' 'selfish,' 'altruistic' – anything you like. The only proviso is that those desires generate a preference ordering; that is, the person can always say whether he or she prefers one bundle to another or is indifferent between them, and that the ordering satisfies the following conditions … (of reflexivity, completeness, consistency, and continuity). (Heap et al. 1994, 5)

To clarify this passage, preferences are "complete" if one can rank bundles A, B, and C in terms of which is best, worst, and intermediate, and preferences are "consistent" if one prefers A to B, B to C, and A to C. This is unproblematic from an Islamic (or any other religious) perspective. The problem comes with the "continuity" axiom, as the following example suggests. Imagine that we have the authority to prevent an evil act, and someone is trying to bribe us to permit it. Although we may be unwilling to accept any amount of money to permit the evil act, we may also have a limit on how much we would be willing to pay to stop the same event that others have the authority to prevent. The two situations are different in the sense that the former is an "act" in which we participate (through accepting the bribe) to accomplish an evil, whereas the latter is an "event" that others perform which perhaps we cannot afford to stop. The continuity axiom, however, requires that the amount of our willingness to accept (WTA) be equal to the amount of our willingness to pay (WTP). This excludes the ethical values of one who "cannot be bought at any price," although it can accommodate the unethical preferences of a miser or a hedonist. In fact, if we constrain choice to alternatives that equate WTA and WTP, no alternative is more "right" or "wrong" than any other (in the absence of special assumptions that the cost of eliminating the damage equals WTA, the only basis on which it *might* be morally justifiable to accept a particular sum of money to compensate for the damage in permitting an otherwise evil act[15]). Unconditionally equating WTA and WTP therefore implies arbitrary choice from a normative point of view and denies a rational basis for ethics, reducing values to tastes. In such cases, there is a "pre-existent motivation, not subject to criticism, unaffected by understanding" (Griffin 1986, 28).

---

[15] Here Michael Sandel might object that even if WTA is sufficient to undo the damage, this is a "degrading market" that should not be permitted. See Sandel (2013).

This is very different from choices involving values in which there are judgments about what preferences *should* be, requiring the possibility that WTA *not* equal WTP. In such cases, the question arises whether "the desire by which… [a man] is moved is either the will he wants or a will he wants to be without" (Frankfurt 1988, 19). The divergence between WTA and WTP in choices involving values occurs because costs and benefits are not always qualitatively the same, or "commensurable," and therefore require ethical judgment over priorities.

This has massive implications for economic theory and policy, because technical market solutions cannot address such questions. To clarify this, imagine a manufacturer polluting to maximize profits, a hedonist who derives pleasure from viewing a landscape with clean air, and St. Francis of Assisi, the patron saint of the environment and the poor in the Roman Catholic Church. If WTA/WTP of the manufacturer is greater than the WTA/WTP of the hedonist, then the manufacturer will always demand more money than the hedonist is willing to pay to stop pollution on one hand, and the manufacturer will always be willing to pay more to pollute than the hedonist is willing to accept on the other hand. The only thing that changes is the distribution of income, not the level of pollution regardless of how the government allocates property rights over the air. But this "market solution" does not apply in the case of St. Francis, whose WTA diverges from WTP. The government must therefore make a moral judgment, and the separate domain argument fails once again. The claim that neoclassical theory accommodates any set of values or tastes thereby smuggles psychological hedonism into economic policy while suppressing the need for substantive philosophical debate over these policies.

Jeremy Bentham was arguably the first to introduce this reduction of quality to quantity into economic thought through his crass hedonism claiming that the attraction of pleasure and avoidance of pain was the only motivating cause in which all pleasures and pains were qualitatively the same but quantitatively different (El-Ansary 2005). Although John Stuart Mill objected to Bentham's hedonism for assuming a single motivating cause, Mill believed that he could add constant causes such as greed to "disturbance terms" such as generosity to predict the aggregate result of economic phenomena, just as Newton added constant forces such as gravity to "disturbance terms" such as friction to predict their aggregate effect (Mill 1884, xiv). The "conflicting forces" of different motivating causes were analogous to the "conflicting forces" of mechanics, perpetuating the reduction of quality to quantity in economics.[16] In this sense, Mill attempted to build on Bentham just as Newton built on Galileo, adding disturbance terms to economic analysis just as Newton added them to mathematical physics.

But John Ruskin rightly objected that disturbance terms such as generosity were not of the same quality as the supposedly constant force of greed, and the two could not be aggregated. He summarized and critiqued Mill's position in the opening paragraphs of his renowned *Unto This Last*:

---

[16] It is ironic that Mill laid the foundation for this "mono-utility" economic methodology while he also argued for the existence of "higher" and "lower" pleasures in his utilitarian ethics, compounding one internal inconsistency with another.

> [Mill's approach] would be a perfectly logical and successful method of analysis, if the accidentals afterwards to be introduced were of the same nature as the powers first examined… But the disturbing elements in the social problem are not of the same nature as the constant ones; they alter the essence of the creature under examination the moment they are added; they operate, not mathematically, but chemically, introducing conditions which render all our previous knowledge unavailable. (Ruskin 1938, 115)

Ruskin therefore maintained:

> The modern Liberal politico-economist of the Stuart Mill school is essentially of the type of a flat-fish – one eyeless side of him always in the mud, and one eye, on the side that *has* eyes, down in the corner of his mouth, – not a desirable guide for man or beast. (Ruskin 1903–1912, 27:180)[17]

Fortunately, the discoveries in physics during the last century have completely refuted the notion of a strictly mechanistic universe in which purely *quantitative* "billiard ball particles" are the basis of reality. Indeed, quantum mechanics has demonstrated that the supposed "particles" of classical physics are merely "potentialities" which have yet to be "actualized" into existence, prompting a fierce debate about what should replace pre-quantum materialism (see, e.g., Smith 2005). This is crucial for the present discussion, since the reduction of quality to quantity in economics is one logical consequence of the reduction of quality to quantity in the sciences of nature during the Scientific Revolution (El-Ansary 2005).

According to Wolfgang Smith, the prodigious Catholic mathematician, physicist, and philosopher, quantum mechanics requires us to distinguish between the "corporeal" world of perceptible *qualities* and the "physical" world of measured or measurable *quantities* that concerns physicists. What is crucial here is that the physical realm of potentiality is below the corporeal level of actual manifestation. Smith points out, "In light of these considerations, we are able, at last, to perceive the full magnitude of the Cartesian deviation. For it appears that in rejecting the qualities or so-called 'secondary' attributes, Galileo and Descartes have cast out what is primary: the very essence of corporeal things" (Smith 2005, 92). Accordingly, "jettisoning Cartesian bifurcation" is the key to resolving quantum paradox on one hand and integrating the findings of physics into higher orders of knowledge on the other (Smith 2005, 81). Fully understanding this point clarifies the limits of physics. But as Nasr notes,

> this limitation is rarely fully understood and therefore it is difficult for many caught in the web of reductionism to see that the reduction of the corporeal realm to the physical renders the physical itself ontologically incomprehensible. The result is the loss of grip upon reality about which some contemporary physicists have complained. To quote Smith, "Strictly speaking, one knows neither the corporeal nor the physical, nor has any clear conception of what physics is about. Is it any wonder, then, that physicists should have (in the words of the physicist Nick Herbert) 'lost their grip on reality'?" (Nasr 1997, 152)

[17] Ruskin gives the following more charitable assessment of Mill in another passage: "Mr. J. S. Mill is assuredly strong in some directions of thought, and entirely, by his nature, shut out from following others" (Ruskin 1903–1912, 17:478).

All this has catastrophic implications for economic theory, because the rejection of Cartesian bifurcation implies that economic theory erroneously conflates the corporeal with the physical realms in reducing quality to quantity and must therefore engage the incommensurability of costs and benefits associated with ever-present externalities for which ethical judgments rather than technical market solutions are necessary.

Moreover, it is significant to note that Muslim philosopher-scientists such as Ibn Sīnā (d. 1037 CE), 'Umar Khayyām (d. 1131 CE), Naṣīr al-Dīn Ṭūsī (d. 1274 CE) by contrasting *al-jism al-tabī'ī* (natural body) with *al-jism al-ta'līmī* (mathematical body), made the same distinction that Smith does between the corporeal world of perceptible *qualities* and the physical world of measured or measurable *quantities* that concerns physicists (Nasr 2006, 171). Mullā Sadrā (d. 1640) developed the thought of these philosopher-scientists into a grand synthesis of Islamic theology, philosophy, and mysticism and in doing so provided the metaphysical foundation for a contemporary science capable of interpreting all natural phenomena through a spiritual perspective that responds to the limitations of modern science without denying its factual discoveries. (It is ironic that Mullā Sadrā was a contemporary of René Descartes.) This explains why an Islamic economic theory of choice based on Islamic metaphysics and cosmological sciences could never reduce quality to quantity in the manner of neoclassical theory. With qualitatively different goods fulfilling different needs or wants (or combinations of the two in the case of goods with multiple use values such as water), neoclassical theory fundamentally misunderstands agents' choices, for changes in allocation involve changes in "each of the items in relation to the *whole*, rather than in relation to each other... changes happen at the *center* rather than at the margin" (John Hobson, quoted in Lux and Lutz 1988, 335).[18] In a word, values transform the economizing process with all this implies for the analytical tools necessary to model it.

The preceding analysis also has implications for the internal consistency of the neoclassical theory of choice itself. This is because the neoclassical approach requires an aggregate devoid of any qualitative differences whatsoever, an aggregate that can only apply to the physical realm below the level of corporeal manifestation, as previously discussed. Although egoistic preferences reducing quality to quantity may be consistent within a *limited* range of choices, such preferences cannot be consistent over any *global* range of *corporeal* choices from the Islamic perspective. In fact, although people often try "in the modern world to achieve integration by bringing forces together on a single plane of reality," this is impossible according to Islamic metaphysics in which integration (as well as every other positive quality) comes "from above" (Nasr 2004b, 2). If only a transcendent Principle can integrate the various elements on a lower level of reality, it is, therefore, impossible to

[18] Hobson provides vivid examples of the "fallacy of allocation by marginal comparison" in neoclassical theory, ranging from a mother's response to a price increase for medicine required by a sick baby to an artist's response to a price increase for a pigment for a painting to charitable contributions. In all such cases, the comparison of marginal utilities is unconvincing and represents a fragmented rather than holistic view.

simultaneously combine the consistency and continuity axioms in the neoclassical theory of choice, since doing so would render it internally inconsistent.[19] Accordingly, no one has ever had a "mono-utility function" and no one ever will.

This fact has further damaging implications for the separate domain argument, because without consistent preferences, "maximizing efficiency for beneficent outcomes" is meaningless. Inconsistent preferences imply there is no stable goal as the object of efficiency and no way to define beneficent outcomes for the separate domain argument in principle.[20] Accordingly, neoclassical theory draws the wrong welfare and efficiency implications for ethical constraints over hedonistic desires for markets such as internet pornography. Indeed, policies that institutionalize unethical preferences in the name of utility maximization lead individuals to internal disintegration and the community into social chaos.

Finally, the preceding arguments over the spiritual significance of work have major implications for the definition of economics, which non-economists are often surprised to know is a major source of debate among economists. As Lindley Fraser points out, economists have generally defined economics in one of two ways, that is, the investigation of a particular *department* of affairs and the investigation of a particular *aspect* of affairs in general (Fraser 1947, ch. 2).[21] For example, the definition of economics as "the science of exchange" fits the first category, whereas the definition of economics as "the science which studies human behavior as a relationship between ends and scarce means which have alternative uses" fits the second category.[22] The latter focus on "economizing processes" presupposes that

> … means and ends can be *given* and defined independently of their relationship – with the latter and not the former being the only concern of the economist. In particular, it is implicitly assumed in this definition that the variables that the economist studies show a peculiar kind of stability: they are either means or ends, and they never switch their role by crossing into intermediate stages in which they are both means and ends at the same time. (Pagano 1985, 172)

Accordingly, human activities are divided into two "sets":

> 1) leisure activities, which affect social welfare but do not affect production (i.e., they are only ends);
> 2) work activities, which affect production but do not affect social welfare (i.e., they are only means). (Pagano 1985, 172)

But human activities do not fit this rigid definition according to Islamic principles, because work can be both a means *and* an end (even a form of prayer). This implies

---

[19] In Islamic philosophical terms, the "unity" required for consistency and the "uniformity" required for continuity are polar opposites. The former is associated with infinite quality whereas the latter is pure quantity.

[20] Satisfaction of desire is particularly vulnerable as a welfare criterion if preferences change. As Hausman points out, "If one says that satisfying past desires does not count, because giving people what they no longer want brings them no 'satisfaction,' then one has shifted from a preference-satisfaction model to a mental-state theory of welfare" (Hausman 1996, 76).

[21] For a survey of definitions of economics, see Kirzner (1960).

[22] For the classic statement and defense of the second definition, see, for instance, Robbins (1962).

that Islamic economics must be defined in terms of a particular department of affairs, not an aspect of affairs.

However, the definition of economics as the investigation of a particular *department* of affairs is consistent with either an Islamic or mechanistic worldview. The difference is that Islamic economics denies the separate domain argument, with all this implies for economic theory and policy, whereas the classical economics of Adam Smith and contemporary neoclassical economics affirm it. In fact, the classical Arabic meaning of *al-iqtisād*, the modern Arabic word for economics, is related to properly managing the affairs of one's household (consistent with the original Latin meaning of *oeconomicus*, itself of Greek origin). The word is derived from the root *qasd*, which literally means "equilibrium" or the "state of being even, equally balanced, or evenly in between."[23] The classical meaning of *al-iqtisād* is therefore intimately related to ethics at both the individual and collective levels. Nasīr al-Dīn Tūsī's widely read classical treatise on philosophical ethics was an examination of the ethical management of one's self, establishing a hierarchy of spiritual and other needs and refuting egoism; the ethical management of the household, or cooperative production and distribution within the smallest traditional community, based on the aforementioned spiritual principles; and the ethical management of the city or state based on the spiritual significance of the division of labor, vocational occupations, and justice in commercial exchange along with distributive justice and cooperation in the larger community in the context of political philosophy (Tūsī 1964). Accordingly, economic solutions require virtue at the individual, household, and political levels and cannot be looked upon in isolation from these other spheres given the ubiquity of incommensurable externalities and the moral limits of markets. Economics is therefore continuous with other practical sciences ranging from ethics to politics and is not an independent domain separated from the rest of social life.

13.5 Conclusion

Recovering Islamic economic theory and practice requires recovering the Islamic intellectual heritage and applying it to the creation and support of holistic production and exchange processes. Thus, the effort to recover Islamic metaphysics and sciences of nature is indispensable to the recovery of Islamic and any other sacred economics. Indeed, in Islam economics is above all a *moral* code governing modes of production, trade, and exchange to benefit the collective good of society. There is no "invisible hand" that guides individuals' economic activities toward some higher collective good, except that it be the Hand of God guiding those who believe in Him. Islamic economics recognizes no distinction between arts and crafts. The

[23] For this etymology and some of its economic implications, see, for instance, Nasr (2004a, 144–147).

reward of work is not only payment in currency to purchase goods and services, but the satisfaction of providing products and services that are works of artistic beauty and excellence. Such work not only enriches the consumers of those services and products, but it also honors and supports the dignity, virtue, and spiritual journeys of those whose talents and efforts provide those products and services, and whose manner of production has as an integral component the protection of the environment for future generations.

An economy that does not provide such satisfaction to all of its laborers and managers and professionals, who are simultaneously consumers, cannot meet their basic psychological and spiritual needs, and its attempts to meet the insatiable demands for material enrichment threaten to destroy the very environment that enables the essential physical needs of human beings to be met. A mechanistic approach to economics destroys a quality of life that could satisfy our highest aspirations as human beings, let alone our basic physical needs. The anxiety, alienation, anomie, despair, frustration, and hopelessness in modern Western (and Westernized) societies began with the disenchantment of the world and corresponding desacralization of work. And it ends in anger, resentment, envy, xenophobia, fear—and possibly chaos and violence, when the laborers deprived of the satisfaction of pride in their work also lack hope for a secure and adequate income. Not only are they faced with accelerating environmental problems, but also the realization that prospects of a fair share in any increase in the income from temporary improvements–improvements that clearly could not occur without their labor–in the economy are beyond their reach.

The question of holistic Islamic production processes is thus central to all other aspects of the Islamic economy and has important interconnections with other aspects of Islamic economic law that are necessary for integrated solutions to economic problems. Such economic practices and institutions cannot cohabit with secularized production processes in the long-term, just as Islamic ethics cannot cohabit with a secular view of science, with all this implies for responding to the environmental crisis. In light of the ubiquity of incommensurable externalities and the moral limits of markets, economics cannot be *amoral* without becoming *immoral*. Economic theory *cannot* be value-free, for every theory presupposes a view of man and nature requiring metaphysics (whether implicit or explicit), as well as epistemology and ethics. The Islamic intellectual and esoteric heritage is therefore central to the foundation of Islamic economic theory and praxis. It is only on this basis that Islamic or any other sacred economics can foster an appreciation by workers, homemakers, professionals, and executives that their work and professions can serve not only to provide well-crafted, beautiful products, and render life-enhancing services, but can also constitute a form of prayer that will support them in realizing their spiritual destinies.

References

Abdul-Rauf, Muhammad. 1984. *A Muslim's Reflections on Democratic Capitalism*. Washington, D.C.: American Enterprise Institute.

Al-Ghazzali. 1982. *Ihyā' 'Ulūm al-Dīn*. New Delhi: Kitab Bhavan.

Baer, Gabriel. 1964. *Egyptian Guilds in Modern Times*. Jerusalem: Israel Oriental Society.

Bakar, Osman. 1991. *Tawhid and Science: Essays on the History and Philosophy of Islamic Science*. Penang: Secretariat for Islamic Philosophy and Science.

Bakar, Osman. 2014. *Islamic Civilization and the Modern World*. Bandar Seri Begawan: UBD Press.

Buchanan, James M., and Robert D. Tollison, eds. 1984. *The Theory of Public Choice*. Ann Arbor: University of Michigan Press.

Campbell, T. Colin. 2013. *Whole: Rethinking the Science of Nutrition*. Dallas: BenBella Books.

Charles HRH The Prince of Wales. 2010. *Harmony: A New Way of Looking at Our World*. New York: HarperCollins.

Coomaraswamy, Rama, ed. 2004. *The Essential Ananda K. Coomaraswamy*. Bloomington: World Wisdom.

Corbin, Henry. 1993. *History of Islamic Philosophy*. New York: Kegan Paul.

Cutsinger, James S. n.d. *Paths of Return: Introducing the World's Religions*. https://www.cutsinger.net/wp-content/uploads/2019/08/paths_of_return.pdf

Dellapenna, Joseph W. 2010. *Behind the Red Curtain: Environmental Concerns and the End of Communism*. Villanova University School of Law Working Paper Series, no. 152. http://digitalcommons.law.villanova.edu/wps/art152/

Economic Policy Institute. 2024. The Productivity-Pay Gap. https://www.epi.org/productivity-pay-gap/

El-Ansary, Waleed. 2005. The Traditionalist Critique of Contemporary Economic Theory. *Sophia: A Journal of Traditional Studies* 11 (1): 79–118.

El-Ansary, Waleed. 2017. Hindu and Islamic Economics: On the Need for a New Economic Paradigm. *The Muslim World* 107:299–331.

Foley, Robert. 2006. *Adam's Fallacy*. Cambridge, MA: Harvard University Press.

Frankfurt, Harry. 1988. *The Importance of What We Care About*. Cambridge: Cambridge University Press.

Franta, Benjamin. 2021. Early Oil Disinformation on Global Warming. *Environmental Politics* 30 (4): 663–668.

Fraser, Lindley. 1947. *Economic Thought and Language: A Critique of Some Fundamental Economic Concepts*. London: A. & C. Black.

Gomaʿa, Ali, ed. 1997. *Revealing the Islamic Economic Heritage (Takshīf al-Turāth al-Islāmī al-Iqtiṣādī)*. Vol. 17 and 19. Cairo: International Institute of Islamic Thought.

Gray, John. 2003. *Al Qaeda and What It Means to Be Modern*. New York: The New Press.

Griffin, James. 1986. *Well-Being*. Oxford: Oxford University Press.

Guénon, René. 1973. *Al-Faqr* or 'Spiritual Poverty. *Studies in Comparative Religion* 7 (1): 16–20.

Hausman, Daniel. 1996. *Economic Analysis and Moral Philosophy*. Cambridge: Cambridge University Press.

Heap, Shaun Hargreaves, Martin Hollis, Bruce Lyons, Robert Sugden, and Albert Weale. 1994. *The Theory of Choice: A Critical Guide*. Oxford: Blackwell.

Hughes, John. 2007. *The End of Work: Theological Critiques of Capitalism*. Oxford: Blackwell.

Hunt, E. K., and Mark Lautzenheiser. 2011. *History of Economic Thought: A Critical Perspective*. London: M.E. Sharpe.

Ibish, Yusuf. 1999. *Traditional Guilds in the Ottoman Empire*. Islamic World Report.

Khan, Muhammad Akram. 2013. *What Is Wrong with Islamic Economics? Analysing the Present State and Future Agenda*. Cheltenham: Edward Elgar.

Kirzner, Israel. 1960. *The Economic Point of View: An Essay in the History of Economic Thought*. New York: D. Van Nostrand Company.

Lewis, Bernard. 1937. The Islamic Guilds. *Economic History Review* A8 (1): 20–37.

Lux, Kenneth, and Mark Lutz. 1988. *Humanistic Economics: The New Challenge*. New York: Bootstrap Press.
MacIntyre, Alasdair. 1984. *After Virtue: A Study in Moral Theory*. Notre Dame: University of Notre Dame Press.
Médaille, John. 2014. Private Correspondence, August 20.
Michon, Jean-Louis. 1999. Titus Burckhardt and the Sense of Beauty: Why and How He Loved and Served Morocco. *Sophia: A Journal of Traditional Studies* 5 (2): 113–140.
Mill, John Stuart. 1884. *System of Logic*. New York: Harpers and Brothers.
Mishan, Ezra J. 1986. *Economic Myths and the Mythology of Economics*. Atlantic Highlands: Humanities Press International.
Nasr, Seyyed Hossein. 1982. Review of Ethics and Economics – An Islamic Synthesis. *Hamdard Islamicus*. 5: 89–91.
Nasr, Seyyed Hossein. 1989. *Knowledge and the Sacred*. Albany: SUNY Press.
Nasr, Seyyed Hossein. 1994. *Ideals and Realities of Islam*. San Francisco: The Aquarian Press.
Nasr, Seyyed Hossein. 1997. Perennial Ontology and Quantum Mechanics: A Review Essay of Wolfgang Smith's *The Quantum Enigma: Finding the Hidden Key*. *Sophia* 3:137–159.
Nasr, Seyyed Hossein. 2001 (rev.; or. 1975). *Islam and the Plight of Modern Man*. Chicago: Kazi Publications.
Nasr, Seyyed Hossein. 2004a. *The Heart of Islam: Enduring Values for Humanity*. New York: HarperOne.
Nasr, Seyyed Hossein. 2004b. *Sufism and the Integration of the Inner and Outer Life of Man: The L M Singhvi Interfaith Lecture for the Year 1999*. Kent: Temenos Academy.
Nasr, Seyyed Hossein. 2006. *Islamic Philosophy from Its Origin to the Present: Philosophy in the Land of Prophecy*. New York: State University of New York Press.
Nasr, Seyyed Hossein. 2007. The Contemporary Islamic World and the Environmental Crisis. *Sophia* 13 (2): 12–35.
Nasr, Seyyed Hossein. 2010. *Islam in the Modern World: Challenged by the West, Threatened by Fundamentalism, Keeping Faith with Tradition*. New York: HarperCollins.
Nasr, Seyyed Hossein. 2012. *Islam in the Modern World: Challenged by the West, Threatened by Fundamentalism, Keeping Faith with Tradition*. San Francisco: HarperOne.
Nasr, Seyyed Hossein, Caner K. Dagli, Maria Massi Dakake, Joseph E. B. Lumbard, and Mohammed Rustom, eds. 2015. *The Study Quran: A New Translation and Commentary*. New York: HarperOne.
Ollman, Bertell. 1979. *Social and Sexual Revolution: Essays on Marx and Reich*. Cambridge, MA: South End Press.
Pagano, Ugo. 1985. *Work and Welfare in Economic Theory*. Oxford: Basil Blackwell.
Putterman, Louis. 1990. *Division of Labor and Welfare: An Introduction to Economic Systems*. Oxford: Oxford University Press.
Quadir, Tarik. 2013. *Traditional Islamic Environmentalism*. New York: University Press of America.
Robbins, Lionel. 1962. *An Essay on the Nature and Significance of Economic Science*. New York: St. Martin's Press.
Ruskin, John. 1903–1912. *The Works of John Ruskin*. Edited by Edward T. Clark and Alexander Wedderburn. 30 vols. London: George Allen.
Ruskin, John. 1938. *Unto This Last and Other Essays*. New York: E.P. Dutton & Co.
Sandel, Michael. 2013. *What Money Can't Buy: The Moral Limits of Markets*. New York: Farrar, Straus, and Giroux.
Sandler, Todd. 1992. *Collective Action: Theory and Applications*. Ann Arbor: University of Michigan Press.
Schumacher, E. F. 1974. *Age of Plenty: A Christian View*. Edinburgh: St. Andrew Press.
Schumacher, E. F. 1979. *Good Work*. New York: Harper & Row.
Smith, Adam. 1812. *An Inquiry into the Nature and Causes of the Wealth of Nations*. Vol. 3 vols. London: Cadell and Davies.

Smith, Wolfgang. 2005. *The Quantum Enigma: Finding the Hidden Key*. Hillsdale: Sophia Perennis.

Speth, James Gustave. 2008. *The Bridge at the End of the World: Capitalism, the Environment, and Crossing from Crisis to Sustainability*. New Haven: Yale University Press.

Tūsī, Nasīr al-Dīn. 1964. *The Nasirean Ethics*. Translated by G. M. Wickens. London: G. Allen & Unwin.

Watts, William. 2025. Corporate Profits Near All-Time Highs, While Wages Are near Lows. How Long Can This Last? *Market Watch*, February 5, 2025. https://www.marketwatch.com/story/corporate-profits-are-near-all-time-highs-while-wages-are-near-lows-how-long-can-this-last-0b0885e7

Weber, Max. 2004. Science as a Vocation. In *The Vocation Lectures*. Translated by Rodney Linvingtone. Edited by David Owen and Tracy B. Strong. Cambridge: Hackett Publishing Company.

Wolff, Jonathan, and David Leopold. 2021. Karl Marx. In *The Stanford Encyclopedia of Philosophy*, ed. Edward N. Zalta. https://plato.stanford.edu/archives/spr2021/entries/marx/.

Wood, Barbara. 1984. *E.F. Schumacher: His Life and Thought*. New York: Harper & Row.

Waleed El-Ansary is the Helal, Hisham and Laila Edris El-Swedey University Chair in Islamic Studies at Xavier University, where he teaches courses on comparative religion, Islamic studies and religion and science. He holds a PhD in Islamic and Religious Studies from George Washington University and MA in Economics from the University of Maryland. He has published numerous articles on the intersection between religion, science and economics.

Chapter 14
Epilogue: World Religions, Empires, Markets, Virtues and Vices

Govert J. Buijs and Jordan J. Ballor

Inspired by Max Weber's seminal work, in this volume we have travelled from one 'world religion' to another, from the modern West to the Far East and back to the West via India and the Middle East. For Weber the journey was primarily a search for precursors and signs of 'rationalization', which eventually would burst out in the open in the West, in Protestantism, with its injunctions to a fully rationalized behavior, culminating in (secular) utilitarianism. And this was 'the spirit of capitalism'.

We mentioned in the Introduction already Karl Jaspers' theory about the "Axial Age", developed in his 1949 book *Vom Ursprung und Ziel der Geschichte* (*The Origin and Goal of History*). Jaspers uses it to refer to an—in itself already very extensive—period between 800 and 200 BCE, in which all the major religions emerged, most of which are discussed by Max Weber. In Jaspers' work Max Weber is mentioned only a couple of times in passing (the work of his brother Alfred Weber is actually referred to more frequently), although Jaspers and Max Weber were intimately acquainted.[1] That doesn't concern us here. Neither would we like to go into all the fiery debates about the adequacy of the identification of one 'Age' (Jaspers omitted Akhenaten and Moses at the front and Jesus and Mohammed at the end, and

[1] Jaspers, who was also a psychiatrist, had a full autobiographical memoir of Max Weber, in which he had extensively analyzed his own psyche, as a kind of therapeutic exercise. After Weber's early death, Jaspers did not feel at liberty to keep this and destroyed the entire piece.

G. J. Buijs
Faculty of Social Sciences and Humanities, Vrije Universiteit, Amsterdam, The Netherlands
e-mail: g.j.buijs@vu.nl

J. J. Ballor (✉)
Center for Religion, Culture & Democracy, First Liberty Institute, Plano, TX, USA
e-mail: j.ballor@crcd.net

G. J. Buijs, J. J. Ballor (eds.), *In Search of the Spirits of Capitalism*, Sophia Studies in Cross-cultural Philosophy of Traditions and Cultures 44,
https://doi.org/10.1007/978-3-032-01137-4_14

also left out Hinduism altogether, which indicates that his idea of an 'Age' is somewhat forced). But there is one interesting thing about this conception that is worth singling out: there is a kind of common core in all these religions. According to Jaspers, the common core of the 'world religions' is not rationalization versus magic or ritualism, but it is the emergence of a new type of consciousness. As he puts it, "Man becomes conscious of Being as a whole, of himself and his limitations. He experiences the terror of the world and his own powerlessness. He asks radical questions. Face to face with the void he strives for liberation and salvation. By consciously recognizing his limits he sets himself the highest goals" (Jaspers 2021, 9). Jaspers speaks as well about a "spiritualization" of the world (Jaspers 2021, 10).

Others have formulated this differently, but the heart of the matter is the same: all these religions/worldviews (and Jaspers includes Greek philosophy as well) make a basic distinction between the present situation, the *status quo*, and a possible normative order that we may use as an ideal to measure the justness of the current order and inspire us to move toward it.[2] Eric Voegelin, in his seminal work *Order & History*, has placed this type of breakthroughs within the context of empires that had emerged in very different parts of the world (Voegelin 1956–1987). Their violent and oppressive nature gave rise to questions of meaning, order and justice, both in justifying the empires (that developed impressive symbolic justifications, political theologies, to manifest the cosmic legitimacy of their existence and actions) and in the search for ways to criticize them. Is 'empire' the real world, or is it an aberration of mankind? One can elaborate this point of view further: at a certain time in history—actually at very different times in very different contexts—it is no longer man's place in nature that is his only or primary spiritual concern, but he tries to find a way to critically relate to his own creations, like empires and other social structures, such as the *polis*, as a 'second nature'. And these human socio-political artefacts do raise questions also about humans themselves: what is man (who apparently creates these kind of structures)? And what is the good human life, amidst these artifacts? The (first)nature-oriented spiritualities or religions are now accompanied by society- and human-oriented spiritualities and/or religions.

For centuries and even millennia, many of these critical questions, emerging from the 'world religions', have remained focused primarily on political structures, and partly as well on household life and good behavior in the family. There is an impressive 'history of political philosophy', from Plato's *Politics* until today, comprising both insights regarding the institutional structure of a healthy political order, be it a monarchy, an aristocracy or a polity (and analyses of structural derailments of political order such as tyranny, oligarchy or democracy/ochlocracy[3]). And there

[2] Max Weber's contemporary Abraham Kuyper distinguished between two fundamental perspectives, that of the 'normalists' and the 'abnormalists', corresponding to whether one viewed the current state of the world as a normative baseline (e.g., naturalism) or whether one's worldview considered the status quo as corrupt, fallen, or in need of some radical correction (e.g., supernaturalism). See Kuyper (1931, 132–135).

[3] We allude here to the famous Book VI of Polybius' *World History* where he describes the 'anacyclosis', the cyclical transition from one political form to another, alternating between a 'good' form

are sundry sketches, both philosophical and theological, of the ethical and spiritual characteristics of good (or bad) political leaders, such as the 'Mirrors for Princes' (*speculum principum*). There is also an impressive harvest focusing on personal ethics, personal behavior, personal meaning and salvation, as well as (in Confucianism for example) on interpersonal relations.

Regarding economic structures, such as markets and businesses, or the personal characteristics of good market behavior, the harvest is much less impressive. That of course has to do with the fact that 'The Economy', as a more or less freestanding institutional sphere only developed in modern times, more or less in the eighteenth century (and Adam Smith was perhaps the first to really treat it as such). The work of Marx is focused on exactly this, the entire organization of a society, the bourgeois society, around 'capital'. Karl Polanyi later spoke of a process of "disembedding" of economic activities, the moment land, labor and capital become 'commodities' in themselves (Polanyi [1944] 2001, 71–80). Charles Taylor speaks of 'the economy' as one of the manifestations of the "modern moral order", and as an "objectified reality" a rather new phenomenon (Taylor 2007, 176–185; Taylor 1991).

This phenomenon was also what Weber's work was primarily focused on: how could this 'economy' emerge as an independent system, an institutional sphere on its own? For Weber the heart of this new institutional sphere was rational calculation, and his key question actually was: how did rationality emerge as the ultimate orientation for human action—the theme of 'disenchantment'? This results in a curious observation: in spite of the name under which his pertinent works has been published, Weber was not really interested in the specific *ethical* content of the world religions but primarily on their impetus toward rationalization. The title of his work therefore should perhaps better been something like, 'The rationality-potential of the world-religions'.

But beware: one of the essential outcomes of the Axial Age is not just, as was Weber's focus, rationality. Rather, much more important for the key players themselves is the discovery of new orientation in life, a new *ethos*. The dominant opposition for them, and for the many millions of followers of the prophets and sages, is not *mythos* versus *logos*, but, if one wants to use this framework, *mythos* versus *ethos*, or even more specifically *kratos* versus *ethos* (*kratos* means force, violence, power over people, victory). This dynamic is key to understanding what the various religions/worldviews are trying to identify as a perspective on the good life for humans beyond the temptation of empire, and what this requires from humans in terms of self-knowledge and dealing with the self (even to the point of reaching the non-self, the *anatta,* in Buddhism). So, in a way, Weber's understanding is as well a procrustean bed for these religions/worldviews. Weber was of course well aware of this, but given what he was after, this was the direction he chose.

But then, if we apply Jaspers' and Voegelin's insights into the nature of the 'Axial Age' as attempts to develop an ethical and/or religious critique of the existing institutions, i.e., of empires, then another question comes to the fore: will we be able to

that then deteriorates into a bad form, after which a new form is instituted.

find a morally and spiritually inspired way to check, to reign in, to limit, the manmade institutional world not only of empires, but also of the new manmade institutional world of the economy, of capitalism? There is an emerging literature, often but not exclusively at the political left, that interprets the current development of gigantic new corporations as 'neo-feudalism' (Kotkin 2020) or 'techno-feudalism' (Durand 2024). The sheer scale of money involved in today's economy, compared to the GDP of quite a few countries, is beyond comprehension. A remarkable comparison is apt: the quite incisive decision of the UK to leave the EU ('Brexit'), came at a cost of €35 billion, a kind of divorce money at an international scale, involving large economic zones, which is only half of the cost of the divorce settlement of Bill and Melinda Gates that came with double that amount! And the divorce of Jeff and MacKenzie Bezos was settled at €35 billion as well. But it is not only the sheer financial size of some business moguls and corporations, but even more the power they exert over the lives of billions of people that reminds one of the empires of old. The analogy between the ancient kings and emperors and modern business moguls is not new. An interesting case in point is the motivation given by American Senator John Sherman for introducing the anti-trust law, which was passed under his name:

> If we will not endure a king as a political power we should not endure a king over the production, transportation, and sale of the necessaries of life. If we would not submit to an emperor we should not submit to an autocrat of trade with power to prevent competition and to fix the price of any commodity (1890).

As indicated in the introduction to this volume, Weber regarded the emergence of the modern economy as a self-contained system to be an irreversible development, an 'iron cage'. Modern man had entered this new phase of the second nature forever after and cannot escape: we not only live in a world dominated not only by state-bureaucracies (in line with the millennia old history of empires), but also, and perhaps even more so, in a world dominated by a capitalist market economy, for which we can now use also 'empire-like' characterizations.

In the Introduction we suggested some qualifications: there is a variety of capitalisms, and the earlier religions and worldview play an important role in this respect, until today regardless all the talk about secularization. A recent Research Paper by the Munich Center for Economic Studies gives an overview of recent research in this area, and the results are overwhelming (Becker et al. 2025). Religion continues to shape societal norms and institutions and impact economic development, the authors conclude. There are both direct influences—many people do find religious viewpoints important in their lives, and allow it to influence their way of life, their *Lebensführung*, as Weber would call it—but also indirect influences, such as religious institutions promoting literacy and education, or stimulating a high trust society.

The influence of religion on public life is in some cases the result of lengthy processes of 'sedimentation' but in other cases it is also the result of conscious attempts to influence the population at large, well beyond the confines of the religious communities. In these latter cases we see a transition from what Weber called *ausserweltliche Askese* to *innerweltliche Askese*. The famous case in point is of course Protestantism and its abandonment of the monastic life. Van Bijlert shows that a similar movement can be seen in Hinduism, which by Rammohun Roy and others was transformed into a source for freedom and social justice, providing the soil from which someone like Gandhi could emerge.

One might ask how it is possible that religions have an impact on the economy, as they originate in a period in which the economy as we know it today—the economy as autonomous sphere or system—did not yet exist? This is not hard to understand for two reasons. These religions have shaped cultures for millennia, affecting their, what Hofstede called, "software of the mind" (Hofstede 1991; cf. Harrison & Huntington 2000). Although there is a risk of reification if expressed in this way, nevertheless 'cultures' or 'civilizations' influence the people who live in their orbit, and influence also the patterns of response to new phenomena, such as the rise of modern capitalism.

But a more specific reason why religions/worldviews influence the way the economy is shaped is more mundane. Key ingredients of this new institutional sphere have been around for millennia: money, credits, trade, markets, as well as the potential, and often actual, clearly destructive ways of using these, such as usury, fraud, greed, accumulation and poverty. 'The economy' may be something new, but economic actions and behavior go back millennia. That gives the insights from the world religions a lasting relevance, even though they do not address the modern 'systemic' issue directly. One certainly can expect indirect insights on capitalism as a system, based on the direct insights and recommendations regarding these ancient ingredients of what later came to be called 'capitalism'. However, given the history of the reflection on economic phenomena, it should not come as a surprise that the harvest of the 'Axial Age', as we have been gathering some of it in this volume, should primarily be focused on personal ethics more than on a comprehensive analysis and critique of the current capitalistic market economy.

Indeed, this volume has provided plenty of such perspectives on economic ethics. Thus we provide a brief, impressionistic survey, rather than attempting to give a representative summary (and therefore doing injustice to the richness that is presented). In a positive sense we find appreciations of the value of work, as 'calling/vocation' in Christianity (Herdt and Van der Kooi), or as 'analogy of God's artistic action', hence sacred (El-Ansary) and of the creativity involved in economic activity (Lifshitz). We find positive appreciation of trade and tradesmen (Lifshitz, Reda, Saliya). From all religions/worldviews presented in this volume comes the call for virtuous behavior as essential for good markets and for them to contribute to human flourishing. The Analects call for joy, filiality, reciprocity, and righteousness (Szto). In Hinduism, *dharma* is central, which according to Dutt refers to an entire gamut of virtues, such as charity, honesty, helping others, courage, truthfulness and which should be in balance with the pursuit of well-being (*mokṣa*). Justice, doing unto others as you wish others do unto you, often called the 'golden rule', and behaving like responsible vicegerents, is called for (Reda). One should strive for the integration of ethical values, compassion and mindfulness into economic life (Saliya). Honesty, fairness, generosity, social and ecological responsibility are called for (Friedman).

However, there is also an avalanche of warnings about the moral and spiritual risks that are particularly related to trade, business, money, markets. We find warnings about the risks accompanying wealth and luxury, in Christianity (Herdt, Van der Kooi), the risks of selfishness, loneliness and isolation (in Confucianism—Herrmann-Pillath). The Analects warn against greed, disloyalty, disrespect for elders, and despair (Szto). In Buddhism, the dangers of 'greed, hatred and delusion' are identified (Magnuson). The Talmud warns against 'behaving with deceit', 'lack of honesty', and even a whole range of very smart tricks to deceive customers are explicitly denounced (Friedman).

Regarding capitalism as a system we certainly do find engagement as well. Perhaps the most trenchant is Herrmann-Pillath's question whether Weber's identification of capitalism and rationality is not a mistake in itself: is there not something deeply irrational about believing that the world could be subject to a totalizing sphere of purely formal rationality? Capitalism builds on fictions, according to Herrmann-Pillath, "dreams of transforming the world according to human desires, defined mainly in terms of material progress." It looks indeed like a myth, we would suggest. El-Ansary dives into the root causes of the environmental crisis and economic instability in the 'invisible foot' of exploitation.

In the Introduction we referred to the work of Ulrich Beck and collaborators (Beck et al. 2003). They call for a rather different approach to the modern world, compared to Weber: do not regard it as an unchangeable system, an 'iron cage', but look for ways to give new direction to it. To be able to do this, we cannot rely simply on the supposedly 'rational' knowledge that has created it. For a 'reflective modernity' we need different types of knowledge. In short, in our terms, the economy is too important to leave to the economists. We need a much broader dialogue, and need to draw on other resources, to find ways to deal with 'second nature', the institutions and practices that we as humans have created and are enacting on a day-to-day basis. We need a 'multi-stakeholder dialogue', in which there is full space as well for what Balkenende and Buijs (2024) call 'imaginative reflection', among which are the traditions that offer a perspective on a different world than the present one, be it political or economic 'empires', the religious traditions that somehow put *ethos* over against *kratos.*

In the Introduction to this volume, we gave the following as leading question for the contributions:

> From the perspective of one of the world religions, do free markets contribute to human flourishing, and what from these perspectives is the role of morality and especially virtues, in realizing this contribution?

In conclusion we can say as a general answer, coming from the world religions: yes, free markets do contribute to human flourishing, but only under three specific conditions.

First, when all those involved in the market economy, both persons and corporate institutions (and we may include governments here), behave virtuously.

Second, when all those involved in the market economy, take seriously the many admonitions against the vast temptations of wealth, money and greed. So—although the particular words originate from one tradition, it may easily resonate with all traditions—they constantly should say the following prayer or do meditative work with similar effects: 'Lead us not into temptation, but deliver us from evil.'

And a third exhortation, immediately connected to this, here in the Buddhist formulation, but to be found as well throughout the various traditions: "Look both inwardly, deeply into ourselves, and outwardly to the conditions of our surroundings. This is the inner and outer work." (Magnuson). Interiority should not be seen as the opposite of exteriority. Inner transformation and the transformation of the outer world, capitalism as a system, are intimately connected.

References

Balkenende, Jan Peter, and Govert Buijs. 2024. *Capitalism Reconnected. Toward a Sustainable, Inclusive and Innovative Market Economy in Europe*. Amsterdam: Amsterdam University Press.

Beck, Ulrich, Wolfgang Bons, and Christoph Lau. 2003. The Theory of Reflexive Modernization. *Theory, Culture & Society* 20 (2): 1–33.

Becker, Sascha O., Amma Panin, Steven Pfaff, Jared Rubin. 2025. *Religion and Economic Development: Past, Present, and Future*. CESifo Working Paper No. 11724. CESifo. Munich. https://www.cesifo.org/en/publications/2025/working-paper/religion-and-economic-development-past-present-and-future. Accessed 7 Apr 2025.

Durand, Cédric. 2024. *How Silicon Valley Unleashed Techno-Feudalism. The Making of the Digital Economy*. London/New York: Verso Books.

Harrison, Lawrence E., and Samuel P. Huntington. 2000. *Culture Matters. How Values Shape Human Progress*. New York: Basic Books.

Hofstede, Geert. 1991. *Cultures and Organizations. Software of the Mind*. London: McGraw-Hill.

Jaspers, Karl. 2021 [1949 Or./1953 Eng. Tr.]. *The Origin and Goal of History*. New York: Routledge.

Kotkin, Joel. 2020. *The Coming of Neo-Feudalism. A Warning to the Global Middle Class*. New York: Encounter Books.

Kuyper, Abraham. 1931 [1898]. *Lectures on Calvinism*. Grand Rapids: Eerdmans.

Polanyi, Karl. [1944] 2001. *The Great Transformation. The Political and Economic Origins of Our Time*. Boston: Beacon Press.

Taylor, Charles. 1991. *The Malaise of Modernity*. Don Mills: Stoddart Publishing.

Taylor, Charles. 2007. *A Secular Age*. Cambridge: Belknap.

Voegelin, Eric. 1956–1987. *Order & History* (5 Vols. *Israel and Revelation 1956*; *The World of the Polis 1957*; *Plato and Aristotle 1957*; *The Ecumenic Age 1974*; *In Search of Order 1987*). Baton Rouge: Louisiana University Press.

Govert J. Buijs studied political science, philosophy and theology at various institutions in the Netherlands and Canada and holds a PhD in political philosophy of the VU University ('Vrije Universiteit') in Amsterdam, the Netherlands. He currently holds the Goldschmeding Chair Societal and Economic Renewal which is combined with the Abraham Kuyper Chair for Political Philosophy & Religion at the philosophy department of the Faculty of Social Sciences and Humanities of VU University Amsterdam. His book *Het goede leven en de vrije markt* (*'The Good Life and the Free Market'*, co-authored with Ad Verbrugge and Jelle van Baardewijk) won the Dutch Socrates Prize for the best book in philosophy in 2019. Recently, he published with the former Dutch Prime Minister Jan Peter Balkenende the book *Capitalism Reconnected. Toward a*

Sustainable, Inclusive and Innovative Market Economy in Europe (Amsterdam University Press, 2024).

Jordan J. Ballor is executive director at the Center for Religion, Culture & Democracy at First Liberty Institute (USA). He has previously held research positions at the Acton Institute for the Study of Religion & Liberty and the Vrije Universiteit Amsterdam as part of the Moral Markets project, and has doctorates in reformation history from the Universität Zürich and in moral theology from Calvin Theological Seminary.

Index

G. J. Buijs, J. J. Ballor (eds.), *In Search of the Spirits of Capitalism*, Sophia Studies in Cross-cultural Philosophy of Traditions and Cultures 44,
https://doi.org/10.1007/978-3-032-01137-4

GPSR Compliance

The European Union's (EU) General Product Safety Regulation (GPSR) is a set of rules that requires consumer products to be safe and our obligations to ensure this.

If you have any concerns about our products, you can contact us on ProductSafety@springernature.com

In case Publisher is established outside the EU, the EU authorized representative is:

Springer Nature Customer Service Center GmbH
Europaplatz 3
69115 Heidelberg, Germany

Batch number: 09582748

Printed by Printforce, the Netherlands